Oracle® Data Warehousing and Business Intelligence Solutions

Oracle® Data Warehousing and Business Intelligence Solutions

Robert Stackowiak
Joseph Rayman
Rick Greenwald

1807
WILEY
2007
BICENTENNIAL

Wiley Publishing, Inc.

Oracle® Data Warehousing and Business Intelligence Solutions
Published by
Wiley Publishing, Inc.
10475 Crosspoint Boulevard
Indianapolis, IN 46256
www.wiley.com

Published simultaneously in Canada

ISBN-13: 978-0-471-91921-6
ISBN-10: 0-471-91921-7

Manufactured in the United States of America

10 9 8 7 6 5 4 3 2 1

1MA/RS/RS/QW/IN

For general information on our other products and services or to obtain technical support, please contact our Customer Care Department within the U.S. at (800) 762-2974, outside the U.S. at (317) 572-3993 or fax (317) 572-4002.

Library of Congress Cataloging-in-Publication Data: Available from publisher.

About the Authors

Robert Stackowiak is Vice President of Business Intelligence in Oracle's Technology Business Unit. He has worked for over 20 years in business intelligence, data warehousing, and IT-related roles at Oracle, IBM, Harris Corporation, and the U.S. Army Corps of Engineers. His papers regarding business intelligence and computer and software technology have appeared in publications such as *President & CEO Magazine*, *Database Trends and Applications*, and The Data Warehousing Institute's publications. He also co-authored the books *Oracle Essentials: Oracle Database 10g* (currently in 3rd Edition, February 2004, O'Reilly), *Oracle Application Server 10g Essentials* (1st Edition, August 2004, O'Reilly), and *Professional Oracle Programming* (1st Edition, June 2005, WROX).

Joseph Rayman leads the Oracle Consulting Business Intelligence Practice in North America with over 20 years of business experience in a vast array of industries, including financial services, manufacturing, retail, telecommunications, healthcare, and federal government. His technical and business leadership spans enterprise architecture design, enterprise data modeling, VLDB system tuning, data warehouse design, data mining, and quality assurance activities for data warehouse practices. Joe is a key contributor in defining and authoring Oracle Consulting's Data Warehousing Methodology. Prior to joining Oracle, Joe designed and deployed business intelligence and statistical analysis solutions for a large food manufacturer and provided real-time trading and analysis solutions for a major international financial organization.

Rick Greenwald has worked in the IT field for over 20 years for major vendors, including Oracle, Gupta Technologies, Cognos, and Data General. He has coauthored more than a dozen books, including *Oracle Essentials: Oracle Database 10g* (currently in 3rd Edition, February 2004, O'Reilly), *Oracle Application Server 10g Essentials* (1st Edition, August 2004, O'Reilly), and *Professional Oracle Programming* (1st Edition, June 2005, WROX). Mr. Greenwald currently works for Ingres Corporation.

Credits

Executive Editor
Robert Elliott

Senior Development Editor
Tom Dinse

Production Editor
Angela Smith

Copy Editor
Michael Koch

Editorial Manager
Mary Beth Wakefield

Production Manager
Tim Tate

Vice President and Executive Group Publisher
Richard Swadley

Vice President and Executive Publisher
Joseph B. Wikert

Project Coordinator
Adrienne Martinez

Graphics and Production Specialists
Carrie A. Foster
Stephanie D. Jumper
Barbara Moore
Heather Ryan
Alicia B. South

Quality Control Technicians
Jessica Kramer
Brian H. Walls

Book Proofreading
Techbooks

Indexing
Stephen Ingle

Anniversary Logo Design
Richard Pacifico

Contents

Acknowledgments

We begin by acknowledging the support of our families, especially our wives who realize that authors sometimes get a bit cranky and difficult as deadlines approach. Although they probably hope there is not another book coming from any one of us soon, we realize such an undertaking would not be possible without the support of Jodie Stackowiak, Donna Rayman, and LuAnn Greenwald.

Special thanks to the folks at Wiley Publishing who worked their magic to turn the documents and screen-captured images from our laptops into the book you have in front of you. We would especially like to thank Tom Dinse, our Senior Development Editor, and Bob Elliott, Wiley's Executive Editor who understood the need for such a book.

Within Oracle, we have had the great fortune to work with many people skilled in this area. From Oracle Development, we would like to acknowledge the following who have provided us with guidance over the years that was especially relevant for this book: George Lumpkin, Robert Ash, Hermann Baer, Andrew Holdsworth, Paul Narth, Jean-Pierre Dijcks, Paul Rodwick, Chris Leone, and Ray Roccaforte. We would also like to acknowledge the contributions of business intelligence specialists in the Technology Business Unit, especially Louis Nagode, Gayl Czaplicki, Derrick Cameron, Jim Bienski, Alan Manewitz, Joan Maiorana, and the Enterprise Technology Center under Jim Olsen where we were able to illustrate some of the large-scale management capabilities.

Oracle also has a great many business intelligence specialists within sales, consulting, and other organizations around the world who remind us of the day-to-day challenges that their customers face when building these solutions. Some of the key individuals who influenced the content in this book include David Pryor, Susan Cook, Steve Illingworth, Nick Whitehead, Jon Ainsworth, Kevin Lancaster, Craig Terry, Joe Thomas, Rob Reynolds, Rich Solari, Nuge Ajouz, Ken McMullen, Brian MacDonald, and Patrick Viau. There are many more, of course.

Lastly, much of the content in this book is based on the experience of the authors. Some of the descriptions of what to avoid are based on observations we made of less successful techniques used by Oracle's customers. But many of Oracle's customers and partners provide innovation and techniques that take product features and turn them into useful solutions. We have had the fortune of dealing with both types of customers, and this book is much stronger and realistic because of what these customers and the Oracle partners have shared with us. So, thank you to all of you whom we have worked with over the years. We especially hope you find this book to be of value as you build and develop your own solutions.

Introduction

We are now decades into deploying decision support systems, data warehouses, and business intelligence solutions. Today, there are many books that describe data warehousing and design approaches. There are many books that describe business intelligence. There are many books that describe the Oracle database. So you may be asking, why did the authors decide to write this book?

The fact is, the authors of this book still hear comments from many of you that business intelligence and data warehousing projects are problematic. This seems to be true regardless of database technologies or business intelligence tools selected and deployed. While the wealth of Oracle skills and resources that exist might make this less true where Oracle technology is part of the solution, the number of implementations that face significant issues and the repetition of mistakes convinced the authors that too few projects are approached holistically. Not many of the books that are available as resources look at Oracle business intelligence and data warehousing in such a manner.

This book attempts to give you a single reference that covers a diverse range of relevant topics in providing a holistic approach. It covers the database and platform technology, of course. But it also covers business intelligence tools, emerging business intelligence applications, architecture choices, schema selection, management and performance tuning, requirements gathering, and justifying the project. Tips are included throughout the book based on real experience and implementations.

Your tendency might be to jump to sections you know something about or suspect as being a possible solution to a problem in order to further develop your knowledge of a specific topic. Although you should find value in using this book that way, keep in mind that the reason many implementations struggle is due to ignoring areas that should be understood and are outside the core competencies of those engaged in the project.

To sum it up, the goal of this book is more than about gaining academic knowledge. If this book attains its objective, you will gain knowledge that you can apply to your own project such that your deployed solution will be viewed as successful technically within Information Technology (IT), but also successful because it delivers the business value that your business community recognizes.

Who This Book Is For

This book should appeal to a wide audience. Although those in IT will find it particularly useful, more technically inclined business analysts and managers should also find value in topics such as justifying projects and evaluating deployment choices.

Within IT, the day-to-day management and modification of such an infrastructure often falls on database administrators, programmers, and systems managers. Certainly, we cover topics of interest to this group. Unfortunately, the value of architects and project managers in deploying and updating such solutions is often overlooked. There is plenty in this book that should also appeal to that audience.

How This Book Is Organized

This book is divided into three parts:

Oracle Business Intelligence Defined

Custom Built Data Warehousing Solutions

Best Practices

Part I: Oracle Business Intelligence Defined

Part I provides a broad background as to possible Oracle-based solutions and how you might deploy them. The database and business intelligence tools are introduced here, but other related topics are covered as well in the following four chapters.

Chapter 1: Oracle Business Intelligence

A broad introduction of Oracle business intelligence is provided. Topics introduced include Oracle's transactional business intelligence, integration components, and components in custom-built data warehouses and business intelligence solutions.

Chapter 2: Oracle's Transactional Business Intelligence

Sometimes called operational business intelligence, this chapter describes Oracle's Daily Business Intelligence modules, Balanced Scorecard solution, and Data Hubs (used in master data management). You are provided with guidance as to where such solutions might be particularly useful and why a data warehouse might also be deployed to augment such a solution.

Chapter 3: Introduction to Oracle Data Warehousing

The introduction of this topic covers the wide array of features in the Oracle database that are relevant in data warehousing. More detailed explanations are provided in Part II of this book. In addition, the chapter covers the data models that Oracle provides for its applications as pre-built data warehousing solutions.

Chapter 4: Choosing a Platform

The basics of choosing a hardware platform are covered including scaling up versus scaling out and how to size your choice. Specifics addressed under these broad topics include high availability considerations, manageability considerations, and approaches to benchmarking.

Part II: Custom-Built Data Warehousing Solutions

Most business intelligence solutions today are custom built. Part II describes design approaches and deploying and managing business intelligence tools and an Oracle data warehousing database. These are explained in the following five chapters.

Chapter 5: Designing for Usability

Covering approaches to design, topics in this chapter include how to leverage Oracle features and an illustration of how these features can be used to provide solutions to needs driven by a business scenario. Schema approaches are described including third normal form, star schema, hybrids, and Online Analytical Processing (OLAP).

Chapter 6: Business Intelligence Tools

This chapter introduces using and deploying Oracle's wide array of business intelligence tools, including portals, reporting, and ad hoc query and analysis tools. The Oracle Business Intelligence Suites (Standard Edition and Enterprise Edition) are covered. In addition, the Oracle database support provided by business intelligence tools available from other vendors is described.

Chapter 7: Data Loading

Embedded extraction, transformation, and loading (ETL) features provided by the Oracle database are described in this chapter. Oracle Warehouse Builder's role in ETL, target data warehouse design, data quality analyses, and metadata management is also described.

Chapter 8: Managing the Oracle Data Warehouse

Oracle Enterprise Manager provides a useful interface often used in managing Oracle data warehouses as described in this chapter. The Grid Control interface for managing clusters is illustrated, as are interfaces for basic performance monitoring, administration, and maintenance.

Chapter 9: Data Warehouse Performance Tuning and Monitoring

Typical performance challenges are described and proven approaches to solving such challenges are presented. We then illustrate using such approaches to tune the data warehouse first described in the business scenario presented in Chapter 5.

Part III: Best Practices

Understanding the technology is great, but is no guarantee of success. Part III will help you identify potential risk and best approaches for mitigating risk as you develop and deploy your solution. These best practices are described in the following three chapters:

Chapter 10: Scoping the Effort and an Approach for Success

This chapter describes how to uncover initiatives by your business community, securing business sponsorship, endorsing a methodology, project staffing, and managing risk.

Chapter 11: Understanding Business Needs

Business needs for better business intelligence might be driven by a poorly designed solution or by a new business requirement. Examples of less optimal solutions and how they can impact the business are first described in this chapter. Typical project drivers driven by business requirements are then presented followed by suggestions on how to build support for a project.

Chapter 12: Justifying Projects and Claiming Success

Getting the go-ahead to build a solution often requires financial justification. This chapter identifies the potential costs you should consider and where business benefits might come from. Financial benefits are computed for a variety of scenarios and computing return on investment (ROI) is described.

Illustrations in the Text

Oracle product illustrations in the text are captured from recent Oracle software versions. You should be able to leverage similar capabilities regardless of your Oracle software version provided you have Oracle Database 10g, Oracle Business Intelligence 10g, or newer releases of these products. We frequently indicate when key features were introduced in these products so that if you have older releases deployed, you can understand limitations you might face.

From Here

To become an expert on this topic usually requires years of practice and learning, implementations for a variety of companies and organizations, and the uncommon ability to feel equally at home discussing needs and details among both IT and business co-workers. For those that grow in such expertise, there is great opportunity and potential reward.

This book is intended to help lay that foundation. Of course, your success will depend not only on what you read in the following chapters, but also on how you put what you learn here into practice in the solutions you work on. As you now start reading this book, it is our hope that it will help you avoid many common pitfalls and that you will gain a better perspective on how to attain professional success in building and deploying such projects.

PART

Oracle Business Intelligence Defined

Oracle Business Intelligence

Business intelligence can be defined as having the right access to the right data or information needed to make the right business decisions at the right time. The data might be raw or might have been analyzed in some way. Having access to such information enables management of the business by fact instead of by primarily relying on intuition.

This is a broad definition of business intelligence and is not limited to data warehousing alone. Although a data warehouse is often used to provide such a solution and is the primary focus of most of this book, we'll broaden the discussion to also include business intelligence gained from on-line transaction processing solutions. Business analysts and users of business intelligence don't really care about — or want to understand where their information comes from. They simply want access to such sources. So the solution you choose to deploy will depend on the kind of information that is needed.

This chapter provides a broad discussion of Oracle's business intelligence offerings and should help you better understand all of the solution types available for deployment. We conclude this chapter by discussing some of the emerging business needs that will lead to a further blending of data warehousing and transactional systems. In subsequent chapters in this section of the book, we provide more details as to how and why you'd deploy transactional business intelligence and data warehousing solutions. We also discuss some of the platform strategies for deployment.

After the introductory first section of this book, we describe in much greater detail the area of business intelligence that you are probably most interested in: custom-built data warehousing solutions using Oracle databases. We provide examples of how you can design, use, and manage various capabilities of the Oracle database and Oracle business intelligence tools. In the final section of this book, we discuss best practices and strategies for deployment of such solutions.

Although the primary audience of the book is information technology (IT) professionals, we begin this book with the following warning: building a business intelligence solution as an IT project without sponsorship of or buy-in by the lines of business is likely to end in very limited success or career-limiting failure. For many of you, the non-technical portions of this book in the best practices section might initially be of the least interest, because your interest is centered in IT and implementing technology platform solutions. However, applying techniques described in that section could determine whether your project is viewed as successful.

Business Intelligence and Transactional Applications

Transactional applications generally provide business intelligence to business users through reports that reveal current data in transactional tables. Oracle's E-Business Suite of applications, PeopleSoft applications, JD Edwards applications, and Siebel Customer Relationship Management applications all provide this level of business intelligence. Reporting is selected and deployed based on key business requirements (KBRs) and most commonly displayed as key performance indicators (KPIs) in a dashboard using portal technology.

Most companies also deploy business intelligence solutions that rely on a complementary data warehousing strategy when reporting and analysis becomes more complex and summary level information is appropriate. Oracle's PeopleSoft and JD Edwards' EnterpriseOne applications are often surrounded by the PeopleSoft Enterprise Performance Management (EPM) data warehouse to enable such reporting through analytical applications. Oracle's Siebel Customer Relationship Management (CRM) applications are similarly often surrounded by Business Analytics Applications built upon a relationship management warehouse model. Other application vendors (such as SAP with their Business Warehouse) have such data warehouse models that often are deployed on Oracle databases.

The Oracle E-Business Suite leverages more of a blended approach to delivering business intelligence applications as many of these applications rely on data in summary levels of transactional tables. The Enterprise Planning and Budgeting application, a more complex analytical application, leverages Oracle OLAP technology in a separate multi-dimensional cube.

At the time of publication of this book, Oracle has described many aspects of Project Fusion, Oracle's future single set of transactional applications that provide a migration path for current deployments of the E-Business Suite, PeopleSoft, JD Edwards, and Siebel CRM applications. The business intelligence solutions provided for this next generation of applications will continue to provide a blending of transactional business intelligence and incorporate data warehousing concepts.

Among Oracle E-Business Suite and PeopleSoft EPM offerings, a number of common business intelligence applications are provided including a balanced scorecard, activity-based management, and enterprise planning and budgeting applications. In addition, the Oracle E-Business Suite has Daily Business Intelligence. We'll briefly describe what these applications do in this chapter, and describe them in more detail in Chapter 2.

Where multiple transaction processing vendors' data models are present, a variety of integration approaches are also possible. We include a discussion of some of those in this chapter.

Daily Business Intelligence

To speed deployment of management reporting showing real-time transaction-level data, the Oracle E-Business Suite features Daily Business Intelligence. Many key management roles are pre-defined, including roles of Chief Executive Officer, vice president of operations, vice president of procurement, vice president of service contracts, project executive, marketing manager, sales manager, manager of e-mail, profit center manager, and cost center manager.

A performance management framework is provided to define KPIs (or measures) and dimensions, set targets, and subscribe to alerts. Out-of-the-box, over 250 key measures are predefined, including revenue, expenses, costs of revenue, contribution margin, gross margin, percentage margin, total headcount and average salary per employee, lead activity, lead conversion, purchase order purchases, contract leakage, inventory turns, and project revenue. Common dimensions are supported across the E-Business Suite modules, including time, geography, customer, supplier, item, warehouse, currency, manager, organization, project organization, sales group, and operating group.

Reports are typically at the day level with period-to-date calculations available for any day. Data is aggregated at multiple levels of the time dimension, including day, week, month, quarter, and year. Report pages are provided out-of-the-box for profit and loss, expense management, compliance management, HR management, operations management, order management, fulfillment management, project profitability management, product lifecycle management, profit operations management, quote management, marketing management, leads management, sales management, sales comparative performance, opportunity management, procurement management, procure-to-pay management, and service contracts management.

Figure 1-1 shows a dashboard view provided by Daily Business Intelligence for sales management of forecasts with KPIs available for sales group and direct reports forecasts, pipeline and weighted pipeline, and won to period.

Balanced Scorecard

Executives have long sought a strategic management tool based on measurements of financial status, customer feedback and other outcomes, and internal process flows that illustrate the state of the business and expose areas where improvement might be desirable. In 1992, Drs. David Norton and Robert Kaplan developed such a tool and named it the Balanced Scorecard. This tool is often used at companies focused on Total Quality Management (TQM), where the goals are measurement-based management and feedback, employee empowerment, continuous improvement, and customer-defined quality.

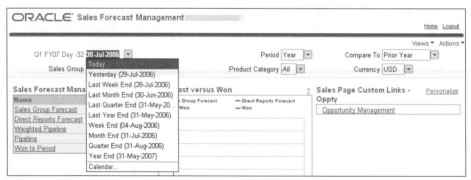

Figure 1-1: A sales manager's view within Daily Business Intelligence

A Balanced Scorecard incorporates a feedback loop around business process outputs and the outcome of the business strategies. This double-loop feedback provides a comparison to financials that results in a more balanced approach to business management. Typical metrics viewed show present status of an organization, provide diagnostic feedback and trends in performance over time, indicate which metrics are critical, and provide input for forecasting.

Oracle's E-Business Suite and PeopleSoft brands offer Balanced Scorecard products that will be merged into a single product in Oracle's next generation Fusion applications. KPIs are viewed through a desktop interface enabling achievement of business goals to be monitored and strategic actions to be taken and recorded. The E-Business Suite Balanced Scorecard can leverage KPIs present in Daily Business Intelligence. Scorecards and associated reports are created with design tools present in the products.

Figure 1-2 shows a typical balanced scorecard strategy map showing the status of various processes.

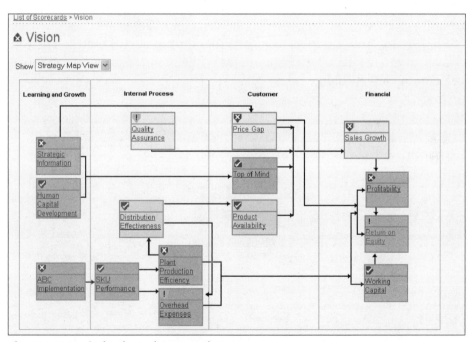

Figure 1-2: Typical Balanced Scorecard strategy map

Enterprise Planning and Budgeting

Chief Financial Officers (CFOs) and their staffs plan budgets, forecast financial achievements, and monitor and analyze the results. Oracle's E-Business Suite and PeopleSoft brands each offer Enterprise Planning and Budgeting (EPB) tools (see Figure 1-3) that will be merged into a single offering when Oracle releases the next generation Fusion applications. Since EPB solutions provide updates to the transactions systems, each branded version of EPB today features seamless integration with corresponding general ledger products. The E-Business Suite tool leverages Oracle's database OLAP Option for analysis and leverages the Enterprise Performance Foundation (EPF) that includes predefined schema, open interface tables, and loader engines. The PeopleSoft version leverages the EPM schema and loading capabilities.

By deploying an EPB solution, what-if budgeting analyses can be compared. EPB can enable consistent and repeatable methodologies to be put into place for planning budgets and agreeing upon forecasts. Models can be shared. The analyses results can be viewed through a portal or shared through e-mail, worksheets, briefing books, or spreadsheets.

EPB reports and budgets can include multiple currencies. Historic results can use the actual exchange rates while planned projects can incorporate budgeted exchange rates.

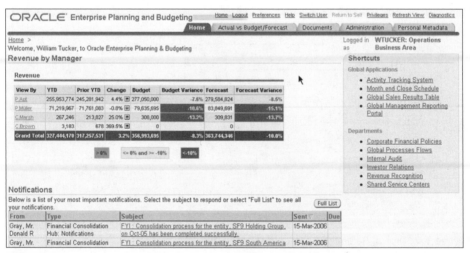

Figure 1-3: Oracle E-Business Suite Enterprise Planning and Budgeting

Activity-Based Management

Although transactional applications typically show costs of components, gaining an understanding of total costs of product, services, or customers can require a more targeted application. Activity-Based Management (ABM) solutions provide a means to map these individual costs including activities, materials, resources, and products or services. As a result, it becomes possible to understand the profitability of customers, products, channels, and markets. Oracle's E-Business Suite and PeopleSoft brands each offer ABM tools. These will be merged into a single offering in Oracle's next generation Fusion applications. Today, each is integrated with the brand's corresponding general ledger offering.

Using an ABM solution, activity costs can be analyzed for setting appropriate charge-back rates, establishing performance benchmarks, and target costing of new product development. Activities, materials, and other costs can be mixed and matched in preparation for bids or based on sales volume projections. Unused capacity costs can be tracked.

Oracle Integration Components Enabling Business Intelligence

A classic approach to providing a single version of the truth, where multiple transactional applications exist, is to build a data warehouse. This is common practice where the goal is to store and analyze years of transactional history and where data quality in source systems is a known issue. However, alternative integration strategies are sometimes used where only recent transactions are needed for business intelligence. Solutions based on Oracle technology components are enabled through what is called Oracle Fusion Middleware, also known as the Oracle Application Server.

A variety of solutions exist. Data hubs can be leveraged to create a master data model where the goal is a common representation of key performance indicators around customers, financials, and other areas. Business activity monitoring can provide an alert-based solution for viewing transactional changes from a variety of sources. BPEL can be used to define business processes among different systems. An Enterprise Messaging Service can be deployed to link data feeds among widely differing sources.

Integration strategy is a lengthy topic and covering it in detail is not a goal for this book. However, we do provide an introduction to some of the key concepts here.

Data Hubs

Data hubs are centralized repositories used to reconcile data from multiple source systems. They are often used where companies have deployed multiple vendors' transactional solutions with different data definitions and where it is desired to have a single location where an official definition lives. Reconciled data can be enriched with other data, viewed, and created or updated. In some situations, data might be sent back in a correct form to source systems (although this can introduce additional workload on those systems, so it is less common in practice). Although hubs are sometimes confused with operational data stores (an ODS is shown in Figure 1-5 later in this chapter), a hub is different in that it usually points to data residing in the originating systems without physically moving the data into the hub.

Oracle's first hubs were based on the E-Business Suite schema and include the Customer Hub, Financial Consolidation Hub, Product Information Management Data Hub, Citizen Data Hub, and Financial Services Accounting Data Hub. Because of this, Oracle's hubs are well integrated with Daily Business Intelligence and the Balanced Scorecard products. Oracle also offers a Customer Master Data integration hub created by Siebel prior to the acquisition by Oracle.

Business Activity Monitoring

Business Activity Monitoring (BAM) enables the monitoring in real-time through dashboards of business services and processes, including correlation of KPIs to business processes. The goal is to enable business executives to take corrective action in a much more timely fashion.

Unlike traditional business intelligence tools that rely on periodic polling to update information, BAM uses an alerting infrastructure to update the dashboard when changes occur. Hence, BAM is a true monitor of changes and can be paired with traditional business intelligence tools where further analyses may be necessary. BAM can also be used as an infrastructure for custom dashboard monitoring across multiple source systems. Business managers can define and modify their own dashboard pages.

Oracle also builds and provides BAM-based applications such as the PeopleSoft Customer Relationship Management (CRM) dashboards. For example, the Enterprise Sales Dashboard provides a real-time view into revenue attainment, pipeline status, and sales-team performance. The Enterprise Order Capture Dashboard displays the status of orders, revenue quotas, and order throughput. Enterprise dashboards for Service, Helpdesk, and Human Resources Helpdesk monitor case and e-mail throughput, service-level adherence, and agent and group case workload levels.

BPEL Process Manager

As companies move toward a service-oriented architecture (SOA) for deployment of business processes, assembling these reusable processes together into business process flows is desirable. The Business Process Execution Language for Web Services (BPEL) is an XML-based language that enables the building of such process flows. The Oracle BPEL Process Manager is Oracle's tool providing the necessary infrastructure to design, build, and monitor the flows. It has support for asynchronous interactions, flow control, and compensating business transactions.

When using Oracle BPEL, you first synchronously define needed services to be invoked, then define exception handling procedures, build assignments of relevant XML information that should be leveraged in the decision making process, define triggers for callback services, and define conditional branches. Oracle BPEL includes an automated testing interface, including audit trails and debugger. Figure 1-4 shows the BPEL Console interface.

After testing, you can deploy to a J2EE application server (most commonly Oracle Fusion Middleware Application Server). In production, the business asynchronous flow is initiated, then asynchronous callbacks are received, and the process flow subsequently branches to and presents the appropriate business outcome.

Enterprise Messaging Service

In SOA and other deployments where trickle feeds of data are needed in order to integrate distributed applications, Enterprise Service Bus (ESB) solutions are becoming common. The ESB provides an underlying messaging infrastructure.

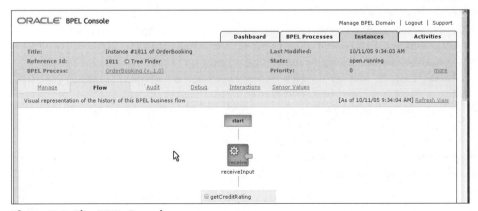

Figure 1-4: The BPEL Console

Oracle provides an ESB solution through the Oracle Enterprise Messaging Service (OEMS). OEMS is built upon the standards-based Java Message Service (JMS) and the J2EE Connector Architecture (J2CA). It can be integrated with non-Oracle messaging infrastructures such as IBM WebSphereMQ (MQSeries), Tibco Enterprise JMS, and SonicMQ. Various service levels are possible for persistence and recovery, including in-memory, file system, and database-backed message persistence.

Custom Data Warehouse Solutions

In the late 1980s and early 1990s, decision support databases began to be deployed separately from transactional databases and were instead deployed into what became known as data warehouses. This model of separating the workloads was driven by the need to report on, query, and analyze increasingly large amounts of data with varying levels of complexity. An important goal was not to impact the transactional systems while doing this. There was much debate during the 1990s as to whether a single enterprise data warehouse with a third normal data model was appropriate as the separate database, or whether the right solution was departmental data marts deployed with star schema. As the decade progressed, the tradeoffs associated with each approach became understood.

THIRD NORMAL FORM AND STAR SCHEMA

In a normal form database, all attributes are atomic and contain unique values (not sets) and cannot have nested relationships. A database is considered to be a second normal form if all relationships of nonprimary attributes are based on the primary keys. In a third normal form, nonprimary attributes are linked using keys to foreign keys. There is no discernable pattern in this linkage. Third normal form schema are common in transaction processing databases and enterprise data warehouses.

By comparison, a star schema appears to be in the shape of a star in a schema diagram. It consists of a relatively large transaction or fact table surrounded by and linked to dimension or look-up tables through foreign keys. The dimensions contain hierarchies representing the roll-up of summary levels. One of the dimensions is almost always time. The star schema is ideal for posing queries similar to: "How many transactions occurred in a specific location over a specific period of time?" As a result, such schema are considered ideal where business analysts access a database and want to perform ad hoc queries or their own analysis.

Enterprise data warehouses were initially proposed as a single repository of all historic data for a company. In many companies, this approach became bogged down in the politics of creating a single data model and gaining corporate-wide approval. Inevitable delays resulted and little or no business value was delivered in a timely fashion. Where only enterprise data warehouses were created during this time, the schema design was typically third normal form enabling flexible update strategies but not providing the ease of use many business analysts expected.

The alternative exercised in many companies was the building of data marts as departmental initiatives. These marts could be more quickly deployed when driven by local business needs, but they were often designed and deployed without any inter-departmental coordination. Questions that crossed two departments could be asked of separated data marts and two different answers would often be obtained. Data marts were typically deployed with star schema enabling business users to more easily submit ad hoc queries and perform analyses.

A solution that emerged in the late 1990s to address the downside of both of these deployment models was the incremental building of an enterprise data warehouse at the same time dependent data marts were built using consistent data definitions. The marts were often fed from the enterprise data warehouse that became the single source of truth. Figure 1-5 is a representation of this commonly deployed business intelligence topology where an operational data store is also present as a gathering point of transactional data.

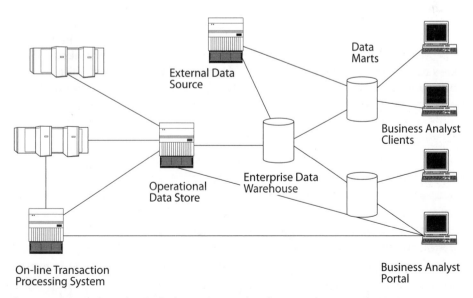

Figure 1-5: Topology that includes an enterprise data warehouse and marts

Today, many companies are leveraging the advanced data warehousing features in databases such as Oracle to consolidate the data mart schema into the same database as the enterprise data warehouse. The resulting hybrid schema is the third normal form for the detailed data and star schema or OLAP cubes for the summary-level data.

The Oracle database is capable of supporting such hybrids and features embedded analytics and star optimization for business analysis combined with advanced management capabilities enabling ongoing maintenance of very large implementations. Oracle's business intelligence tools can leverage many of the database analysis features. The focus of much of this book will be on how to deploy the database for data warehousing and how to appropriately set up and use the business intelligence tools. For example, Chapter 5 describes tradeoffs of the various design approaches we introduced here.

The Role of the Oracle Database

The Oracle database is the heart of a data warehousing and business intelligence solution. Oracle's long history as a relational database vendor dates back to the late 1970s with an initial focus on online transaction processing workloads. As deployment of data warehouses for decision support and business intelligence became popular, Oracle began adding features to address such workloads, most notably beginning with Oracle7 in 1991. Today, the Oracle database contains a rich set of features designed for today's most demanding business intelligence environments.

For example, Oracle added performance features such as extensive parallelism, static bitmap indexes, advanced star join techniques, materialized views and embedded analytic functions, multi-dimensional cubes (OLAP), and data mining. As the databases have grown in size and complexity, Oracle developed more extensive management and self-management capabilities including Enterprise Manager's specific features for data warehousing management, automatic degree of parallelism, memory allocation at query time, a database resource manager, table compression, the Automatic Database Diagnostics Monitor (ADDM), and the Automatic Storage Manager (ASM). Of course, as data warehouses obtain their data from other sources, Oracle added and optimized many data movement capabilities within the database including SQL*Loader for direct path loading, extraction, transformation, and loading (ETL) extensions to SQL, transportable tablespaces, and Streams for advanced queuing and replication.

These features are all necessary; although a data warehouse can start small and relatively simple, providing the right data to make fundamental business decisions often requires more historical data over time in finer granularity and detail. Analysis needs might require near real-time access to the data. As business analysts evolve in their understanding of the data, simple reporting is often not enough and many begin to augment their decision making with ad hoc queries and sophisticated analyses.

Since business needs continue to evolve in most companies, most data warehouses are never considered to be complete. Rather, a data warehouse is deployed in an evolutionary way in order to match business requirements when business needs change.

We'll spend much of the focus of this book not only explaining what the previously mentioned features do, but also how they can be applied and the best practices that should be considered. As we are also covering how the business intelligence tools fit in an overall deployment strategy, we'll now provide a brief introduction to those tools here.

Oracle Warehouse Builder

Oracle Warehouse Builder (OWB) is an infrastructure builders' tool most often used during the design and deployment of data warehouses. The data warehouse design might include schema in third normal form, star schema, OLAP cubes, or as a hybrid schema of multiple types. OWB provides an interface to also define the source to target data extraction, transformation and load (ETL) mappings, generate the ETL script, coordinate workflows, and perform metadata management. Figure 1-6 shows the Design Center in OWB where projects and connections are defined and components shared.

OWB-generated scripts can pull data from other Oracle databases, other relational sources accessible via ODBC or Oracle Transparent Gateways, and from flat files with fixed width or delimited columns. Integrators are available to enable ease in building extractions from source tables in the Oracle E-Business Suite, PeopleSoft, or SAP applications. The generated scripts can be scheduled using Oracle Enterprise Manager or other popular schedulers and can leverage Oracle Workflow.

A library of standard data transformations is provided and custom libraries can be built and shared. Name and address cleansing can be incorporated in the ETL scripts using libraries available from third-party vendors for various geographies around the world. Oracle Warehouse Builder also added data profiling capabilities as part of a Data Quality Option first released in 2006. Formerly packaged in the Internet Developer Suite, the OWB base version is now included with the database. Other options in addition to the Data Quality Option include Enterprise ETL and the previously mentioned Applications Connectors.

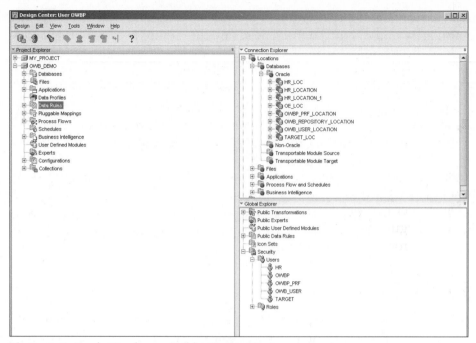

Figure 1-6: Oracle Warehouse Builder Design Center

All development done with OWB, including importing of source definitions, mapping of sources to targets, building of custom transformations,
and added descriptions, are stored in the OWB repository that the OWB
client is linked to. This metadata is stored consistent with a version of the
Common Warehouse Metamodel (CWM) definition, a specification from
the Object Management Group. Data lineage and impact analysis diagrams
can be viewed through a browser. Metadata bridges are provided for many
tools, including Oracle tools such as Discoverer. In addition, third-party
bridges from the OWB version of CWM to other repository formats are
available.

Oracle Business Intelligence Standard Edition

The two BI tools that form the basis of Oracle Business Intelligence Standard Edition are Oracle Discoverer and Reports. We begin this discussion
with the Oracle business intelligence tool that historically was the most
commonly used by business analysts, Discoverer.

Discoverer

Discoverer was first introduced as an ad-hoc query tool, but added capabilities enabling more extensive analysis (through support of Oracle's OLAP Option) and user-based reporting (including creation of Adobe PDF format and e-mail distribution of reports). Although Discoverer is most often used with data warehouses, it can access any database and is bundled with some versions of Oracle applications. Discoverer is based on concepts that most business users are familiar with: workbooks that define broad business areas and worksheets for specific areas such as you might find in a spreadsheet.

Discoverer has web-based clients named Discoverer Plus and Discoverer Viewer. (Figure 1-7 shows creating a new calculation leveraging analytic functions from within Discoverer Viewer.) An older client-server version named Discoverer Desktop was still available when this book was published. As most deployments are web-based today, Oracle's focus in providing new functionality is limited to the web-based clients. These clients are also part of the Oracle Application Server Enterprise Edition in addition to being packaged with Oracle Business Intelligence Standard Edition.

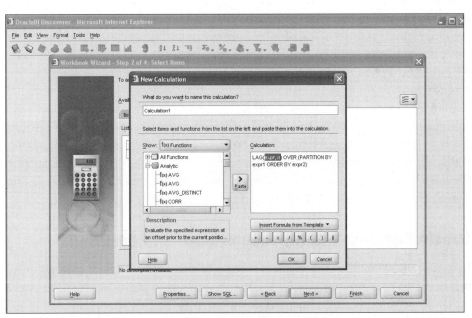

Figure 1-7: Discoverer Viewer showing new calculation creation

Although Discoverer can access any relational database via ODBC, it most commonly is used to access an Oracle database. In fact, it supports features that are specifically enabled by only the Oracle database. For example, in addition to the Oracle OLAP Option support, Discoverer also has integrated Oracle database materialized views creation capabilities for when summary levels in the database would speed queries and usage analysis of those created views.

Discoverer metadata resides in what is called the End User Layer (EUL). Discoverer Administrator software is included in the Oracle Internet Developer Suite, and provides the capability to manage users and the EUL.

Reports

Oracle Reports is an IT-class reporting tool packaged in Oracle Business Intelligence Standard Edition enabling development and deployment of web-based and paper reporting against a variety of data sources, including Oracle relational and OLAP, JDBC, XML, and text files. The Reports services reside in the Oracle Application Server and the Reports Developer is part of the Oracle Internet Developer Suite.

Reports can be generated in batch operations from the command line or using a command file. The command file can be useful if you are running several reports using the same set of arguments. The generated reports can be published to a variety of formats including PDF, XML, HTML, HTMLCSS, PostScript, PCL, delimited text, RTF, and using Java Server Pages (JSPs).

Oracle Reports distribution capabilities enable you to design a report with multiple output formats and distribute the report to multiple destinations from a single run. Distributions can be created for entire reports or individual sections of reports. You might generate, in a single run, HTML output, send a PostScript version to a printer, publish the report to a portal, and e-mail any or all sections of the report to a distribution list or individuals.

Oracle Business Intelligence Enterprise Edition

In 2006, Oracle acquired Siebel, a company primarily known for customer relationship management (CRM) software. Included in the acquisition was a suite of business intelligence tools known as Siebel Business Analytics. Today, these are packaged in Oracle Business Intelligence Enterprise Edition consisting of:

- **Answers** — ad-hoc query tool with basic pivoting, reporting, and charting

- **Intelligence dashboard** — role-based dashboard, displays Answers content

- **Reporting and Publishing** — report building tool

- **Intelligent Interaction Manager** — embeds results in operational systems

- **Offline (Mobile) Analytics** — Dashboard, analysis when disconnected

- **Sense & Respond (Delivers)** — analytics alerting and scheduling

- **Analytics Server** — a mid-tier engine, metadata repository, and cache

Answers, illustrated in Figure 1-8, is deployed as a thin client leveraging HTML and DHTML. It is designed to provide optimal query performance for a variety of popular databases by leveraging the Analytics Server in the middle tier. The Analytics Server provides a query integrator and calculation engine, caching, and a physical SQL generation engine. Database version features are recognized and taken into account when optimizing queries. Where data mining is deployed, Answers processes mining in this mid-tier. Metadata is also stored in this tier, including presentation, logical, and physical metadata. Administration is through the Analytics Server Administrator for managing the catalog and repository.

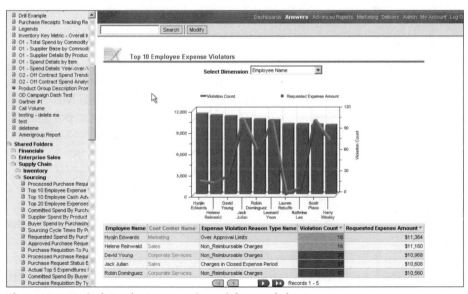

Figure 1-8: Typical Oracle Answers view of data and chart

Prior to the Oracle acquisition, Answers was primarily deployed to analyze only relational data. However, Answers can support Oracle's OLAP Option using the SQL access that the OLAP Option supports. It also has MDX support for Microsoft SQL Sever Analysis Services. Integration with the Oracle Portal is through JSR 168 support.

BI (XML) Publisher

BI Publisher, also known as XML Publisher, is a template-based publishing solution used to develop custom report formats using popular desktop tools such as Adobe Acrobat or Microsoft Word that are familiar to business users. After incorporating XML data extracts, the reports are then created using the Extensible Style-sheet Language Formatting Object (XSL-FO) as the underlying technology for the layout templates.

BI Publisher was originally created to leverage XML data from the Oracle E-Business Suite of Applications to enable easy creation and reuse of highly formatted reports. For example, the XML data can be merged with PDF-provided forms from third parties such as the government. BI Publisher continues to evolve as part of Oracle's business user reporting solution.

Reports can be generated in various output formats, including PDF, RTF, HTML, Excel, XML, and eText. Figure 1-9 shows a sample report layout created using BI Publisher. Conditional formatting is supported. Where multiple languages are desired, BI Publisher can generate a XLFF file for each translation.

Oracle Portal

Oracle Portal enables companies to easily build, administer, and deploy enterprise-class dashboards or portals that display the business' key performance indicators from a variety of sources. Different user communities within a company might be restricted to seeing different aspects of the company's business within the portal. For example, the Human Resources Department portal would show very different key performance indicators than that of the CFO.

Portal administrators have the ability to define regions on the Portal page including graphics, links to other web sites, and dynamic regions known as portlets. Other users of the portal can customize these content areas to some degree, depending on the permission levels they are granted.

BILL OF LADING

Date: <?DATE?>

Page: <?fo:page-number?>

SHIP FROM

Name: <?SHIP_FROM_ADDRESS?>
Address:
City/State/Zip:
SID#:   FOB: ☐

Bill of Lading Number: <?CF_MBOL_NUMBER?>

<?CF_ADD_MBOL_BARCODE1?>
<?CF_MBOL_WITHAI?>

SHIP TO

Name: <?SHIP_TO_ADDRESS?>   Location #:_____
Address:
City/State/Zip:
CID#:   FOB: ☐

CARRIER NAME: <?CF_CARRIER_NAME?>
Trailer number: <?TRAILER_NUMBER?>
Seal number(s): <?SEAL_NUMBER?>
SCAC: <?CF_SCAC_CODE?>
Pro number: <?PRO_NUMBER?>

THIRD PARTY FREIGHT CHARGES BILL TO:

Name: <?CF_FREIGHT_TERMS?>
Address:
City/State/Zip:

<?if:CS_MPRO_NUM_FLAG='Y'?>
<?CF_ADD_PRO_BARCODE2?>
(9012K) <?PRO_NUMBER?><?end if?>

Freight Charge Terms: *(freight charges are prepaid unless marked otherwise)*

SPECIAL INSTRUCTIONS: *Underlying Bill of Lading Numbers*:

| <?if:CS_M_CF_PAID='Y'?> Pre-paid: ☒<?end if?><?if:CS_M_CF_PAID='Y'?> Pre-paid: ☐<?end if?> | <?if:CS_M_CF_COLECT='Y'?> Collect: ☒<?end if?><?if:CS_M_CF_COLLECT!='Y'?> Collect: ☐<?end if?> | <?if:CS_M_CF_THIRD_PARTY='Y'?> 3ʳᵈ Party: ☒<?end if?><?if:CS_M_CF_THIRD_PARTY!='Y'?> 3ʳᵈ Party: ☐<?end if?> |

<?CS_BOL_LIST?>

☒
(check box)

Master Bill of Lading: with attached underlying Bills of Lading

CUSTOMER ORDER INFORMATION

CUSTOMER ORDER NUMBER	# PKGS	WEIGHT	PALLET/SLIP (CIRCLE ONE)		ADDITIONAL SHIPPER INFO
<?for-each:G_DELIVERY_ID?>cust_order num	pkgs	weight	Y	N	additional shipper <?end for-each?>
<?if:CS_COUNT_DELIVERY<1?>			Y	N	<?end if?>

Figure 1-9: Sample report layout created using BI (XML) Publisher

Oracle Business Intelligence suites and Balanced Scorecard are examples of some of Oracle's portlet and Portal content providers. For example, Discoverer portlets include the list of worksheets portlet, worksheet portlet, and gauges portlet. The Oracle Portal has been packaged as a stand-alone product but has more often been purchased as part of the Oracle Application Server Enterprise Edition since that also includes Discoverer and Reports.

Figure 1-10 shows a typical Oracle Portal view with multiple portlets. In this example, the portlet on the right with the analyze link enables the business user to open Discoverer Viewer for further analysis and other customizations. The portlet on the left is from Answers. The output shown in the portlets can be automatically refreshed according to preset schedules.

Spreadsheet Add-ins

Just about every business analyst is familiar with Microsoft Excel and uses this spreadsheet tool to gain intelligence about the business. A growing trend among providers of analytic platforms is to provide spreadsheet support into their platforms. Oracle does this through spreadsheet add-ins for OLAP and for Data Mining.

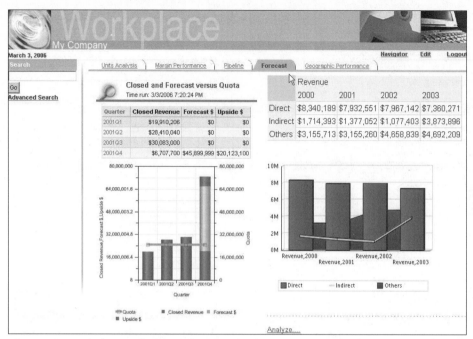

Figure 1-10: Oracle Portal with multiple portlets for various types of business analysis

In the spreadsheet add-in for OLAP, Oracle provides the OracleBI add-in that enables direct access to the OLAP cubes for building queries and calculations. Figure 1-11 shows the OracleBI add-in. The query builder wizards are identical to those present in Discoverer since the same Business Intelligence Java Beans are used. When the query results appear in the spreadsheet, the business user can use standard Excel functionality including Excel graphing and formatting.

The Data Mining spreadsheet add-in has a different purpose in that it provides a simplified introduction to using some of the data mining algorithms in the database. However, like the other add-in, results are returned to the spreadsheet for further manipulation and sharing.

By using spreadsheet add-ins against base data in the Oracle database (as opposed to downloading and manipulating the base data in the spreadsheet), when query results are pulled into the spreadsheet, the original base data remains intact and unchanged in the Oracle database. This can be beneficial where, to meet compliance requirements, you must go back to the original historically accurate data. Of course, for the data stored in the database, you have much more control over access rights and who can change it.

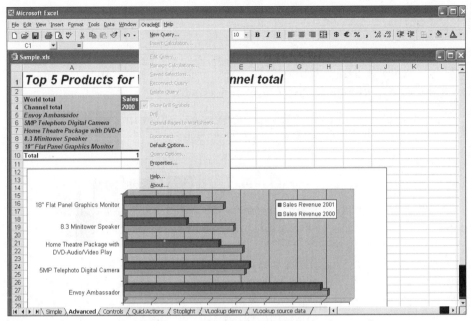

Figure 1-11: The Oracle OLAP spreadsheet add-in pull-down for Excel

Building Custom Business Intelligence Applications

In some situations, commercially available business intelligence tools don't fully match business requirements and customized tools are desired. However, reuse of some of the components that are present in tools such as Oracle Discoverer, the Spreadsheet Add-in, and Enterprise Planning and Budgeting would be useful. For this reason, Oracle made available the same Business Intelligence Java Beans present in Oracle's business intelligence tools available for use with Oracle JDeveloper (an Oracle Development Suite tool).

The BI Beans available include presentation beans (for over 70 graph types and for crosstabs), data beans (providing query and calculation builders), and persistence services for deployment in HTML client and Java client applications. The BI Beans provide a number of Development Wizards enabling creation of objects without coding. Further customization is possible using Java visual editing tools.

Since the applications are Java based, they can be deployed into Java desktop applications or web applications such as Java Server Pages and Servlets. The Beans are also J2EE compliant enabling deployment to Application Servers that support J2EE.

Emerging Trends

Several common requirements are often expressed by business intelligence and data warehousing architects in companies that have mature business intelligence experience. These point to needs for:

- Easy access by a wider group of users to right-time information of high quality when making critical decisions.
- Faster speed of deployment and sharing of results.
- Deployment of enterprise-wide data on lower-cost platforms.

As these requirements are consistent with Oracle's capabilities and focus, we'll briefly discuss the alignment here and practical implementations later in this book.

The need for easy access by a wider group of users is addressed by the common look and feel and shared metadata that the Oracle BI tools provide and the tight integration with the database. Since the database is capable of storing structured and unstructured data in a variety of ways (including relational, OLAP, spatial, object, XML, text, audio, and video), a single version of the truth can be established in a single database. A single database is also desirable for simplification, lower cost, and for enabling corporate compliance. Thus, many companies are consolidating data marts into single larger data warehouses. Of course, the database can be updated in a variety of ways, ranging from batch to trickle feed, to match business requirements and deliver data at the right time.

As we mentioned earlier in this chapter, the building of such an infrastructure is dependent on business drivers and these drivers are often felt in ways that require a rapidly deployed solution. Companies often start building a solution by leveraging generic data models available from consultants or data warehousing solutions from applications providers. Many such solutions are deployed in 90- to 180-day deployment increments today to more quickly establish business value. When these solutions are deployed, it is often desired to share the interesting results of analysis by using collaboration tools for e-mail and web conferences such as the Oracle Collaboration Suite.

Historically, deploying such an infrastructure was quite costly as scalability limits of individual high-end hardware platforms were reached and required replacement. An emerging approach is to deploy instead lower-cost commodity platforms, usually with four CPUs each, as nodes in a Grid infrastructure. Oracle's Real Applications Clusters (RAC) enables deployment of Oracle instances on each node that can then function as a single database across the nodes. Such an infrastructure is often deployed with reliability, availability, and serviceability in mind. Oracle's Grid Control provides a single point of management for using Automatic Storage Management (ASM), Flash Recovery, Flashback, Data Guard, and Information Lifecycle Management (ILM) capabilities. As this infrastructure can enable the sharing of data with bigger and wider communities, security considerations emerge, including deployment of single sign-on, managing data encryption, and maintaining patching and provisioning.

Now that we've introduced the scope of Oracle's business intelligence and how some of these technologies and strategies for deployment are changing, it is time to provide some detail. We begin by covering Oracle's transactional business intelligence in Chapter 2, including Daily Business Intelligence, the Oracle Balanced Scorecard, and Oracle's data hubs.

Oracle's Transactional Business Intelligence

The use of the term *business intelligence* is a signpost for the evolution of technology in today's business climate. Many years ago, the use of computers was referred to as *data processing*, highlighting the core purpose of that technology — to collect, store, and manipulate data. This term was superceded by the term *information technology*, focusing on a higher-level use of data — not just raw data, but information that is more usable by humans. *Business intelligence* brings it all back home, zeroing in on the ultimate purpose of technology in a business environment — to help organizations increase efficiency, profits, and revenue, as well as using data to make intelligent decisions. Business intelligence is gained by the timely display of data to business analysts enabling them to make the best possible business decisions and helping organizations steer their ships of commerce, rather than simply acting as the fuel to run those boats.

This chapter looks at a number of offerings Oracle has created to deliver business intelligence from the data collected by and residing in Oracle's enterprise transactional applications. We'll also cover the role of Oracle's Balanced Scorecard and using Oracle's data hubs to create a master data reference in order to access data from a variety of transactional applications. All of these products are designed to deliver timely business intelligence to the less-technical user — from business analysts to business executives who will be making decisions based on that information.

Transactional Business Intelligence

Before moving on to specific concepts and products, you should understand the meaning of the title of this chapter. Transactional business intelligence is a term that highlights gaining business intelligence in real-time through access to data that resides in online transaction processing (OLTP) databases.[1] In Oracle's E-Business Suite of Applications, this data is stored in a unified data model. Since data across many business areas is represented in this unified data model, Oracle can create pre-build applications that deliver business intelligence in an easy-to-use and consistent format.

By using a single data model, users can easily see across the boundaries sometimes imposed by separate functional areas of a business and executives can look back over limited historical data (since data is not typically retained for long periods in an operational system) and project into future scenarios for the entire business of the organization. And, of course, a single data model makes it much easier for Oracle applications to deliver a standardized set of reports and metrics for business analysts and executives.

This solution is a bit different from creation of data warehouses that are separated from the stores of transactional data. Data warehouses are typically deployed to isolate the potential performance impact of complex unplanned queries operating on large amounts of data, or to create different data designs to efficiently service these queries, or to store a consolidated cleansed source of data apart from the different sources. By their nature, classic data warehouses often have somewhat older data than transactional systems, with data loads ranging from every minute to hourly to daily to weekly. (We cover classic data warehousing in most of the other chapters in this book.)

Business Terminology

Business people will sometimes complain that technologists speak language that they cannot understand using a set of descriptions and concepts that they find foreign. However, a business intelligence discussion can introduce another set of jargon that can appear just as confusing. This section is intended to define and describe some key concepts that are used throughout this chapter. If you already are familiar with them, feel free to jump to the next section.

---

[1]Companies may have their own reasons to isolate business intelligence functionality on different servers, but this choice is usually due to organizational reasons. The Oracle database enables data warehouses and OLTP databases to share the same data.

Corporate Performance Management

Corporate performance management (CPM) is the process of using business intelligence to assess how well a business or portion of a business is performing. Reports are leveraged that highlight the most important metrics measuring this performance. Oracle often uses this term to categorize all business intelligence offerings that are built on transactional applications, data hubs, and application-specific data warehouses. CPM is sometimes also referred to as business performance management (BPM).

In Oracle's E-Business Suite, the offerings provide access to transactional business results and include a feedback loop to allow users to track the effects of process changes to continually refine the processes. Similar PeopleSoft and JD Edwards applications capabilities are delivered through the PeopleSoft Enterprise Performance Management (EPM) data warehouse described in Chapter 3. The Siebel applications also have a data warehouse solution primarily focused on customer relationship management (CRM) that is also described in Chapter 3. Oracle announced, in 2006, a stated direction to combine all of these business intelligence models into a unified analytic and CPM model referred to as Fusion Business Intelligence.

Key Performance Indicators

Key performance indicators (KPIs) are the metrics used to determine how well a business or business unit is performing. Simple KPIs might include metrics like profit and loss, but even simple metrics can become quite complex in larger organizations. An example KPI would be the percentage of the overhead of a shipping department that is charged for individual units shipped. The process of simply defining appropriate metrics to measure and track this type of information can provide significant insight into the way a business operates. KPIs can be defined within horizontal business areas (for example, Financial, Human Resources, Supply Chain) or can be industry vertical specific (for example, airplane landing and take-off turnaround).

Dashboard

A business intelligence dashboard provides a function similar to the dashboard in your car in that it displays the most important information you need to drive your business. In more technical jargon, it is simply a portal page that displays key performance indicators as data and charts and can provide a means to further drill into detail. A dashboard or portal page can contain multiple portlets representing different results and interfaces.

COMPLIANCE AND CORPORATE PERFORMANCE MANAGEMENT

When delivering solutions to satisfy a dizzying array of compliance regulations (Sarbanes-Oxley, Graham-Leach-Bliley, Bassel II Accords, HIPAA, Patriot Act, and others), CPM and business intelligence compliance initiatives should also provide additional business value. But, delivering KPIs to CPM dashboards only fulfills part of compliance requirements. Compliance regulations also introduce a need for more data auditability, more control of who accesses data and can change it, improved system testing procedures, and the ability to verify the accuracy of data at any given point in time.

As previously mentioned in this book, business intelligence projects require close coordination between business users and IT. In compliance projects, typical key business partners to IT should include the Finance and Legal departments within an organization. Many organizations choose to create formal compliance teams that include all of these key parties when implementing such solutions.

For example, each page in an Oracle Daily Business Intelligence module or an Oracle Balanced Scorecard is displayed as a portal page. These portal pages can also be displayed as portlets and with other portlets on a single page.

Dashboards have been called the killer application for business executives, since a dashboard can present information from a variety of sources and provide a quick and easy-to-understand high-level view of business operations. Simple views can be misleading when they inaccurately represent the actual state of the underlying business operations. Although key performance indicators used in Oracle applications such as Daily Business Intelligence and Balanced Scorecard have been carefully chosen and designed to monitor appropriate business data, even these KPIs might be misleading if the data residing in the source systems is not valid.[2]

Oracle's Daily Business Intelligence

Business intelligence can be defined as the process of taking large amounts of data, analyzing that data, and presenting a high-level set of reports that condense the essence of that data into the basis of business actions. Daily business intelligence (DBI) is a term used by Oracle to describe high-level reports and charts that display KPIs from data in transaction tables in Oracle's E-Business Suite, enabling management to make fundamental daily business decisions. DBI was introduced in 2003. It was made available as

---

[2]This, however, is an individual corporate problem far beyond the ability of Oracle to address.

an Oracle patch to E-Business Suite release 11i.9 and has been included in Oracle E-Business Suite applications since release 11i.10.

Each subsequent release of DBI has delivered an increasing number of KPIs. Since the reports and charts are pre-built around Oracle's E-Business Suite of Applications, deployment is greatly accelerated. Business people can quickly gain access to these reports since administrators and developers do not have to spend time creating the infrastructure from scratch. Figure 2-1 illustrates the E-Business Suite Navigator that is used to access to various DBI modules. Typical key steps in an implementation start with determining which dashboards to deploy and which KPIs to disable, and then determining user responsibilities and assignments, whether you want to customize buckets (how data is grouped) in the dashboards, set-up of item dimensions, and determining whether you want to hide any dashboard regions.

DBI currently comes with almost 300 KPIs and close to 800 reports. You can also create your own KPIs for display, and additional reports and charts to expand on indicators summarized in the KPIs. Although the standard KPIs that come with DBI modules only access data in tables used by Oracle applications, you can create your own KPIs that access data in other tables, including tables in external systems.

KPI portlets and associated metadata reside in a Performance Management Framework. A DBI Administrator will typically customize the DBI dashboards to match the needs of the business either by selecting appropriate reports and KPIs, rearranging existing reports and charts, or by adding new reports and charts to the dashboards. Portlets communicate with each other on a single page through a page-level parameter portlet that contains the common parameters. These reside in the Performance Management Viewer.

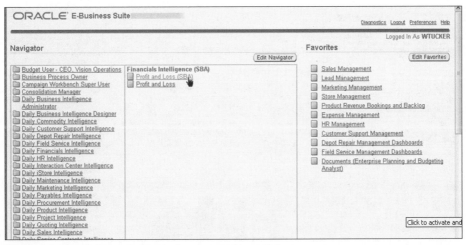

Figure 2-1: E-Business Suite Navigator to DBI modules

Dashboards displaying DBI data can also be deployed using Oracle business intelligence tools. In Figure 2-2, we illustrate a Financials dashboard for profit and loss in an Oracle Business Intelligence Enterprise Edition dashboard.

Different Oracle application modules have different dashboards, presenting the most relevant information for that particular area of business. What users will see is also determined by their roles in the organization. Later, this chapter will provide summaries of the functionality of the various DBI dashboards available at the time that this chapter was written.

There are several noteworthy aspects to the dashboards. The first is that the presentation is within a browser. Since all DBI dashboards are web-based, this eliminates the need for full-scale PCs as clients, as well as the need to install and update client-based software on many different client machines, or require a heavy-duty machine for the use of the dashboard. Any heavy lifting required to create this business intelligence is done on the server or middle tier, which is easier than having to deal with dozens, hundreds, or thousands of client machines. The browser-based interface does not impede on the layout or attractiveness of the DBI dashboard.

The second important aspect of the DBI dashboard is the inclusion of KPIs in the prominent position. This display gives users an immediate understanding of how their business is doing.

Such dashboards typically contain a set of drop-down boxes that let a user quickly specify the basic parameters of the information displayed, such as the date of the displayed information, the time period the information covers, and the currency used in the displays, as well as organization-specific parameters, such as the particular sales group the information relates to.

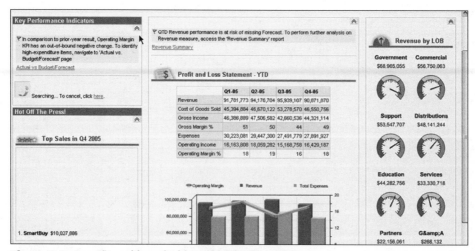

Figure 2-2: A profit and loss dashboard built using DBI

One final aspect of a dashboard comes from the nature of its browser interface and directly addresses the needs of users. There are links to relevant reports, as you would expect in a browser presentation. In addition, for some of the pieces of summary data, such as for KPIs, there are also links, so that clicking the summaries takes users directly to more detailed information on the KPI.

The drill-down mechanism echoes the natural discovery process. The high-level pages give an overview of business conditions. This high-level overview is useful both as a summary and as a guide to areas that require further investigation. A user can simply click the relevant topic to see more information to help further determination of the cause of any anomaly. Oracle E-Business Suite of Applications includes hundreds of reports for multiple levels of drill-down detail.

Information presented in dashboards can be shared in several ways. You can export the data from any report or chart into an Excel spreadsheet file or as a PDF document. You can also e-mail entire dashboards to other users.

How DBI Works

As mentioned previously, a key to the flexibility of DBI is the unified data model. This model provides users access to and extended reporting of data as it resides in transactional systems. A number of common dimensions are supported across business areas, including currency, customer classification, inventory organization, item, operating unit, organization, person, sales group, and time.

Simple drill-down or drill-up to summary-level data is common in business intelligence applications. A specific feature of the Oracle database, known as a materialized view, enables this reporting to work more efficiently. A materialized view is actually summary-level data stored in a physical table and is also commonly used in Oracle data warehouses. Materialized views are used to pre-calculate various totals, making the creation of management reports much less resource intensive. Instead of calculating aggregations on the fly, reports can simply read the summary level data from the materialized views.

Materialized views are updated based on scheduling defined by the DBI administrator. Incremental refreshes are commonly used to provide timely updates of summary-level data. The E-Business Suite Concurrent Manager triggers the updates. The responsiveness delivered by materialized views enables DBI to provide simple drill-down capabilities in a transactional application. DBI uses its standard views and materialized views for the base information in creating the reports used as data sources for the KPIs.

Of course, Oracle's Multi-Version Read Consistency (MVRC) also helps make such an approach practical. Simply put, with MVRC, data readers do not block data writers, and vice versa. This scheme means that read-intensive business intelligence operations will not necessarily interfere with the performance of mission-critical OLTP operations.

The illustration in Figure 2-3 shows the architecture that supports DBI. The Oracle database supporting the Oracle E-Business Suite provides the detailed transaction data that is used to create DBI metrics. On top of that core data is a set of views consisting of base summaries and materialized views (providing appropriately aggregated data) used to create reports. These reports are then summarized as a number of key performance indicators, which are, in turn, used to build the various DBI modules.

Figure 2-3 also illustrates various ways to populate the E-Business Suite with data from external sources.

Varieties of DBI

As mentioned previously, Oracle applications include DBI offerings for various areas of business focus. All of these use the same architecture but each of them has a targeted set of metrics or KPIs and reports for specific business areas. So each DBI area uses relevant tables and data from specific areas of the E-Business Suite.

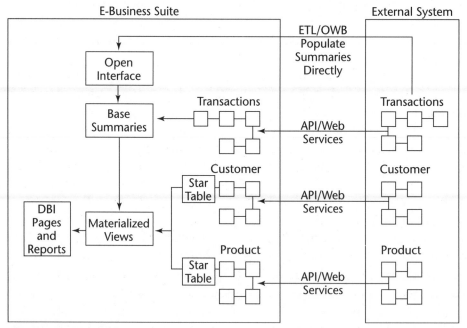

Figure 2-3: DBI architecture

DBI components can take a very wide view of business activities — over time, over separate functions, such as development, sales and inventory — and present easy to comprehend metrics to rate the overall affect of various individual functions. But since each DBI is oriented towards a specific operational area, each can also deliver concise yet pithy metrics to address the needs of different functional groups or roles within an organization.

Oracle is continually adding new DBI offerings. The remainder of this section provides brief descriptions of existing DBI offerings at the time this book was published. The following descriptions present a very high-level view of the type of intelligence delivered by the DBI modules, but will hopefully give you an idea of how they can help you improve the operational efficiency of your business.

Daily Business Intelligence for Compliance

Daily Business Intelligence for Compliance (DBI-C) tracks compliance progress by leveraging data from the Oracle Internal Controls Manager in the Oracle E-Business Suite. Key areas tracked include audit opinions, compliance environment change, business process certification, organization certification, and financial statement certification. Negative evaluations and certification results are reported as KPIs in the Internal Controls Manager so you can drill down from DBI-C into the more detailed reports.

The DBI-C main dashboard is called the Financial Statement Certification Dashboard. KPIs include significant account evaluation status, organization certification status, and process certification status. Drill-downs are provided to the account evaluation reports, organization certification and process certification reports, the open issues report, the open remedial action report, and the compliance environment change report.

Daily Business Intelligence for Customer Support

In this DBI module, the key entity tracked is support requests typical in a customer support organization. Data comes from the Oracle TeleService application. Broad DBI for Customer Support (DBI-CS) metrics include backlog, activity, resolution, and closure. Individual KPIs provided include service request backlog, unresolved service request backlog, unresolved escalated and unowned service request backlogs, service request opened and closed activities, mean time to resolve service requests, and service request close time.

DBI-CS is particularly useful for a customer support manager. Backlogs can be analyzed by severity and by problem escalation. In addition,

DBI-CS can identify rate of closure and support requests that have been re-opened, a phenomena that reduces both customer satisfaction and the efficiency of the support department.

Daily Business Intelligence for Depot Repair

DBI for Depot Repair (DBI-CR) provides metrics customized to the needs of organizations that repair products. KPIs provided include repair order backlog, past due percent, repair order margin, completed repair orders, late completion percent, and mean time to repair.

Since items only come into repair depots when there has been a problem, promptly addressing such problems can have a significant impact on customer satisfaction and loyalty. Repair Depot managers can determine the amount of time it takes to complete repairs, how long repairs have been in process, and whether the time to repair is improving or getting worse. Data comes from Oracle Depot Repair, TeleService, Order Management, Inventory, Work in Process, and Order Management applications.

DBI-DR can help to avoid problems by prioritizing repairs based on how quickly the repair was promised to the customer. Managers can use all of these indicators to help determine how effective their repair operation is. They can also determine the amount charged for a repair, the cost, and the margin.

Daily Business Intelligence for Field Service

Field Service is a business area where technicians are assigned tasks such as installation, service, and repair on a daily basis. Having an accurate, up-to-date source of information about active requests is required in implementing efficient field service departments. DBI for Field Service (DBI-FS) displays a broad range of metrics involved in field service operations including inventory of parts, mean time to repair, and service technicians travel or labor rations. This DBI module also enables managers to compare reported travel times to similar locations, enabling them to spot variances that could lead to improved scheduling or other corrective actions.

DBI-FS reports include technician utilization and utilization trends, usable inventory days on-hand, travel time and distance (and trends), travel time and distance distribution, travel time and distance variance, travel time and distance variance distribution, and task travel detail. KPIs include technician utilization, inventory usage value, on-hand inventory value, average travel time (in minutes), average travel distance, task backlog, task closed activity, first time fix rate, and mean time to resolve (in hours).

Daily Business Intelligence for Financials

DBI for Financials (DBI-F) can help managers across all lines of a company's business to react to changes in the financial status of the company much faster. In organizations without access to this type of solution, financial information is typically compiled on a quarterly basis and then shared within the company. DBI-F enables authorized users to get a daily view of revenue and expenses for the entire organization as well as different segments, making it possible for the company to take an active role, rather than reactive role, in addressing potential issues. Within DBI-F, you can incorporate budget and forecast information. The two content areas displayed by DBI-F are general ledger revenue and expense reporting, and payables reporting.

General ledger revenue and expense reporting dashboards include profit and loss, profit and loss by manager, expense management, expense analysis, and funds management, payables management, and payables status. Part of the set-up includes determining which set of books to collect data from and rules to follow for including journals. You also define which segments in the chart of accounts the dimensions will be based on, build hierarchies for financial dimensions (such as cost), and specify budgets to be extracted from Oracle General Ledger.

The profit and loss dashboard includes reports for cumulative revenue, revenue summary, revenue by sales channel, cost of goods sold, gross margin, expense summary, and operating margin. KPIs include revenue, expenses, operating margin, and operating margin percent. The profit and loss by manager dashboard includes similar reports with similar KPIs.

The expense management dashboard reports include an expense summary, headcount and expenses trend, expenses per head, travel and entertainment expenses, and top ten spenders. The KPIs include expenses, percent of forecast, forecast versus budget, expenses per head, travel and entertainment expenses per head, and headcount. Expense analysis dashboard reports include expense and revenue summaries, expense and revenue rolling trends, and cumulative expense trends. KPIs displayed include expenses, budget, percent of budget, forecast, and percent of forecast.

The funds management dashboard enables public sector (state and municipal government and higher education institutions) to see budget, encumbrances, actual expenses, and available funds for each fund, cost center, and expense category. KPIs include funds available, percent available, budget, encumbrance balances due to commitments, encumbrance balances due to obligations, encumbrance values not due to commitments or obligations, and actual expenses. Dashboard reports include funds available, budget summary, budget trend by account detail, encumbrance summary, encumbrance trend by account detail, and funds available trend. There is also a link to the expense summary report in the expense analysis dashboard.

The payables management dashboard displays reports for invoice activity, invoice detail, invoice types, electronic invoices, electronic invoices trend, paid invoices, electronic and paid late invoices, paid late invoices, paid invoice discounts, holds activity and trend, past due invoices, and invoice activity detail. KPIs include invoices entered, electronic invoices, invoices paid, percent of invoices paid late, invoice to payment days, number of payments, and percent discount offered and taken. A payables status dashboard includes reports providing an open payables summary, invoices due aging summary, invoices past due aging summary, invoice aging, past due invoices, discount opportunities summary, holds summary, invoices on hold discount summary, holds categories summary, hold trend, and invoice status detail. KPIs displayed include open payables amount, invoices due amount, number of invoices due, weighted average days due, invoices past due amount, discount remaining and offered amounts, and total and percent of invoices on hold.

Daily Business Intelligence for Human Resources

Human Resources may not seem like a department that could benefit from business analysis as much as some of the other operational areas already described. But every part of an organization is composed of human components, and DBI for Human Resources (DBI-HR) tracks both the overall headcount and various aspects of staff turnover, by manager at different levels in the organization. DBI-HR can take into account different types of employment, including hourly workers or suspended workers. DBI-HR can also take these measurements and combine them with salary information to highlight the impact of salary on factors such as turnover.

DBI-HR reports include annualized turnover, turnover status, detail and trend, salary by job function, job family and detail, and headcount reports including hire detail, transfer detail, termination detail, and country, budget and salary trends. KPIs include headcount of employees, salaries of employees, average salary, and total annualized turnover.

Daily Business Intelligence for Interaction Center

DBI for Interaction Center (DBI-IC) is designed to deliver advanced analytic information for call center management at several levels. The measures are shown in DBI-IC dashboards that track e-mail activity and trends and inbound telephony operations. The ability to track and compare across historic levels helps management to improve efficiency and identify any particular bottlenecks in the operation.

Email Center reports include overall activity, activity by agent and customer, response performance, backlog aging, resolution, and outcome result and reason. KPIs include percentage of emails replied within service levels, transfer rate, delete rate, one and done resolution, service level goal, customer wait time, number received, replied to, in backlog, and composed, service request created, leads, and replies per agent hour.

Inbound Telephony reports include overall activity and activity by agent and customer. KPIs include inbound service level, average speed to answer, abandon rate, transfer rate, inbound calls handled, agent dialed calls, web callbacks handled, agent availability rate, agent utilization rate, average talk time per call, average wrap time per call, calls handled per agent hour, service requests created, leads created, and opportunities created.

Daily Business Intelligence for iStore

DBI for iStore (DBI-iS) is designed to provide a comprehensive view of sales, products sold, and customer orders in Oracle's eCommerce web store. Since the entire sales cycle, from browsing to ordering, takes place in a computing environment, DBI-iS can transform data collected over the range of eCommerce activities into meaningful business intelligence. DBI-iS dashboards include a store management dashboard and a store top activity dashboard.

The store management dashboard displays new customer count, cart and order activity reports, cart to order conversion ratios, average order value and discount, activity by product category reports, and total booked and campaign related order amounts. The store top activity dashboard displays top orders, top products sold, top customer orders, and top carts by sales amount.

Daily Business Intelligence for Marketing (DBI-M)

Marketing is usually one of the most squishy areas of a business since it is difficult to tie explicit marketing expenses to specific sales and profitability gains. DBI for Marketing (DBI-M) helps your organization understand the impact of marketing activities by providing dashboards for marketing management and lead management with an aggregate view of the entire range of marketing activities and an ability to drill down to look at specific campaigns. Where enough history is stored in transactions tables, DBI-M allows comparisons over time.

Marketing management KPIs include leads from customers, leads from prospects, top or « A » leads, new opportunities sales credit sum, won opportunities sales credit sum, cost per lead, revenue per lead, lead to opportunity conversion, number of campaigns started, and number of events started. Lead management KPIs include amount opportunities converted from leads, number and percentage of leads converted to opportunities, new leads, open leads, top or « A » leads, average lead age in days, and average « A » lead age in days.

Users can map campaigns to various sales groups within the company and compare marketing activities with sales results. Sales impact can be broken into direct impact and inferred impact, thus comparing marketing activities to overall sales trends regardless of whether sales were designated as marketing driven. All of this intelligence can be used to calculate realistic return on investment (ROI) from marketing activities, useful in validating marketing budgets.

Daily Business Intelligence for Maintenance

DBI for Maintenance (DBI-Mt) is organized around the entities common to maintenance organizations, such as work orders. Managers can examine various aspects of work orders moving through the system through a Maintenance Management dashboard. Some of the work order information available includes work order number, type, asset and asset group, activity to be performed, status, assigned department, actual incurred cost, cost breakdown by material, labor and equipment, total estimated cost, cost variance, and variance percent.

A number of key reports are provided in DBI-Mt, including work order cost detail and summary, asset downtime, work order completion, late completion detail and aging, request to completion distribution, work order backlog, past due work order detail and aging, and labor backlog. Maintenance KPIs include work order cost, asset downtime in hours, completed work orders, late to schedule completion percent, work order backlog, past due to schedule percent, and request to completion in days.

Maintenance managers can gain a full appreciation of how their business is performing by using DBI-Mt. For example, managers can identify problem areas and drill down to specific work orders to determine if the anomalies spring from a general performance problem or a small number of exceptional work orders.

Daily Business Intelligence for Procurement

Managing an organization's vendors effectively can help to reduce acquisition costs. DBI for Procurement (DPI-P) enables sourcing of new items, developing a commodity strategy, and analysis of supplier performance and money spent. DPI-P provides numerous dashboards to enable this capability, including dashboards showing procurement status, procurement performance management, procurement management, procure-to-pay management, commodity spend management, and commodity supplier management. Common users can be defined to have access to relevant procurement or commodity dashboards. Procurement and commodity managers have additional responsibilities for set-up of DBI-P and are provided with additional access to dashboards for expense management, human resource management, management of payables, and payables status.

In order to present these dashboards, DBI-P uses data from a variety of E-Business Suite applications, including Oracle Purchasing, iProcurement, Payables, Services Procurement, and Sourcing. KPIs include unprocessed requisition lines, unprocessed requisition lines past an expected date, unprocessed requisitions amount, unprocessed average age (days), unfulfilled requisition lines, unfulfilled requisition lines past an expected date, unfulfilled requisitions amount, unfulfilled average age (days), processed requisition lines and amount, processed average (days), fulfilled requisition lines and amount, fulfilled average age (days), percent fulfilled past an expected date, contract and non-contract purchases rate, contract leakage rate, PO purchases growth rate, invoice amount growth rate, price savings amount, quantity change amount at benchmark price, price change amount, return amount, return transactions, receipt date exception amount rate and transactions rate, payables leakage rate, and manual invoices rate.

DBI-P can be used to aggregate vendor purchases and increase discount levels. Since companies typically try to delay procurement and the subsequent payment for procurement, being able to see daily information on procurement status can help maximize savings. You can also analyze procurement trends and drill down to find the source of trend changes. DBI-P also helps organizations understand the effectiveness of their own procurement personnel.

Daily Business Intelligence for Product Lifecycle Management

DBI for Product Lifecycle Management (DBI-PLM) is designed to help managers understand the costs and profitability of products throughout their entire lifecycle, from design to deployment, as well as examining the profits created by sales of the product over time. DBI-PLM tracks the overall complexity of a product throughout the development lifecycle, based on objective measures such as part count and the number of levels in the bill of materials for the product. Dashboards are provided for product management and for product management engineering.

The product management dashboard displays data from the following Oracle E-Business Suite applications: General Ledger, Inventory, Order Management, Receivables, Sales, and Service. KPIs include revenue, cost of goods sold, gross margin, product margin, sales forecast, and booked and backlog amounts.

The product management engineering dashboard displays data from Oracle's E-Business Suite, including Oracle Inventory, Advanced Product Catalog, Cost Management, Bill of Materials, and Engineering. KPIs include unit cost, part count, bill of material levels, manufacturing steps, new and open change orders, and change order cycle times.

For a full understanding of product expenses, you would also set up and leverage DBI for Financials along with this module. To further understand fulfillment, return and inventory items, you would also set up DBI for Supply Chain when deploying this module.

Daily Business Intelligence for Projects

Daily Business Intelligence for Projects (DBI-Prj) provides reports for data residing in E-Business Suite applications for project costing, billing and resource management. Key reports provided in the DBI-Prj dashboard include project profitability, project operations, capital projects cost, and contract projects cost. Reports are available in project summary, trend, and detail versions. Key performance indicators include bookings and backlog, cost, forecast cost, capital cost, percent of cost, expense, billable cost, non-billable cost, revenue, and margin.

DBI-Prj presents tracking information on projects, but also ties these projects to other financial data so that you can determine whether projects are within the boundaries of their budgets. DBI-Prj highlights out of bounds projects, and provides drill down enabling investigation of the causes of the problems.

Daily Business Intelligence for Quoting

Daily Business Intelligence for Quoting (DBI-Q) hones in on a particular phase of the sales process. You would use DBI-Q for analysis when quotes are created, then follow them through the rest of the procurement cycle. The intelligence provided by DBI-Q helps managers to track quotes as they make their way through the system, but also helps them spot bottlenecks in the quote approval process. DBI-Q displays data from Oracle Quoting and Oracle Approvals Management.

Since DBI-Q also associates quotes with orders, you can see the impact of factors like discounting on the ability to turn quotes into revenue. For example, how do you know if discount levels are too high (leaving unclaimed revenue), too low (losing sales), or just right? The information that comes from DBI-Q can help you to make these types of high-impact decisions based on historical fact.

Reports provided include quote summary by sales group, quote summary by product category, quote summary by adjusted price, top quotes, approval summary by sales group, and approval rules summary. KPIs displayed include total, converted, and open quotes (number and amount), converted amount percent, average days to convert, number of all quotes submitted, number of processed submissions that completed approval process, approved percent of all submissions, approved percent of completed submissions, average number of days for approval, and average number of approvers.

Daily Business Intelligence for Sales

Unlike marketing, the direct impact of sales activities in sales-oriented companies are usually extremely visible — from the details of whether an individual sales representative is meeting his or her quota to the company revenue attained. In many organizations, however, the basis for much of this information resides in reports created by sales representatives. Daily Business Intelligence for Sales (DBI-S) brings a more analytical view of the entire process by tracking opportunities as they change over time. This enables management to judge the performance of sales reps more effectively, as well as forecast future sales revenues more accurately.

DBI-S provides three main dashboards — sales forecast management, sales management, and opportunity management. Additional dashboards include lead management, product revenue bookings and backlog, and quote management. To have access to all data possible in these dashboards, you should also deploy DBI for Marketing and DBI for Supply Chain as DBI-S displays information from both.

Sample sales forecast reports include forecast versus won trend, forecast overview, and top open opportunities. Sales forecast management KPIs include sales group forecast, direct reports forecast, weighted pipeline, pipeline, and deals won to period.

Sample sales management reports include sales results versus forecast, sales group forecast by product category, leads and opportunity and backlog, forecast versus won trend, lead opportunity by campaign, and top/bottom sales performers, extended forecast versus won trend, and extended forecast versus pipeline trend. KPIs include revenue, net booked, sales group forecast, direct reports forecast, (sales credit) won, weighted pipeline, and pipeline.

Opportunity management reports include opportunity win/loss, opportunity win/loss with counts, forecast and pipeline and won trend, opportunity activity, weighted pipeline, pipeline trend, and win/loss trend. KPIs include (sales credit) won, (number) open opportunities, pipeline, weighted pipeline, (sales credit) lost, win/loss ratio, and sales credit marked as no opportunity.

Daily Business Intelligence for Service Contracts

Daily Business Intelligence for Service Contracts (DBI-SCt) focuses on the process of fulfilling and renewing service contracts and is used by service contracts managers and service sales managers. Dashboards are provided for service contracts management (showing both new contracts and renewals) and service renewals management (showing renewals only).

KPIs that will be of interest to service contracts managers include beginning active service contracts, expired value, activated new business value, activated renewals value, terminated billed value, terminated remaining value, and current active service contracts. Service renewals management KPIs include booked value, forecast, uplift, period renewals value, period booked value, period renewal rate, period uplift, booked to renewal ratio, and past due percent.

Daily Business Intelligence for Supply Chain

DBI for Supply Chain (DBI-SC) provides supply chain professionals with high-level summaries that help them quickly identify areas in need of improvement in the overall action of the supply chain. Dashboards include customer fulfillment management, shipping management, inventory management, manufacturing management, product cost management, plan management, product revenue bookings and backlog, warehouse management, and transportation management. In addition, supply chain managers have access to dashboards for expense management and human resources management.

DBI-SC is extremely rich in the number of reports provided. Customer fulfillment management reports include fulfillment performance, booked order and book to fulfill, requested lead-time, backlog, past schedule, past due, and returns. Shipping management reports include lines shipped, book to ship, past due schedule lines, and backorders. Inventory management reports include inventory value, on-hand and in-transit inventory detail, inventory turns, cycle count, and hit/miss summary.

Manufacturing management reports include production to plan, actual production job detail, manufacturing cost, current unrecognized variance, open job detail, material usage, resource, and scrap. Among product cost management reports are product gross margin, material usage, resource, manufacturing cost, current unrecognized variance, and open job detail. Plan management reports include planned revenue, margin, organization, costs, performance, inventory, shipments, and resources.

Product revenue bookings and backlog reports include trends, details, and revenue. Warehouse management reports provide a view into pick-to-ship times, put-away cycle times, storage and capacity utilization, and operation plan performance. Finally, transportation management reports include rated freight costs, on-time arrival rates and trends, carrier billing and payment, and freight cost recovery.

Of course, the richness of many of these reports makes them useful to others in an organization as well. A sales manager would also likely find the product revenue bookings and backlog reports to be of interest.

As might be expected, set-up of this module can require quite a bit of thought. For example, you have the ability to map this module to discrete manufacturing processes, define measures in a way most appropriate in your organization, and provide appropriate access to sales based on sales hierarchies when access is provided to those users.

Balanced Scorecards

When a company's visions and strategies are converted into specific and quantifiable objectives, measurements, targets, and initiatives, business leadership will often express a desire to be able to monitor business performance in an intuitive fashion. Balanced scorecards can be deployed to leverage metrics tracked in applications, data hubs, and data warehouses and provide a framework and interface for easily understanding their impact and the cause-and-effect relationships present in meeting business goals. Viewing these relationships through a balanced scorecard can be especially enlightening when the relationships cross lines of business.

Drs. David Norton and Robert Kaplan originated the concept of balanced scorecards in 1992. The premise behind the balanced scorecard (BSC) is straightforward — nothing, including key business objectives, can be improved without measurement. By measuring an organization's achievement of key business goals, or lack thereof, these organizations are better able to reach those goals. They can also quickly diagnose issues that are preventing them from achieving those goals.

Oracle's implementation of balanced scorecards was first released in 1999. With the Oracle Balanced Scorecard (OBSC), individuals can create simple dashboards that give an immediate simplified indication of the performance of a particular business area or process — even if they are not technologists. A user can also perform what-if analysis as they plan and forecast business scenarios. The building process, as well as the final result, takes place within a browser environment, making the balanced scorecard accessible from many different types of clients. The data viewed can be extracted from an Oracle database or other external source, such as an Excel spreadsheet.

OBSC can leverage all of the KPIs included in DBI modules. You can also create your own KPIs to supplement DBI metrics, or deploy OBSC completely independently of the E-Business Suite. Most commonly, however, OBSC is deployed in order to leverage KPIs in Oracle Financials, General Ledger, and DBI for Financials.

Oracle Balanced Scorecard Structure

The Oracle E-Business Suite Balanced Scorecard visually presents information at three levels, with drill-down to further detail at each lower level. The multi-layer structure of OBSC makes it easy for business users to not only spot potential problem areas, but also to investigate quickly and intuitively potential causes for any unexpected results.

At the top level, the OBSC business objectives are presented in purely business terms as shown in Figure 2-4. OBSC includes color-coded health alarm icons to quickly show how well a business objective is being achieved. In addition, each entry on this level is actually a link that provides users access to more detailed levels in the Scorecard.

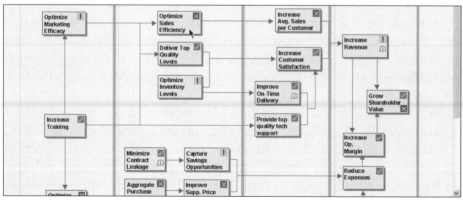

Figure 2-4: A portion of a top-level Oracle Balanced Scorecard

The next level of the OBSC, shown earlier in this book in Chapter 1 in Figure 1-2, lays out the business blueprint or strategy map. Although this view looks a bit complex, it provides the cause-and-effect relationship between the sub-topics presented in the high-level business objectives. This level also includes health indicators so that a user can quickly determine if a problem in one area is cascading down to other areas, or if the issues represented by poor health indicators are unrelated.

On this OBSC page, a user can add annotations to entries. This provides quick links to documents providing further information on any of the business objectives detailed in the blueprint. A user can also add links directly to DBI reports on this page.

The third level of the Oracle Balanced Scorecard, shown in Figure 2-5, provides more detailed information about the KPIs that are used in determining the health of the business as shown in the other two levels. A user can modify what information is shown on this page to determine if there is any particular dimension of this business activity showing unexpected data or trends.

Although we have described accessing levels of the OBSC through drill-down techniques starting in the Balanced Scorecard tool itself, all of the information could also be displayed as a single page in an Oracle Portal or in a Performance Management Framework dashboard. You would build the Balanced Scorecard into the Performance Management Framework using the Performance Management Designer interface. A page in the Performance Management Designer is illustrated in Figure 2-6.

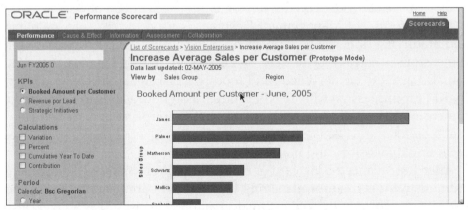

Figure 2-5: Detailed reports in the Oracle Balanced Scorecard

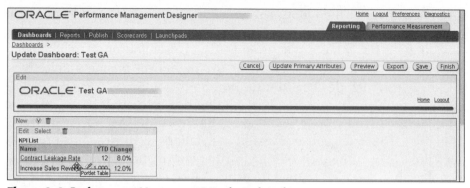

Figure 2-6: Performance Management Designer interface

OBSC Architecture

OBSCs can use all the intelligent aggregation and reports that are pre-built for use with DBI. OBSCs can also use custom KPIs that access other data in the E-Business Suite database, other databases, or Excel spreadsheets. This ability to access data outside of the E-business Suite is the feature that allows OBSC to be used without the presence of any Oracle applications.

Creating an Oracle Balanced Scorecard

An OBSC is built with the Oracle Business Intelligence Builder or Performance Management Designer (shown previously in Figure 2-6) with naming of this feature dependent on the version of the product you have.

The Performance Management Designer is used for creating, deleting, and modifying dimensions, dimension objects, and relationships between dimensions. It can also be used to create, modify, and delete measures. You can also use it to create, delete, and modify KPIs, create, delete, and modify KPI groups, assign KPIs to KPI groups, assign measures to KPIs, create dimension sets, assign dimensions to dimension sets, and define color methods for the KPIs. Designers can lock objects when making changes including dimensions and measures assigned.

After the Balanced Scorecard is created, the Performance Management Administrator is used for managing loading and administering users and security. It replaced the older Oracle Balanced Scorecard Manager, also known as the OBSC Manager. Loader functionality includes OBSC input, managing OBSC dimensions and calendars, and deleting data from OBSC tables. The Administrator functions include managing users, security, and indicator security.

Data Hubs

Certainly, there are many KPIs that can be displayed using Oracle DBI as gathered from the E-Business Suite. But, in many organizations, federated solutions are deployed consisting of many different data models and much of the needed data does not reside in Oracle's E-Business Suite. How do you bring this information together with common KPIs as if the data resided in a single transaction processing system? Data hubs can provide this solution.

Since business intelligence is only as useful as the data it is based on, it is important to remember that the usefulness of base data will be reduced if:

■ The data is incorrect due to bad manual or automatic entry and incomplete validation.

■ The data is incomplete at entry time or because it comes from different sources with different sets of attributes.

■ The data is incompatible because of differing formats or meaning in different sources.

A data hub can provide an infrastructure that provides consistent data definitions for master data management from diverse sources ensuring that it is both correct and compatible in format and attributes. When a data hub is established, business intelligence tools can leverage more meaningful data. Data hubs can also be deployed in order to eliminate duplication of data and duplication of business processes. In providing an accurate centralized source of master data definitions, data hubs can help organizations comply with regulatory requirements.

A conceptual view of a typical Oracle data hub is illustrated in Figure 2-7. The Integration Services typically deployed as part of this solution include Oracle Fusion Middleware, Web Services, and other popular ETL and integration products.

The Oracle Customer Data Hub

To understand data hubs more completely, we look at a piece of data that is central to almost every enterprise system — the customer description. Customer descriptions can come from different systems such as supply chain management and customer relationship management applications. Customer descriptions might also be obtained or supplemented from outside sources, such as Dun & Bradstreet information. Given the importance of customer data, it is no surprise that Oracle's first data hub was the Oracle Customer Data Hub.

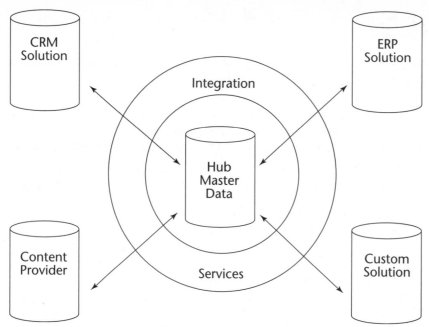

Figure 2-7: Oracle Data Hub illustration

The Customer Data Hub brings together customer data from multiple available sources. It provides a master customer identity, centralized data storage for data maintenance, reconciliation, and enrichment, integration services, high data volume import for data quality management, the ability to dynamically build master records, and a viewer across all information. The Customer Hub is based on the Trading Community Architecture (TCA) registry of core data elements present in Oracle's E-Business Suite of applications.

The end point of the Customer Data Hub is called the master customer identity. This identity is a set of physical tables that contain all the attributes for a customer and provide a common representation for all customer records. Built into this identity are a variety of validation and resolution capabilities including address validation and the ability to create blended records from duplicate entries in multiple source systems.

The Customer Data Hub uses mapping to specify the relationship between source data and the master identity. Oracle Fusion Middleware or other middleware products are used to transport data from the source systems to the hub. A connection between each source system and the Customer Data Hub is called a customer data spoke. This hub and spoke architecture enables you to access as many data sources as necessary without a corresponding increase in complexity.

How Data Hubs Work

The Customer Data Hub (CDH) has a multi-step process for creating a rich customer record. The first step is to consolidate customer data records by importing source data into the CDH and TCA registry, often by using the Oracle Data Librarian. This provides the ability to cross-reference the data sources from a single point. The Hub is kept synchronized with data sources through Data Librarian's support of SOAP-based XML Web Services and business event-based triggers provided by Oracle Workflow. The Librarian also provides data cleansing including matching, merging, and de-duplication.

As data is cleansed, it can be sent back to the source system to help create an infrastructure providing a single source of truth across multiple systems. In addition, this resynchronization means that you can make changes to the customer model in the CDH and automatically have these changes ripple down into source data models.

The process is repeated for each source of customer records. Once all the data has gone through this process, the customer records can be enriched with data from external sources, and the enriched customer records are once again synchronized with the sources.

Other Oracle Data Hubs

At the time of publication of this book, Oracle had also introduced the Product Information Management Data Hub (PIM Data Hub) and Financial Consolidation Data Hub. Oracle had also announced future plans for data hubs for the public sector and government agencies.

The PIM Data Hub is useful where organizations have some form of product that is central to their operations. The PIM Data Hub performs standardization and transformation for products and creates a central product master in a manner similar to the approach the Customer Data Hub uses with customer data. The PIM Data Hub can be used to manage both sell-side and buy-side products and create standardized Bill of Materials for all products. The PIM solution can be extended using Data Librarian to deliver product data to trading partners through synchronization with UCCnet using the Global Data Synchronization Network (GDSN).

The Financial Consolidation Data Hub provides similar single source of truth benefits for managing the business. Since all financial data records are accessible through a single hub, it is also much easier to comply with regulatory requirements for auditing and reporting. Relevant balances can be automatically extracted from Oracle General Ledger and data from other sources can be submitted using spreadsheet loaders.

This hub is particularly useful for companies involved in mergers and acquisitions. For example, the Financial Consolidation Data Hub can be set up to automatically eliminate inter-company balances, enforce materiality thresholds for various types of inter-company activity, calculate minor interest for partially owned subsidiaries, apply equity accounting, eliminate investment in subsidiaries, calculate goodwill, and reflect real and projected results of acquisitions and disposals.

Is Transactional Business Intelligence Enough?

Can you provide all of the business intelligence an organization needs using only the products in this chapter? The answer depends heavily on whether the KPIs supported in these products match how you measure and run your business. You should also consider whether most of your data resides in Oracle's E-Business Suite (since all of the products are designed to have a high degree of affinity to the E-Business Suite). You should also evaluate the importance of analyzing long periods of history, something you would not likely do in a transaction processing system.

Certainly, if you do most of your transactional processing using the E-Business Suite, evaluating and deploying these products should be your first step in a business intelligence strategy. These products can provide tremendous business value quickly. But if your analysis needs or sources of information are quite different, you will likely begin to evaluate data warehousing solutions. Chapter 3introduces Oracle data warehousing.

CHAPTER 7

Introduction to Oracle Data Warehousing

The solutions outlined in Chapter 2 provide business intelligence gleaned from transactional data. Such solutions can provide reporting and simple drill-downs to more detailed data and, in some cases, rely on data warehousing features present in the Oracle database. In this chapter, we'll introduce Oracle database features and describe how they might be used if you deploy a classic data warehouse solution. We'll also describe some of the data warehouses available today for some of Oracle's applications that will be merged in Oracle's next generation Project Fusion business intelligence applications.

In subsequent chapters, we'll explore how to leverage these features and deploy a data warehouse solution in more detail. Chapter 4 describes some of the hardware platform configuration choices. Chapter 5 describes database schema design choices and types of analyses these choices enable. We describe Oracle's business intelligence tools and how they are used in Chapter 6. In Chapter 7, we'll describe loading options that might be used in populating a data warehouse. In Chapter 8, we describe manageability of an Oracle data warehouse in much greater detail.

But, given that we described in the previous chapter how some business intelligence solutions might be deployed as extended applications in transaction processing systems, you might need more detail on why a separate and largely custom data warehouse could be necessary. So, we begin with a more detailed discussion as to why you might need to build such a data warehouse.

Oracle Data Warehousing Basics

Transactional applications are usually deployed to provide a view of the status of the business at a current moment or since the most recent transaction. The status can change as often as new transactions are introduced. For example, in a retail company, new transactions at point-of-sales devices (cash registers) are captured every time a sale is made. Such transactional systems are designed so that updates to sales data occur reliably and quickly, even during peak sales periods. Where reporting is deployed using transactional databases, such reports are contained so as not to impact update performance. The amount of historical data kept in such systems is often limited to what is necessary to provide a current view of the business.

However, retaining a large amount of historical data is desirable when strategizing about future initiatives, analyzing how well current initiatives are doing compared to what has occurred in the past, or for forecasting. The workloads for such queries and analyses can be fundamentally different from transactional systems with full-table scans, large result sets returned as a result of queries, and CPU-intensive computations. For these reasons, the data warehouse emerged in many companies as the place to handle such workloads and as a home for historical data. Although initially envisioned by some as a place for summarized history, today's warehouses often are the location for holding the official single version of company truth, in both summarized and detailed record form. As noted in Chapter 1, the schema deployed is often a hybrid of third normal form for the detailed data and star schema with summary levels (Oracle's materialized views) or Online Analytical Processing (OLAP) cubes stored in the relational database.

The data might be extracted and loaded into a separate data warehouse for other reasons. Data in transactional systems is not always checked for validity. Multiple transactional systems can become silos of information and the data can be inconsistently represented in the different systems. So, the warehouse is often the location where data is cleansed of bad information and brought together in a consistent format with consistent meaning.

Data cleansing is a very important topic as it consumes much of planning and design work needed during extraction, transformation, and loading (hence, we'll cover this topic in the data loading discussion in Chapter 7).

Oracle has embarked on a technology and applications product development path that begins to blend together data warehousing and transactional systems. Deploying a single database across a grid infrastructure consisting of clustered hardware platforms where some nodes can be designated for transactional workloads and others for data warehousing is an important part in this vision. But for many companies, source data will remain in silos of legacy applications for years to come and, even where the applications are consolidated, data quality in these transactional source systems will remain an issue. Building a separate data warehouse infrastructure will likely continue to make sense for many well into the future.

Given that you are probably now convinced you'll need to build a data warehouse as part of your business intelligence solution and need to better understand what is in the Oracle database to help you, we will next introduce some of the database features that can enable better analysis and creation of a manageable infrastructure.

Oracle Database Analysis and Schema Considerations

When companies began to build customized standalone decision support systems and data warehouses on Oracle prior to the 1990s, they found that an Oracle database could be difficult for novice business users to navigate. The typical database schema was third normal form matching that of transactional systems and even though access to any of the data through SQL, PL/SQL, and later Java programs and business intelligence tools was possible, knowing where that data was located was not always intuitive. Query performance was also not predictable due to a large number of needed joins, so a Database Administrator (DBA) was often enlisted to create views and add rules for the optimizer to follow to guarantee fast query performance.

Oracle7 was introduced in the very early 1990s and was the first Oracle database version to feature a cost-based optimizer. The cost-based optimizer determines a cost associated with solving a query and the most optimal path to provide an answer to that query. As Oracle evolved through subsequent releases, features were added to make the database easier and more functional for business intelligence and data warehousing. The cost-based optimizer was improved to better leverage these enhancements. Table 3-1 denotes the introduction of several of these features. As of Oracle Database 10g, the cost-based optimizer became so advanced that Oracle announced desupport of the old rules-based optimizer.

Table 3-1: Oracle Database Versions Introducing Analysis Features

FEATURE	DATABASE VERSION(S)
Static bit-mapped indexes	Oracle7
Cartesian product star joins	Oracle7
Parallel bit-map star joins	Oracle8
Materialized views	Oracle8i
SQL analytic functions	Oracle8i, Oracle9i, Oracle Database 10g
OLAP Option	Oracle9i (and later release enhancements)
Data Mining Option algorithms	Oracle9i, Oracle Database 10g
XQuery	Oracle Database 10g

Today's Oracle database has a rich set of features that can be leveraged in the database design for your data warehouse. Brief descriptions of these features follow.

Star Joins

Star joins are used to solve queries where data resides in the star schema that was introduced in Chapter 1. As a brief review, a star schema exists in the database as a large fact table surrounded by multiple dimension tables (also known as look-up tables) with a foreign key relationship. Usually time is one of the dimensions making the schema ideal for answering queries searching for the number of transactions that occurred in a given period of time in a given geography or other dimension. Figure 3-1 illustrates a simple star schema. Relational database optimizers were originally not capable of recognizing such schema or solving them in a cost-efficient fashion. In early versions of Oracle, each individual dimension table was joined one-at-a-time to the fact table. Since the fact table is usually very large, these multiple joins could take considerable time.

The Oracle7 version of the database was the first in which the optimizer recognized the star schema and took a different approach to solving the query. Cartesian products were generated for the dimension tables and then a single join took place back to the fact table saving time in solving the query. This technique works well where there are only a few dimensions and sparseness of data is not a problem. Cartesian product joins remain one solution the optimizer might use to solve queries to this day.

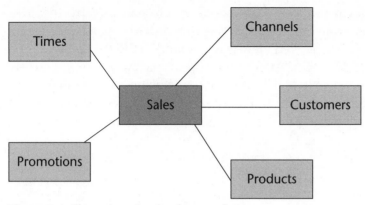

Figure 3-1: Illustration of a simple star schema

Oracle8 added another technique the optimizer could use to solve queries more appropriate for situations when there are large numbers of dimensions in the schema (since Cartesian products can get extremely large) or where data is sparse (and needless computation of Cartesian products would have occurred). The second technique is referred to as parallel bitmap star joins. Parallel bitmap star joins use bitmaps that are created on the foreign keys to dimension tables. Thus, they account for sparseness while efficiently handling large numbers of dimensions. These star joins are performed in parallel to further increase the speed with which query results are returned.

Materialized Views

Queries that are best answered by transaction-level data rolled up to a subtotal at summary levels are common in assessing the state of the business. For example, a sales manager might wish to understand total sales in various territories that they manage without seeing individual transactions. The Oracle8i version of the database introduced the ability to create summary tables in a defined hierarchy as materialized views. Hierarchies can be defined for fact tables and/or dimension tables. Where materialized views exist, queries are transparently redirected to the right level of the hierarchy during query rewrite and expensive queries against base detailed data tables can be avoided. As of Oracle Database 10g Release 2, if a single materialized view cannot provide results for a query but a combination of existing materialized views can, then the optimizer will perform a query rewrite that includes joining the needed materialized views together.

Materialized views can be recommended automatically by the SQL Access Advisor in Oracle Enterprise Manager in order to speed queries. So, one way to create a materialized view is to respond to the recommendation through Enterprise Manager. Alternatively, you may want to proactively create materialized views in anticipation of how business users will use the data warehouse. The following statement shows the typical syntax for creating a materialized view:

```
CREATE MATERIALIZED VIEW sh.cust_sales_mv
BUILD IMMEDIATE
USING INDEX
REFRESH FORCE
ENABLE QUERY REWRITE
AS
SELECT customers.cust_id,
       SUM(amount_sold) AS sales_in_dollars
FROM sh.sales, sh.customers
WHERE sales.cust_id= customers.cust_id
GROUP BY customers.cust_id;
```

When detailed data in the database is updated, materialized view tables can be defined to be refreshed in one of four ways. A complete refresh will completely refresh the summary by removing old data and reloading. A fast refresh only applies changes as detected during SQL*Loader incremental loads or from INSERT, UPDATE, or DELETE SQL tracked in the MATERIALIZED VIEW LOG. A force refresh (the type designated in the sample script above) will do a fast refresh if possible or a complete refresh if not possible. When data is partitioned using the Partitioning Option, a partition change-tracking refresh will fast refresh rows in those partitions where data is changed.

Bit-map Indexes

In Oracle7, static bitmap indexes were introduced as a technique to speed results of queries where low cardinality data exists. Data is said to be of low cardinality data if the ratio of the number of distinct rows in a table compared to the total number of rows is relatively low, usually 10 percent or less (although some Oracle documentation suggests values as low as 1 percent). The data is stored as bitmaps (zero if a value is not present, one if the value is present) and since the cost-based optimizer looks for such bitmaps, joins will be very fast. An additional benefit is that storage of data as static bitmaps often uses less disk storage space.

Oracle's optimizer can combine static bitmaps with other access methods for the same table. Where static bitmaps are not pre-created, the optimizer might alternatively generate bitmaps dynamically if performance will be improved.

For an example of creating a static bitmap, gender might be a great candidate within an employee table since one can reasonably assume there are relatively few distinct rows in comparison to the number of rows in the table. Typical statement syntax might be:

```
CREATE BITMAP INDEX employee_gender_bix
ON sh.emp (gender_id)
LOCAL;
```

Since building static bitmaps can take some time after a data load, this technique is sometimes used in data warehouses where all data is loaded into a new range partition defined using the Partitioning Option and where older partitions do not need new local indexing.

The CREATE BITMAP INDEX statement can also be used to create a bitmap join index across two or more tables. A typical application of a bitmap join index is to create an equi-inner join between the primary key column in a dimension table and the foreign key column of a fact table. Syntax to create a bit-map join index between sales and customer tables might appear as follows:

```
CREATE BITMAP INDEX sales_cust_src_id_bjix
ON sh.sales(sh.customers.cust_src_id)
FROM sh.sales, sh.customers
WHERE sh.sales.cust_id= sh.customers.cust_src_id
LOCAL;
```

In this example, the indexed fact table is a sales transactions table and the indexed key is sh.customers.cust_src_id.

SQL Analytics

Since data warehouses of many terabytes in size are increasingly common and the business intelligence tools that access them are often HTML-based with no footprint on the desktop, it can make a lot more sense for data analysis to take place in the database instead of moving the data into the tool. To accomplish this, Oracle introduced many SQL analytic extensions in the database in a series of database releases. These extensions can be accessed directly through SQL or through business intelligence tools that generate SQL, such as Oracle Business Intelligence Standard Edition (Discoverer) and Enterprise Edition (Answers), or tools from vendors such as Business Objects, Cognos, and others.

Oracle initially added CUBE and ROLLUP extensions to Oracle8i for exactly this purpose. In 1999, ISO standard SQL Analytic functions were introduced to the Oracle database. These functions include:

- Windowing functions, including cumulative and moving sums
- RANK and DENSE_RANK
- CUME_DIST and PERCENT_RANK
- ROW_NUMBER
- PERCENTILE_DISC and PERCENTILE_CONT
- Hypothetical Rank and Distribution
- WIDTH_BUCKET
- Linear Regression group, Correlation, and Covariance

For example, you might want to rank values using a SQL statement. An example of the use of the RANK function syntax follows:

```
SELECT product_id,
    TO_CHAR (quantity_on_hand, '9,999,999') QUANTITY,
    RANK() OVER (ORDER BY quantity_on_hand) AS quantity_rank
FROM oe.toronto_inventory;
```

Oracle Database 10g added many additional statistical functions beyond the ISO standards. Some of the extensions Oracle provides include:

- LAG and LEAD
- RATIO_TO_REPORT
- NTILE
- FIRST_VALUE and LAST_VALUE
- FIRST and LAST aggregates

OLAP Option

Multi-Dimensional Online Analytical Processing (MOLAP) technology was introduced as a stand-alone database solution over 25 years ago to enable queries to leverage fact tables and dimensions with roll-up hierarchies in a fraction of the time that relational databases were capable of. Oracle was once a leader in standalone MOLAP database engine technology with a product named Express Server. The MOLAP engines retrieved query results faster, because all combinations of joins between the fact table and the dimension tables were pre-computed and the optimizer would not need to figure out the joins at query time. In this approach, the data is sometimes represented as stored in cubes (for example, for three dimensions) as represented in Figure 3-2. However, deploying standalone MOLAP engines also has its disadvantages. Loading of these cubes can take longer than loading relational tables. The cubes are managed and accessed in a separate location from detailed data. The access language is usually non-SQL based.

Many businesses decided to simplify their architecture by storing the data in a single relational database by deploying a star schema with materialized views. This approach remains popular where frequent updates occur, although performance is not as great as with MOLAP engines since the optimizer must figure out the proper joins.

Beginning with Oracle9i, Oracle began offering an OLAP option that embeds MOLAP cubes (Oracle calls them analytic workspaces) within the relational database. These analytic workspaces are accessible via a Java OLAP API (JOLAPI) or, more commonly, via SQL. They are especially useful where a large number of dimensions are desired. An example of such a query would be one to find persons who bought certain stocks in the final trading hour of the year from a discount broker located in New York City and who also bought those stocks in the previous three quarters but not through such a broker. Since the OLAP option is designed to scale and perform well for cubes of over a terabyte in size, such OLAP cubes are sometimes partitioned for manageability using the Oracle Partitioning Option.

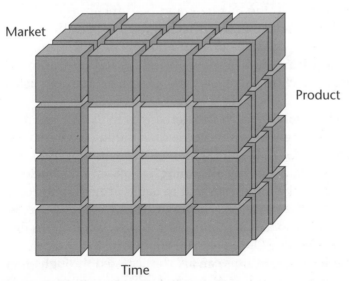

Figure 3-2: MOLAP cube illustration

Oracle's Business Intelligence Standard Edition (Discoverer and Spreadsheet Add-in) access the analytic workspaces using the Java OLAP API. Custom OLAP applications can be created with Oracle JDeveloper using the same Java development BI beans for presentations, graphs, and calculations that Oracle uses in developing products such as Oracle Discoverer, Enterprise Planning and Budgeting, and the Spreadsheet Add-in. As a result, your custom-built applications can look and behave like Oracle products.

Oracle's Business Intelligence Enterprise Edition (Answers) and other tools from Oracle partners such as Business Objects and Cognos ReportNet access the analytic workspaces through SQL. Such access is more seamless and continues to improve due to continued enhancements in recent versions of many of these business intelligence tools and the Oracle database.

OLAP cubes can be designed using Oracle Warehouse Builder (OWB) where code generation of star schema hierarchies can be switched easily to OLAP cubes, and vice versa. Where data is stored in a star schema in the database and the goal is to populate an OLAP cube using that data, Oracle's Analytic Workspace Manager (AWM) is used to build simple mappings from relational tables to the cubes.

Data Mining Option

Data mining can be defined as the application of mathematical algorithms to build predictive models for rarely occurring events. Such events might have very noticeable impact to the business and be difficult to model or predict using other business intelligence techniques, especially where there are a large number of variables present and lots of data. Common business solutions built using data mining include fraud and criminal intent detection, customer churn analysis, and customer market basket analysis.

The classic approach to solving such problems was to extract the relevant data out of the data warehouse into special data mining engines. Oracle once offered a product for data mining named Darwin that used this method. The volume of data in typical mining exercises led Oracle to reevaluate this approach in the mid-1990s and to begin providing the data mining algorithms within the database. The algorithms were made accessible through PL/SQL and a Java data mining API. Today, applications that leverage the Oracle Data Mining Option can be built using the Oracle Data Miner tool. The data mining algorithms can also be accessed through other tools from Oracle partners such as InforSense and SPSS Clementine.

Oracle first introduced Association and Naïve Bayes algorithms into Oracle9i Release 1 of the database. Release 2 of Oracle 9i added Adaptive Bayes Networks, Clustering, and features such as attribute importance, a model seeker, automated binning, limited Predictive Model Markup Language (PMML) support, and asynchronous mining tasks. Oracle Database 10g Release 1 added Support Vector Machines (SVM) and Nonnegative Matrix Factorization algorithms and Release 2 extended SVM for anomaly detection and added Decision Trees.

Storage and Retrieval of Multiple Datatypes including XML

Storage and retrieval of other datatypes such as spatial, text, audio, video, and images from the data warehouse will sometimes fulfill additional business needs. For example, you may want to deploy Oracle Mapviewer (included with the Oracle Application Server) to display spatial data on maps and images in response to specific queries.

An increasingly popular format for storing semi-structured and unstructured data is XML. Oracle began offering storage of native XML datatypes and featuring an XML repository for managing XML data beginning with the Oracle 9i Release 2 database. In Oracle Database 10g Release 2, the W3C standard XML Query (XQuery) syntax was officially introduced enabling the writing of XML expressions and the retrieval of data stored natively in Oracle in XMLDB or in Oracle relational schema where XML views exist. The SELECT XMLquery function transmits an XQuery statement to the database and returns an XML document (XMLType value).

Table 3-2 provides a quick summary of some of the data formats that can be stored in Oracle.

Table 3-2: Formats That Can Be Stored in and Retrieved from Oracle

UNSTRUCTURED DATA TYPE	FORMATS
Text/document	ASCII, Microsoft Word, Excel, PowerPoint, HTML, XML, Adobe Acrobat (PDF)
Audio	AU, AIFF, WAV, MPEG
Video	Apple QuickTime, AVI, MPEG, MP4, RMFF
Image	BMPF, CALS, FPIX, GIF, JPEG, PBMF, PGMF, PPMF, PPNF, PCX, PCIT, PNGF, RPIX, RASF, TGAF, TIFF, WBMP, and multiple additional compression formats

ORACLE BUSINESS INTELLIGENCE TOOLS PARTNER SUPPORT

Oracle has a wide variety of partners for business intelligence tools covering the range of reporting, ad hoc query and analysis, data mining, and extraction, transformation, and loading. Each Oracle software partner determines the degree to which they'll leverage more advanced Oracle database features in their tools. Most provide native (Oracle*Net) access to the Oracle database due to the popularity of Oracle-based data warehouses among their customers, thus enabling better performance than generic interfaces like ODBC can provide. Some provide specific support and guidance for gaining access to the Oracle database SQL analytic functions, the OLAP option, or Data Mining option. In addition, some of these tools can be deployed on the Oracle Application Server and leverage other Oracle business intelligence components such as the Oracle Portal.

We have indicated some of the support provided by certain partners in the previous sections at the time of publication of this book. However, the level of support can change over time and for various Oracle software versions. You will want to investigate support for the Oracle versions you plan to deploy if you have specific partner tools in mind.

Oracle also offers products competitive to most of these tools that we will discuss in this book. Most organizations that evaluate the various tools compare features and function, usability, ability to expose needed database features, cost, and the level of integration with other tools and components already present.

Managing an Oracle-based Data Warehouse

Published surveys describing deployment of very large data warehouses often show a doubling of data volume at these sites every one to two years. Decreasing storage costs can lead companies to keep older and less frequently accessed data on disk that formerly was archived to tape. Deployment to smaller but lower-priced computer hardware nodes while online data and numbers of users grow can lead to larger numbers of nodes in clusters. All of these factors combine to make database manageability considerations even more important than they were in the past. The usage of business intelligence and data warehousing for tactical decision making also introduces new requirements for availability as part of the management planning.

These trends led Oracle to introduce additional manageability capabilities over a period of years that are very appropriate for data warehousing. Table 3-3 summarizes the introduction of some of these key features and capabilities.

Table 3-3: Oracle Database Versions Introducing Manageability Features

FEATURE	DATABASE VERSION(S)
Oracle Enterprise Manager	Oracle7
Oracle Parallel Server	Oracle7
Partitioning (range, list, and other types)	Oracle8, Oracle8i, Oracle9i
Dynamic Resource Manager	Oracle8i, Oracle9i
Virtual Private Database	Oracle9i
Grid Control	Oracle Database 10g
Self-tuning/management: ADDM, ASM and related features	Oracle Database 10g
Information Lifecycle Management	Oracle Database 10g (and later release enhancements)

Many IT organizations change their management procedures to leverage these advanced features and tools when new versions of the Oracle database are deployed. Today, primary management responsibilities often fall upon a single DBA when the data warehouse is deployed on a newer Oracle database version, even for very complex workloads or very large implementations. A second DBA is usually assigned to provide coverage when the primary DBA is unavailable or needs additional assistance.

We'll describe management best practices and explore using these features in more detail in Chapters 8 and 9, but a brief introduction to the tools and features follows here.

Enterprise Manager and Grid Control

Oracle Enterprise Manager was initially introduced as a GUI-based database management interface with Oracle7. The interface evolved from a client-server version to a Java applet version to today's HTML browser-based client. Enterprise Manager's current version can be used for management for an Oracle database, Application Server, Collaboration Suite, or E-Business Suite Application. Enterprise Manager Grid Control can be used as a single front end in data warehousing implementations where there are multiple databases, multiple database instances in Real Applications Cluster (RAC) configurations, and multiple Applications Servers. Figure 3-3 shows a sample home page in Grid Control.

Grid Control provides tabs that lead to links for individual targets, deployment information, alert information, policy descriptions, job status, and reporting. Through Grid Control, you can reach the Enterprise Manager interface for each individual database.

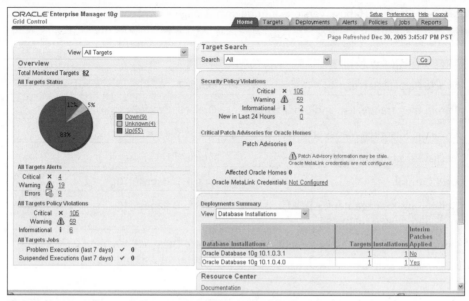

Figure 3-3: Oracle Enterprise Manager Grid Control home

Grid Control provides tabs that lead to links for individual targets, deployment information, alert information, policy descriptions, job status, and reporting. Through Grid Control, you can reach the Enterprise Manager interface for each individual database.

Within the Enterprise Manager interfaces to individual databases, you'll find tabs to multiple database management pages. The home page shows status of the database instances including instance and listener names, Oracle home location, links to the Automatic Database and Diagnostics Monitor (ADDM) findings, high availability settings, and jobs status. The administration page has links to instance, storage, redo, data warehouse, schema, and workload administration and to the Database Resource Manager. The maintenance page has links to utilities, recovery set-up, backup management, and Oracle software management (patching). The performance page contains graphs showing parameters such as host run queue length, paging rate, and instance service and throughput.

Database Self-Tuning and Management

Ad hoc queries and analyses commonly occur in business and this infers that many queries will be unplanned. Most business analysts submitting queries will not be aware of the potential impact on the system they are querying. Business intelligence tools further shield this complexity from business users since the tools typically generate SQL transparently. To maintain levels of service, database self-tuning and pro-active manageability is necessary. Oracle's database releases have added self-managing features and tools while pre-setting a growing number of initialization parameters to simplify deployment.

The Database Resource Manager is one such tool and first appeared in Oracle8i as a means for the database administrator to classify business users by consumer groups and limit the amount of CPU utilization by group. Using the Database Resource Manager in this fashion enables certain groups of users to have higher priority in order to meet service-level agreements. For example, giving prioritization to creating critical business reports in a mixed workload environment is possible. The Database Resource Manager was extended in Oracle9i with the addition of a proactive query governor (based on costs computed by the cost-based optimizer), automatic queuing, and dynamic reprioritization. Queries that would dominate a system and have a very negative effect on the query performance experienced by other business users can instead be automatically executed at lower priority levels with a negligible impact on others.

Improved database manageability was a major focus of the initial Oracle Database 10g release and subsequent database releases. Many more features were added to enable more self-tuning and monitoring including:

- Automatic Database Diagnostic Monitor (ADDM) that analyzes statistics automatically gathered by the database.

- Automatic SQL Tuning Advisor that reviews ADDM recommendations and provides better SQL profiles.

- Automatic Shared Memory Tuning that uses self-tuning algorithms to automatically configure the System Global Area (SGA) buffer cache and shared pool.

- Segment Advisor that provides recommendation on objects to shrink on-line and in-place.

- Single command FLASHBACK DATABASE and FLASHBACK TABLE that brings a database or table back to its state at a previous point in time.

- Automatic Storage Manager (ASM) that enables striping and mirroring to be set up through Oracle Enterprise Manager.

Striping and mirroring of data in an Oracle database is critically important for data warehouse performance and availability. This task was often delegated to a system administrator in the past and required coordination between the administrator and the DBA. Since the introduction of ASM, the DBA can also be responsible for storage management utilizing Enterprise Manager.

Additional storage management capabilities first emerged in Oracle Database 10g Release 2 with the introduction of Information Lifecycle

Management (ILM) and has subsequently been improved. ILM now provides an interface to set up the automatic migration of older and less frequently accessed data to higher capacity and slower disk drives that are also less expensive. This can help make it cost effective to keep all data desired in the data warehouse online.

Highly Available Database

With growing usage of Oracle data warehousing databases for tactical decision-making, critical data must be highly available and accessible. Today, a variety of approaches are used, often in combination.

Disk availability can be guaranteed using popular Redundant Arrays of Inexpensive Disk (RAID) approaches and devices. Full mirroring has been historically popular in business intelligence and data warehousing where the goal is to also optimize the speed of data loading (since creating a full duplicate of data on disk is faster than building parity on disk). Alternatively, RAID 5 (striping of a single copy of data with distributed parity to enable recovery of lost data) can be used with very high performance disks with fast write times. However, as disks become less costly, space savings associated with RAID 5 appears to be less of an advantage and so full mirroring remains popular.

From a system standpoint, physical and logical database standby systems (for example, Oracle Data Guard) can be deployed to meet a variety of availability needs. Disks can be connected to multiple nodes such that when a primary node fails, the disk is made available to a secondary node. Oracle supports transparent application failover such that queries submitted to a failed node can automatically be resubmitted to a surviving node.

Given the length of time it takes to cleanse and load data, many companies do not want to repeat the process in the event of a disaster. As the price of hardware continues to drop, especially for large-scale Linux-based or Windows-based implementations using Oracle Real Applications Clusters (RAC), deploying full duplicate backup sites has become a viable option. Advanced Queues or replication can be used to keep the Oracle data warehouse databases in sync with each other in the different locations.

Oracle Database Partitioning Option

The Oracle Partitioning option is often used as part of a database availability strategy where large-scale data warehouses are deployed. The Partitioning option enables data to be partitioned by ranges of values (such as dates) or, using list partitioning, by discrete values (such as geographies) within the database. A composite range-list partitioning enables distribution of list groups within ranges of values in a partition (see Figure 3-4).

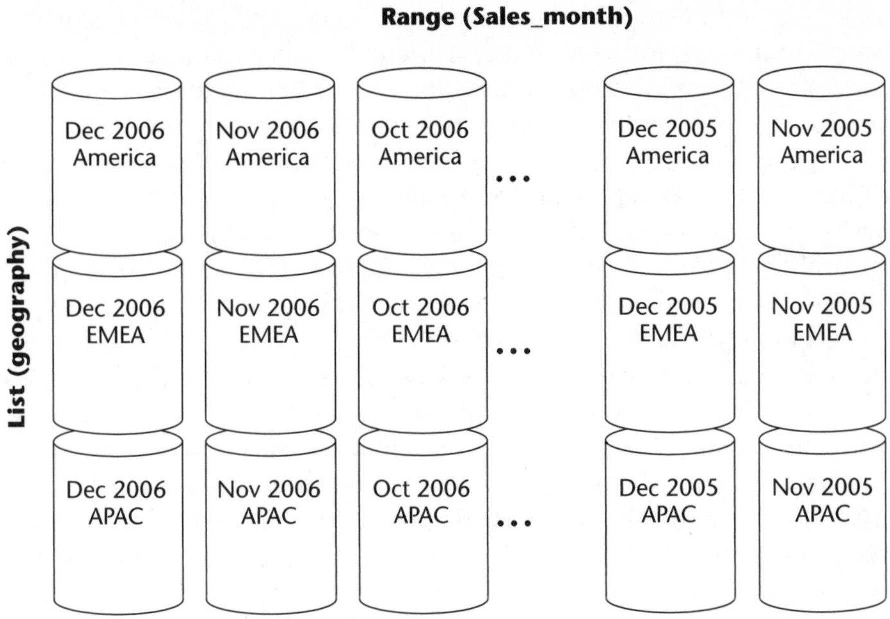

Range (Sales_month)

Figure 3-4: Illustration of composite range-list partitioning

Individual partitions can be taken off-line for maintenance. Data can be loaded to a new partition via direct path loading, local indexing can be applied, and the new partition be made available and appear instantaneously to business users without impacting the rest of the database. Where partitions are by date range, older partitions will often contain data that is non-changing and therefore needs no further backup to other devices. In large-scale data warehouses, this can reduce backup times substantially.

In addition to range and list partitioning, hash partitioning is provided in order to evenly distribute data using a hashing algorithm. Since this would somewhat defeat the manageability that other partitioning types provide, it is usually used in a composite range-hash partition.

Partitioning data can also help speed query performance. The cost-based optimizer recognizes if data requested by a query will not be present in specific partitions and will eliminate those partitions when the query is executed.

Security

Secure access to data is of increasing concern for many, especially where data in a data warehouse is shared outside of a company with partners, distributors, suppliers and others. Understanding and securing who is allowed to see and change data is also important when meeting financial and information compliance regulations.

Passwords provide the first line of security. It is common knowledge that if users are forced to have many different passwords, they'll write reminders to themselves and increase the risk of exposure of those passwords. The need to enter different passwords multiple times can also negatively impact productivity. For these reasons, Oracle's business intelligence tools and the database support single sign-on. The Oracle Internet Directory provides a LDAP compliant repository that stores user and group privilege information and can be synchronized with Active Directory if needed. Business users can log in once and gain access to multiple tools and databases.

Once users have access to the database, each user can be limited through policies set by the DBA to only see data appropriate for them. The Advanced Security Option and Row Level Label Security can restrict users to access only selected sets of rows, thus creating a virtual private database for that user. Oracle automatically appends additional criteria to each query limiting the rows returned to the user regardless of the tool that submitted the query. This eliminates one of the primary drivers to create views on top of data and provides a much more secure solution.

You can store data in specific fields as encrypted in Oracle to ensure that only authorized users can see data in those fields. Data can also be encrypted when moved over network connections and can be stored on backup media as encrypted to ensure that even if such data is intercepted or obtained by unauthorized users, it can't be viewed.

Where to Start?

Thus far in this book, we've described a range of applications and technologies useful in business intelligence and data warehousing deployment using Oracle. So, where should you start in deploying a solution at your company?

We indicate in Chapter 1 that the right place to start any such project is to gain an understanding of the key business requirements driving your company and the business unit(s) sponsoring your project. The business users in these units will have in mind a set of key performance indicators (KPIs) they'll need in order to understand how the business is functioning. Once you have gathered their requirements, you are ready to identify where the data currently resides in your systems that will provide the information needed for the KPIs.

If this data exists in transactional systems and if transactional business intelligence applications exist that provide access to these key performance indicators in an out-of-the-box fashion, then you should explore deploying such applications. Unfortunately, these applications might only provide some of the needed key performance indicators. In performing a gap analysis, you can compare the out-of-the-box functionality to what your business users tell you they need. If the gap is relatively small, you might deploy the application solution and possibly customize it. For example, Oracle's Daily Business Intelligence provides the ability to modify some out-of-the-box content. Alternatively, you might augment the out-of-the-box content with a small data mart and unify user access to needed information through a portal interface or common dashboard. If the gap is quite large, you might decide you are better off building the entire solution as a custom data warehouse.

Possible solutions that provide an out-of-the box starting point but also provide flexibility available in deploying a data warehouse solutions include pre-defined data warehouses that Oracle acquired with People-Soft, Siebel, and other applications (such as Retek). In this section, we'll briefly introduce two of the most popular that cross industry verticals — the Oracle/PeopleSoft Enterprise Performance Management (EPM) data warehouse and Oracle/Siebel Business Analytics applications.

These product suites share a number of common components. They enable much faster deployment at a lower cost than a completely custom-built solution since extraction, transformation, and loading (ETL) maps and code are pre-defined in an ETL tool. Additional sources can be added since source to target maps can be extended or custom-built using the ETL tool. Data is then loaded into a pre-defined data warehousing data model provided in the product. Business intelligence tools are available with pre-populated business metadata and can display pre-defined key business metrics or KPIs supported in the data model. Figure 3-5 illustrates a simplified view of this architecture.

Oracle/PeopleSoft EPM

PeopleSoft first shipped a version of EPM in 1998. The product has gone through major changes in various releases and enhancements since then. Prior to the EPM 8.9 release in mid-2005, the product included the Informatica ETL tool, staging tables, a series of operational data warehouse tables, and data marts (most commonly in a star or snowflake schema). Over 1700 source-to-target ETL maps are included in EPM 8.8. Four separate data marts are provided for Human Resources, Financials, Supply Chain Management, and Customer Relationship Management (CRM) in EPM 8.8, though it lacks conformed dimensions (causing information silos) or surrogate key support. Over 1200 business metrics are available and a variety of business intelligence tools provide sample reports and metadata including Cognos for Human Resources, Business Objects for Financials, and MicroStrategy for Supply Chain Management.

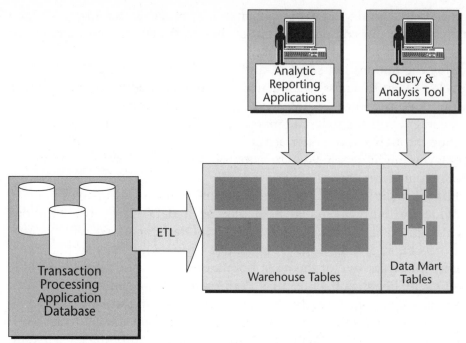

Figure 3-5: Common components in application-based data warehouse products

PeopleSoft EPM 8.9 was released as a product after the acquisition of PeopleSoft by Oracle. The ETL tool bundled in this release and EPM 9.0 is IBM's Ascential DataStage along with MetaStage for metadata management. Maps were redesigned from previous EPM releases and mapped to a single target. EPM 8.9 and more recent data marts feature conformed dimensions and support for surrogate keys. Table 3-4 provides a list of these data marts. In addition to PeopleSoft applications supported out-of-the-box source systems, maps from J.D. Edwards' application sources were added. Business intelligence tools with business metadata support for this release include Oracle Business Intelligence Standard Edition (Discoverer) and Enterprise Edition (Answers and the Dashboard), and Business Objects.

Table 3-4: PeopleSoft EPM Data Marts in Performance Management Warehouse

PERFORMANCE MANAGEMENT WAREHOUSE PACKAGE	DATA MARTS
Human Capital Management/HR	Compensation, workforce, recruiting, learning and development
Financials	General ledger and profitability, accounts receivable, accounts payable, advanced cost accounting, real estate, enterprise service automation

Table 3-4 *(continued)*

PERFORMANCE MANAGEMENT WAREHOUSE PACKAGE	DATA MARTS
Supply Chain Management	Fulfillment and billing, procurement, spend, inventory, manufacturing, supply chain planning
Customer Relationship Management	Sales, service, marketing, customer

EPM 9.0, released in mid-2006, added a student administration data mart. As you are reading this book, additional changes may have been announced for supported tools and future releases as Oracle merges these analytical models and those from the former Siebel business analytics applications into the Fusion unified analytics and CPM data model.

Oracle/Siebel Business Analytics Applications

Included in Oracle's acquisition of Siebel's Customer Relationship Management products and business in 2006 was the Siebel relationship management warehouse. This data warehouse infrastructure includes over 60 pre-defined subject areas, pre-built mappings and ETL built using Informatica that contains over 10,000 attributes, and over 2500 KPIs either computed or stored. Pre-built business adapters are also available for leveraging source data from the Oracle e-Business Suite and PeopleSoft applications, SAP, and others. Table 3-5 contains a list of the analytics applications that rely on the relationship management data warehouse and the focus areas of each.

Table 3-5: Oracle/Siebel Business Analytics Applications

ANALYTICS APPLICATIONS	FOCUS OF APPLICATIONS
Sales Analytics	Pipeline, triangulated forecasting, sales team effectiveness, up-sell/cross-sell, discounting analysis, lead conversion
Service and Contact Center Analytics	Churn propensity, customer satisfaction, resolution rate, service representative effectiveness, service cost analysis, service trend
Marketing Analytics	Campaign scorecard, response rates, product propensity, loyalty and attrition, market basket analysis, campaign return on investment
Financial Analytics	Cost, customer profitability, product profitability, regulatory compliance, expense management, cash flow analysis

(continued)

Table 3-5 *(continued)*

ANALYTICS APPLICATIONS	FOCUS OF APPLICATIONS
Supply Chain Analytics	Supplier performance, inventory analysis, bookings/billings/backlog, partner portal, partner service, partner campaign return on investment
Workforce Analytics	Staffing costs, compensation analysis, performance reporting, skills analysis, and turnover rates

Metadata for report definitions resides in the Analytics Server. Reports are typically delivered to Oracle Business Intelligence Enterprise Edition (Answers for ad-hoc query and the Dashboard). Embedded support is provided through the Intelligent Interaction Manager and agents can send alerts to devices through Oracle Delivers. A SQL API is provided into the Analytics Server allowing access from other non-Oracle business intelligence tools.

Choosing Completely Custom

If you decide that data warehouses offered as applications are not a good match for your business either and you determine it is better to build a custom data warehouse, you could have additional choices. Consulting companies and systems integrators sometimes have libraries of data warehouse schema for industry verticals that may begin to deliver the key performance indicators your business community needs. You may even find useful models in books and publications. Such schema will probably also have gaps since everyone runs their business in a unique manner, but such models can speed initial deployment and provide an early return on investment. If you can't find such a model or believe the customization of such a model will be so great as to not make it worthwhile, you should begin to consider the best way of creating a schema of your own design or with the help of a systems integrator or consultant.

Now that you've read this chapter, you realize there are many Oracle data warehousing features that can provide faster and easier access, more complete analysis, and be deployed in a way that is more easily managed. You should also consider levels of security and availability needed. But, remember that how you deploy your data warehouse solution and the success you will have will be driven by meeting business requirements.

The second major section of this book describes how to leverage much of what was introduced here to build a custom data warehouse. But before we discuss those approaches, we next look at common hardware platform deployment strategies.

Choosing a Platform

Oracle's database developers have focused, since the 1980s, on giving the Oracle database the flexibility to be deployed on any leading computer hardware platform at any given moment in time. Available platform choices change over time as some disappear and are replaced by newer and more cost-effective configurations. For example, massively parallel processing (MPP) computers, popular for data warehousing in the early 1990s and once available from many vendors, are no longer sold in the open systems market (for example, where the platforms support databases from multiple vendors). Today's platform choices are more straightforward since you likely will simply evaluate whether to deploy your data warehouse on a single symmetric multi-processing (SMP) system or to a cluster of similar systems utilizing Oracle's Real Applications Clusters (RAC).

Deciding which platform and deployment strategy to use should be driven by a combination of business and IT priorities in your organization. You will likely evaluate the scalability, manageability, and price of each of the platforms considered. You may have business-driven service-level agreements to meet that include performance and availability goals. This chapter should help you make a more informed decision as you consider each of these requirements.

When you pick a platform, you will need to size the configuration of the hardware. Sizing is a collaborative effort. You should start by working with your business community to understand their immediate needs and also future analysis and reporting plans. After gathering this information, you should then work with your favorite hardware platform vendor to determine possible configurations. You might also engage Oracle in this process. The sizing estimate should take into account your confidence in the information you gather from all parties involved. In this chapter, we will describe some of the information you should gather for sizing and discuss the roles that emerging reference configurations and benchmarks can play in this process.

Scaling Up Platforms Versus Scaling Out

As noted in other chapters, data warehouses are continuing to grow in size because of the need to store more history and greater detail. When coupled with the increasing business intelligence workload present in many organizations, it is no surprise that platform scalability is extremely important when determining a deployment strategy.

As you develop your strategy, your computer hardware platform providers will likely describe the benefits of scaling up a single SMP system capable of holding tens of CPUs compared to scaling out many systems or nodes that each have a capacity of a few CPUs. In the scale-out approach, individual nodes with four CPUs are often considered ideal when deploying the Oracle Database and RAC. However, RAC configurations with just a few nodes consisting of much larger SMP systems are sometimes deployed where there are extremely large workloads and data.

The Oracle database can leverage all of these deployment models since Oracle's processes execute in parallel for queries, data manipulation language (DML) tasks, including insert, update, and delete, data definition language (DDL) tasks, and data loads. For example, an Oracle query can leverage intra-operation parallelism in full table scans, order by and other operations, and also inter-operation pipelined parallelism between the operations. The degree of parallelism when a query is submitted is independent of data partitioning or the type of hardware architecture. Oracle will determine the appropriate degree of parallelism based on the number of CPUs available and the workload present.

At the time of writing, a growing number of data warehouses are being deployed using Oracle RAC on low cost nodes featuring Intel or AMD processors. The largest configurations of this type had as many as 16 nodes containing four CPUs each and hosting databases of over 50 terabytes in size. Of course, additional disks are present in such configurations for availability and planned growth. Where fewer nodes of larger SMP systems were deployed, the largest databases had also reached over 50 terabytes in size. In both scenarios, since an Oracle RAC configuration can support as many as 100 nodes, the room for growth is exceptional. Very large data warehouses can also be deployed on single large-scale SMP configurations — the largest database on a single SMP system exceeded 100 terabytes in size at the time of publication. When you read this book, these numbers likely will have grown much larger since data warehouse sizes tend to grow by a factor of two to three every two years.

Which style of deployment should you consider? You will want to compare scalability, but also the relative cost of platforms, manageability, and availability capabilities in each of these approaches. We'll describe some of the tradeoffs in each approach here, but first we will provide a background on these hardware platforms for those of you less familiar with them.

Hardware Platforms

Hardware platform configuration scalability is based on a number of factors. Total processing power is a function of processor speed and the number of CPUs. Larger amounts of memory can speed performance where commonly accessed data can be cached. Memory block sizes for reads are typically set to larger sizes (for exampled, 16 KB) in Oracle databases used in data warehouse deployments. Throughput (or I/O) is critical in delivering large amounts of data during tasks such as full table scans in response to queries.

The most commonly deployed hardware platforms under Oracle data warehouses are SMP systems. Early computer systems were single CPU and so they were known as uniprocessor systems. Although processors have a history of doubling in performance every 12 to 18 months, processor performance limits were sometimes reached as the business workload grew more quickly than new processor performance. SMP systems became the more popular platform to deploy by providing scalability through the addition of multiple CPUs. Figure 4-1 represents a typical SMP system that might also serve as a node in a cluster.

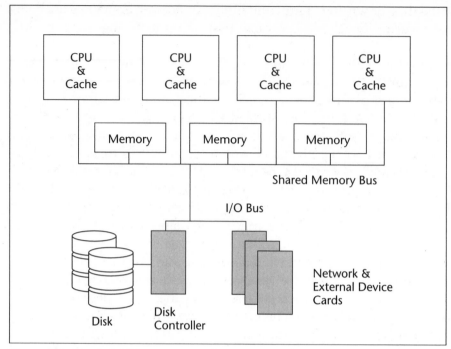

Figure 4-1: A typical SMP system or node

Since Oracle's built-in parallelization enabled it to very efficiently take advantage of additional CPUs in SMP systems, the ability to scale memory often became the next resource that determined performance limitations. Today's 64-bit SMP servers are capable of holding much more addressable memory than previous 32-bit systems, so memory capacity is rarely an issue today. That leaves I/O as the next potential bottleneck and, in fact, inadequate I/O is the most common bottleneck in Oracle-based data warehouses today. Reaching performance limitations due to inadequate I/O is especially likely where the system designers fail to recognize the importance of disk performance and provide an inadequate number of disk spindles on an I/O backplane that is not fast enough.

Clustering systems or nodes using RAC can help overcome each of these limitations since multiplying nodes scales the CPU, memory, and I/O backplane throughput capacities. Deployment of large numbers of nodes is often referred to by Oracle as Grid computing. Grid computing configurations can consist of a combination of Oracle database and Oracle Application Server nodes. Figure 4-2 illustrates Grid deployment including RAC deployed on a cluster of nodes and a blade server.

Application Server Blade   Database Blade   Database Cluster

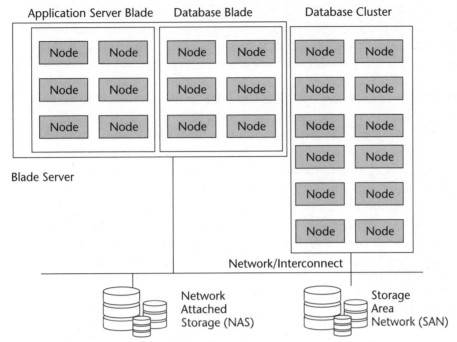

Blade Server

Network/Interconnect

Network Attached Storage (NAS)

Storage Area Network (SAN)

Figure 4-2: Illustration of a Grid including a blade server and clustered systems

RAC's availability as a product dates back to Oracle9i when it was introduced as a replacement for Oracle Parallel Server (OPS). RAC leverages Cache Fusion in using the high-speed interconnect between nodes to transmit locking information held in memory. This is a much different architecture from OPS where large numbers of reads and writes of locks to disk often resulted in high latency that led to performance challenges.

As of Oracle Database 10g, integrated clusterware is provided in the database for all operating systems where RAC is available. The clusterware synchronizes concurrent access to the database and manages the cluster's configuration. Whenever a database connection is established, that connection is made to the database instance that will provide the best service.

When systems are linked together as nodes in a networked cluster or Grid configuration, interconnect speed is also an important factor in achieving performance, especially to support locking and access to data that is not local to a node. The most common interconnect used in larger RAC and Grid configurations as this book was published is Gigabit Ethernet. The signaling rate of Gigabit Ethernet is 1 Gb per second with peak bandwidths of about 120 MB per second. For greater scalability, Infiniband has a base signal rate of 2.5 Gb per second. It is possible to configure multiple link channels or widths when using Infiniband, with four being the most common (providing a signal rate of 10 Gb per second). Peak bandwidths of 880 MB per second have been observed using Infiniband with four link channels.

We will discuss sizing the platform later in this chapter. But remember that as you work with your platform provider, the key is to create a balanced system design. It will be of no use to deploy a solution with adequate processing power if the CPUs are starved for work by disk throughput incapable of delivering needed data in a timely enough fashion. It is common for business analysts to want more and more data, but you should avoid the temptation to purchase higher capacity disk drives that lack performance in an attempt to hold down costs. Deploying such a system can result in a system unable to deliver performance that meets business requirements as well as one that wastes available computer processing resources.

Cost Considerations

The appeal of deploying lower cost hardware platforms that feature mass-produced CPUs from Intel and AMD (including Opteron) is growing. Such systems can be deployed as nodes in RAC configurations to support tens of terabytes of data and hundreds of users. Since these are often deployed in configurations that also include lower cost disk technology, such configurations can be as little as half the price of more traditional UNIX based solutions.

These configurations are most often deployed using Linux as the operating system, although there are also examples of such configurations deployed on Windows and Sun's Solaris. Scaling these operating systems to large numbers of nodes on commodity CPUs is a fairly recent development.

The maturity and robustness of the operating systems and the hardware components must be weighed. Lower-cost nodes and disks are more likely to have components with less mean time between failure (MTBF). Since failure rates are often higher, you should carefully plan how the system will meet the availability requirements that the business requires before deploying such nodes and disks.

Availability Considerations

Early data warehouses and business intelligence systems were used almost exclusively for long-term strategic business planning. They were often deployed on platforms where taking the database off-line for maintenance was expected. Planning and deploying for high availability was not considered necessary, even if unplanned downtime occurred.

More recently, the data warehouse has assumed a new role in enabling tactical decision-making. The growing popularity of updating a data warehouse using near real-time data feeds is one indication of this change. So, an important part of a business intelligence and data warehousing deployment strategy now is minimizing downtime during working hours when critical business decisions are made. As more companies become global, the need for 24-hours-per-day availability increases.

Recent versions of the Oracle database have added features to enable a reduction in downtime in the event of database problems caused by hardware, software, or human error. For example, the Fast-Start Recovery Fault capability available since Oracle Database 10g can be used to place bounds on database on database crash recovery time. The database automatically performs checkpoint processing in a manner that assures the desired recovery time can be met.

Flashback capabilities were introduced in Oracle9i and have improved with every database release since. Today, Flashback Query enables an administrator or user to query data at a previous point in time and is useful if any data has been accidentally deleted or changed. Flashback Versions Query enables viewing of changes at the row level and Flashback Transactions Query enables viewing of changes made by a transaction. Flashback Table can bring a table back to a previous point in time. Flashback Database can bring an entire database back to a previous point in time. Flashback Drop enables database objects that have been accidentally dropped to be brought back from a Recycle Bin.

Fault Tolerant Disk Configurations

Failure of disks and storage subsystems and nodes or systems will occur at some point. Even the most expensive components have an MTBF rating. High-availability planning simply becomes more important where less expensive components are deployed with a lower MTBF and the business expects a high level of service. For example, if lower priced disks are part of the configuration, it becomes even more important to have a second copy of the data available on other disks or to have the ability to recreate that data using parity if a primary disk fails.

Oracle's Automatic Storage Management (ASM), introduced in Oracle Database 10g, enables striping (for performance) and mirroring (providing a backup copy). This is sometimes described as a Redundant Array of Inexpensive Disks (RAID) configuration of level 0+1. Oracle Enterprise Manager provides the management framework used around ASM.

Other configuration levels of RAID have been deployed in data warehousing, although not as often as mirroring. Table 4-1 lists some of the common choices. RAID 5 is sometimes considered where parity is desired as a method to restore data that resided on inoperative or corrupt disks. Where RAID 5 is used, a very high performance disk is needed to meet loading windows thus limiting viability for use in a data warehouse. Any financial gain from using less storage on disk to store parity instead of a full data mirror is often offset by the higher cost of the disk.

System Downtime and Fault Tolerance

Lack of access to critical business data can be minimized through deployment of Oracle Data Guard. Where Oracle RAC is not deployed, a standby database is often desirable for use when the primary database fails or is unavailable. Primary and standby databases deployed using Data Guard are managed through Oracle Grid Control. Data Guard has various methods for updating the standby database. The method you choose should be determined by how quickly you need access to complete data in the event of failure. Both the primary and secondary databases can also be returned to an earlier time using Flashback (as of Oracle Database 10g).

Table 4-1: Descriptions of RAID Levels Commonly Considered

RAID LEVEL	DESCRIPTION
RAID 0	A striped array with no fault tolerance.
RAID 1	Full mirroring so two copies of data exist and data can simply be recopied during rebuild of failed disk.
RAID 0+1	A mirrored array where segments are striped. Failure of a single disk returns the entire array to RAID 0.
RAID 3	Data blocks are striped onto disk with parity recorded on a parity disk. RAID 53 is a higher performing variation where a striped array (RAID 0) has segments in RAID 3 for better I/O.
RAID 4	Entire blocks are written to disk with parity recorded on a parity disk.
RAID 5	Entire blocks are written to disk with parity distributed among disks. RAID 6 is a variation with a second distributed parity scheme.
RAID 10	A striped array where segments are RAID 1 (mirrored) for very high performance with availability equal to RAID 1.

The standby database can be kept consistent with the primary database through usage of Data Guard Redo Apply as updates occur. As of Oracle Database 10g, the redo data can be applied as soon as the standby receives it. A logical standby database can also be updated using Data Guard SQL Apply where archive logs are converted into SQL transactions and applied. If zero data loss is necessary, Data Guard can synchronously write redo log updates to either type of standby database as they occur.

Although RAC is increasingly deployed so that lower cost nodes can be used for scalability, it also provides the most highly available infrastructure in the event of system or node failure. In RAC deployment, all of the disk storage where data resides is shared and all nodes have access to all of the data. If a node fails, RAC provides fast and automatic connection and service relocation and failover. In the event of failure of a primary system or node where a query is being processed, the Oracle database has Transparent Application Failover (TAF) such that the business user will not need to resubmit that query. Instead, after a brief delay, the query will be automatically resubmitted and processing will continue at the standby system or on a secondary node.

Since RAC configurations using low-cost nodes and storage can be less than half the cost of traditional large SMP solutions, an increasingly common method of deployment combines RAC and Data Guard. Duplicate RAC configurations are deployed at secondary locations and provide both a high availability and disaster recovery solution.

Manageability Considerations

A large SMP system provides the simplest management model since there is a single operating system and single database instance to administer. However, as we indicated above, you may need to introduce a second system to assure availability meeting service level agreements. Since the cost of smaller SMP nodes can be a compelling driver to deploy a larger number of nodes, the need for a single interface to simplify management of multiple database instances can lead to deployment and use of Oracle's Grid Control.

Grid Control makes it feasible to manage an RAC or Grid configuration with the same number of database administrators (DBAs) as you would deploy supporting an Oracle data warehouse running on a single system. It provides a view of the target database instances that you can group to be managed as a single unit. You can analyze alerts, define policies, execute jobs, and view reports in your defined group. You can also clone instances, automate patching, and gain access through Grid Control to Enterprise Manager running on the same nodes as each instance.

Oracle provides integrated clusterware as part of RAC (since Oracle Database 10g) eliminating the need for a non-Oracle cluster file system under the database. This greatly simplifies installing RAC since the clusterware is installed using Oracle's Universal Installer. When installed, Oracle provides the ability to manage down to the disk level through Automatic Storage Management (ASM). Using ASM, you can set up striping and mirroring.

Management of the Oracle database under a data warehouse is an extensive subject. We cover this topic in more detail in Chapter 8 where we include in-depth descriptions of Grid Control and Enterprise Manager, ASM, the Automatic Database Diagnostics Monitor, Partitioning, and other related topics.

Sizing the Platform

Proper sizing of a platform on which you will deploy a data warehouse depends on many factors, most of them driven by the business. Data warehouse architects have sometimes been known to estimate platform configurations without understanding how the data warehouse would be used by the business. Some have attempted use industry benchmarks such as TPC-H or vendors' customer references to estimate configurations. But using this method can be wildly inaccurate for a number of reasons. Your business user query, reporting, and analysis workload will likely be quite different from the workload in other organizations. Available hardware configurations also change over time, so processor speeds and I/O contention comparisons can be difficult.

ORACLE AND DYNAMIC HARDWARE RECONFIGURATION

As hardware deployment becomes more flexible and dynamic, the most recent versions of the Oracle database enable it to adjust to these changes. For example, Oracle can adjust to CPUs added to or removed from an SMP server. In RAC configurations, Oracle automatically adjusts as nodes are added to or removed from a cluster. You can add or remove database disks while the database is online and move datafiles online. Oracle can automatically rebalance I/O workloads across storage and tune online memory dynamically by growing and reducing shared memory.

In the context of Grid computing, these capabilities sometimes are described under the heading of provisioning. These provisioning features in the database and the use of Grid Control for management are the keys to success where a large number of nodes are deployed.

For these reasons, you should always first try to understand your organization's potential workload as best as you can. In addition, you should try to determine likely future changes in workload and growth in database size. In doing so, you will be gathering some of the key metrics that your platform vendor will need in order to provide more accurate computer hardware platform sizing configurations.

Most hardware platform vendors have created software-driven tools that can use the information you gather and provide sizes and types of their platform solutions as output. These tools are calibrated by using configuration and usage information gathered at data warehousing sites in production. This information is also leveraged when they make projections of how similar workloads will perform on newer hardware configurations.

Information Needed for Warehouse Hardware Sizing

Data warehouse database information you gather should include measurement and projections of raw data size and, if you are using Oracle's compression capabilities, an estimate of the size after compression. In addition, you should include estimates of the size of temporary space and the space utilized by indexing. Deploying a high-availability solution will double the disk space required if full mirroring is going to be used, or incremental space should be added to build parity if other RAID levels, such as RAID 5, are to be used.

You should gain an understanding of the query workload by estimating the number of users, the number of queries (including concurrency), the mix of queries submitted, and the desired response time. Queries are usually defined by type as simple, intermediate, or complex. Simple queries are sometimes defined as queries solved with no intermediate result sets while the most complex queries might be solved using multiple intermediate result sets and rely on analysis features in the database. The workload can be defined in percentages of each type of query.

Sizing the platforms for the database does not take into account the type of business intelligence tools used since most business intelligence tools submit SQL to the database. These tools are usually deployed on a middle-tier application server, not on the data warehouse platform. Those platforms are sized separately, as we discuss subsequently in this chapter.

Extraction, Transformation, and Loading

If you are using a generic extraction, transformation, and loading (ETL) tool that processes much of the workload outside of the Oracle database, you will need to size the platform for that tool. Oracle's ETL tool, Oracle

Warehouse Builder, is designed to leverage the Oracle database's embedded ETL functionality. So from a sizing standpoint, some of the workload you include in sizing the database platform might include ETL. This will be especially true if you are providing near real-time data feeds on a continuous basis such that ETL processing is occurring at the same time as queries and analyses.

It is more common, however, to build batch feeds from your source systems into the Oracle data warehouse. In companies where there are two or more nodes deployed for the data warehouse, a common practice is to perform the data loading during off-peak hours and use underutilized or standby nodes for this activity. If this is your deployment model, you will simply need to determine your batch window, speed of ETL, and how many nodes are needed to process the load in parallel to order to meet the loading time window. The nodes could simply be sized based on the query and analysis workload if you have more than enough processing available to meet the load window.

Reference Configurations

Beginning in 2005, Oracle's hardware platform partners, including IBM and Hewlett Packard, began to produce reference configurations for Oracle-based data warehousing workloads. These reference configurations are typically a matrix of platform types and configurations based on the parameters we previously described. At a minimum, you'll be asked to by your computer hardware vendor to provide them with the number of active users, query workload description, and raw data size.

The configurations are generated by each platform provider using the previously mentioned sizing tools that each has developed. Typically each vendor can provide a variety of possible deployment possibilities that include scaling up of large SMP configurations or scaling out less expensive hardware platform nodes by leveraging RAC.

The reference configurations are meant to provide rough sizing information as a starting point. Each hardware vendor ultimately will want to provide a recommended hardware sizing especially designed to meet your needs.

Benchmarking

Benchmarks, where projected workloads are tested on platforms under consideration, are an expensive undertaking for all parties involved. They will require a significant investment in resources by your team as well as the vendors involved to be truly meaningful. When evaluating technologies and platforms, beware of companies that introduce benchmarking in the first conversation. This is usually an indication that they have specific benchmarking teams who try to limit workloads in such a way as to make their platform look good. They will often focus on only a small subset of what your solution needs to deliver to business users or may already deliver today.

To be useful, your benchmark should be based on what you anticipate to be a typical real workload. Take control of the benchmarking effort by assuming the role of project manager. Key to proper preparation is involving the business users. If there is no such business intelligence workload today, find out what sort of queries the business users will submit, the expected timing of when these queries will be submitted, and the needed response time. If such a workload exists and concern is about scalability, you will need to identify planned growth and gain agreement with the business users on how you will simulate this.

Keep in mind that you will want to develop a reasonable benchmark scope. Both you and your platform providers will likely have limited time available for such tests. Ideally, you will do such testing close to their development sites in order to engage their most knowledgeable people and the right mixture of hardware. Many vendors provide network access into their sites if evaluation team members can't travel to those sites.

The benchmark should be deployed in a manner that is consistent with your skills. So, it is a good idea to gain agreement very early as to the rules you want followed. For example, you might stipulate that the database and operating system only contain currently available features in production products. You might test the configuration for both performance and manageability. You might introduce a surprise workload based on user demands during the testing just to see how flexible the configuration really is, since your business users likely will do the same on your production system.

Before reaching the benchmark site, your test query workload scripts, database creation scripts, and data load and backup scripts should be written and debugged. Obviously, the vendors would rather not be faced with debugging your code in your presence. You should also convey your flexibility regarding indexing during the benchmark and where you might want indexing. You might also want to prioritize the running of the query workload scripts and execute the most important first just in case you run out of time.

Since preparation is so important, make sure your benchmark team is in regular contact with all involved parties before the benchmark is run. Ideally, the team will be small and consist of members of your organization, Oracle, and the hardware platform vendor.

The final step in the process is the presentation of the results. Plan ahead regarding how you want the results presented. If you are considering several vendors, consistency will be important to provide a valid comparison.

Benchmark Configuration Considerations

If you decide to build a benchmark, run the benchmark on what you plan to buy. Hardware vendors will sometimes under-configure solutions to meet your available budget, so getting the configuration right is sometimes a justification for doing benchmarks. For example, disk storage, host-based adapters, and switches should provide throughput consistent with system performance expected. Under-configured I/O is common in badly run Oracle benchmarks. A good rule of thumb is to make sure that the system provides 1 GB per second of I/O for every four CPUs with a minimum of 2 GB per second provided.

During testing, queries may be submitted using Java-based applications or business intelligence tools from middle-tier applications servers. If you plan to deploy these on separate hardware platforms in your home environment, do so during the benchmark as well to avoid placing an unrealistic workload on the database platform.

Unsuccessful Benchmarks

Benchmarks can fail for a variety of reasons even if the above criteria are followed. For example, a benchmark started without solid project funding or business involvement can be a waste of everyone's time. After all, what good are the results if the project is put on hold and the tested configuration is no longer available when funding becomes available? The results might also be considered meaningless when the business and IT organizations disagree as to whether a realistic workload was tested.

Assuming the right sponsorship, funding, and agreed-upon workload for testing is defined, the most common reason for failure is poor execution of the benchmark itself. Do not assume the vendors have everything under control and have taken all of the proper planning steps. You should take the lead in assuring that the right hardware and software for testing is in place, your scripts and data are realistic and debugged, the right people from all participants are involved, and a proper scope has been defined.

Success criteria should be understood by all engaged in the benchmark. Providing the fastest benchmark is not always most important when mature organizations evaluate the results. Remember that if multiple platform providers are successful in meeting your business requirements for performance in the benchmark, you can then focus on other criteria such as cost, support, vendor viability, and your relationship with them as you decide what platform to select.

Sizing Hardware for Business Intelligence Tools

Thus far, our discussion has centered on how to properly size and deploy the platform for the data warehouse. Of course, the business intelligence infrastructure also includes tools used by the business analysts and users. Today's web-based business intelligence tools leverage application servers as part of their deployment. You might take a less rigorous approach in sizing these platforms since they are relatively inexpensive and you can simply roll in another server when mid-tier scalability limits are reached. However, getting the sizing right such that deployed platforms match the workload is a good idea if you want to avoid the perception that your entire infrastructure is inadequate. Given this, we will provide some guidance on sizing here.

Oracle generally recommends an architecture consisting of Oracle business intelligence tools (for example, Oracle Business Intelligence Standard Edition Discoverer or Oracle Business Intelligence Enterprise Edition Answers) on a server configured with two to four CPUs and a second (single CPU) server for running the application server infrastructure. Sizing is based on the number of users submitting simple and complex queries and the number of simple and complex viewer users. For more accurate sizing, you might also want to consider the impact of think times and adjust concurrency accordingly. This combination is used in determining the number of MHz of CPU processing needed and the amount of memory required.

Oracle defines typical simple tasks and queries as connecting, opening the workbook, paging through results, changing the page axis item, switching to a cross tab, pivoting an item, drilling once, and disconnecting. Complex tasks include all of the above plus a second drill, switching to an average cross tab, exporting to Excel, displaying a graph, switching between a big table and small table, and printing the worksheet (including graph).

After initial deployment, you should monitor CPU usage, free memory available, and disk space available on the application server. Disk I/O on the database server should also be monitored. If CPUs or memory become the issue, you might either upgrade the application server computer (if not at capacity for CPUs or memory) or add additional servers. If all of these parameters are high, you probably need to replace the application server computer with a bigger machine or add additional servers.

If you are deploying Oracle Business Intelligence Enterprise Edition, the recommended configuration also includes a gateway server that supports accessing multiple database types. As these software configurations change from release to release, we recommend that you consult Oracle's configuration guides for the specific release you are deploying.

Your Strategy

In this chapter, we outlined platform choices as you deploy a data warehousing and business intelligence solution, and we provided some guidance on how to size the platform. Our focus here was on determining the right configurations for your production platform. You should, of course, also plan a development and test strategy that might include additional dedicated platforms. Keep in mind that testing to scale can be very important in business intelligence and data warehousing since scalability testing can expose hardware and software issues that are not otherwise visible.

This concludes the section of the book where we cover a broad set of deployment possibilities and introduce both pre-built solutions and software components used in a custom solution. You should now have a pretty good notion as to what sort of strategy you can use to solve your own business intelligence needs and how you might deploy such a solution.

In the next section of the book, we explore data warehousing in more detail as it most commonly is deployed — as a custom solution. We begin by providing more detail on design choices in Chapter 5, then use subsequent chapters to discuss Oracle's business intelligence tools, how to load and manage your data warehouse and performance tuning.

PART

II

Custom-Built Data Warehousing Solutions

In This Part

Designing
for Usability

Business analysts and designers use data modeling to represent ideas about information in a uniform and organized manner. Data models expose an abstraction of business processes, events, and time to provide a comprehensive view of the business. Relational database technology enables data modelers to focus on creating logical representations of the business that remain independent of physical storage and access methods. While such logical abstractions are envisioned to withstand the test of time, continued enhancements in database technology enable evolving physical design approaches that offer better flexibility and performance. Therefore, there is an increasing emphasis on physical design to ensure that business requirements are satisfied. With many design alternatives available for performance and usability, it is important to select an approach that is flexible to meet today's needs and future requirements.

This chapter highlights the approaches and principles used in designing business intelligence solutions in an Oracle environment. These principles for physical database design support a full spectrum of uses including pre-defined reporting, ad-hoc queries, trending, and forecasting analysis. Although this chapter does not address the techniques and benefits associated with logical data modeling, it will highlight the necessary constructs and best practices common in successful implementations. In addition, we will discuss the advantages and disadvantages of these approaches in an Oracle environment.

Approaches for Design

Although there can be an argument regarding the best modeling technique to use, the Oracle database has been designed to deliver flexibility and superior performance for a variety of physical designs. The most prominent design solutions today include normalized, dimensional, hybrids, and online analytical processing or OLAP. Well-designed and best-in-class Oracle enterprise data warehouses often utilize multiple physical design approaches in order to achieve flexibility and deliver performance that meets the needs of demanding users. In the following sections, we will discuss each design approach and apply best practices in an example business scenario deployed on Oracle.

Key Design Considerations

When determining the best design approach to use, it is important to consider the intended purpose of the data warehouse or business intelligence solution in order to ensure the design aligns to business requirements. Tradeoffs between flexibility and cost of improved performance should be avoided. Increasing data volumes should be accounted for.

Failures can occur where logical data modelers capture the essence of the business needs but fail to properly communicate the critical success factors that will be supported by the design. The physical design is sometimes designated to the database administrator who has responsibility over several initiatives and may not be fully versed in the specific business details needed to make informed design decisions. In organizations that staff a data architect, there is a higher success rate in matching requirements to the enterprise vision.

Although it may be difficult to ascertain all the answers during the initial design of the solution, there are several critical success factors to consider as illustrated in Figure 5-1. These include gaining a deep understanding of the business user community, data volumes, and design volatility, understanding the types of queries, analyses, and data architecture, and understanding performance and service level expectations. Understanding these factors will help you align current requirements to a long-term solution that delivers needed functionality and meets or exceeds anticipated service levels.

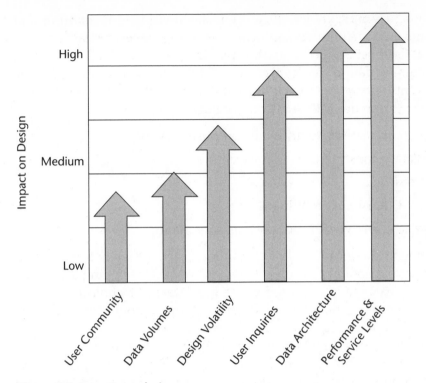

Figure 5-1: Impacts on design

User Community

In order to understand the project objectives, you should also understand the types of business users that will be utilizing the solution. Business users have diverse needs and may simply initiate infrequent and simple queries (for example, for activities such as customer service requests) or they may perform advanced analyses that scan through years of information to identify emerging trends. Understanding user community needs will help when prioritizing design considerations and ensure the highest levels of functionality are achieved.

Data Volumes and Granularity

Identifying data that matches reporting needs, including the granularity of such data, will heavily impact the overall size and cost of a data warehouse or business intelligence project. When evaluating transaction systems to capture data from, a decision to capture data at the atomic level may appear to be a simple choice since it enables the greatest reporting and analysis flexibility. Although capturing the lowest level transactions can ensure that the most detailed analysis is possible, the cost of loading, storing, and maintaining data at this level can be prohibitive. So in determining the level of granularity of data to capture, it is important to consider the following factors that impact the overall design:

- Users requirements to drill to detail during analyses
- Budgetary constraints for infrastructure
- Service levels
- Future extensibility requirements
- Advanced analytical needs such as data mining

When determining the level of granularity, capacity planning can help determine the overall impact on system resources. Developing a comprehensive capacity plan is a task shared by the data and technical architects and enables an organization to determine the amount of hardware resources and storage required to support the project.

Granularity and resulting data volumes also have a significant impact on the overall design's ability to meet flexibility and performance service levels. As data volumes increase, more emphasis is placed on techniques such as indexing, partitioning, parallelism, and compression to ensure that performance service levels can be maintained. Archiving and information lifecycle management (ILM) solutions are also considered.

Design and Volatility

Although some business data models withstand fundamental change for long periods of time, this is the exception since business conditions more often change, especially where reporting and analysis solutions are deployed across the enterprise. Understanding the likelihood of volatility is important when selecting the most appropriate design approach.

Where there is more volatility that can impact the design, there should be more flexibility built into the design in order to support the business without drastic change and rework. For example, when solutions are deployed in organizations actively engaged in mergers and acquisitions, diverse data from newly acquired organizations needs to be integrated quickly. Flexible designs are more capable of rapid integration and enable faster visibility into the newly added data.

User Inquiries and Analysis

Taking into account how users intend to query the data will have a large impact on the physical design. To better describe the variety of queries possible, user queries are often classified as Type I, Type II, and Type III.

Type I queries are operational in nature, scan only a few rows, and execute in a minimal amount of time. Type II queries include complex operational queries and historical queries where large sets of data are scanned, providing results of varying size. Type III queries are very complex and scan large sets of data while performing multiple calculations that consume large amounts of computing resources. Understanding the mixture of query types that will be present provides the data architect a better understanding of capacity and performance requirements.

Data Architecture

Establishing the right architecture that enables effective storage, retrieval, and analysis of data is an important part of creating a successful business intelligence solution. An approach that often leads to problems is to initially focus on just the needs of a single department or line of business. As the requirements grow, the architecture needs to support growth in size and function. If not considered initially, it can be difficult to extend or scale the solution to meet emerging requirements.

When the data architecture is flexible, the architect can select from multiple designs that best meet the needs of the business while providing the highest levels of functionality and performance. For example, such an architecture can include operational data stores, functional subject areas, dependent data marts or combinations that can be adopted to provide best in class solutions.

Performance and Service Levels

Performance of the solution must meet specified service levels established by the business. This requirement demands a comprehensive understanding of business functionality, user data access, concurrency, infrastructure configuration, and the overall size of the environment. For the architect, the success of the initiative can be based on ensuring that service levels are preserved, often by leveraging one or more design techniques.

Features for Design — Enhancing Performance

The Oracle database provides comprehensive support for the most commonly accepted design approaches for data warehousing and business intelligence. Although data architects must ensure that their solution satisfies all key design considerations, success of the project can be judged based on performance delivered. Newer Oracle database releases continue to deliver additional performance features optimized for business intelligence while improving ease of use and scalability. Some of these distinct features available for use include partitioning, indexing, parallelism, summarization, and query optimization.

Although features alone cannot guarantee the success of a solution design, leveraging them can help satisfy key design goals. In this section, we will highlight the top performance features, shown in Figure 5-2, and how they are applied to the most accepted design approaches.

Partitioning Approach

The exponential growth of data volumes for business intelligence solutions has created performance challenges that cannot be solved using traditional indexing approaches alone. First introduced in Oracle8, the Partitioning Option provides the data architect and database administrator with a means to meet performance profiles while improving the manageability of large data volumes. In Chapter 8, we'll describe in more detail how partitioning aids in manageability.

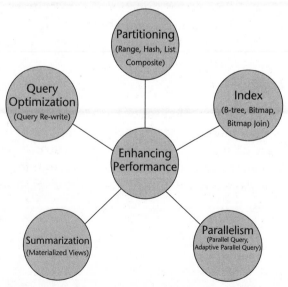

Figure 5-2: Design features for enhancing performance

Partitioning involves dividing data into smaller, more manageable pieces allowing the optimizer to isolate a small portion of the total volume of a table for data access activities. Oracle provides several partitioning methods to increase performance and manageability and continues to introduce new variations of partitioning. You should check the database documentation for the version of Oracle you are deploying for a complete list of your options. The most frequently used partitioning types are:

- **Range** — The most common partitioning method that allows the data architect to segregate data based on the ranges of data values or intervals within a column. Range partitioning is most commonly used for time series data.

- **Hash** — Hash partitioning provides an alternative to range partitioning where data is evenly distributed across multiple partitions based on a hashing algorithm. Hash partitioning is most often applied generically to tables that lack time series data but possess significant volumes that require data to be equally isolated.

- **List** — Although list partitioning is a lesser-used partitioning method, it enables the data architect to address real-world challenges with the ability to divide data into discrete, finite subsets for organizational and management purposes. List partitioning is most often applied to data that can be segregated by organization, geography or other logical classifications.

- **Composite Partitioning** — To enhance the flexibility of partitioning and to add additional granularity of data within each partition for data access performance, Oracle offers multiple composite partitioning capabilities. Composite partitions most commonly in use today are:

  - **Composite Range-Hash** — Range-hash partitioning is becoming widely adopted as it combines the flexibility and manageability of range partitioning with the ability to distribute data for optimal performance, but within each range, based on a hashing algorithm.

  - **Composite Range-List** — Range-list partitioning provides the flexibility of range partitioning with the ability to sub-partition each range into discrete, finite lists. The most common application includes time series data (range) that is subdivided by organization, geography or other logical classifications.

Most data warehouse and business intelligence solutions will leverage one or two partitioning methods. When determining the partitioning method that is most appropriate, it is important to understand the types of queries that are valuable to each user community. This will help ensure that the physical design aligns to the business solution providing the highest levels of flexibility and performance.

Indexing Approach

Indexing is the most common approach used by data architects to satisfy performance requirements. Indexing is leveraged to increase the overall efficiencies of data access by reducing disk I/O. Oracle provides several indexing methods that can be utilized to increase performance of a data warehouse or business intelligence solution. These include B-tree, bitmap, and bitmap join indexes.

B-Tree Indexes

B-tree indexes are often utilized to enforce uniqueness for high cardinality data or provide enhanced performance for commonly searched or joined data. (*Cardinality* is defined as the number of unique data values in a column compared to the total number of rows. For example, low cardinality might be defined as where the percentage of unique values is 10 percent or less.) B-tree indexes provide excellent retrieval performance for queries that specify ranges or exact matches of data and do not degrade in performance as the size of the table increases. For volatile or hybrid environments that encounter high rates of insert, update, and delete activities, B-trees are more effective and remain balanced to maintain performance. In data warehousing and business intelligence solutions, B-tree indexes commonly provide:

- Uniqueness of data enforced through primary key constraints or unique constraints.

- Increased performance for foreign key relationships that have high cardinality to facilitate joining of tables.

- Increased performance for one or more specific columns of high cardinality that are often searched.

ABOUT PRIMARY KEYS

Primary keys are one or more columns in a relational table that ensure the uniqueness of a row of data. Often, primary keys are represented by natural or business keys (and, in fact, the primary key and business key might be the same) or can be represented by surrogate or system generated identifiers.

B-tree indexes can be implemented across partitioned tables to provide access to the entire set of rows. Better known as global indexes, DDL activities on the partitioned table invalidate the global index requiring a costly rebuild. Since Oracle Database 10g, global B-tree indexes can be implemented without previous invalidation limitations. While global indexes should only be implemented in special situations that cannot be solved by local indexes, they can provide a complete solution to enhance performance and provide uniqueness.

Bitmap Indexes

Bitmap indexes have been available since Oracle7 and are most commonly used in a data warehouse or business intelligence solution where the column of data has low cardinality. These indexes are considerably smaller in size compared to B-tree indexes and provide faster response storing only the ROWID and a series of bits in a compressed format. Bitmaps are extremely efficient for set-based operations and are integral to optimization techniques like star transformation. Unlike B-tree indexes, bitmaps include all rows of a table including NULL values, providing advanced filtering capabilities not available in B-tree indexes. For data warehousing and business intelligence solutions, bitmap indexes commonly enhance performance for:

- Table joins where one or more columns have low cardinality (for example, in a dimensional model, joining a fact table that has many transactions to dimension tables used for look-up of parameters such as time and geography).

- Frequently searched columns that have low cardinality.

- Filtering conditions on specific columns that are NULL or contain equality conditions like AND, OR, and NOT.

Bitmap indexes can be utilized in partitioned tables where they map to only the rows found within that partition. Known as local bitmap indexes, they are aligned to the table partition and provide significant optimizations for parallel operations.

Bitmap Join Indexes

Available since Oracle9i, bitmap join indexes can be used to facilitate faster joins between tables. Bitmap join indexes pre-join foreign key values of a large table with primary keys of supporting tables providing a magnitude increase in performance. The capabilities of bitmap join indexes enable multiple columns to be included with multiple table joins. The benefit to the data architect and users include:

- Pre-joining of common access paths that include filtering columns that can be resolved entirely within the index, thus eliminating the need for a physical table join.

- Storage efficiency over traditional indexing methods.

Although there are some restrictions when implementing bitmap join indexes, their use is well aligned with dimensional modeling. Although available for some time, relatively few organizations have deployed bitmap join indexes in their data warehouse solutions. In organizations that have discovered their value, superior performance has been achieved especially when join paths are well understood.

An indexing strategy can have a dramatic impact on the overall performance of a business intelligence solution. When you're unsure about which indexes will yield the highest benefits, the SQL Access Advisor can provide insight for candidate index optimizations. We will discuss the database advisors in Chapters 8 and 9.

Parallelism Approach

One of the most effective methods for improving query access is to divide the work effort into multiple units of work that execute concurrently. Parallel capabilities have existed since Oracle7 and have become integral to enhancing business intelligence performance, especially with the advent of faster and cheaper hardware.

There are many parallel capabilities within Oracle, including parallel data loading, parallel Data Definition Language (DDL), parallel Data Manipulation Language (DML), and parallel query. Each of these capabilities provides the data architect, database administrator, and business user the ability to increase performance of operations by dividing the workload and distributing it across available resources.

Parallel Data Loading

One of the most resource intensive activities for a business intelligence solution is loading data. A common misconception is that this activity is the most time-consuming data warehouse activity. However, loading data often requires only a fraction of time compared to extraction and transformation operations (the ET in ETL). In environments that have shrinking processing windows, parallel activities can be applied to data loading activities to meet service levels.

Oracle provides two effective approaches for loading data when using the SQL*Loader utility: direct path and parallel data loading.

Direct path data loading is a technique that bypasses traditional internals like the buffer cache and directly formats data to be asynchronously written to disk limited only by the bandwidth and speed of the I/O storage subsystem. While there are limitations to direct path loading of tables, most of these restrictions can be overcome with proper design and control. Best practice approaches leverage direct path loads into stand-alone tables that are void of indexes and complex constraints and rely on bulk ETL operations to provide advanced transformation and cleansing activities.

The *parallel data loading* approach provides the database administrator the ability to spawn multiple sessions to load a subset of a larger data set. This approach can reduce the overall time to load data by dividing the work into smaller increments. Several restrictions and additional preparation are required to enable parallel data loading that should be evaluated before adopting this strategy. Automating this process is more complex and requires additional management by an administrator. If service levels can be successfully met using direct path loading, that strategy should be adopted over a parallel data loading strategy.

Figure 5-3 illustrates the relative performance and restrictions when using various data loading approaches.

Parallel DDL

Parallel DDL provides the data architect and administrator flexibility and efficiency when creating tables and indexes. One of the most efficient data preparation and dissemination operations is the CREATE TABLE...AS SELECT or CTAS statement. The CTAS operation is routinely used to create a table that represents large data volumes and is created based on a sub-query that reads data from one or more tables. CTAS efficiency can be significantly increased through parallelism and performing the operation in an unrecoverable mode. This makes the CTAS operation one of the most efficient methods of moving raw data into a structured format for querying and analysis.

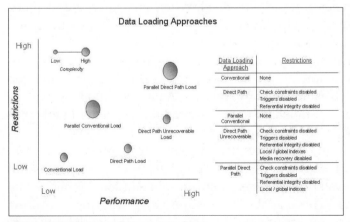

Figure 5-3: Data loading approaches

In addition, parallel operations can be applied to moving, splitting, and coalescing partitions within a table. Parallel DDL is one of the most frequently used operations for preparing and maintaining data within a business intelligence solution. As with tables, indexes benefit from parallel DDL reducing the amount of time for construction and maintenance. Parallel DDL is the operation of choice for architects and administrators to move and maintain data within an Oracle database, providing performance, flexibility, and scalability.

Parallel DML

Parallel DML is useful for efficiently maintaining existing data. Explicit to INSERT, UPDATE, DELETE, and MERGE operations, parallel DML is ideal for large batch operations that refresh or restate existing information. Parallel DML operations have many restrictions that, when improperly applied, can translate into serial operations without notification. While fully understanding the restrictions and validating execution plans can help you avoid this unexpected behavior, parallel DML operations are best performed in quiescent environments or during dedicated batch loading cycles where concurrent access to target data is restricted.

Parallel Query

Parallel query provides significant improvement in the speed of data retrieval operations. Parallelization of queries starts when the optimizer determines the most effective plan of execution and the parallel execution coordinator determines the most efficient method of parallelization based on the degree of parallelism and the number of parallel execution servers to invoke.

Parallel query can be initiated in a number of ways. The simplest method for invoking parallelization for queries is for the data architect or administrator to enable parallelism at the table level. When a user executes a query, the optimizer determines if parallelism will benefit response time and determines the optimal degree of parallelism.

The alternative method to invoke parallelism is to specify a hint as part of the query. *Hints* are directives to the optimizer that specify the intended optimization approach established by the user. A parallel hint specifies the table and the degree of parallelism to be initiated for a specified table provided there are sufficient resources.

More recent releases of Oracle provide an adaptive degree of parallelism that will, by default, reduce the degree of parallelism of new queries if it determines that the system load exceeds current thresholds established by database parameters. This capability ensures that no single process monopolizes system resources impacting other users. Although hints were often necessary in older versions of Oracle, in currently supported database releases, the optimizer is significantly more sophisticated and the use of hints is discouraged within applications and other solutions.

Summarization Approach and Query Optimization

An Oracle-based data warehouse can be designed to optimize queries by leveraging database features such as bitmap indexes and partitioning. Optimizer behavior will vary based on the type of design and the complexity of the query. For example, for normalized models that join several large tables, a partition-wise join can leverage partition elimination (for example, eliminate partitions from the query that contains only irrelevant data) and parallelism to increase efficiency for complex queries.

Another common optimization technique is the star transformation used to solve dimensional models. By leveraging bitmap indexes on foreign keys of a fact table, the optimizer transforms the query into subqueries where each of the bitmaps to each dimension are scanned. Needed rows are filtered and combined to matching fact rows. Since the bitmap indexes are compressed and very efficient, this filtering operation facilitates the join of the fact table to each dimension to produce the final result set.

Often, large volumes of data, possibly consisting of millions of rows, are required to produce aggregate results requiring significant processing resources. To ensure the highest levels of performance for common queries that require summarized information, data architects would often create stand-alone structures in older Oracle database versions to meet service levels and reduce the resource consumption. However, the need to provide synchronization, the complexity in determining change, and the need for additional storage often negated the value of this summarization approach.

Oracle simplified this by providing materialized views, a schema object that provides a method to pre-join complex queries and performs commonly requested aggregates with full transparency to the end user or application developer. Materialized views support a variety of update scenarios in order to keep the summary data consistent with detailed data. In addition, the materialized view structure is made transparent to business users and application developers by leveraging an optimization capability called query rewrite.

A *query rewrite* operation occurs when the optimizer analyzes a query and determines it can be satisfied by one or more materialized views at a lower optimization cost compared to accessing the base-level structures. The optimizer will then rewrite the query (transparently to the user or application) to take advantage of the materialized view. This transparency assures the application developer that application code is preserved, eliminating the need for rework if design changes become necessary, and it provides the data architect and administrator considerable flexibility to increase performance without the need to modify the existing design or application code.

The Oracle database also has several advisors that provide guidance to determine if materialized views can improve query performance. We will discuss database advisors and the use of materialized views in Chapter 9.

Business Scenario

The following business scenario will be used in the upcoming sections to illustrate design approaches while highlighting the benefits of each.

An electronics manufacturer has recently acquired a competitor to extend its existing product line. The acquisition has provided them with an established customer base in a new geographic region that was considered for development. The manufacturer plans future acquisitions to strengthen the current portfolio and enable growth. While the acquisition presents new opportunities for expansion and growth, competition across existing product lines and higher raw material costs have limited their ability to expand. In addition, the manufacturer has encountered several internal challenges that have limited growth. These challenges include:

- Latency and inaccuracies in receiving sales information.
- Inability to determine profitability by product and product line.
- Poor quality of information.
- Difficulty in forecasting sales leading to higher inventory carrying costs.
- Inaccuracies in calculating sales commissions.
- Needed information regarding sales, inventory levels, and manufacturing commitments to raw materials for product managers.
- Use of spreadsheets in analysis of sales, manufacturing, and finance data extracted from ERP systems.
- Difficulty in identifying root cause of manufacturing issues due to the inability to access supporting detailed data.
- Inability to accurately predict the most marketable bundles of products that maximize profits, utilize excess manufacturing capacity, and reduce inventory levels.
- Difficulty in satisfying the reporting needs of diverse user communities due to multiple tools, inconsistent definitions, and complexities encountered in finding and understanding data.

This manufacturer has set aside a budget to construct a sales reporting solution to help solve many internal reporting challenges. The proposed solution will be used by sales, finance, and manufacturing to answer the most significant queries. Some of the most notable questions to be answered include:

- Sales analysis:
  - What are the sales by quarter, sales representative, and geography?
  - How are sales trending to industry forecasts?
  - How do sales compare in the Northeast to Southwest?
- Product profitability:
  - Which product lines are the highest revenue producers this year?
  - Which products and product lines are the most profitable this quarter?
  - Which product lines are above seasonal forecasts?
- Sales representative analysis:
  - Who are the top five sales representatives by sales volume?
  - Who are the most productive sales representatives in divisions, regions, and territories?
  - Which sales divisions, regions, and territories generate the highest revenues and margins?
- Customer analysis:
  - Who are the best customers?
  - Who are the most profitable customers?
  - What percentage of sales is generated from the top five customers?
  - Which customers purchase the most products by product line?
  - Which industry has experienced the fastest growth over last year?

Figure 5-4 shows the number of transactions the manufacturer anticipates in the next three years and the historical transactions that are significant to support the analysis.

Anticipated Transaction Volumes					
Table	Historical	Current Year	Year 2	Year 3	Tota
Products	30,000	10,000	5,000	5,000	50
Customers	160,000	50,000	10,000	10,000	230,
Sales Reps	2,000	800	300	500	3
Rep Commissions	400,000	160,000	60,000	100,000	720,
Sales Items	80,000,000	30,000,000	60,000,000	80,000,000	250,000,

Figure 5-4: Anticipated transaction volumes

Normalized Design

Database normalization is a structured design technique used for eliminating data anomalies and redundancies within data. Pioneered by E.F. Codd in the 1970s, data normalization establishes dependencies between data, reducing duplication and inconsistencies. Although normalized designs provide flexibility and efficiencies in active transactional implementations, they do not by themselves typically provide needed levels of performance and ease of comprehension for business analysts when used for business intelligence. But the chief goal of some implementations is simply to cleanse and gather all data centrally in an enterprise data warehouse. In the early 1990s, Bill Inmon and others created a foundation for constructing such an enterprise data warehouse by introducing best practice designs that were based on third normal form techniques.

The Oracle database provides comprehensive support for physical designs based on third normal form. Recent versions of Oracle leverage advances in parallelism, indexing, and partitioning, enabling normalized designs to have the highest levels of flexibility and performance. Today, some of the largest data warehouses built upon Oracle use third normal form as the basis of their designs. Examples exist in a variety of industries, including Internet content providers, telecommunications, manufacturing, and financial services. In many of these, the reason for normalizing the design is to provide flexibility. Many of these solutions are enterprise repositories that provide a single point of consolidation of information from many disparate data sources. Using our business scenario, we will next highlight the potential benefits provided by a normalized approach.

Business Scenario: Normalized Design

The following example represents a third normal form design to support the sales process and is illustrated in Figure 5-5. This view of the manufacturer's sales process is designed to capture only the information that is significant to current reporting and analysis needs and is not intended to represent a comprehensive view of the enterprise. Some of the operational data was not made available due to its limited value to reporting, thus helping to improve performance and lower the cost for supporting infrastructure.

During analysis and design, it is important to identify candidate data elements that are anticipated to provide value for both operational and strategic analysis. Although many organizations take the approach to capture as many data elements as possible, the cost and level of effort associated with assessing quality, reporting value, and construction activities often render this approach prohibitive. It is often more cost effective to use the so-called 80/20 rule in selecting data elements. Choose to focus on providing data elements that are used most often (for example, in 80 percent of queries) to deliver a solution faster while also eliminating potential data quality issues in data that would be used less frequently.

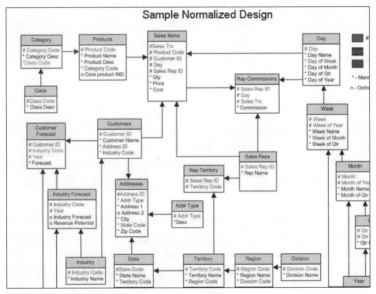

Figure 5-5: Sample third normal form design

In our business scenario, the manufacturer has encountered several challenges that may benefit from constructing a normalized design. Their needs include:

- **Single version of the truth** — The manufacturer has encountered challenges in providing accurate information caused by extracting data from disparate data sources, subjecting it to many interpretations of business rules and formatting. Poor quality of information has plagued the manufacturer causing difficulties in satisfying simple business requests for information. A normalized model will provide a single repository for information, providing the organization with a centralized source for sales information.

- **Acquisition of data from disparate sources** — The manufacturer has recently undergone an acquisition that requires this new information to be integrated to provide both cross product and geographic analysis.

- **Business representation** — A normalized design will provide the best representation of the business in this scenario since such models provide the most flexible structures for extending existing designs during acquisitions.

In a later section, we will discuss the key factors that must be considered in deploying normalized designs to ensure that they are aligned to business requirements. In addition, we will highlight specific Oracle features that can be deployed for design optimization.

Dimensional Design

Dimensional design is a denormalization technique used in providing an intuitive view of historically correct information that corresponds to the needs of users. Commonly referred to as star schema design, dimensional designs are subject-oriented structures comprised of fact tables and dimension tables.

Fact tables represent processes, events, or activities that are used in measuring a business. A fact table is comprised of two types of columns: foreign key references to dimension tables and to measures. Foreign key columns are provided to join the fact table to dimension tables that enable the filtering and constraining of data. Measures or metric columns provide information about the event that is classified as additive, semi-additive, or non-additive values. *Additive* measures support discrete arithmetic operations along all of the dimensions, *semi-additive* measures support arithmetic operations along only some of the dimensions, and *non-additive* measures are typically descriptive and provide no arithmetic value.

Dimension tables contain attributes and hierarchies that enable a logical grouping and constraining of data. Dimension attributes are normally descriptive and represent details about the dimension. Hierarchies within a dimension provide a natural summarization of information ranging from the lowest level of detail to the highest summary level. The most common hierarchy in dimensional designs is the time hierarchy that provides multiple levels that typically range from day, week, and month to year. Pioneered by Ralph Kimball, dimensional modeling has gained popularity for simplicity in building, ease of maintenance, ability to perform, and business user comprehension.

If a goal is to extend a solution to support multiple business processes using dimensional designs, the definitions of dimensions should be consistent. Better known as conforming dimensions, such dimensional structures provide consistent definitions that can be leveraged for multiple business processes. This approach enables dimensional designs to support enterprise business intelligence solutions crossing multiple business areas.

Since Oracle7, specific data warehousing features have been introduced providing improvements in performance, manageability, and scalability when dimensional designs are used. These specific enhancements include:

- Partitioning solutions that provide performance and manageability to support the most complex access needs.

- Bitmap and bitmap join indexes for efficient storage.

- Optimization techniques such as star-transformation and query-rewrite for query optimization.

- Materialized views enabling transparent summarization and efficient drill-to-detail.

Many large subject-oriented data warehouses built on Oracle use dimensional designs as the basis of their enterprise data warehouse and data mart solutions. This approach can also be found in virtually all industries. Next, we return to our business scenario and highlight the benefits provided by a dimensional approach.

Business Scenario: Dimensional Design

The model in Figure 5-6 represents a dimensional design example to support our manufacturer's sales process. While portions of the model possess similar characteristics found in a normalized model, numerous textual attributes have been consolidated and denormalized into dimension tables. The consolidation of attributes provides an efficient and intuitive method to enable users to constrain and filter data.

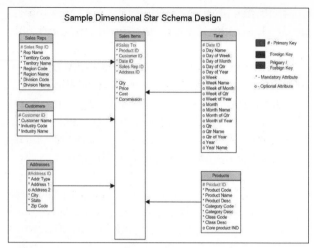

Figure 5-6: A Sample dimensional model design

In our example, the consolidation of attributes can be found in the time, product, customer, and sales representative dimensions. In many dimensional designs, there are fewer operational data elements than captured in normalized designs since many of these elements might provide little or no value to the core analysis.

A dimensional design provides unique capabilities to answer ad-hoc queries against large volumes of data requesting results at different levels of granularity without special tuning in advance. The model is comprised of the detailed information for sales items captured at the day, sales representative, customer, and product level. Notice that unlike in the normalized model, commission information can be collapsed into the sales items since the required details for commissions are captured at the same granularity as sales items.

In our business scenario, the manufacturer has encountered several challenges that may benefit from dimensional design. The most notable business needs include:

- **Subject-area analysis** — The manufacturer understands challenges caused by a lack of visibility into sales performance and forecasting accuracy problems. A dimensional design is a superior approach for providing solutions to specific business processes such as sales analysis due to flexibility provided to answer most known and ad-hoc queries. By defining subject areas, you are more likely to deliver functionality that meets the immediate needs of the business in a shorter time frame. Although such an approach is specific to a selected business process, if designed properly, it can be expanded to satisfy the demands for enterprise reporting.

- **Ad-hoc requirements** — The manufacturer has identified four user communities with distinct reporting and analysis needs that include product profitability, sales commission, customer, and sales representative analysis. A dimensional design provides extensive flexibility in providing answers using centralized measures stored in fact tables and supporting attributes used for constraining and filtering in dimension tables. Since the join paths between fact and dimension tables are established to produce what is known as a star query, the Oracle optimizer can produce the most efficient execution plan.

- **Ease of use** — The manufacturer has encountered challenges in reporting and analysis for multiple user communities. Some of these challenges are due to design complexities and difficulty in finding necessary information. A dimensional design simplifies this since measures or metrics are exclusively stored in fact tables and supporting descriptions and hierarchies can be found in dimension tables. Since a dimensional design is based on a specific business process, usage is confined to answering specific questions about a given process and the business user training can be process specific.

- **Time to market** — Many organizations fail to deliver successful business intelligence solutions due to increasing size and scope of the project. One key approach in reducing the overall risk is to start with a smaller initiative that can be delivered in a shorter duration. Dimensional designs are subject-oriented and focused on a specific business process so scope can be naturally limited.

- **Historical view** — There are several techniques that map well to dimensional designs that allow a historical view of information to be preserved when attribute values change over time. Better known as slowly changing dimensions, these techniques allow designers to determine the most effective method of tracking history for a business intelligence solution.

Dimensional designs provide an intuitive view of a business process for answering known and ad hoc queries. In a later section, we will discuss key factors that should be considered when deploying dimensional designs that are aligned to business requirements. In addition, we will highlight specific Oracle features that can be leveraged to ensure design optimization.

Hybrid Design

Hybrid designs leverage the best characteristics of normalized and denormalized design techniques to provide a flexible and extensible solution. Commonly referred to as snowflake design, this approach utilizes fact and dimension tables but focuses on normalizing dimensions to reduce redundancy. This approach is especially useful when dimensions contain a significant number of attributes or when hierarchies contain many levels comprised of a significant number of attributes. A significant reduction in storage may be realized by normalizing dimensions when there are a significant number of text attributes or attributes that possess low cardinality.

Snowflake designs can provide additional flexibility especially when resolving a many-to-many relationship that cannot be easily captured in a dimension table. This approach prevents the dimension table from containing multiple levels of granularity that can be confusing to business users when they determine the attributes to be used in constraining and filtering queries.

The same features in the Oracle database that support normalized and dimensional designs can be applied to hybrid designs. These include partitioning, bitmap indexes, specific optimization techniques, and materialized views for transparent summarization. Most large data warehouses built on Oracle technology base their foundation on hybrid designs to leverage the best features of normalized designs when capturing data from disparate sources and dimensional designs to support efficient data access. In our business scenario, we will next highlight the benefits provided by a hybrid approach.

Business Scenario: Hybrid Design

The model illustrated in Figure 5-7 represents a hybrid design supporting our manufacturer's sales process. Although the model appears similar to a dimensional star-schema design, several dimensions are in snowflakes and resemble a normalized design. The benefits achieved in this design include the ability to remove many of the sparse and verbose text attributes associated with dimensions like demographic information about customers.

Dimensions such as *products* that historically possess a significant number of attributes are candidates for snowflake designs. This allows attributes specifically associated with each level of the hierarchy to be independently isolated, improving clarity and reducing the impact of data volatility. Although this model provides the same capabilities to answer known and ad hoc queries, its performance may be diminished against large data volumes compared to dimensional solutions. This trade-off in access performance must be considered when determining the proper balance between manageability, flexibility, and performance.

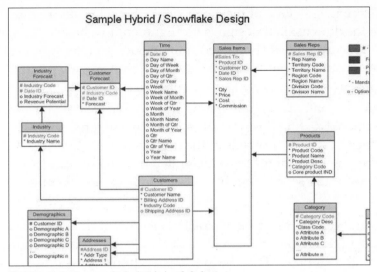

Figure 5-7: A sample hybrid model design

An additional benefit provided by a hybrid design is the ability to efficiently manage many-to-many relationships that are coupled to dimensions. In our scenario, we can easily compare revenue to customer and industry forecasts efficiently using an optimization technique called a partition-wise join. A *partition-wise join* is an optimization technique that reduces query response time by minimizing the amount of data exchanged by parallel processes during parallel query operations. This operation is extremely efficient when partitioning methods between large tables are consistent.

In our business scenario, the manufacturer has encountered several challenges that may benefit from a hybrid design. The most notable business needs include:

■ **Flexibility to extend** — A hybrid design provides benefits of normalizing specific dimensions by easing integration of new data from future acquisitions. The data architect can determine when and where to denormalize attributes based on known existing query patterns. In addition, this design is flexible enough to withstand multiple iterations as new functionality is added ensuring that current investments can be extended without the need of unnecessary rework.

■ **Ease of use** — The manufacturer has encountered previous challenges in supporting reporting and analysis needs of business user communities. Although not as intuitive as a purely dimensional design, the most significant dimensional attributes in the hybrid design are represented as part of the star-schema so most queries remain simple and intuitive.

- **Subject-area centric** — One of the key benefits that a hybrid design shares with the dimensional design is its alignment to a business process. Extraneous data is eliminated from the design to ensure that known and ad hoc queries can be efficiently solved.

- **Quality initiatives** — Ensuring high-quality information can be a difficult task especially when integrating new sources of data into an existing solution. Existing business rules must be validated and new ones introduced to meet the needs of the organization. A hybrid design enables new attributes to be integrated into the solution rapidly by physically separating the data until the quality is fully reconciled.

Hybrid designs leverage the best characteristics of normalized and denormalized design techniques to provide a flexible and extensible solution that meets design and query needs. In a later section, we will discuss the key factors that must be considered when deploying hybrid designs to ensure that they are aligned to business requirements. In addition, we will highlight specific Oracle features that can be deployed to ensure design optimization.

Online Analytical Processing Design

In many organizations, reporting solutions have a limited scope of analytic requirements and the majority of queries can be solved using standard SQL and relational technology. Where advanced analytics and statistical functionality is required, online analytical processing (OLAP) can provide a multi-dimensional modeling technique that provides such functionality. OLAP allows complex calculations along multiple dimensions enabling analysis that cannot be easily replicated by purely relational solutions. Some example calculations that would leverage OLAP include ranking product sales quarter over quarter, determining top products purchased ranked by the top five new customers, and trending of actual sales compared to a forecast for the top revenue categories.

In the past, OLAP solutions were often costly and confined to separate, stand-alone environments that limited their widespread use across the organization. Such solutions introduce delivery latency caused by the necessity to extract data from relational systems, security provisions that are often immature and inconsistent with other solutions, a need to administer a separate platform, and a lack of high availability and recoverability. Although many database vendors now recognize the need to provide solutions that can analyze multidimensional and relational data, Oracle's OLAP Option was the first to be truly embedded in the relational database and offer similar functionality to stand-alone multidimensional servers such as Oracle Express.

Available since Oracle9i and improved in releases since, today's Oracle OLAP Option, provides many important features valuable in business intelligence solutions including:

- SQL access to multidimensional structures enabling high performance access by traditional relational applications and tools.

- Cube compression that optimizes dynamic aggregation and significantly reduces storage of multidimensional data based on patterns of sparseness.

- Multiple partitioning methods that enable faster data loading, multi-write access and ease of management optimizing I/O for faster data update and access.

- Parallel processing for high-speed maintenance, data loading, and aggregation leveraging server resources.

Oracle OLAP can be leveraged to provide business users a near real-time solution for complex financial and statistical analysis that complements an existing data warehouse, all within the same platform environment.

Business Scenario: Online Analytical Processing Design

In our business scenario, we will view our sample OLAP design as an extension to our existing relational solution instead of as a replacement solution. One of the benefits of having relational and OLAP technology within the same platform is that there is no need for solution functionality to overlap. This provides the data architect and administrator the flexibility to choose the most appropriate technology to ensure the highest ease of use, flexibility, and performance.

The Oracle OLAP engine uses what is called an analytic workspace as a multidimensional data structure to support analytic processing. When constructing our OLAP design, the analytic workspace is built by logically defining dimensions, levels, hierarchies, attributes, cubes, measures, and mappings prior to physically loading data from a relational source. Each analytic workspace is stored in a relational table as a large binary objects data type, thus the administrator can manage OLAP solutions in the same manner as relational solutions.

Similar to relational solutions, these dimensions categorize data and form the edges of a logical cube and are used in our example to constrain and measure *sales* (see Figure 5-8). The dimensions include *customers*, *products*, *sales reps*, and *time*. The *time* dimension has many special characteristics that enable it to support historical business analysis through complex time-series analysis. This enables comparisons of data between periods such as current quarter compared to the same quarter last year. Dimensions are further defined through levels, hierarchies, and attributes.

A level establishes a one-to-many or a parent-child relationship among data within a dimension that is ultimately used to establish a hierarchy. Levels can be used to drill up and down a hierarchy providing insight into trends. In this example, the base level of information in the *product* dimension is the *product_code*. Although detailed analysis at the product level is important, many users want to view product information at various summary levels. These levels include the *category*, *class*, and a level to support all products.

A hierarchy establishes a navigational drill path within a dimension based on a predefined ordering of levels. Hierarchies are extremely flexible, providing solutions to solve most complex data relationships. The simplest hierarchy is specified using levels. The most common example of a level-based hierarchy is time-based where days roll up to weeks, months, quarters, and years. Hierarchies can also be defined by specifying a parent for each dimensional value. Parent-child or value-based hierarchies are often used when the relationships within the dimension are not meaningful or where data is flat with little to no relationships. A key advantage of OLAP is its ability to support multiple hierarchies within a dimension. In our example, multiple hierarchies allow users to analyze data in the *time* dimension along calendar and fiscal boundaries.

Dimensional Hierarchies and Levels

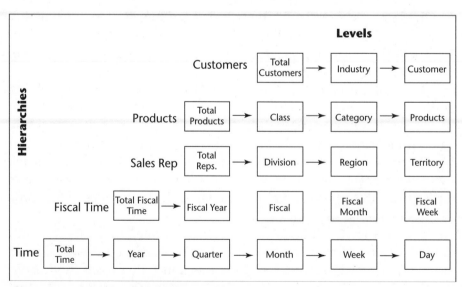

Figure 5-8: Dimensional hierarchies and levels

Attributes provide descriptive information about the individual members in a dimension. As in relational solutions, dimensional attributes are used for selecting, filtering, and displaying data, although this represents only a small subset of overall attributes found in their relational counterparts.

The OLAP cube provides a logical multidimensional representation used to organize metrics that share the same relationships for analysis. The edges of a cube represent the dimensions used for filtering and constraining while the body of the cube contains one or more metrics or measures used in measuring a business process or event. In our example, we created a *sales* cube that is dimensioned by *time, customer, product*, and *sales rep* in a manner similar to the dimensional model.

Measures or metrics represent the information that is to be measured about a business process or event. Measures represent information that is specific about one or more dimensional values. In this example, the measures captured are *quantity, sales, profit*, and *commission*.

The final step in the OLAP design is to provide the physical mapping of relational data to the OLAP cube. This process involves mapping the normalized model, star-schema, or snowflake schema to the *sales* cube (shown in Figure 5-9). While mapping a dimensional model is relatively straight forward, additional work may be required in mapping the hybrid and normalized models to our *sales* cube such as creating relational views to flatten and combine dimensional hierarchies.

The diagram represents information that was created using Oracle Analytic Workspace Manager (AWM). AWM provides a graphical interface for defining, mapping, and loading data into analytic workspaces. Table 5-1 highlights the detailed steps (as numbered in Figure 5-9) that are required in constructing a multidimensional design.

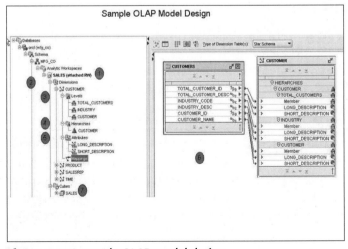

Figure 5-9: A sample OLAP model design

Table 5-1: Steps for Constructing a Multidimensional Design

ITEM	ELEMENT	DESCRIPTION
1	Analytic Workspace	Supported by *customer*, *product*, *sales rep*, and *time* dimension and *sales* cube.
2	Dimension — Customer	Framework for customer information, including levels, hierarchies, attributes, and mappings.
3	Levels — Customer	Comprised of total customers (summary), industry and customer (most detailed) levels.
4	Hierarchies — Customer	A single hierarchy representing customer levels.
5	Attributes — Customer	Comprised of short and long descriptions only.
6	Mappings — Customer	Enables a graphical drag-and-drop mapping of the relational customer table to the OLAP customer dimension. The mapping is straightforward since its source is a star-schema design.
7	Cube — Sales	The sales cube represents the sales, quantity, and profit measures that are associated with the customer, product, sales rep, and time dimensions. It also includes any calculated measure like month, quarter, or year-to-date summaries that are value for business analysis.

Other Considerations

The ability to leverage important database features, including partitioning, indexing, and summarization, can influence the design. In the following sections, we will discuss the advantages and disadvantages of each approach and highlight best practices as they relate to our manufacturing business scenario.

In our business scenario, we need to provide the most comprehensive design in the shortest time based on competitive and market pressures. There is a need to store several years of historical sales data obtained through a recent acquisition. In addition, one or more additional acquisitions are anticipated introducing additional sales data and volatility into the design. So, before transforming a logical model into a specific design approach, we should also look at some of the fundamental business requirements and physical factors that may impact the appropriateness of our design choices.

Business Scenario: Partitioning

As previously highlighted, partitioning has a significant impact on improving the performance and manageability of a large table. In our business scenario, the *sales_items* table will initially support 80 million rows, and over 250 million rows within three years. Tables with a large number of rows can benefit from increased query performance provided by partition elimination or have significant historical data that could benefit from compression or enhanced maintainability. There are several steps that should be considered in selecting the most appropriate partitioning method. These steps include:

- **Access** — Understand business functionality and the types of anticipated queries. In our scenario, many of the queries have a time-series component making range partitioning a prime candidate.

- **Manageability** — Understand the life cycle of information and how it will be maintained over time through capacity planning. In our scenario, we anticipate storing six years of data in which three years are historical. Compression combined with range partitioning allows historical data to be stored efficiently and easily archived when appropriate.

- **Granularity** — Determine the granularity of data based on service levels, types of queries and overall data volumes to establish the number of partitions. In our scenario, we know that 80 million rows will be loaded by the end of the first year. In Figure 5-10, our analysis shows that monthly partitions provide a manageable number of blocks per partition and the granularity of monthly partitioning provides the necessary manageability for compression and archiving. Sub-partitioning by product enables us to further divide monthly sales into smaller increments since many queries are product-centric within a specific time-series. The quantity of hash partitions should be based on a power of two to avoid any skewing of rows. In our scenario, we selected four based on the number of data blocks per partition and support for parallelism. If a mistake is made in selecting the optimal granularity, with some work, either splitting or combining partitions can fix it.

ESTIMATING THE NUMBER OF ROWS PER DATA BLOCK

In our example, we allocated a 16K database block size for our data warehouse. To estimate the number of rows per data block, we loaded a representative sample of data, estimated statistics, and utilized the average row size found in the data dictionary view user_tables to assist in sizing.

Initial Sizing & Partitioning Estimate

Table: sales_items	Historical	Previous Year	Last Year	Current Year
Partitioning Solution: Range / Hash	24 Range 4 Hash/Range	12 Range 4 Hash/Range	12 Range 4 Hash/Range	12 Range 4 Hash/Range
Rows	30,000,000	25,000,000	25,000,000	30,000,000
Rows / Partition	1,250,000	2,083,333	2,083,333	2,500,000
Rows / Hash	312,500	520,833	520,833	625,000
Rows / DB Block (16K)	256	256	256	256
Avg DB Blocks / Range	407	678	678	814
Avg DB Blocks / Sub-Partition Blocks	81	136	136	163

Figure 5-10: Business scenario — initial sizing and partition estimate

The partitioning solution is independent of our selection of data model designs since large tables most often require partitioning to ensure the highest levels of manageability and performance.

Business Scenario: Indexing

The overall goal of indexing is to increase the performance of data access by reducing disk I/O. Although commonly used in all design techniques, the approach to indexing is dramatically different when implementing normalized, dimensional, or hybrid solutions.

Indexing of normalized models is based on known query patterns or a full index model. Most normalized models are designed to answer a series of known queries, so the indexing structure often reflects this approach. Under this approach, primary keys, foreign key columns to support specific table joins, and columns used in filtering are routinely indexed. This approach can be sufficient given that queries are well known and experience little variance.

More commonly, data architects choose to fully index a normalized model by placing B-tree indexes on all primary and foreign keys while creating additional indexes on specific columns commonly used in filtering activities. In our business scenario, if we were to deploy a normalized model, we would adopt the latter approach by indexing all primary key columns with B-tree indexes for both uniqueness and performance. Although indexing many smaller tables like *addr_type* or *division* will not benefit performance, it is often useful to include the index to ensure data integrity of the model. For low cardinality columns, bitmap indexes provide efficiency, performance, and storage. Examples where bitmap indexes will benefit the scenario include:

- Foreign key values in the *sales_item* table since these columns have low cardinality ratio (less than 1 percent in our scenario).

- Frequently searched columns that have low cardinality like *core_product_indicator* in the *products* table.

- Filtering conditions on specific columns that are NULL or contain equality conditions like AND, OR and NOT.

Figure 5-11 illustrates a sample indexing design for a normalized model in our scenario.

Table	Column	Index	Purpose	Table	Column	Index	P...
Sales Items	Sales Trx	B-tree	PK / FK / Unique	Addr Type	Addr Type	B-tree	PK / U
	Product Code	Bitmap	FK / Ref Integrity	Industry	Industry Code	B-tree	PK / U
	Customer ID	Bitmap	FK / Ref Integrity	Industry Forecast	Industry Code, Year	B-tree	PK / U
	Day	Bitmap	FK / Ref Integrity	Rep Commissions	Sales Rep ID, Day, Sales Trx	B-tree	PK / U
	Sales Rep ID	Bitmap	FK / Ref Integrity	Sales Rep	Sales Rep ID	B-tree	PK / U
Products	Product Code	B-tree	PK / Uniqueness	Rep Territory	Sales Rep ID, Territory Code	B-tree	PK / U
	Product Name	B-tree	Performance	Territory	Territory Code	B-tree	PK / U
	Core Prd Ind	Bitmap	Performance		Region Code	B-tree	FK / R
	Category Code	B-tree	FK / Ref Integrity	Region	Region Code	B-tree	PK / U
Category	Category Code	B-tree	PK / Uniqueness		Division Code	B-tree	FK / R
	Class Code	B-tree	FK / Ref Integrity	Division	Division Code	B-tree	PK / U
Class	Class Code	B-tree	Performance	Day	Day	B-tree	PK / U
Customers	Customer ID	B-tree	PK / Uniqueness		Day of Week	B-tree	FK / R
	Customer Name	B-tree	Performance	Week	Week, Week of Year	B-tree	PK / U
Customer Forecast	Customer ID, Industry Code, Year	B-tree	PK / FK / Unique	Month	Month, Month of Year	B-tree	PK / F
Addresses	Address ID	B-tree	PK / Uniqueness	Qtr	Qtr, Qtr of Year	B-tree	PK / F
State	State Code	B-tree	PK / Uniqueness	Year	Year	B-tree	PK / U

Figure 5-11: A sample indexing approach for normalized design

The index design technique for dimensional models is simple and straight-forward in its implementation. To ensure the highest levels of performance for dimensional models, it is important that the optimizer can leverage a star transformation as part of its plan using bitmap indexes. In our business scenario, we will start by indexing the fact table. Fact tables in dimensional models can leverage bitmap indexes on foreign keys since the cardinality of values is low and the size of the index structure is compressed and very efficient. These include column references for *product, customer, date, sales rep*, and *address* dimension tables. Since the fact table is partitioned, the indexes would be local indexes specifically aligned to each partition. For dimension tables, all primary keys would be indexed and represented by B-tree indexes supporting uniqueness and facilitating joins to fact tables. Figure 5-12 illustrates a sample indexing design for a dimensional model in our scenario.

The index design technique for hybrid models is a combination of methods found in both dimensional and normalized solutions. Bitmap indexes are used extensively for dimensional portions of the model to enable star transformation, while standard B-tree indexes provide uniqueness for dimensional tables and join paths for snowflake tables. Leveraging bitmap join indexes to flatten the snowflake portions of supporting dimension tables can enhance the performance of a hybrid model. This approach provides the design flexibility of normalized dimensional structures and the performance provided by bitmap join indexing.

Business Scenario: Summarization

Summary structures are common in business intelligence applications where the data architect and administrator optimize performance for a class of queries that routinely request information at higher levels of a hierarchy. While the motivation for summarization is clear, there were often side effects in previous approaches to existing infrastructures and applications limiting usage.

Table	Column	Index	Purpose
Sales Items	Product ID	Bitmap	FK / Ref Integrity
	Customer ID	Bitmap	FK / Ref Integrity
	Date ID	Bitmap	FK / Ref Integrity
	Sales Rep ID	Bitmap	FK / Ref Integrity
	Address ID	Bitmap	FK / Ref Integrity
Products	Product ID	B-tree	PK / Uniqueness
Customers	Customer ID	B-tree	PK / Uniqueness
Addresses	Address ID	B-tree	PK / Uniqueness
Sales Rep	Sales Rep ID	B-tree	PK / Uniqueness
Time	Date ID	B-Tree	PK / Uniqueness

Figure 5-12: A sample indexing approach for dimensional design

In comparison, Oracle provides application transparency through a process called query-rewrite that is enabled through the creation of materialized views. This approach for summarization satisfies performance service levels without adversely impacting existing applications or designs. In addition, the same management techniques that we use for managing and loading large relational tables are appropriate for materialized views.

In our business scenario, a materialized view could significantly enhance the performance of sales inquiries summarized by quarter, year, or period over period comparisons. Other opportunities where materialized views could significantly enhance performance are along the organizational hierarchy for *sales reps* and *products*. It is important to review the consolidation and compression ratios of rows that will be achieved in creating a summary. If the number of rows reduced is relatively small, the value of the materialized view is significantly diminished. See Figure 5-13.

Implementations of materialized views can range from overuse requiring significant maintenance and administration to very limited use or no use. There are also permutations of materialized views that could be created across many dimensional levels. This opens the debate of whether an OLAP solution could be more beneficial than its relational counterpart, especially when queries become more complex. The best way to determine if materialized views will benefit your application is to leverage the SQL Advisor. We describe an example in Chapter 9.

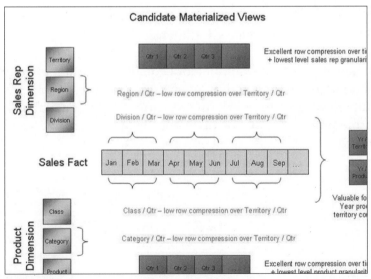

Figure 5-13: Candidate materialized views

Selecting the Best Approach

The ongoing debate over the optimal design approach for data warehousing remains alive and well after over 20 years. Although the different design techniques have benefited from advances in hardware and software, many organizations still fail to provide extensibility, performance, or flexibility during the lifetime of a business intelligence solution. Proper design and planning will significantly enhance your opportunity for success.

Many database vendors favor specific designs based on optimizations they support. The Oracle database provides great flexibility through support for normalized, dimensional, hybrid, and OLAP designs. But, with such wide choice, you may wonder how to determine the best approach.

Selecting the optimal approach for your business intelligence project will require a deep understanding of the business, the scope of the project, the quality of data, priority of requirements, and optimal duration. Ideally, you also have the proper sponsorship for the project. The best design approach will address the following:

- Meet or exceed service-level requirements.
- Provide flexibility to meet immediate and near-term needs.
- Provide simplicity to aid user comprehension.
- Provide extensibility to support change and growth.
- Provide support for analysis tools favored by business analysts.

No matter if your design is normalized, dimensional, hybrid, or OLAP, Oracle will continue to enhance the database features that make constructing and maintaining such solutions optimal. But equally important to your success will be an ongoing understanding of emerging business problems and potential solutions by gathering information from all of your available sources. At the same time, you must be open and flexible to change since change is guaranteed.

CHAPTER 6

Business Intelligence Tools

This chapter describes business intelligence tools commonly used by business executives, analysts, and other users. Since entire books are written about specific tools and we are covering this topic in a single chapter, our intent is to give you a broad perspective regarding the types of tools available and how they are used and deployed. We will focus mostly on Oracle's business intelligence tools in this chapter. These include products used for deploying dashboards that present key performance indicators (KPIs) such as Oracle Portal, reporting tools that include Oracle's BI (XML) Publisher and Oracle Reports, Oracle Business Intelligence ad hoc query and analysis tools, and data mining tools that include Oracle Data Miner.

The decision to deploy Oracle business intelligence tools compared to other vendors' tools in each of these areas will involve various trade-offs. Benefits of buying tools from a single vendor include more simplified metadata management, enterprise security management, better integration, better access to more advanced Oracle database features, and a more common look-and-feel across the tools. In addition to these technical benefits, many organizations prefer to deal with a single point of support when problems occur.

Of course, we recognize that many of you also deploy other products around Oracle data warehouses. Business users sometimes select tools based on look-and-feel, perceived ease-of-use, or critical needs that other vendors may have more proactively demonstrated solutions for. Wide availability of a tool can also influence the choice of tool used in an organization. For many, the most popular business intelligence tool in common use is Microsoft Excel. So, we will describe how you can use Excel to access data residing in an Oracle data warehouse and describe levels of Oracle support provided by some of the other business intelligence tools you might deploy.

Oracle Portal and Portal Products

Many of today's business intelligence tools include software used to create dashboards that enable easy access to the reports published by the tools. An enterprise portal is a more sophisticated dashboard in that it provides a framework for viewing content and re-usable components (or portlets) within a collection of pages, leveraging information provided by a variety of business intelligence tools and sources.

Oracle's portal products have had a variety of names. Oracle's history in portal development dates back to the introduction of a portal product named WebDB in 1997. WebDB was designed to be a self-service product for publishing structured and unstructured content. In 2000, Oracle introduced the Oracle Portal integrated into the Oracle Application Server and featuring a distributed portlet architecture based on the Simple Object Access Protocol (SOAP). The version released in 2002 featured more tightly integrated deployment functions, including caching, identity management, administration, and monitoring along with more simplified deployment. Ongoing development and subsequent releases of Oracle's portal products have focused on improving information unification, process integration, content management, collaboration, and ease of management.

Oracle portals have supported the Java Specification Request (JSR) 168 standard for portal and portlet interoperability since version 10.1.4 of Oracle Portal. JSR 168 defines the application programming interfaces (APIs) for portlets and provides additional standardization for portlet requests, portlet responses, deployment packaging, and user preferences, information and security. This enables Oracle and other vendors (for example, Business Objects) to deploy portlets in the Oracle Portal by adhering to the standard.

Within an Oracle Portal page, portlets are rendered as HTML table cells. Multiple cells can appear on a page. Figure 6-1 shows the initial Build page in the Portal Builder. This page consists of several portlets, including one in the illustration labeled as Recent Objects. Portlets typically include a header with portlet title, a border around the title and content to separate the portlet from other content on the page, a personalize link for personalizing portlet attributes (that may be turned off by the page designer), a portlet refresh icon, and an icon for expanding or collapsing the portlet.

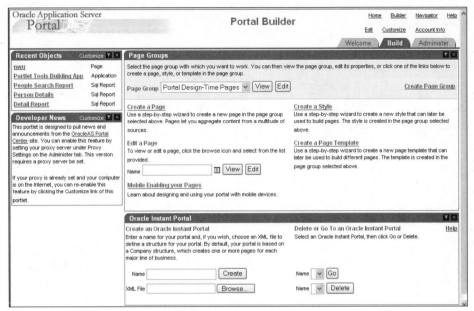

Figure 6-1: The Portal Builder Build page consisting of multiple portlets

Using Oracle Portal

Portal users are most commonly non-technical business executives and analysts. Since Oracle Portals are more often deployed to serve an enterprise, they are usually built and deployed by developers and designers. In the next section, we describe some of the development and design tools and features.

Users are presented with an easy-to-use interface requiring minimal instruction on usage since most are familiar with accessing commercial Web sites today. Most of the time, users will simply follow links from page to page. Figure 6-2 pictures such an informational portal, the Oracle.com web site. When a user isn't sure where to find certain information, they might use Oracle Portal's item search, page search, and category search capabilities. If Oracle Text is also enabled, search words can be found in any appropriate content that is accessible through the Portal.

In general, the user of an Oracle Portal deployed for business intelligence will need to understand how to login and change their password, view pages, find information, and possibly subscribe to a page or item. More advanced users might seek privileges to personalize their environment by editing or adding content to a page, or privileges to create their own pages. Users are managed through an Administer interface in the Portal Builder (see the portlets on the right side of Figure 6-3).

Figure 6-2: Home page of the Oracle.com site built using Oracle Portal

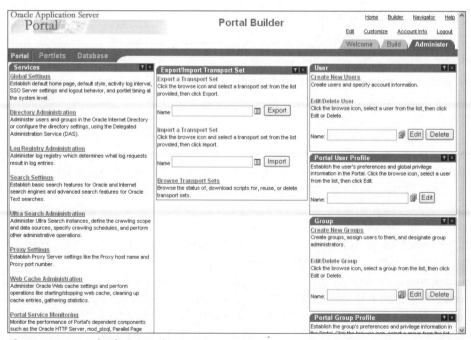

Figure 6-3: Portal Administration page

Pages can be seen when users are granted view privileges by the Portal administrator. Users can refresh pages or individual portlets when they want to see the most current content. Where subscriptions are provided for pages or items, users can select to subscribe so that they will receive an alert every time the page or item is updated. With proper privileges, they can view their subscriptions in a My Notifications Portlet.

Users have control over various aspects of their Account Info. For example, they can change their login password. They can also change their default home page and the style of pages presented (see Figure 6-4 illustrating the screen where account information can be edited).

More advanced users can personalize a page by adding a portlet to a page, arranging portlets in a page region, moving portlets to different regions or tabs, hiding a portlet on a page, removing a portlet from a page, arranging the order of tabs in a region, hiding a tab on a page, applying a new style to a page, personalizing a page parameter, or removing page personalizations. Their ability to perform these will depend on the privileges granted. With full privileges, they can personalize a page in all of the ways previously stated. However, it is possible to be granted only limited privileges for just adding portlets, hiding or showing portlets, or only changing the style.

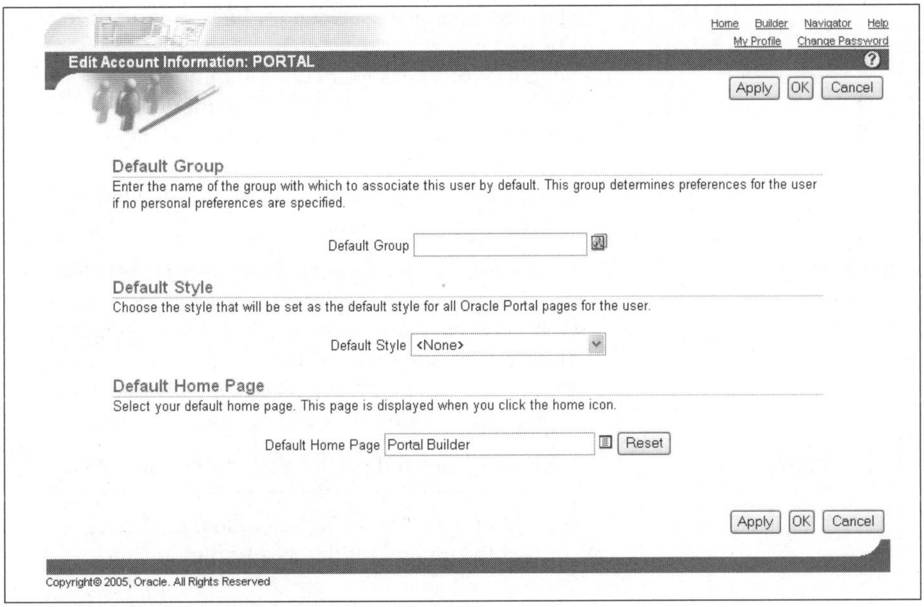

Figure 6-4: Portal Account Info editing page

Building and Deploying Oracle Portal and Portlets

Complexity in building and deploying an Oracle Portal can range from using packaged components in Instant Portal's point-and-click interface, to deploying pre-built portlets in a custom Oracle Portal, to building home grown programmed portlets and deploying them in a very highly customized Oracle Portal. Many of Oracle's business intelligence tools provide portlets for deployment in Oracle Portal including Oracle Business Intelligence (both the former Siebel and Discoverer components), Reports, and BI (XML) Publisher. Oracle also includes a number of pre-built and pre-registered portlets in a Portlet Repository in the Oracle Application Server. The Portlet Repository's main page includes links to pages for Portlet Builders, the Survey Builder, Content Portlets, Additional Portlets, the Portlet Staging Area, Published Portal Content, Shared Portlets, and Administration Portlets. Included in these Portlets are a number of tools to speed Portal and Portlet development as described in Table 6-1.

Table 6-1: Description of recommended Oracle Portal and Portlet development tools

DEVELOPMENT TOOL	DESCRIPTION
Instant Portal	Intended for small and medium businesses and included with Application Server Standard Edition One, the interface provided for building portals in this tool is point and click. Out-of-the box, the home page includes links for news, announcements, new content, and favorite content. The interface provides a great deal of flexibility including the ability to edit pages, define tabs, define child pages, define news items, and manage levels of access as defined by the portal administrator.
OmniPortlet	Page designers and portlet developers can publish data from a variety of sources, such as CSV, XML, Web Services, Web pages, and SAP. Pre-built layouts provided include bulleted lists, forms, charts, and news. Data can be personalized for individual users by applying filtering.
Web Clipping	Page designers and portlet developers use a Web browser to navigate to Web pages holding desired content and the Web Clipping Studio to choose content to clip and render as a portlet in Oracle Portal.
Portlet Factory	Developers tool that enables assembling of builders into portlets presenting data from Oracle's PeopleSoft and JD Edwards applications and SAP.

The Portlet Builders page that contains the OmniPortlet, Web Clipping, Simple Parameter Form, HTML, Report, and Form portlets is pictured in Figure 6-5. If you are building surveys, tests, or polls, you should explore the Survey Builder page in the Repository. There, you'll find a Survey Builder, Form, Chart, and Reports portlets.

Portlets for controlling content on pages, subscriptions, and searching are found in the Content Portlets page. These include Set Language, Favorites, Advanced Search, Basic Search, Custom Search, My Approval Status, My Notifications, Page, My Page, Pending Approvals Monitor, Saved Searches, and User Managed Pages portlets. You'll also see a link in the Repository to Additional Portlets that include Calendar, Chart, Data Component, Dynamic Page, Hierarchy, Menu, and MobileXML portlets.

Administration Portlets include a single sign-on/Oracle Internet Directory (SSO/OID) page, a database page, a Portal page, and a Reports Security page. The SSO/OID page includes portlets for external applications, login, SSO Server Administration, User, Group, People Search, Portal Group Profile, and Portal User Profile. Portlets on the database page include the Database Navigator, Schemas, Roles, Database Information, Database Memory, Consumption and Transactions and Locks, Database Storage, and Batch Results portlets. On the Portal page under Administration, you'll find portlets for Mobile Logs, Most Recent Mobile Log Entry, Oracle Instant Portal, Recent Objects, Remote Providers, the Portlet Repository, Services, Find, Providers Navigator, Page Group Navigator, Database Providers, Remote Provider Group, Export/Import Transport Set, Clear Cache, Error Message, and Page Groups portlets. The Reports Security page includes Reports Security, Reports Server Access, Reports Definition File Access, Reports Printer Access, and Reports Calendar Access portlets.

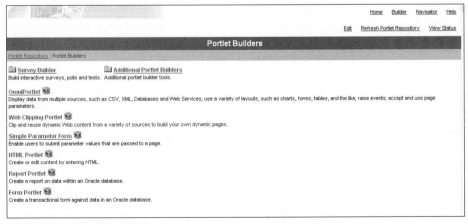

Figure 6-5: Portlet Builders page

In addition to Oracle developed portlets, Oracle maintains a web site where portlets contributed by users and partners of Oracle Portal are posted. At `http://portalcenter.oracle.com`, you will find portlets others have developed for custom charts and calendars, image galleries, renderers, and other useful Portal building blocks. Figure 6-6 shows a portion of a typical Oracle Portal Center web page.

Some prefer a more custom approach in Portal development using programming development tools to generate Java or PL/SQL programs. Development kits enabling calls to portlet APIs include the Portal Development Kit for Java (PDK-Java) and the Portal Development Kit for PL/SQL (PDK-PL/SQL). A number of content management APIs are also provided for Oracle Portal.

Transactional Business Intelligence Portlets

In Chapter 2, we described the concept of transactional business intelligence and tools. Oracle's E-Business Suite is certified to be deployed using the Oracle Application Server and Portal and is integrated with Oracle Identity Management (OIM) solutions. The E-Business Suite provides a number of portlets including the Navigator, Favorites, Daily Business Intelligence (DBI), Work-list, Balanced Scorecard Custom View, Balanced Scorecard KPI Graphs, and Balanced Scorecard KPI lists portlets.

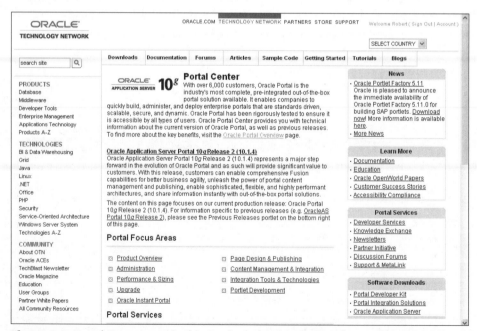

Figure 6-6: Portal Center page in the Oracle Technology Network

Of course, Oracle also offers PeopleSoft and JD Edwards applications and many Oracle database customers deploy SAP applications. The Oracle Portlet Factory was first introduced in version 10.1.4 of Oracle Portal to develop, deploy, and maintain portlets that interact with these applications.

The Portlet Factory includes two builders that act as Portlet adapters. The JSR 168 Adapter generates the appropriate JSR 168 code in the form of a portlet WAR file. The Oracle Application Server Portal Adapter generates native Portal code based on the PDK-Java and supports Application Server Portal 10g functions, including SSO, National Language Support (NLS), Portlet-to-Portlet communications, and content cachability.

Oracle's PeopleSoft applications portlets can be deployed to the Oracle Portal with SSO enabled if you use the PeopleSoft Pagelet Wizard from PeopleTools versions 8.47 or a more recent PeopleTools version along with the PDK-Java. The Portlet Factory added portlet builders for the PeopleSoft Component Interface and PeopleSoft View and Form.

Oracle's JD Edwards EnterpriseOne is certified for deployment on the Oracle Application Server and Portal and can also leverage SSO. The EnterpriseOne Forms Design Aid tool can generate thick client sources from which the portlet generator can produce PDK-Java portlets. The Portlet Factory adds a JD Edwards EnterpriseOne Business Function portlet builder.

For SAP applications, you can use the Oracle Application Server Provider for SAP iViews to integrate SAP MiniApps directly into the Oracle Portal. The Oracle Portal also provides a number of pre-defined portlets based on the SAP Java Connector (JCo) interface, including the Generic SAP Portlet, Employee Details Portlet, Exchange Rates Portlet, Personnel Payroll Results Portlet, and Employee Attendance Records Portlet.

If you plan to build your own SAP portlets, Oracle offers such portlet builders. Using the SAP Data Source for OmniPortlet, you can use a wizard to define BAPI functions from your portlet to SAP R/3 data sources. The Portlet Factory includes SAP View and Form, SAP Function Call, SAP Transaction, SAP BW Data Access, SAP Help Values, and SAP Batch Input builders.

Portlets for Business Process Flows

In some businesses, sensors measure changes in business conditions and mountains of data are fed to the database for analysis. In such scenarios, it can make sense to leverage an alerting infrastructure in the business intelligence tool to automatically trigger a business process flow whenever preset thresholds are reached and a known repeatable action is warranted. Oracle's Business Intelligence Enterprise Edition (formerly Siebel Business Analytics) includes such an alerting infrastructure. Oracle's BPEL tool can be used to build the business process flows. BPEL provides a number of portlets enabling this reporting through the Oracle Portal, including Instance State, Instance Execution Time, and Performance Metrics portlets. (Oracle's Business Activity Monitoring or BAM product might also be used to view changes in status in real time.)

The BPEL Worklist application provides Task Listing and Task Analysis portlets. The Task Listing portlet can show tasks assigned to the Portal user must be acted upon before the tasks are routed forward. Tasks can be assigned to individuals or groups. If a user is a member of the assigned group, they can claim the task and become responsible for routing it forward. The Task Analysis portlets represents tasks assigned to the user on a chart.

Reporting

Reporting tools may seem fairly mundane, yet reports are the most widely used form of business intelligence since their ease of use appeals to everyone, ranging from business executives to temporary employees. Their usefulness is often gauged by the relevancy of the KPIs and the ease of deciphering their meaning. When selecting a reporting tool, a key consideration is often the ease and flexibility of distributing these reports.

BUSINESS PROCESS FLOWS AND BUSINESS INTELLIGENCE

Many visionaries and technology analysts believe that incorporating business process flows in business intelligence solutions will become commonplace. IDC's Dr. Henry Morris sometimes refers to this style of business intelligence as Intelligent Process Automation.

Certainly, one of the promised benefits of a service-oriented architecture (SOA) is to be able to more easily link various applications together. Oracle has described a SOA-based architecture as a key ingredient in the next generation Project Fusion applications. You might do this to better enable execution of business processes across applications modules. Sophisticated and automated business actions might be triggered by alerts being raised as established thresholds of data values are reached.

When this transition to SOA occurs, it is likely that the alerting infrastructure will be shared among the applications themselves. But for now, a viable alternative is to use alerting infrastructures provided within some business intelligence analysis tools to trigger business process flows.

Today, Oracle offers a variety of reporting solutions. BI Publisher, also known as XML Publisher, is Oracle's latest reporting offering and is intended to enable easy report generation (and especially report formatting) by business users. Oracle's older reporting tool is Oracle Reports and is intended for use by IT developers to build and distribute more sophisticated reports. The Oracle Reporting Workbench in Oracle Business Intelligence Enterprise Edition (formerly Siebel Business Analytics) is actually a repackaging of a popular tool from Actuate. We describe each of these in this section.

BI/XML Publisher

Originally introduced as XML Publisher, Oracle BI Publisher is used to create highly customized reports where data is provided in XML format. Examples of such reports can include invoices, government forms, bills of lading (including bar codes), printed checks (with embedded MICR format), journal reporting, and balance sheets. Publisher includes a template builder, repository manager, delivery manager, and XML parser.

Publisher is designed for deployment in Oracle's transactional applications such as the E-Business Suite, or standalone on the Oracle Application Server. When deployed to the Application Server, the main Publisher software is installed as a Java Archive (JAR) file along with the supporting XML Parser.

When XML Publisher was originally introduced, it was designed explicitly for use with the E-Business Suite (where the Concurrent Manager can generate XML). Today you might also generate XML output with Oracle Business Intelligence tools such as Oracle Reports (described in the next section), XQuery (with Java or PL/SQL), XMLGEN (with SQL or PL/SQL), or completely manually. XML generation support is provided in the Java XML Developers' Kit (XDK).

Supported report template types include PDF, RTF, eText (a RTF-based template used for Electronic Funds Transfer and Electronic Data Interchange), XSL-FO, XSL-HTML, XSL-TEXT, and XSL-XML. For example, you might choose to generate PDF forms in a PDF authoring tool such as Adobe Acrobat or reuse a pre-existing PDF form. Of course, Microsoft Word can be used to author RTF forms.

The Template Builder plug-in for Microsoft Word is available for inserting data fields and data-driven tables, forms, and charts into the various template types. Figure 6-7 illustrates a data-driven table containing defined fields. Figure 6-8 illustrates a data-driven chart. Note the appearance of the Template Builder add-in on the Microsoft Word menu.

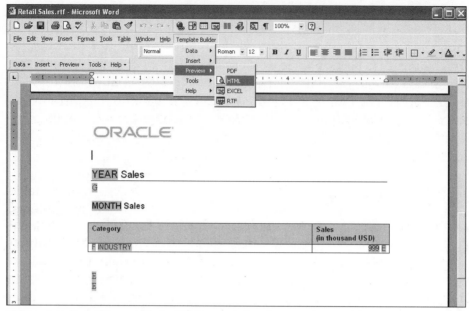

Figure 6-7: Data driven table in RTF format using the Template Builder

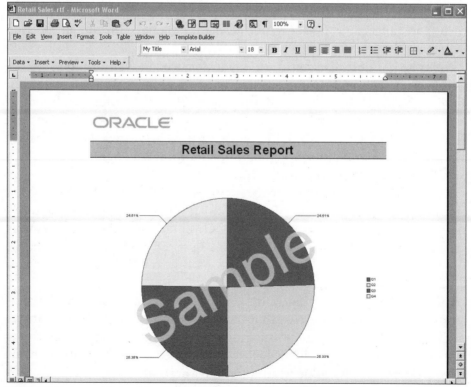

Figure 6-8: Data driven chart in RTF format using the Template Builder

Through the Template Builder, you can also preview the report leveraging XML data stored locally or create XML data through SQL queries you submit to a database connection established through the Builder. In a previous illustration, Figure 6-7, you can see the pull-down menu for loading sample data. Previews can be viewed in PDF, HTML, Excel, or RTF formats. Figure 6-9 shows a portion of the previously defined report viewed in HTML as generated by the Template Builder. Tools provided in the add-in include a field browser, text translation, exports to XSL-FO style sheets and FO formatted XML, and options for user interface fonts and display mode, language in previews, and builds.RTF templates can feature placeholders, repeating fields or groups, multiple headers and footers, table breaks, page-level calculations, sorting, a dynamic table of contents, included images, hyperlinks, XSL-FO and FO elements, and conditional formatting (including column and row formatting and cell highlighting). Advanced reporting layouts for RTF can include batch reporting, cross-tab support, and support of dynamic data columns. PDF templates can feature form field aliasing, page duplication and numbering, groups of repeating fields or rows of repeating items, and overflow data.

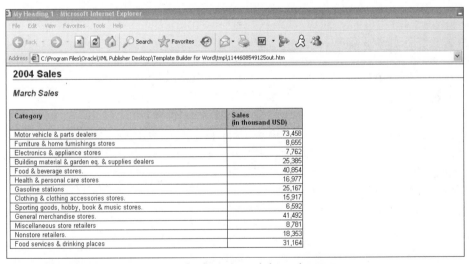

Figure 6-9: Table containing sample data viewed through HTML

Once templates are created, they are registered in the Template Manager repository to be made available to Publisher during runtime. The Template Manager can also be used for viewing, copying, and updating templates and maintaining data definitions for your XML sources. You can create and maintain mappings between PDF fields and XML data elements, export and upload XLFF files for translation, and preview a report template containing sample data. The Manager is accessible by any user who is a Publisher administrator. A template locale can be specified defining a template language and territory. Since a single XML data source can have multiple templates associated with it, you could deploy a single report with multiple language translations such as English, French, and Japanese.

Reports created in Publisher can be delivered to business analysts and users in a variety of ways using the Delivery Manager APIs. For example, reports might be delivered via email, to a printer, via Fax, to WebDAV servers, using FTP, or over HTTP.

Oracle Reports

The Oracle Reports product pre-dates BI/XML Publisher and is most appropriate for IT developers developing and deploying a complex infrastructure for high-quality web-based and paper reporting. The Reports product includes the Developer component in the Oracle Internet Developer Suite and Reports Services bundled in the Enterprise Edition of the Application Server or Oracle Business Intelligence Standard Edition.

A variety of sources can provide data for these reports, including Oracle relational databases, the Oracle database OLAP Option, JDBC connected sources, and XML and text files. Reports can be published in formats appropriate for the web or printed documents, including PDF, XML, HTML, HTMLCSS, using JavaServer Pages (JSPs), PostScript, PCL, delimited text, and RTF. Destinations can also include FTP and WebDAV servers.

The Developer component provides wizards for constructing SQL queries, organizing data, creating reports, graphing, and creating conditional formatting. For example, using Reports Developer, IT users step through the process of defining Reports structures, sources of data, break groups, and summaries. The page frame model enables the use of a variety of formats and a Live Previewer will display the report layout and a page of data after the initial format selection. Report formats can include tables, matrixes, grouped reports, graphs, and combinations. Re-entrant wizards enable further modifications after previewing.

The graphing wizard provides more than 50 different graph types that can be added to reports. Since the graphs are based on the same presentation

Java Beans leveraged in Oracle Discoverer, the graph types are common. Available graph types include bar, horizontal bar, pie, line, area, combination, scatter/bubble, stock, circular, and Pareto types, with some available in both two-dimensional and three-dimensional forms.

When the developer is satisfied with the format, a report file can be generated from the command line or in a batch command file. A command file can be useful if you are running several reports using the same set of arguments. Reports deployed for web use might be specified at runtime to be output in a variety of formats, such as Adobe PDF, plain text, HTML, HTML extension, or HTMLCSS. Web-based reports can also include predefined drill-down capabilities enabling a business analyst to ask to see more detailed data within a report.

Using this variety of web-based formats, the generated reports can be deployed to Oracle Portal. They can also be deployed as portlets by taking advantage of the JSP capabilities in Oracle Reports that enable deployment as HTML. When using JSPs, you can separate static and dynamic content and view data as it is updated in the database. JSPs also support scripting and tags, reuse of components and tags, and can be compiled for faster execution. Single sign-on is supported when deployed in this manner.

Report generation can be triggered by specific events leveraging an event-driven publishing API available as a PL/SQL package. The report jobs are submitted via HTTP and publishing of the reports occurs when triggered by specific database events or using Oracle's Advanced Queuing (AQ). Reports might also be triggered by Java applications using the Web Service interface to the Reports Server in the Oracle Application Server.

When distributing reports, multiple destinations can be specified in a single run and can be created for entire reports or report sections. For example, as you generate HTML output, you might also send a PostScript version of the report to a printer and email sections of a report to individuals using a technique known as bursting.

Oracle BI Reporting Workbench (Actuate)

In the next section covering ad-hoc query and analysis, we describe Oracle Business Intelligence Enterprise Edition (BI EE) that provides ad-hoc query and dashboard capabilities. Oracle BI EE is based on the former Siebel Analytics product suite. A part of this product suite included an advanced Reporting Workbench developed by Actuate. Oracle's stated direction for providing a tool for business user reporting is to focus on adding more functionality in BI (XML) Publisher. However, we provide mention of the Reporting Workbench here for completeness.

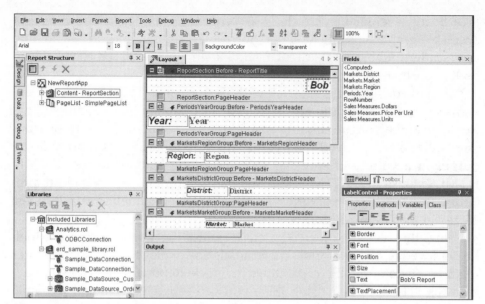

Figure 6-10: Oracle BI EE Reporting Workbench showing report layout (center)

Figure 6-10 shows the Reporting Workbench. The tool is typically used for report design layout and subsequent building and debugging. A toolbox provides the ability to define structure, data sources and filters, controls over labels, text, and dates, graphics primitives, and pages. A number of chart and graph types are also provided.

A typical page in a report contains a header, footer, and details section as illustrated above. The fields in the report typically contain labels or are populated with data from the database. The Reporting Workbench also enables you to define computed fields. For example, you might define a field to contain a sum of several fields.

Ad hoc Query and Analysis

Ad hoc query and analysis tools are designed to enable business analysts to pose their own what-if questions without the assistance of an IT organization. They commonly provide an interface that eases navigation of database tables containing business relevant data. Upon selecting that data, the analysts can create their own reports in tabular form and build relevant charts and graphs. The tools also commonly provide a means to share these user-generated reports with others in the organization.

The tools are important in that they enable the business users to separate valuable business information from less relevant data that sometimes is present in reports. The tools take on added power when combined with analytics provided in the database.

One less useful illustration of the power of these tools is the ability of software vendors to position and sell them directly to business users through contrived demonstrations. Unfortunately, many business users don't understand the work needed in deploying such tools, including management of business metadata, security considerations, and the additional work needed to build and maintain the database that these tools access. In many organizations, a variety of tools are purchased in different departments, thus making this task even more difficult.

Oracle's business intelligence strategy includes partnering with many tools vendors. However, Oracle is also increasingly approaching this market in a more aggressive fashion by selling its own tools. In very early 2005, Oracle introduced a version of Discoverer with a drag-and-drop interface and OLAP support. In 2006, Oracle acquired Siebel and, with it, Siebel's Business Analytics. As this book was published, Oracle offered both products as ad hoc query and analysis tools, positioning Business Intelligence Enterprise Edition (or BI EE, containing the former Siebel Analytics) as the more advanced suite and Business Intelligence Standard Edition (or BI SE, containing Discoverer) as a lower cost alternative. So, in this section, we describe both, and start the discussion with Oracle BI EE. We also describe a couple of the Oracle spreadsheet add-ins that are available — the Oracle BI Spreadsheet Add-in (for OLAP) and the Oracle Spreadsheet Add-in for Predictive Analytics.

Business Intelligence Enterprise Edition

Oracle BI EE consists of a suite of tools based on previous offerings from Siebel, including an ad hoc query tool named Answers, the Intelligence Dashboard, Reporting and Publishing (previously described above), a component named Delivers that provides monitoring, workflow and alerting for delivery to email, dashboards, and mobile devices, and an Office plug-in. Oracle BI EE can be used while connected to a relational database or while disconnected from the network (sometimes called Oracle Mobile Analytics or Disconnected Analytics). The product suite includes a mid-tier Analytics Server engine that contains a metadata repository and cache, an alerting infrastructure, and a scheduling server.

At the time this book was published, Oracle was in the process of rebranding many of the former Siebel Analytics products as Oracle Business Intelligence. Our illustrations in this section show them in a Siebel labeled version.

Using Oracle BI EE and Oracle Answers

Business users of Oracle BI EE access the tools through a browser. Users are first presented with a login screen and specify their user name and password (Figure 6-11). They can also specify the language the interface is to be viewed in.

When logged in, business users are commonly presented with a role-based Intelligence Dashboard (a typical portion is displayed in Figure 6-12). The Dashboard is usually defined by the administrator or designer and provides an easy means to access and deploy generated reports and charts and provide links to other sites. Data might be obtained from a remote database over a network or from a local database if the user is working in disconnected mode. In the Delivers interface, accessible through the Dashboard, a user can create iBots to automatically download data, manage subscriptions, or email reports. The Dashboard can also provide access into the ad hoc query tool (Answers) and advanced reporting.

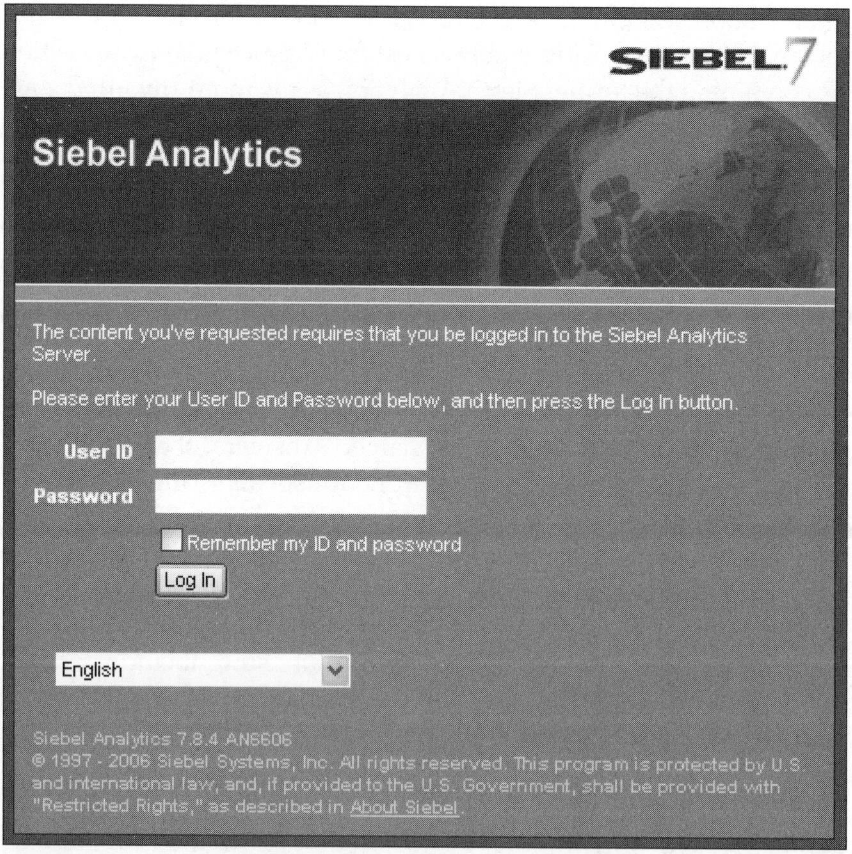

Figure 6-11: Oracle BI EE/Siebel Analytics login screen

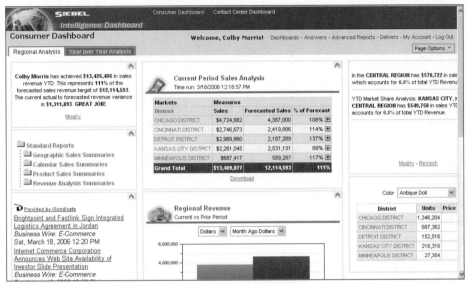

Figure 6-12: Oracle BI EE / Siebel Analytics Dashboard

For large enterprises where an enterprise-wide portal (capable of supporting JSR-168) is deployed, access to these reports and charts can also be provided. For example, this is how Answers portlets can be deployed to Oracle Portal.

When using the Answers tool, a user has access to pre-defined analyses and briefing books through the interface shown in Figure 6-13. A new query or request can occur by selecting a subject area to query from.

The first step in building a new query from a subject area is to define the criteria to be used. The user does this by pointing at and selecting column names to be queried from a list of available columns. Figure 6-14 shows the list of available columns on the left. A base table of accounts with various dimensions and measures has been pre-defined to use in our potential query. We have selected to query the accounts by state (in the United States) in this illustration and also view products by product line, periods of time by fiscal quarter, and measures for closed revenue, closed units, and percent of quarter. In addition, we have placed a filter on the query to only return results for the third and fourth quarters.

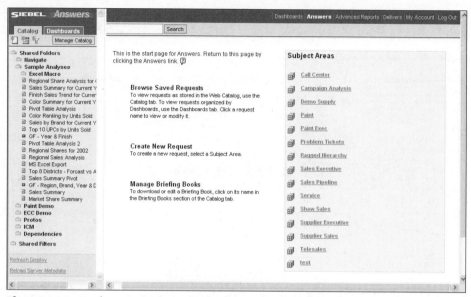

Figure 6-13: Oracle BI EE/Siebel Answers interface to briefing books and analyses

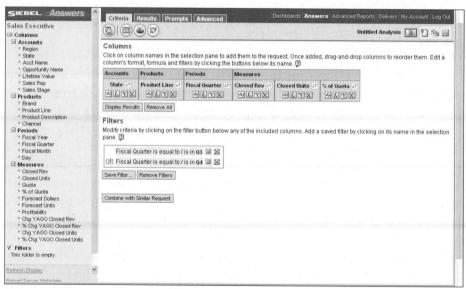

Figure 6-14: Setting query criteria in Oracle BI EE/Siebel Answers

Results can be viewed in several forms, including table, chart, or crosstab. Figure 6-15 shows a typical result in table form for our query.

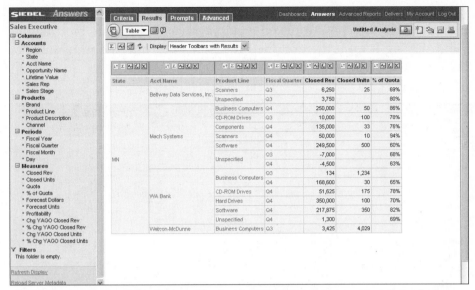

Figure 6-15: Query results displayed in Oracle BI EE/Siebel Answers in tabular form

Charts or graphs can be displayed in a variety of two-dimensional and three-dimensional types. Standard charts provided include area, horizontal bar, bubble, vertical bar, line, line bar combo, Pareto, pie, radar, scatter, and step. Figure 6-16 illustrates a three-dimensional pie chart that shows closed revenue in several states.

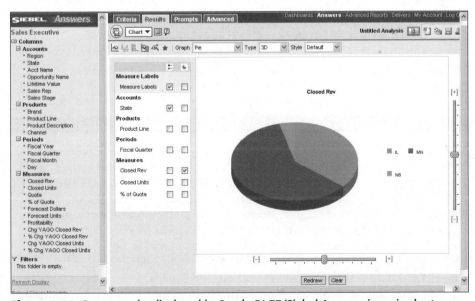

Figure 6-16: Query results displayed in Oracle BI EE/Siebel Answers in a pie chart

When displaying results in a crosstab, you must specify measures used. In Figure 6-17, we chose to use the closed revenue measure by dragging and dropping it from the excluded measures box into the measures box that initially contained no measures.

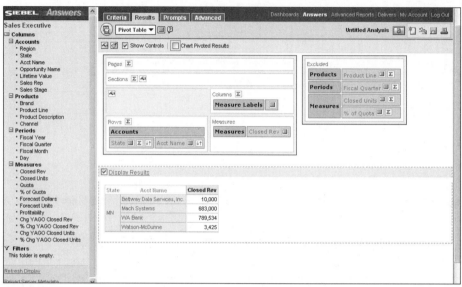

Figure 6-17: Query results displayed in Oracle BI EE/Siebel Answers in a crosstab

The Answers interface also provides more sophisticated capabilities. Under a prompts tab, query prompts can be defined enabling users to select specific values to be used in filtering requests. An interface under the advanced tab enables users to see the SQL generated in a query and generate XML that represents the analysis that has been requested (as shown in Figure 6-18).

REAL-TIME DECISIONS AND ORACLE BI

Oracle's Real-Time Decisions (RTD) was originally targeted at Call Centers as part of Siebel Customer Relationship Management (CRM) implementations and recommends offers that call agents should convey as they try to upsell products and services to customers. In mid-2006, Oracle acquired the intellectual property of Sigma Dynamics, the provider of this predictive analytics software, and announced that Oracle Business Intelligence would leverage RTD for more generic operational decisions. Enterprise business priorities and processes can be mapped using the RTD rules engine. RTD uses data mining to adjust predictions based on the success of previous predictions.

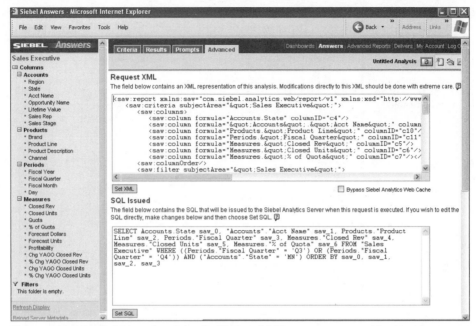

Figure 6-18: Analysis representation in XML and SQL query generated by Answers

Administering Oracle BI EE

Oracle BI EE includes an Administration Tool for managing security and access, defining the user environment within BI EE, and deploying and managing the Analytics Server. For example, the Administration Tool provides a Security Manager interface that defines user access to the Administration Tool and the business tools. The Security Manager is used to configure users and groups, synchronize LDAP users and groups, set access to tables and columns, set filters, and manage when users can access data. Users' connections can be authenticated using operating system, database, LDAP, or external table authentication.

Figure 6-19 shows a hierarchy representation in the Security Manager of administrators with access to the Administration Tool and defined groups of business users given access to the Analytics tools. Groupings of business users are usually defined for the various lines of business and based on level within the organization and their need to access certain information.

Administrators also use the Administration Tool to define and manage the repository that holds definitions of physical databases that are used by business users in their analyses, appropriate business model mappings, and a presentation layer. Figure 6-20 shows all three of these as displayed in summary form after logging into the Administration Tool.

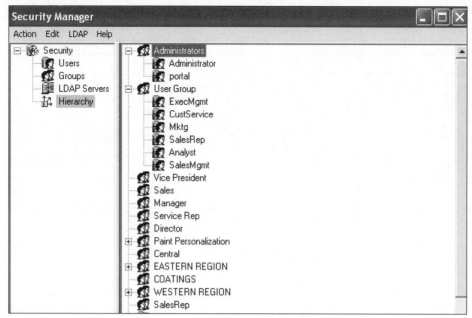

Figure 6-19: Security Manager in Oracle BI EE/Siebel Analytics Administration Tool

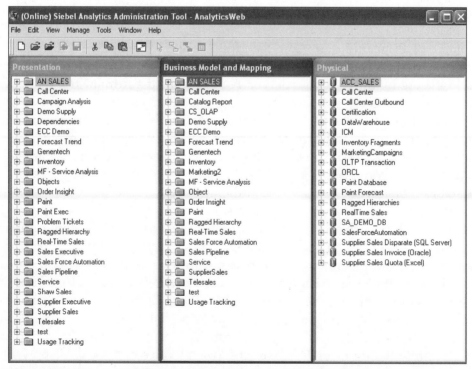

Figure 6-20: Oracle BI EE/Siebel Analytics Administration Tool management areas

The first step in building an environment for users is defining a physical layer. Metadata is typically imported from Oracle and non-Oracle databases to be used in the analyses. For each data source, the administrator also defines a connection pool, including information on the data source name, number of connections allowed, and timeout information.

Our illustration in Figure 6-21 shows the set-up of physical levels in an Oracle database. As shown here, the interface can be used to define access to data stored in both Oracle OLAP Option of the database and Oracle relational tables in the database. The Oracle BI EE tool can access both sets of tables through SQL.

Once physical definitions are set, a business model and mapping layer to the physical sources must be built. This layer should be built based on business requirements gathered from the business users. Data definitions usually include important measures and dimensions for the business and appropriate hierarchies or rollups of key attributes.

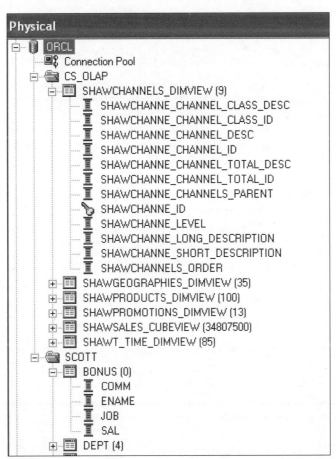

Figure 6-21: Oracle BI EE/Siebel Analytics Administration Tool Physical levels

In Figure 6-22, we see one such logical representation of the business attribute *sales* and a list of column definitions in the table. Logical table and column mappings can be defined from a single data source, but might also be defined to include multiple and heterogeneous data sources such as a mix of Oracle and non-Oracle databases.

The presentation layer is used to manage user views of the business model. For example, an administrator might choose to exclude certain columns, tables, or catalogs in the business model from certain users. Column names can be given more relevant labeling than exists in the business model metadata for specific users.

Administrators also perform a variety of other tasks, including starting up and shutting down the Oracle Analytics server, administering the query log and usage tracking, and Server configuration and tuning. Up to 16 Analytics Servers can be configured in a network domain Cluster Server to act as a single server and share requests. A Cluster Controller can monitor resources and perform session assignments based on workloads or server failure.

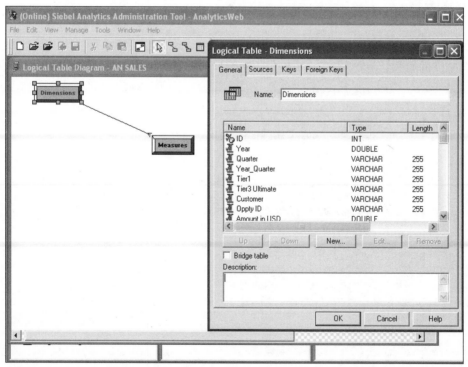

Figure 6-22: Logical tables in Oracle BI EE/Siebel Analytics Administration Tool

A key to Oracle BI EE performance is properly leveraging the cache in the Analytics Server. This cache is designed to store results for later reuse when similar queries are submitted. The Cache Manager in the Administration Tool is used to monitor and define how the cache is used. Figure 6-23 illustrates defining the purging of the cache for some of the Oracle OLAP and relational tables that were part of our previous physical design illustration.

Discoverer and Business Intelligence Standard Edition

Oracle Discoverer is available in Oracle Business Intelligence Standard Edition (BI SE) and the Oracle Application Server Enterprise Edition at the time this book was published. Oracle Reports and the BI Spreadsheet Add-in (for OLAP) are also included in this packaging as is a limited use Internet Development Suite license that includes Oracle Warehouse Builder and Oracle BI Beans. In general, you would likely deploy BI SE if you already have a base of other Discoverer users and are satisfied with the capabilities of today's tool. Oracle has stated it will continue supporting Discoverer indefinitely and continue enhancements, but will also enable metadata migration to Oracle BI EE and Answers by leveraging the Analytics Server where businesses prefer the more advanced interface.

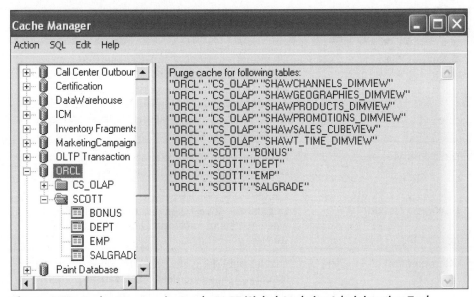

Figure 6-23: Cache Manager in Oracle BI EE/Siebel Analytics Administration Tool

ORACLE BUSINESS INTELLIGENCE STANDARD EDITION ONE

Oracle Business Intelligence Standard Edition One (Oracle BI SE-1) includes the Analytics Server and Answers that are part of Oracle BI EE. Intended by Oracle to appeal to small and medium-sized businesses, Oracle BI SE-1 also includes an entry-level version of the database (Oracle SE-1) and an ETL tool. Dashboard and server-level administration facilities similar to those just described are also provided.

Discoverer can be used to access data residing in relational data sources, especially in Oracle databases, and within the Oracle OLAP Option cubes. The user selects appropriate tables to query and create worksheets that typically contain parameters and calculations similar to the sheets they are familiar with in spreadsheets. A collection of worksheets can be represented as a workbook.

The BI SE product suite includes Discoverer web-based user interfaces that are used by business analysts (Discoverer Plus and Viewer), and an administrative interface (named Discoverer Administration Edition). Worksheets and graphs can be deployed to the Oracle Portal using the Discoverer Portlet Provider. These components are described in Table 6-2.

Table 6-2: Descriptions of Oracle Discoverer Components

COMPONENT	DESCRIPTION
Discoverer Plus	Discoverer's most powerful user interface (downloaded as a Java applet) as it enables creating ad hoc queries for new worksheets and graphs. Also provides advanced capabilities to analyze from relational and Oracle OLAP data sources and share worksheets and graphs with others.
Discoverer Viewer	HTML interface used for analyzing data in worksheets created by Discoverer Plus and Discoverer Desktop.
Discoverer Desktop	Original Windows-based interface used for creating worksheets and analyzing data from relational sources.
Discoverer Portlet Provider	Enables publishing of worksheet and graph portlets, list of worksheets portlets, and a gauges portlet.
Discoverer Administrator	Wizard-driven Windows-based interface used to control user access, manage summary levels, and set up and maintain batch scheduling.

Using Discoverer in Oracle BI SE

Users are typically given a web address that provides access to Discoverer. They are then presented with a login screen and must specify a user name, password, and database to connect to (see Figure 6-24). Locale (language) can be specified or might be obtained from the browser as pictured here. If login details have not been established or previously saved with a connection name, these can be created with proper access rights. The type of data that will be analyzed (relational or OLAP) is specified.

Once logged into the database, users have the choice of using existing Discoverer workbooks or creating a new workbook if they're using Discoverer Plus or Desktop. Existing workbooks can also be edited, copied, or deleted given proper access rights. The workbooks can be shared among users and data can be pre-populated at scheduled times or when the user queries the workbook. When a query is run or is rerun, Discoverer will estimate how long it will take the query to return the results to the first worksheet in the workbook and visually indicate the estimated progress (see Figure 6-25).

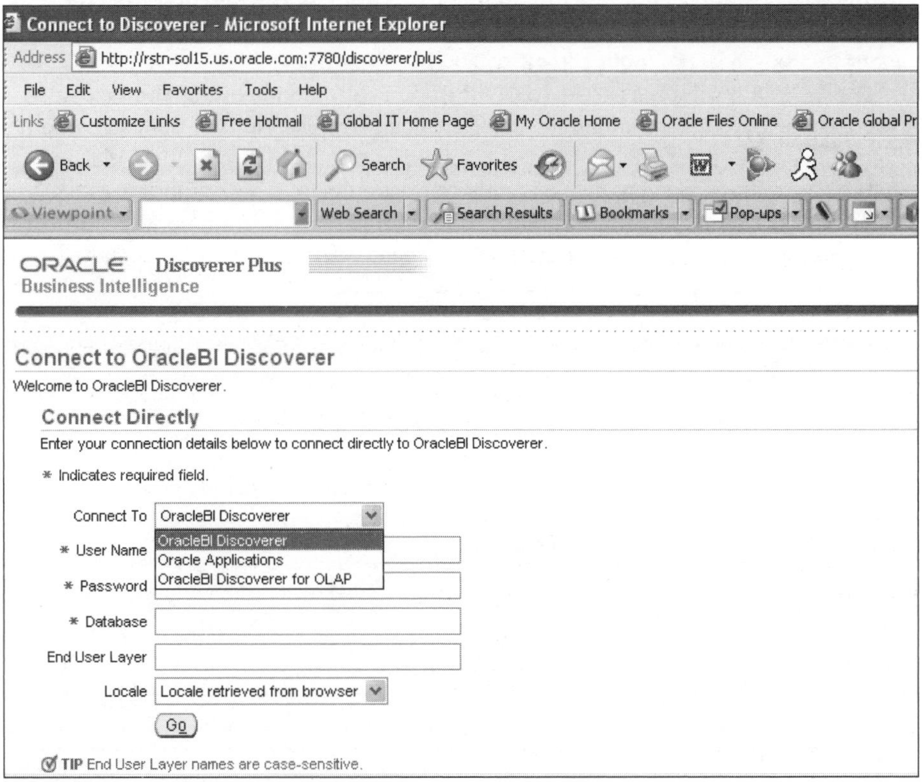

Figure 6-24: Discoverer Login Screen

ORACLE OLAP OPTION, ANALYTIC WORKSPACES, AND CALCULATIONS

We described the Oracle Option in an earlier chapter introducing Oracle data warehousing features. The OLAP Option simply provides multi-dimensional analytical processing cubes that are stored within the relational database and are defined using Oracle Warehouse Builder (OWB) or the Analytic Workspace Manager (AWM).

The AWM tool is mentioned here since it can be useful to business users as well as to IT. AWM simplifies logical dimensional modeling, creation of a physical model, and provides a simpler mapping interface when compared with OWB. Dimensional modeling elements you can define in AWM include dimensions and their levels, hierarchies, and attributes. Cubes, that can be parents of measures and calculated measures, are also defined here. Model designs can be saved to XML files for reuse. AWM is also used for managing the loading, refreshing, and aggregation of the data into cubes.

Query access to the OLAP Option cubes can be through SQL or the Java OLAP API. The more common access mechanism to the Oracle OLAP Option for BI tools is through SQL. Oracle continues to improve SQL access as it introduces new database versions. Tools that access the OLAP Option using SQL, such as Answers in Oracle BI EE or those of third-party vendors, provide seamless access to both the relational data and the OLAP cubes through a single interface.

The Discoverer tool accesses relational data through SQL and accesses the OLAP cubes using the API, hence you are asked to specify the type of data you want to analyze in the login screen shown in Figure 6-24.

The OLAP API provides access to OLAP Option calculations out-of-the-box or you can create your own variations using a calculation wizard. Types of calculation formulae provided include cumulative total, difference from prior period, division, future value, index, moving average, moving maximum, moving minimum, moving total, multiplication, percent difference from prior period, percent markup, percent variance, prior value, rank, ratio, share, subtraction, variance, and year to date.

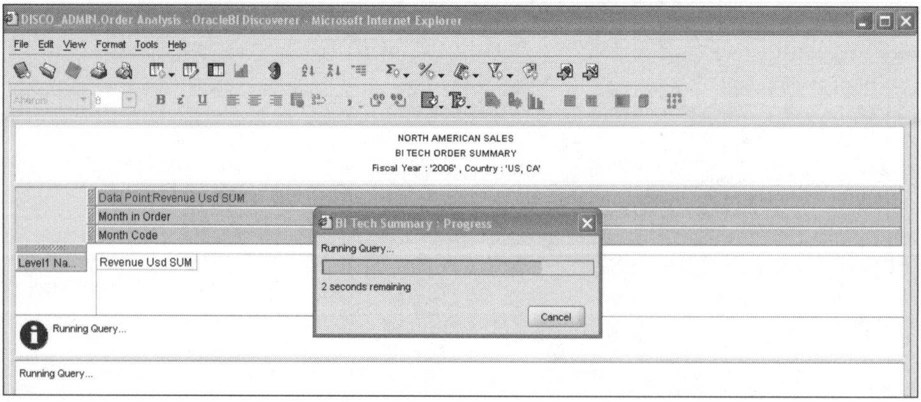

Figure 6-25: Discoverer query estimation

Worksheets within the workbook are used to analyze the data and are presented in tabular form or as crosstabs. When working in a worksheet for a long period of time, a user can refresh it to see the latest data that is available. Users can pivot data items and compare data values, drill up to summary levels or down to more detailed levels, or drill out to data in other applications. They can also create totals, calculate percentages, and create custom calculations. Worksheets can also display data in the form of charts and graphs. A number of standard graph types are available, including two-dimensional area, vertical and horizontal bar, bubble, circular, combination, line, Pareto, pie, scatter, and stock, with some also available in three-dimensional versions.

When submitting a query against a pre-defined workbook, users can be presented with specific selectable parameter values. Figure 6-26 illustrates a workbook pre-defined to provide sales results. Within this workbook, the user can select fiscal year and countries to be displayed.

When an analysis is complete, results can be saved in PDF format for printing, distributed via e-mail, or shared as worksheets in workbooks. Worksheets can also be shared with other users as portlets in Oracle Portal. For high-resolution reporting, the data can also be exported into the Oracle Reports format.

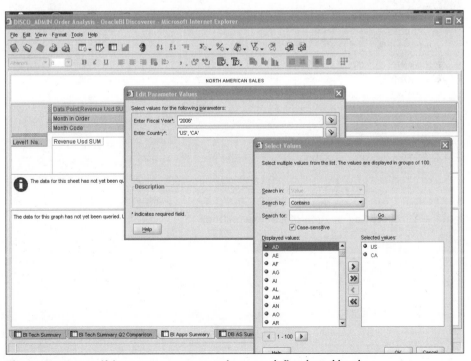

Figure 6-26: Specifying query parameters in a pre-defined workbook

New workbooks are created through a wizards-driven interface. Figure 6-27 pictures the interface Discoverer presents shortly after logging in. Earlier, we described querying existing workbooks, but you can also create a new workbook as you see in this illustration.

The next step is to add items to be selected for our worksheet as pictured in Figure 6-28. In this example, these items are the tables that contain key dimensions and measures used to determine sales. We select the metrics to be used in the workbook by populating the window on the right. We can also place conditions and calculations on the data retrieved in a query through this interface.

Next, the user can choose the layout of the table to be populated after the query is submitted, as illustrated in Figure 6-29. The user can also choose to preview the SQL that Discoverer will generate when querying the database.

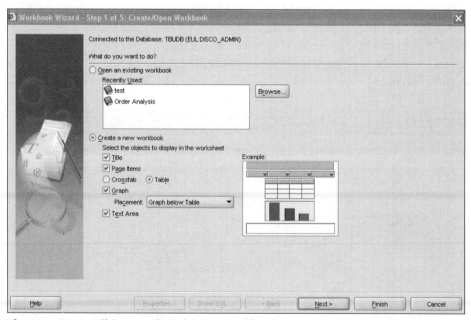

Figure 6-27: Specifying creation of a new workbook

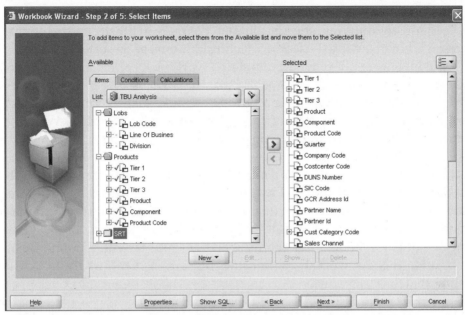

Figure 6-28: Specifying measures and dimensions to be used in the workbook

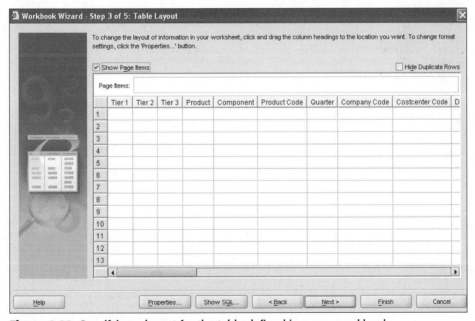

Figure 6-29: Specifying a layout for the table defined in a new workbook

To present the data in an understandable fashion, it will often be desirable to sort columns in a specific manner. Figure 6-30 illustrates this step as presented by the wizard used in selecting columns to be sorted.

When we were querying a pre-defined workbook earlier in this section, we were presented with parameters that allowed us to define the query (see Figure 6-26). As we create a new workbook, such parameter choices are defined in the next step of the workbook creation wizard. We see a place to define the parameters, descriptions, and prompts in Figure 6-31. After this step, the workbook is created.

Discoverer Viewer provides a much simpler HTML interface for analysis of data in worksheets created by Discoverer Plus or Desktop. While creation of new worksheets is not possible, the interface supports limited modification of existing worksheets such as resorting of data or repositioning of worksheet items. Such changes can be saved. As with Plus and Desktop, updating the worksheet via querying and worksheet drilldown is supported.

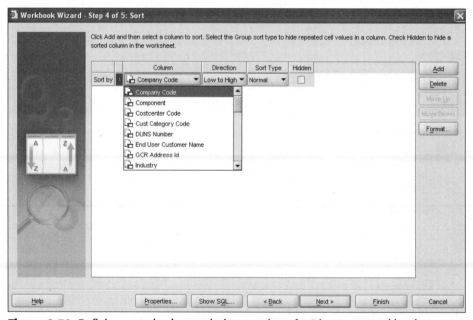

Figure 6-30: Defining sorted columns during creation of a Discoverer workbook

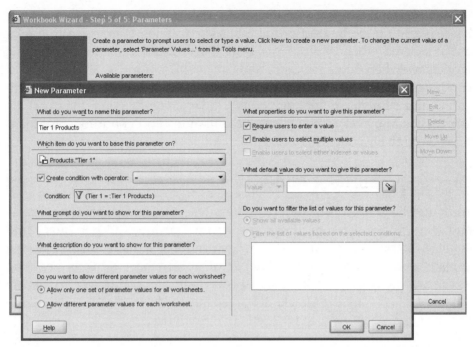

Figure 6-31: Defining parameters users can define in querying Discoverer workbooks

Administering Discoverer in Oracle BI SE

Discoverer is most commonly deployed to analyze data in relational sources. In these environments, the Discoverer Administration Edition is used to manage the Discoverer End User Layer (EUL). It is also used to build and maintain Discoverer business areas as defined by user requirements and map relevant database tables and views containing the data. Structures can be refined according to user needs and conditions can be set such as for the number of returned rows. In addition, calculated items and joins can be created where needed, folders can be combined to create complex folders, and custom folders can be created to represent results sets. Administrators can edit item names and descriptions to make them easier to understand, create item classes and hierarchies, manage summary tables, grant business area access based on user identification or role, and schedule worksheet updates.

Through Discoverer Administration, it is also possible to control the tasks available to users. Users can be restricted regarding their ability to create or edit workbooks, drill to detail, grant access to other users, save workbooks, or collect query performance statistics. The administrator can put limits on allowable times for query execution by user or role.

When using Discoverer to access OLAP data, metadata is stored in the Discoverer Catalog instead of the EUL. The Catalog is mapped to a relational schema when deployed as a ROLAP solution and to the analytic workspace when deployed using the Oracle OLAP Option. The Catalog is configured using Oracle Application Server Control. Dimensions, measures, and dimension hierarchies can be managed using the Analytic Workspace Manager (AWM), while calculations and conditions are managed through Discoverer Plus.

Oracle Spreadsheet Add-ins

Although there are ad-hoc query and analysis tools available from Oracle and many other vendors, one could argue that most ad-hoc query and analysis in businesses and other organizations actually takes place in spreadsheets. Oracle offers a couple of spreadsheet add-ins enabling advanced analysis within spreadsheets that are connected to Oracle databases. These are the Oracle BI Spreadsheet Add-in (for OLAP) and the Oracle Spreadsheet Add-in for Predictive Analytics.

Oracle BI Spreadsheet Add-in

The Oracle BI Spreadsheet Add-in enables business users to access data stored in the Oracle database OLAP Option through the familiar Microsoft Excel interface. Users have access to Oracle OLAP calculations and can create their own leveraging the OLAP Option. (We previously noted the calculation types available in the OLAP Option in this chapter in the section on Oracle BI SE that describes Discoverer.) Users can alternatively leverage the capabilities the spreadsheet provides for building formulas and graphing.

Upon installation of the BI Spreadsheet Add-in, users will see OracleBI as a menu item as illustrated in Figure 6-32. It is through this drop-down menu that new queries can be submitted to the Oracle database in order to populate the spreadsheet.

When this selection is made, users will be prompted to connect to an Oracle database. If a connection has been pre-defined, users are presented with a screen similar to that pictured in Figure 6-33 and will need to provide their Oracle database user name and password. If they need to define the connection, the host name, port number, and database SID must also be provided.

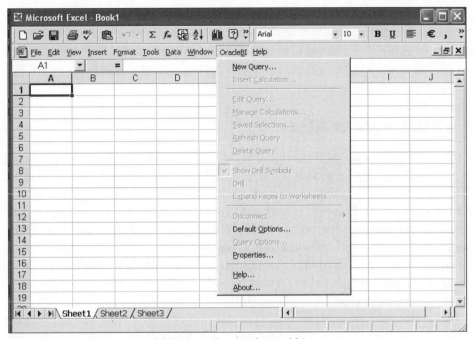

Figure 6-32: Selections available from the OracleBI add-in

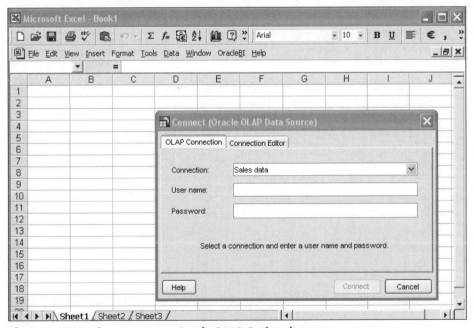

Figure 6-33: Login screen to an Oracle OLAP Option data source

The query wizard is identical to that provided in Discoverer and since we introduced it previously in this chapter, we will not cover it again here. Just as described previously, you can specify measures and dimensions to be used in queries, determine the table layout, select dimension members for each dimension, and create saved selections.

Predictive Analytics Add-in

Application of data mining algorithms has typically been the domain of experts in statistical analysis. Oracle has attempted to make usage of data mining easier by creating a predict-and-explain interface as a spreadsheet add-in based on PREDICT and EXPLAIN procedures included in the Oracle Data Mining Option's DBMS_PREDICTIVE_ANALYTICS PL/SQL package. The Add-in for Predictive Analytics is used to predict the value of a target column and explain or rank attributes in order of their influence in determining the target value. When the add-in is installed, there is an item on the Excel menu bar labeled OraclePA.

Input data for prediction will typically consist of a mixture of records where some have a value in the target column and some records have a NULL value in the target column. The first row of data must contain the column names. Figure 6-34 illustrates a typical sample data set. Data sets can reside in an Oracle database or in an Excel worksheet.

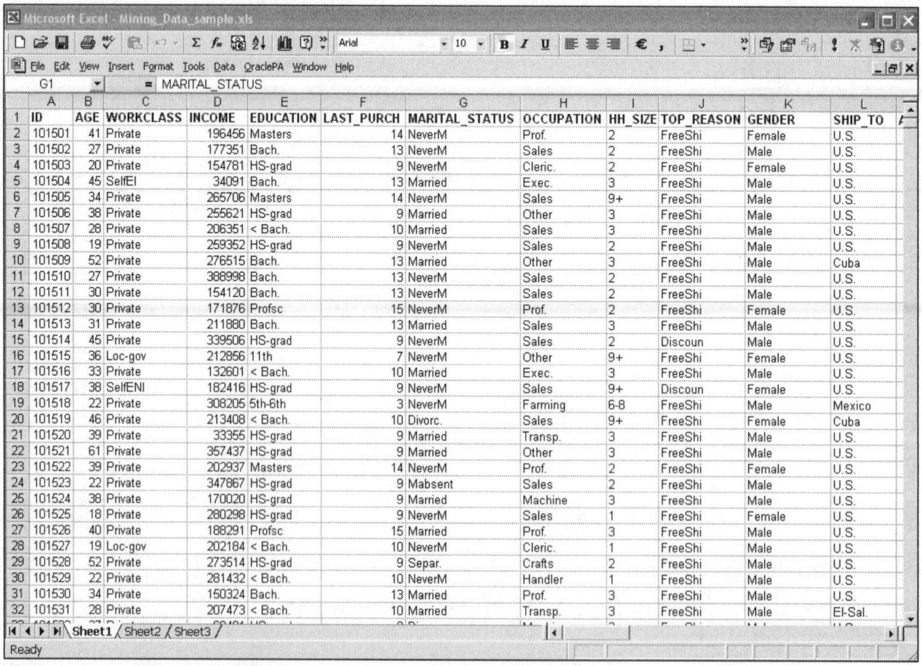

	A	B	C	D	E	F	G	H	I	J	K	L
1	ID	AGE	WORKCLASS	INCOME	EDUCATION	LAST_PURCH	MARITAL_STATUS	OCCUPATION	HH_SIZE	TOP_REASON	GENDER	SHIP_TO
2	101501	41	Private	196456	Masters	14	NeverM	Prof.	2	FreeShi	Female	U.S.
3	101502	27	Private	177351	Bach.	13	NeverM	Sales	2	FreeShi	Male	U.S.
4	101503	20	Private	154781	HS-grad	9	NeverM	Cleric.	2	FreeShi	Female	U.S.
5	101504	45	SelfEI	34091	Bach.	13	Married	Exec.	3	FreeShi	Male	U.S.
6	101505	34	Private	265706	Masters	14	NeverM	Sales	9+	FreeShi	Male	U.S.
7	101506	38	Private	255621	HS-grad	9	Married	Other	3	FreeShi	Male	U.S.
8	101507	28	Private	206351	< Bach.	10	Married	Sales	3	FreeShi	Male	U.S.
9	101508	19	Private	259352	HS-grad	9	NeverM	Sales	2	FreeShi	Male	U.S.
10	101509	52	Private	276515	Bach.	13	Married	Other	3	FreeShi	Male	Cuba
11	101510	27	Private	388998	Bach.	13	NeverM	Sales	2	FreeShi	Male	U.S.
12	101511	30	Private	154120	Bach.	13	NeverM	Sales	2	FreeShi	Male	U.S.
13	101512	30	Private	171876	Profsc	15	NeverM	Prof.	2	FreeShi	Female	U.S.
14	101513	31	Private	211880	Bach.	13	Married	Sales	3	FreeShi	Male	U.S.
15	101514	45	Private	339506	HS-grad	9	NeverM	Sales	2	Discoun	Male	U.S.
16	101515	36	Loc-gov	212856	11th	7	NeverM	Other	9+	FreeShi	Female	U.S.
17	101516	33	Private	132601	< Bach.	10	Married	Exec.	3	FreeShi	Male	U.S.
18	101517	38	SelfENI	182416	HS-grad	9	NeverM	Sales	9+	Discoun	Female	U.S.
19	101518	22	Private	308205	5th-6th	3	NeverM	Farming	6-8	FreeShi	Male	Mexico
20	101519	46	Private	213408	< Bach.	10	Divorc.	Sales	9+	FreeShi	Female	Cuba
21	101520	39	Private	33355	HS-grad	9	Married	Transp.	3	FreeShi	Male	U.S.
22	101521	61	Private	357437	HS-grad	9	Married	Other	3	FreeShi	Male	U.S.
23	101522	39	Private	202937	Masters	14	NeverM	Prof.	2	FreeShi	Female	U.S.
24	101523	22	Private	347867	HS-grad	9	Mabsent	Sales	2	FreeShi	Male	U.S.
25	101524	38	Private	170020	HS-grad	9	Married	Machine	3	FreeShi	Male	U.S.
26	101525	18	Private	280298	HS-grad	9	NeverM	Sales	1	FreeShi	Female	U.S.
27	101526	40	Private	188291	Profsc	15	Married	Prof.	3	FreeShi	Male	U.S.
28	101527	19	Loc-gov	202184	< Bach.	10	NeverM	Cleric.	1	FreeShi	Male	U.S.
29	101528	52	Private	273514	HS-grad	9	Separ.	Crafts	2	FreeShi	Male	U.S.
30	101529	22	Private	281432	< Bach.	10	NeverM	Handler	1	FreeShi	Male	U.S.
31	101530	34	Private	150324	Bach.	13	Married	Prof.	3	FreeShi	Male	U.S.
32	101531	28	Private	207473	< Bach.	10	Married	Transp.	3	FreeShi	Male	El-Sal.

Figure 6-34: Typical Sample Data Set for Predictive Analytics

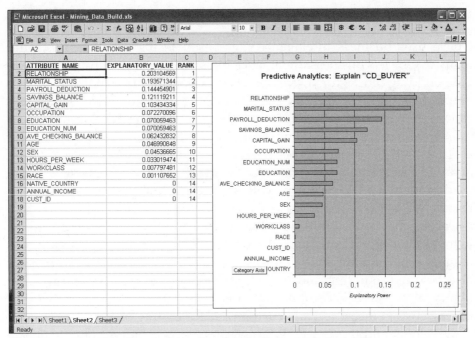

Figure 6-35: Results of an Explain using the Predictive Analytics add-in

To predict values where the NULLs appear, the user would select Predict from the pull-down OraclePA menu and then select a unique case ID column (the first column of the above data set) and the column where predictions should occur. Influence of an attribute is explained by first selecting Explain from the pull-down OraclePA menu, then selecting the column to be explained. Figure 6-35 illustrates the results of an Explain with values closest to 1 showing the highest correlation. In this example, the most significant attribute for CD buyers was their relationship.

Building Business Intelligence Applications

A far less common approach in most organizations is custom building of business intelligence applications. But if your user community has unique analytical needs that are repetitive, you might investigate Oracle's tools that can help enable you to build such applications. The two we briefly cover here are JDeveloper, used in custom building OLAP applications, and Oracle Data Miner, used in building data mining applications and also in data mining analyses.

JDeveloper and BI Beans

Oracle uses Business Intelligence Java-based Beans (BI Beans) to build many of Oracle's business intelligence tools. These same BI Beans can provide building blocks for JDeveloper, a Java development tool, and enable you to more rapidly build and deploy custom HTML and Java-based applications that use the Oracle database OLAP Option. The development environment includes presentation beans for rendering graphs, tables, and crosstabs, OLAP connection beans, query and calculation builder beans, and a BI Beans catalog and metadata manager. Since these beans are also used in many Oracle products, your custom-built applications will likely resemble Oracle's tools.

Development wizards enable the creation of objects and applications without the need to initially write code. A JSP tag library is provided containing reporting objects. Controls are included for editing reporting objects, query building and query modifying, and page navigation. The library also includes additional dialog boxes for building queries and adding custom measures, and customizers for editing objects.

JDeveloper and the Oracle BI Beans can be downloaded from the Oracle Technology Network (OTN). If you're not a member, you simply register to establish your user identification. An installation guide and download information can be found at www.oracle.com/technology/products/bi.

Data Miner

Oracle's Data Miner tool is used for data mining and text mining analysis and also to create and deploy reusable data mining applications that leverage the Oracle database Data Mining Option. If you desire to deploy an application, when a model is ready for usage, a JDeveloper extension is available that will generate the code in Java. Data Miner became available with Oracle Database 10g and replaced an earlier Oracle offering named DM4J.

A typical data mining process consists of preparing the data, building the data mining model, applying it, and testing it. Data Miner supports this entire activity lifecycle through a series of wizards. Figure 6-36 illustrates the build process steps when using the decision tree algorithm, a type of classification activity.

Mining activity types supported include anomaly detection, association rules, attribute importance, classification, clustering, feature extraction, and regression. Figure 6-37 illustrates selection of the activity type in the new activity wizard. The wizard presents appropriate interfaces based on the activity type. For example, if your activity is determining attribute importance, you can choose to view histograms for attributes you select that show the counts for ranges of values (also known as bins).

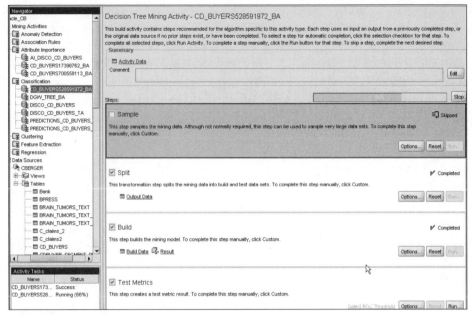

Figure 6-36: Build process steps in Data Miner for decision trees

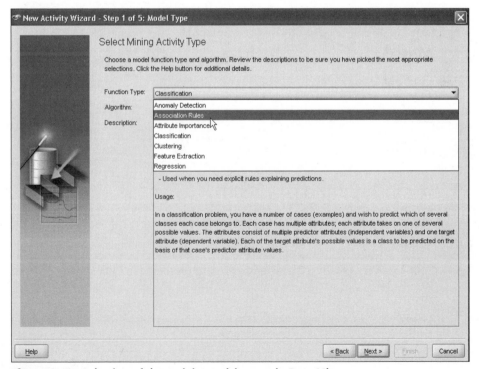

Figure 6-37: Selection of data mining activity type in Data Miner

A variety of results viewers are provided. You can test supervised models (anomaly detection, attribute importance, classification, and regression) using Receiver Operating Characteristics (ROC), a confusion matrix, lift measurements, or test metrics for regression. Figure 6-38 illustrates presentation of typical ROC results. Results from attribute importance, association rules, apply results, decision tree rules, clustering rules, and classification test metrics can be published to Oracle BI SE Discoverer using a Discoverer gateway in Data Miner.

When mining text, you can include a single text column in your mining activity and that text column must be located in a table. Valid data types for such a column are BLOB, CLOB, BFILE, LONG, VARCHAR2, XMLType, CHAR, RAW, and LONG RAW. Text mining leverages the anomaly detection, association, classification, clustering, feature extraction, and regression algorithms. Of course, Oracle Text must be installed in the Oracle database (and by default, it is installed during normal installations).

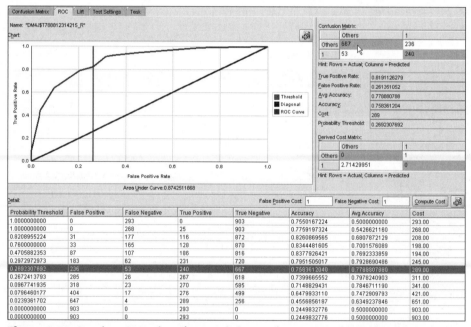

Figure 6-38: Receiver Operating Characteristics results presented in Data Miner

DATA MINING ACTIVITY TYPES

Oracle defines multiple activity types in Oracle Data Miner as previously noted in this section. Anomaly detection predicts whether a value is typical and uses a one-class Support Vector Machine (SVM) algorithm. Association Rules identify relationships between data and their probability of occurrence using the Apriori algorithm. Attribute importance identifies relative importance of each attribute using a Minimal Descriptive Length (MDL) algorithm. Classification is used for predicting new discrete or categorical data and can leverage Naïve Bayes, Adaptive Bayes Network, SVM, or Decision Tree algorithms. Clustering models determine natural groupings by leveraging Enhanced K-Means or Orthogonal Clustering algorithms. Feature Extraction models are used to pull significant data from a set using Non-Negative Matrix Factorization. Regression models use historical data to predict continuous numerical data by leveraging the SVM algorithm.

Other Tools

A number of other tools should be mentioned to round out the discussion of this topic. Since Oracle databases can store location-based data containing spatial coordinates or addresses, a visual presentation of this data returned as the result of a business intelligence query can be desirable. Oracle MapViewer is provided as a J2EE component in the Oracle Application Server and displays such data on maps enabling visualization. MapViewer includes support for XML requests and responses, a Java client API for map interaction (for example, pan, zoom, locate, re-center), and JSP tag libraries for session control and basic viewing.

Although sometimes not considered as business intelligence tools, collaborative tools can be an important part of a business intelligence infrastructure since business decisions are often made during meetings and through other information exchanges. Oracle's Collaboration Suite provides a number of capabilities useful in sharing information among a business community, including web conferencing, file and content management, calendar, voicemail, e-mail, and instant messaging. Workspaces enable a community of users to share documents, hold discussions, and manage tasks.

Of course, non-Oracle business intelligence tools are also commonly deployed to analyze data stored in Oracle databases. The level of Oracle database connectivity and support provided by these tools ranges from a least common denominator approach using ODBC to extensive leveraging of Oracle database extensions and additional support for the Oracle Application Server. Table 6-3 summarizes support among some of the business intelligence analysis tools available at the time this book was published. As always, you should consult your favorite vendor(s) for the most current information.

Table 6-3: Sample of Varying Levels of Oracle Support (Note: can be version specific)

BUSINESS ANALYST TOOL	ORACLE SUPPORT
Business Objects	Native access to the Oracle database from business analysis and reporting tools. SQL access to the Oracle OLAP Option is well documented. Deployable to the Oracle Application Server with portlet (JSR 168) support. Additional support for current Oracle Transactional Business Intelligence modules (EPM).
Cognos	Native access to the Oracle database from analysis and reporting tools. SQL access to the Oracle OLAP Option from ReportNet has been tested. Deployable to the Oracle Application Server with portlet support.
Hyperion	Native access to the Oracle database. OLAP engine extracts data out of the Oracle database. Planning, Budgeting, and Forecasting solution can be deployed in Oracle's Application Server.
Information Builders	Oracle database access, through Oracle Application Server, and to Oracle Advanced Queuing via iWay adapters. Open Portal Services for Oracle Portal.
InforSense	Data mining analysis and visualization tool with support for all Oracle Data Mining Option algorithms and integration with Oracle Portal and BI Beans.
MicroStrategy	Access to Oracle database through ODBC with extended Oracle database SQL support. Generally pulls data into MicroStrategy generated temporary tables. Portal integration kit available.
SAS	Native access to the Oracle database though data is typically pulled into a SAS data store for analysis.
SPSS	Native access to the Oracle database in SPSS statistical tools. Support of Oracle Data Mining Option algorithms in SPSS Clementine.

For an example of how these tools can sometimes leverage extended Oracle features, we will now take a closer look at how one tool, Business Objects Web Intelligence, provides access to both relational data stored in an Oracle database and analytic workspaces created using the Oracle OLAP Option. Figure 6-39 illustrates building a query against an Oracle database using Web Intelligence. In this example, the query is built against an Oracle analytic workspace.

The transparent querying of data in Oracle analytic workspaces using Web Intelligence is made possible by building a Business Objects metadata map, also known as a Universe. Business Objects provides a Universe Builder for Oracle OLAP in order to do this. Using this tool, you first connect to the analytic workspace you want to use in analyses and then respond to a series of wizards. The Universe Builder for Oracle OLAP tool then gives you the option of creating Oracle views or the Business Objects Universe or both. Figure 6-40 illustrates a typical wizard presented during Universe creation.

Wizards presented during view and Universe creation enable you to edit the SQL data type and length for dimensions and measures, edit hierarchy levels, select view and Universe options, verify SQL expressions for relational views and derived tables, and perform the metadata extraction and Universe generation. Once the Universe is generated, it is presented in the Universe Designer similarly to the illustration shown in Figure 6-41.

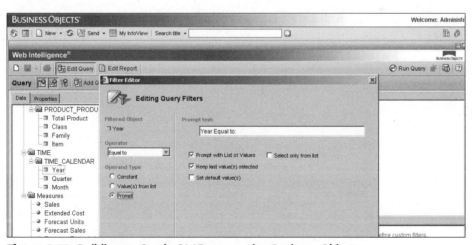

Figure 6-39: Building an Oracle OLAP query using Business Objects

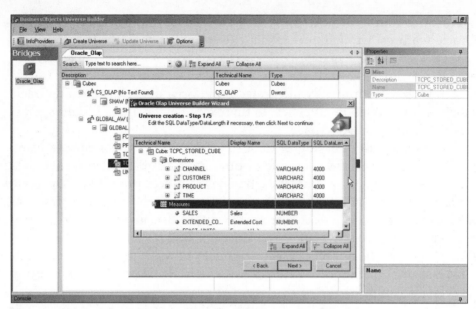

Figure 6-40: Business Objects Universe Builder for Oracle OLAP

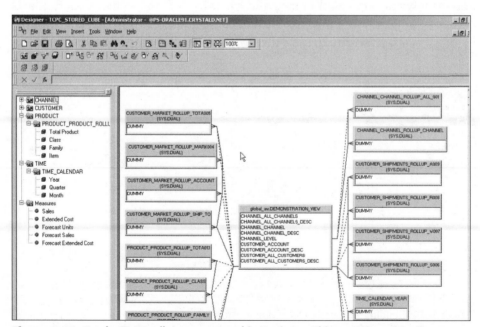

Figure 6-41: Oracle OLAP rollup represented in Business Objects Universe Designer

As noted previously, there is quite a range in sophistication provided by Oracle's business intelligence tools partners in support of extended features such as OLAP. Supported Oracle products and features can change over time and can depend on versions of the Oracle products and the versions of the partner products.

This concludes our overview of business intelligence tools commonly used by business analysts for reporting and analyzing data stored in the database in order to gain business intelligence. We next shift the discussion to ways of getting the data into the Oracle database. Since getting the right data into the database is extremely critical, we include the topic of data quality.

Data Loading

As we noted in early chapters in this book, there are several reasons why a data warehouse is usually deployed in a database separated from an organization's main transactional systems. Common reasons to deploy a separate data warehouse include the desire to keep the unique resource requirements of the data warehouse segregated from transactional systems, the need to consolidate data from multiple operational systems, and the need to cleanse the data to ensure an accurate and consistent view of information.

When deploying a separate data warehouse, the data must be extracted from source systems and loaded into the data warehouse. During this process, data cleansing and consolidation can be part of a transformation process. Together, this extraction, transformation, and loading of data are commonly referred to as ETL. Understanding the data sources, determining the quality of the data, and generating and deploying the necessary ETL scripts usually consume the bulk of the time it takes to develop and initially deploy a data warehouse project.

In this chapter, we will look at how you can leverage an ETL tool, Oracle Warehouse Builder, to greatly automate the building of scripts and maintain a repository of reusable ETL maps. But first, we will take a look at the variety of data loading possibilities where the target data warehouse is deployed upon an Oracle database.

Oracle Database Data Loading Features

When planning a data loading strategy for your data warehouse or data mart, the quality of your source data and the frequency of data loading should be considered. The strategy should be driven first and foremost by business requirements. If data must be near real-time to make proper tactical business decisions, then batch loading of data every day or even every hour may not be considered adequate by potential business users. On the other hand, if the warehouse is used for strategic planning and analysis, day-old data might be perfectly fine.

Data can be moved into the data warehouse in near real-time using trickle feeds provided by Oracle Streams Advanced Queues and change data capture, or for less frequent loading, moved into the data warehouse using scheduled batch jobs. More often than not, data is gathered from multiple data sources and requires reformatting and cleansing for consistency and accuracy. Transformations can be built using Oracle SQL, database languages (for example, PL/SQL), and table functions. But, keep in mind that the availability of data in the warehouse can be delayed by complex transformations and might impact your ability to deploy a truly near real-time solution.

Of course, data loading consumes platform resources and this overhead can impact the other business intelligence operations on a server. In one very important way, the Oracle database minimizes the impact of loading operations because of its multi-version read consistency locking capability that allows read access to data even if there is write activity occurring that is modifying that data. Since a data warehouse workload consists mainly of read operations, there will be little locking overhead from loading operations. Trickle feeds tend to consist of smaller and discrete updates to the data that behave more like a transactional workload, something that the Oracle database is also designed for.

When batch loading of large bulk data occurs, both reading and writing can require I/O operations that impact performance by using up disk access bandwidth. As a result, most organizations schedule batch loading during times when there is relatively little query and analysis activity.

Given the variety of data loading scenarios that Oracle-based implementations must address, it should come as no surprise that the Oracle database includes multiple data loading features and utilities. We will describe those next.

Embedded ETL in the Oracle Database

The Oracle database includes extensions to SQL that can be leveraged in building ETL scripts, most notably a multi-table insert and a MERGE SQL keyword. Multi-table inserts allow data to be inserted into multiple tables using a single SQL statement and are often used in data transformations and for conditional handling. The MERGE keyword in SQL enables, in a single SQL statement, an update of data to occur if the data item pre-exists, or an insert to occur if the data item is new. Both of these capabilities were first introduced in Oracle9i.

Also introduced in Oracle9i was support for external tables enabling flat files to be represented as read-only tables. Since they can be accessed via the languages the database supports, complex transformations can be built and can be applied in scripts to the flat files in parallel. Pipelining of the loading phase in combination with the transformation phase is possible eliminating the need to stage data within the database, greatly improving performance.

Table functions have also been available in the database since Oracle9i to speed performance. Such functions are built using PL/SQL or Java and used as virtual tables in a FROM clause. The result sets that can be gathered from these functions can eliminate the need for intermediate staging tables where complex transformations are needed. The result sets are returned incrementally as soon as they are created for further processing in what is called incremental pipelining. These functions can take cursors as input and can also be parallelized for better performance.

> **USING PARTITIONS TO SPEED LOADING FROM EXTERNAL TABLES**
>
> The Oracle Partitioning Option is most often associated with improving data warehouse manageability and is described in that role in Chapter 8. But, using the Partitioning Option (and range partitions in particular) can speed loading from external tables into your target Oracle-based data warehouse. The first step is to add an empty partition for the time period of the data to be loaded into your data warehouse. This time period will match your frequency of loading, so the partition might be a specific day, hour, 15-minute interval, or other time period. You would next create a non-partitioned temporary table, then load the data from the external table into the temporary table, create bitmap indexes on foreign keys in the temporary table, perform an exchange partition between the temporary table and the newly created partition, and finally drop the temporary table.

During a load process, error conditions sometimes occur such that a load will not complete and, under normal conditions, the operation would be rolled back. As of Oracle9i, the database supports resumable statements for use when space limit and out-of-space errors occur. When such an error occurs, the Database Administrator can correct the error (for example, by adding more free space) and the operation will resume. Specific time limits during which error correction can take place can be set.

A number of utilities providing more complex capabilities are also available for loading data into the database. These include support for direct path loading using SQL*Loader, change data capture, transportable tablespaces, and the Oracle Data Pump. We will cover these topics next. In general, data is usually loaded as uncompressed to optimize loading performance, and then compressed over time in combination with a partitioning strategy where a reduction in required storage is desired.

SQL*Loader

SQL*Loader has long been part of the Oracle database and is designed to optimally load data from sources that provide flat files. Such sources might include other Oracle databases, legacy non-relational databases, and spreadsheet export files. SQL*Loader provides a series of commands to export data into an external file, or to load data into the Oracle database.

The biggest advantage of SQL*Loader is its universal nature in the Oracle world since it has been part of the database for many years. SQL*Loader can be used to dump data from any supported version of the database and load it into any supported version of the database providing a common language for data movement. SQL*Loader is able to achieve this universality because it acts as an SQL client going through the Oracle server to get all the data, and inserting the data back into the database through the server instance.

SQL*Loader has a conventional-path loader where SQL functions are applied to any column during the loading process. More common in data warehousing is the use of SQL*Loader's direct path loading for better performance. Data type conversions and simple NULL handling can be resolved during the direct path loading process. When loading with the direct path option, the target table must have any constraints and triggers disabled. Target tables cannot have any pending transactions during the load, and the target table cannot be clustered.

In addition to direct path loading through SQL*Loader, such loading can be scripted using the Oracle Call Interface (OCI) applications programming interface (API). This API was first introduced in Oracle8i.

Change Data Capture

After data warehouses have been loaded for the first time, you might want to schedule subsequent loading of just new or changed data, not the entire data set. A classic approach to identify changed data is to store time stamps from when data updates occur in the source data table. Data can be determined to have changed based on containing a recent time stamp. Another classic approach is to simply dump a copy of changed data to a flat file as it is changed and use this file for incremental loading.

Change data capture was added to the Oracle database to provide another means to track incremental Oracle-based source data changes for loading into Oracle database targets. Change data capture was first introduced with Oracle9i and provided a synchronous mode in publishing the data to a change table that defined subscribers have access to. This capability was greatly improved in Oracle Database 10g when asynchronous support was added. Today, change data capture is supported where the source databases are Oracle9i release 2 or more recent versions.

When using Oracle's change data capture, all modifications made to source data using an INSERT, UPDATE, or DELETE statement are tracked either synchronously or asynchronously in the separate change table. Data definition language (DDL) changes are similarly tracked.

Change data capture, in synchronous mode, is fired by a trigger that is part of the transaction. This enables the target database updated in real time, though some overhead is introduced. In asynchronous mode, the change data capture is based on Oracle Streams and provides a lighter weight solution by leveraging data automatically captured in redo logs in the source.

ORACLE STREAMS

Oracle Streams can capture and process changes recorded in an Oracle database redo log, stage events in an Oracle Advanced Queue (AQ), propagate events among queues, dequeue events, perform transformations, and detect and resolve conflicts. Streams can be used in loading a data warehouse by themselves or in combination with change data capture. In addition to sending and receiving messages by enqueuing and dequeuing messages among Oracle databases, Streams can also be used to send and receive messages linked to other queuing systems such as IBM WebSphere MQ and TIBCO Rendezvous via an Oracle Messaging Gateway.

Transportable Tablespaces

Transportable tablespaces enable copying an Oracle tablespace from one database to another database, provided the tablespace data dictionaries agree in the source and target databases. This enables high-speed bulk data movement and can also be used to move indexes and constraints. Transportable tablespaces have been available since Oracle9*i* where source and target platforms are the same. All restrictions on use of transportable tables between Oracle databases on different platforms were removed as of Oracle Database 10*g*. So, for more recent versions of the Oracle database, it is possible to move a transportable tablespace between databases residing on different platforms and deployed on different operating systems.

To move a tablespace, you first have to stop activity on the source tablespace by either taking it off-line or making the tablespace read-only. A common approach is to combine usage of transportable tablespaces with range partitioning provided by the Oracle Partitioning Option. A transportable tablespace for a specific time interval partition can be moved from the source to an identical but empty partition on the target. When moved to the data warehouse target, the partition is made available to users and appears to be instantly loaded and available.

Transportable tablespaces also can be used for other purposes in data warehousing. Data can be published to CDs as transportable tablespaces for distribution to users who have similar databases. Transportable tablespaces can also be used as part of a data archiving strategy.

Data Pump

The Oracle database export and import capabilities can be used to copy data and the database structure from a source database to a target. This is less often used as part of a data warehouse data loading strategy since the database structure in an online transaction processing system is often quite different from a data warehouse design. The Oracle Data Pump provides a newer high-speed export and import utility and has been included in Oracle databases since Oracle Database 10*g*. It was designed to replace the previous export and import commands provided in the database, though this previous utility and format continues to also be provided for compatibility.

The Data Pump provides improved performance by taking advantage of direct path unloading and parallel operations in the Enterprise Edition of the Database to further enhance the speed of data export. Similarly, import with Data Pump is much faster than the traditional data import by leveraging direct path loading and parallelism.

In addition to being faster than the old export and import, Data Pump is easier to manage through a graphical interface that is part of Oracle Enterprise Manager, a command line interface, and a built-in PL/SQL package for a programmatic interface. You can estimate the size of an export file before you run the actual job, specify only a subset of database objects (functions, packages or procedures, as well as data) for a particular export, and monitor import and export jobs as they are running.

Oracle Warehouse Builder

Although extraction, transformation, and loading (ETL) scripts can be written from scratch, over the past decade, the use of ETL tools to build maps and generate code gained popularity. Such tools are used since they are faster and less error prone than manual scripting and provide a visual record of the ETL process that can be adjusted when sources or targets change. Our focus in this section is on Oracle Warehouse Builder (OWB), Oracle's tool that provides a framework for the creation of ETL scripts for populating a data warehouse or operational data store.

OWB is noteworthy for especially targeting and taking advantage of the Oracle database features such as set-based and row-based operations, PL/SQL bulk processing and table functions, foreign key constraint manipulation, use of inline views to speed loading, partition exchange loading, external table support, multi-table insert, merge, direct path insert, and parallel operations. However, a number of other ETL tools, such as Informatica and IBM's Ascential, are also popular where Oracle data warehouses are deployed and offer some degree of extended Oracle database features support. In late 2006, Oracle announced acquisition of Sunopsis' tools and technology to further enable ETL and integration to non-Oracle databases.

OWB Packaging

OWB first became generally available in early 2000 and has undergone several major interface and functionality improvements since. Originally packaged in Oracle's Internet Development Suite, Oracle began including a standard version of OWB with the database beginning in 2006 (OWB release 10.2). This version and subsequent versions can be used to generate ETL for Oracle Enterprise Edition, Standard Edition, and SE-1 databases, as well as flat files. A variety of sources can be extracted from including Oracle databases, other relational databases, flat files (with fixed column lengths or delimiters), and mainframe sources. Warehouse Builder Options available provide extended functionality for Enterprise ETL, Data Quality, and Connectors.

OWB is more than simply a mapping tool and ETL script builder since it can also be used to design a target data warehouse, data mart, or operational data store. Designs can be created as star schema (including aggregations featuring summary levels with multiple hierarchies), OLAP cubes, or as third normal form. OWB also offers a metadata browser for viewing metadata reports, data lineage diagrams, and impact analysis of metadata stored in the OWB repository. The runtime component is managed through a comprehensive deployment manager, and HTML-based audit access is provided.

The Warehouse Builder Enterprise ETL option includes support for additional data types including spatial, XML, and custom. Pluggable mappings can be created for reuse. Advanced process flow design, metadata management, and dimensional modeling are also provided in this option. The Enterprise ETL Option supports deployment to Oracle database Enterprise Edition Real Applications Clusters (RAC) implementations.

The Warehouse Builder Data Quality Option is used to determine, correct, and remove bad data. Data profiling can point out data that doesn't fit more common patterns. Data rules can be created and applied to ETL mappings in order to automate data correction.

The Warehouse Builder Connectors Option extends OWB support of popular applications as sources. Connectors for the Oracle E-Business Suite, PeopleSoft, and SAP R/3 enable building and deployment of ETL and process flows and access to these applications' metadata.

Typical Steps when using OWB

The first step when using Oracle Warehouse Builder is often the design of the target data warehouse. As described elsewhere in this book, the design of the warehouse should be driven by business requirements. During this design process, the designer also begins exploring the source data to gain an understanding of which data fields are needed, the quality of the source data, and whether representation of source data items is consistent across the various sources. After this information is gathered, design of the target schema and needed data transformations can begin.

Metadata from data sources is imported from source systems and into the OWB repository using interfaces provided in the OWB tool. Target objects are then further refined including dimensions, levels, hierarchies, attributes, facts, transformations, and calculations. Maps can then be defined from sources to targets through a drag-and-drop interface. Transformations and post-mapping processes are added during this step.

Prior to generating the ETL code, the design can be validated by OWB for such things as type mismatch between sources and targets. After successful validation, the ETL code is generated. SQL*Loader scripts are generated where data will be extracted from flat file sources. PL/SQL is generated for set-based or row-based ETL from relational sources. The objects in the target are then instantiated when the ETL scripts are transferred to the target data warehouse that becomes the transformation and load engine. The scripts are then scheduled to run, usually as Oracle Enterprise Manager jobs. If there are dependencies between jobs, process flows can be created in OWB that define those dependencies.

The PL/SQL scripts connect to Oracle relational databases through database links. For other relational sources such as IBM DB2 and Microsoft SQL Server, ODBC or transparent gateways can provide connectivity.

Since the code created by OWB uses standard Oracle scripting languages (SQL*Loader or PL/SQL scripts), you may be tempted to manually edit the generated scripts for purposes of tuning or small changes. However, since a value in using a tool such as OWB is that you can easily regenerate new scripts as sources or targets change, you might think twice about such editing outside of the tool since you would also need to do so after subsequent changes in the future.

The metadata models in the OWB repository can be exported as a metadata loader (.mdl) file type. As Oracle releases new versions of Warehouse Builder, each newer OWB release has been designed to automatically convert the version of the metadata loader file from the previous OWB release to the current release during the import process.

IS IT ETL OR ELT?

At the time of writing, there was much hype around the changing nature of ETL described as ELT. In traditional ETL, data is first extracted from source tables, and moved to staging tables (usually in an intermediate tier) where transformations occur. The data is then loaded into the target data warehouse.

In ELT, the data is extracted, loaded into the target data warehouse, and then transformed. This can eliminate the need for staging tables and speed the entire process.

Oracle Warehouse Builder-generated scripts are commonly used in combination with an Oracle data warehouse in an ELT type of data flow. The target Oracle database serves as both the load and transformation engine while OWB generates the scripts that leverage the built-in database extensions for loading and transformations.

ETL Design in OWB

Since OWB stores source, mapping, and target design metadata in an Oracle database, the first step in using OWB is to log into the OWB repository through the OWB tool. When logged into the repository, the designer can create a new project or work in an existing project and define or work in predefined project modules. Figure 7-1 illustrates a typical Design Center view including the Project Explorer, Connection Explorer, and Global Explorer panes.

Our illustrated project module in the Project Explorer pane is named OWB_DEMO. Within this window, we have pull-downs for selected database, file, and application sources, defined data profiles and rules, pluggable mappings, process flows, schedules, business intelligence tools, user defined modules, experts, configurations, and collections.

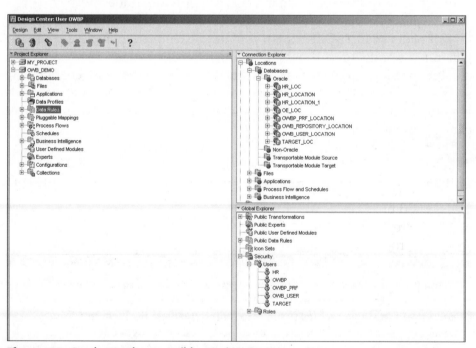

Figure 7-1: Oracle Warehouse Builder Design Center

ORACLE WAREHOUSE BUILDER EXPERTS

Oracle Warehouse Builder Experts are task-oriented utilities that are built in OWB by more advanced designers and then used by the broader design and business user community. First introduced in OWB release 10.2, Experts can be created that call needed user interfaces, contain customized instructions, and prompt users for input in a way such that advanced defined tasks are easier to use.

Experts are built using an Expert Editor and can be limited to use in individual projects or shared publicly. The Expert Editor interface is similar to the interface used in defining OWB process flows, described later in this chapter.

The Connection Explorer pane in the upper right of the previous illustration shows available resources that can be connected to and used in the project such as databases, files, applications, process flows, and business intelligence tools. The Global Explorer shows shared public transformations, public experts, public user-defined modules, public data rules, and icon sets available to the project team. Users and their roles are also defined through this interface.

Out-of-the-box transformations provided in OWB include administration transformations, conditional value conversions, character, date, numeric transformations, transformations on XML objects, other miscellaneous transformations not restricted to data types, and control center transformations used in process flows. Custom transformations can be created using a new transformation wizard in OWB. You can also import PL/SQL packages into OWB to be used in transformations.

As noted previously, metadata from sources is stored in the OWB repository. Figure 7-2 shows that we have several source Oracle databases in our example project. For each database used in the project, we can define mappings, transformations, data auditors, dimensions, cubes, tables, external tables, views, materialized views, sequences, user defined types, and queues. In the illustration, we see the names of the tables residing in the HR Oracle database.

In our project example, we also want to define source data as coming from applications. In Figure 7-3, we see sources can be utilized from the Oracle E-Business Suite, PeopleSoft, and SAP and we have started to define a source for data from an E-Business Suite application. OWB has the ability to generate ABAP code when extracting data from SAP.

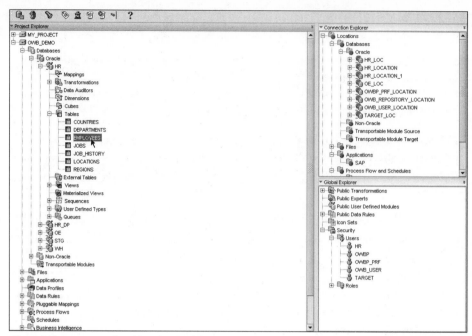

Figure 7-2: Source database and tables as seen in Oracle Warehouse Builder

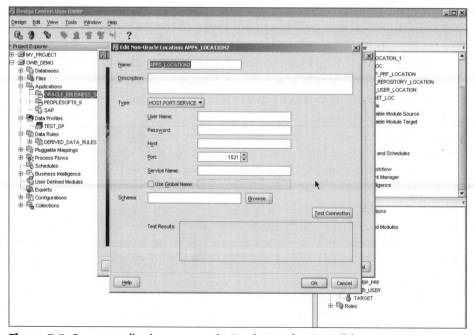

Figure 7-3: Source applications as seen in Oracle Warehouse Builder

Objects are then selected for use in the ETL process and appropriate mappings are built. Such mappings are displayed in OWB as tables and table operators with appropriate connections as created by the designer (as in Figure 7-4) or in more detailed column-to-column mapping levels within the tables.

In addition to a mapping pane in Figure 7-4, you also see a Bird's Eye View in the lower left pointing out what portion of the map is being shown. This is particularly valuable where very complex maps are built. Zooming within the map views is supported. Also shown in the previous Figure are an objects explorer, palette of operators, and table operator properties panes.

The palette of operators includes a variety of operators useful in building maps and transforming data, including data aggregation, filtering, joining of tables, splitting of tables, key lookups, sequence, and sorting operators. Some of these available operators are illustrated in Figure 7-5 in the center palette. Pluggable mappings can be created if you want to reuse maps or portions of your maps in other maps. The Name and Address operator can leverage data available from third-party providers of name and address libraries around the world, and you can use this operator to determine the accuracy of name and address data in your source systems as part of a data cleansing procedure.

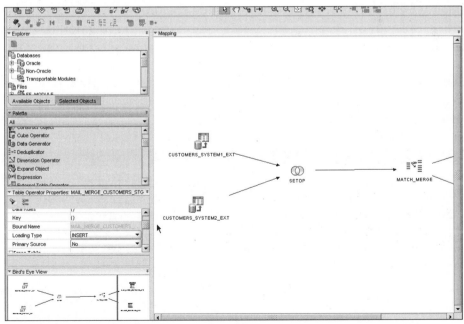

Figure 7-4: Mapping interface in Oracle Warehouse Builder

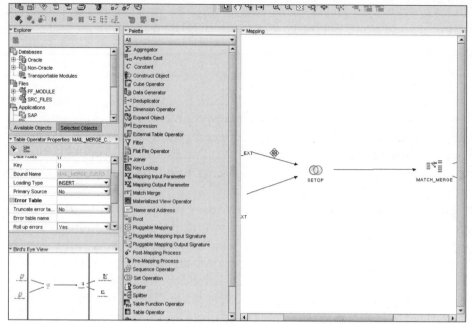

Figure 7-5: Palette of operators available for transforming data in OWB

More advanced data profiling and data rules for understanding and correcting defects in data are available in the Warehouse Builder Data Quality Option. Figure 7-6 illustrates using the property inspector in the data profile editor to set up the load configuration, aggregation configuration, and discovery configurations for use when loading the employees table in our HR_DP source. This interface can also be used to bind data rules, such as the sending of an email message, should certain data profiles be observed. The results can be presented in tabular or graphical form for analysis.

DATA PROFILING STEPS

When using the Warehouse Builder Data Quality Option, first load the data and then define a new data profile using the data profile editor. You can then use the editor to profile the data, view the results and derive data rules, create schema and mapping corrections, define additional rules manually (if needed), and finally generate, deploy, and execute the corrected mappings and data rules.

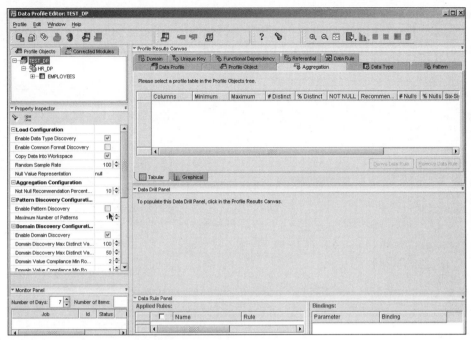

Figure 7-6: The Data Profile Editor in OWB

OWB and Dimensional Models

Although OWB provides the ability to design a variety of schema and mappings, dimensional modeling is popular in many data warehouse designs. The dimensional models can be created in Oracle relational tables or, using the Oracle database OLAP Option, in multidimensional online analytical processing (MOLAP) cubes stored as objects in the database. In fact, relational star schema containing materialized views for hierarchies can easily be converted into OLAP cube designs (or vice versa) using OWB.

It is often desirable to be able to maintain a history of changes within dimensions over a period of time versus restating dimensions as changes occur. This is driven by the business need to do like comparisons over periods of time even as the underlying business definitions for products, geographies, and other attributes may change. Formerly a particularly challenging model to design, this was greatly simplified when Oracle released OWB version 10.2. Using a method referred to as slowly changing dimensions and originated by Ralph Kimball and others, these can now be defined through an interface in OWB by simply selecting the type of slowly changing dimension you want to create (see Figure 7-7).

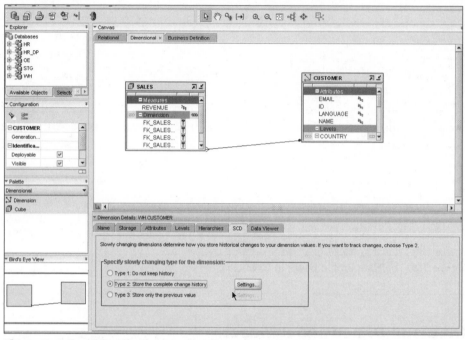

Figure 7-7: Specifying slowly changing dimensions in OWB

TYPES OF SLOWLY CHANGING DIMENSIONS

Slowly changing dimensions are most often defined to be of three types. In Type 1 slowly changing dimensions, only the most recent dimensional values are stored and previous values are over-written. However, where the business requirement is the need to understand how such values have changed over time, Type 2 or Type 3 slowly changing dimensions are typically used.

Type 2 slowly changing dimensions are used when dimensional values have changed but the records would have the same primary keys. A dimensional column is added containing a surrogate key enabling storage and tracking of changing dimensional value records.

In Type 3 slowly changing dimensions, a field is included in the record that contains the previous dimensional value in addition to the current value. This enables determining the value history.

The OWB Process Editor

Once ETL maps are defined, created, and instantiated to the target data warehouse, they are scheduled as jobs. Simple jobs are typically scheduled using Oracle Enterprise Manager or other job scheduling tools. However, such jobs can also be quite complex with the sequence of loading events dependent on the successful execution of other events. OWB includes a process editor used to define the sequence for ETL processing that presents a view similar to the mapping editor.

In Figure 7-8, we see that the process editor view includes a process flow diagram, Bird's Eye View, explorer, palette of operations, and listing of object details. In the illustrated process flow diagram, you see that the loading of data into the channels, customer, product, promotion, and credit limit tables must succeed before the sales table is loaded.

A variety of operators are available for use in building process flows, including assigning values, creating loops and forks, and building monitoring and notifications. Some of the available operators are illustrated in the palette shown in the center of Figure 7-9.

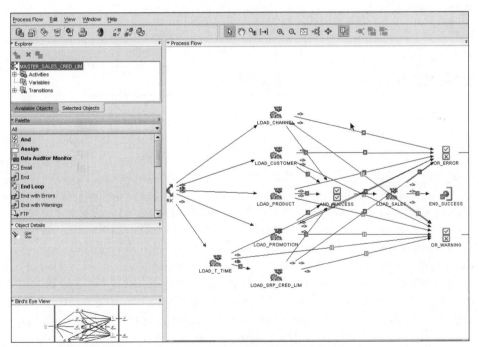

Figure 7-8: Process flow editor in Oracle Warehouse Builder

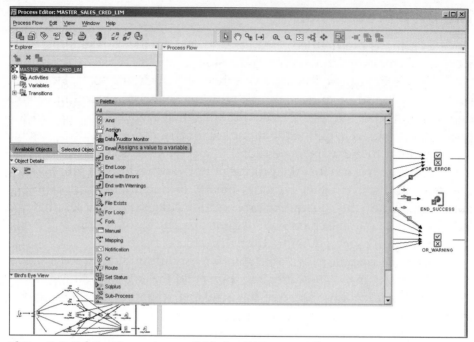

Figure 7-9: Palette of operators available for OWB process flows

Balancing Data Loading Choices

This chapter provided a short overview describing many of the database and Oracle Warehouse Builder features that can be used in deploying an ETL infrastructure for an Oracle-based data warehouse. The Oracle database utilities and features that might be leveraged include the embedded SQL for ETL and extensions in the database, SQL*Loader, the Oracle Data Pump, transportable tablespaces, change data capture, and Oracle Streams. Designers are increasingly using tools to generate ETL scripts and perform data quality analysis and since Oracle Warehouse Builder is included with the Oracle database, OWB is now a popular choice.

As you create your data loading strategy, you will likely need to balance multiple requirements. You could face demands to create a solution that can deliver near real-time data, perform ETL in a very limited time window, validate and improve the quality of your data, and face aggressive design and deployment timelines that may or may not match the skills of your data warehouse and ETL designers. All of these demands need to be evaluated and prioritized in a way that takes into account your organization's business priorities.

For example, what do you do if your business needs near real-time data and you have identified that you have major data quality problems in your source data? Furthermore, you know that the ETL needed to cleanse the data will require extremely complex and time-consuming transformations. In such a situation, you might work with the business users and modify source systems to restrict data input to certain sets of validated values. This could simplify not only the data cleansing needed to deploy a useful warehouse, but also improve reporting accuracy directly out of the transactional systems.

Proper ETL design, generation, and scheduling is often considered key in successfully managing the data warehouse. Of course, managing a data warehouse includes a lot more than simply getting the ETL processing right. In Chapter 8, we will focus on using Enterprise Manager to manage data loading, including topics such as setting refresh options for materialized views when base level detailed data is loaded. But, we will also cover many other aspects important in successfully managing a data warehouse infrastructure.

Managing the Oracle Data Warehouse

Any data warehouse deployed on any database supporting a large and mixed community of business users requires upfront planning to mitigate complications in management or the need for extensive custom programming later. Although it is common to focus on the number of database administrators (DBAs) required to manage a data warehouse, that number is irrelevant if the resulting deployment requires an army of programmers to make the data warehouse understandable to the business users, or if extensive modifications are needed every time business needs change. From a broad perspective, one should consider the number of people, types of skills, and flexibility needed in managing the entire infrastructure over time, including the data warehouse, any data marts deployed, and business intelligence tools.

This section of the book provides focus on managing a data warehouse deployed on the Oracle database. Administrative tools used to create and manage Oracle databases that might be deployed using a hybrid schema are discussed here, since such schema are increasingly used in deploying single, scalable, and understandable data warehouses. Of course, these same tools can be used in organizations that choose to deploy multiple data marts (usually built using a star schema) or a more traditional enterprise data warehouse that has a third normal form schema.

INSTALLING ORACLE

This chapter covers managing the database, but the first step is installing it, of course. Oracle has greatly simplified the database installation process over the years. You can download the Oracle database from the Oracle Technology Network (OTN) at www.oracle.com/technology and run the setup file to install it. A more common approach is to insert a database CD obtained from Oracle, in which case the setup process will begin automatically. Oracle's CD packs come with quick installation guides that describe hardware and software requirements and basic installation steps.

When installing the database, you can choose to perform a basic installation or a more advanced installation. The basic installation requires that an Oracle home location be specified, the version of Oracle you are installing is specified, a database name be given, and a database password for system accounts (SYS, SYSTEM, SYSMAN, and DBSNMP) be entered. You can automatically create a starter database that includes a sample schema to help you familiarize yourself with the database. Many of the examples in this book leveraged the sample schema.

Initialization parameters are largely predefined and the number used has been greatly reduced from earlier database releases. The parameters can be adjusted through Enterprise Manager's administration interface that we'll describe in this chapter.

Oracle manageability features have grown more automated with each release of the database. This chapter touches on newer Oracle database self-managing capabilities in the database, but mostly focuses on Oracle Enterprise Manager and Grid Control management tools. Oracle Enterprise Manager provides interfaces needed to monitor, administer, maintain, and optimize (for performance) Oracle databases. We will describe manageability interfaces for important database features here and include discussions on leveraging Oracle's Partitioning Option to enable higher availability and Oracle's advanced security options. Other features we touch on include the database resource manager, table compression, Automatic Database Diagnostics Monitor (ADDM), and Automatic Storage Manager (ASM).

Oracle Enterprise Manager Grid Control

A key to simplifying data warehouse management after deploying an Oracle database is using Oracle's automated management tools, and especially Oracle Enterprise Manager, in ongoing management procedures. Oracle Enterprise Manager is automatically installed with every instance of the

Oracle database. Enterprise Manager Grid Control enables management of multiple Oracle database instances and databases as well as Application Servers, the Oracle Collaboration Suite, web applications, services, systems, groups, and storage devices, through a common interface. In this chapter, we'll focus on how you can use Grid Control and Enterprise Manager to manage a database deployed as a data warehouse.

As illustrated in Figure 8-1, Enterprise Manager Grid Control provides a single interface to all manageable software targets through a browser. You simply enter the HTTP address for Grid Control and then log into it by providing a user name and password. When logged in, you will first get a view of the number of targets being monitored and their status levels, the number of alerts and policy violations, the number of patch advisories, and deployment summaries by types of targets.

From the home page, you can tab to pages providing more information on the targets, deployment, alerts, policies, jobs, and available reports. For example, through the deployment link, you can access information about hosts and their operating systems and software installations. These tools enable you to compare detailed information concerning various hosts and databases, search Oracle's MetaLink for patches and manage deployment, clone an Oracle database or Oracle home, and manage the configuration collection. A typical deployments page showing database installations is illustrated in Figure 8-2.

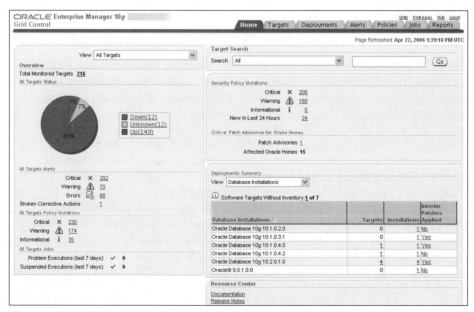

Figure 8-1: Enterprise Manager Grid Control home page

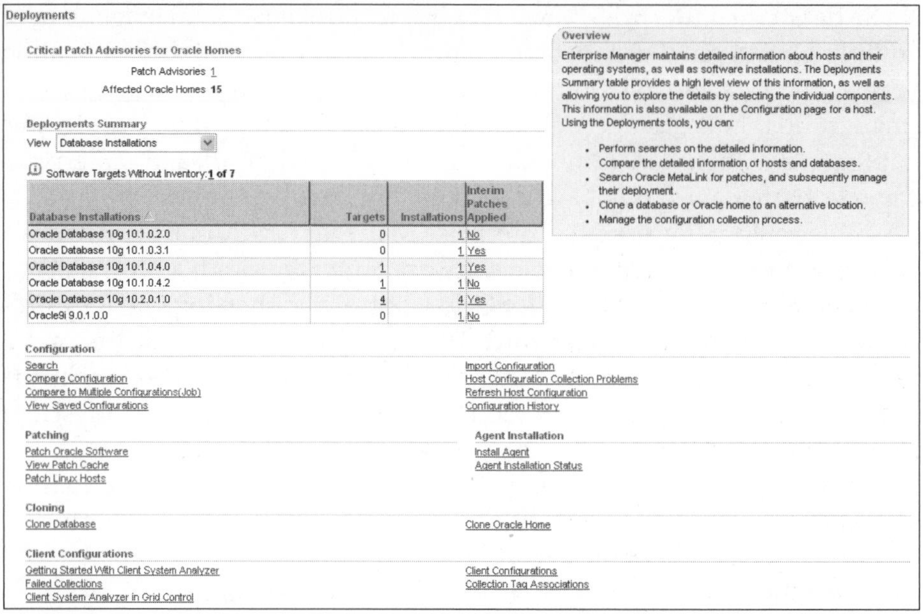

Figure 8-2: Enterprise Manager Grid Control Deployments page

Next, we'll explore an individual database target on a specific server. Figure 8-3 illustrates a typical view of database targets monitored servers and includes their current status, number of alerts, number of policy violations, version, CPU and I/O status, and read activity.

ORACLE SECURITY PATCHES AND CRITICAL PATCH UPDATES

Oracle issues fixes for its database and other software products in the form of patches that are posted to its web-based support site, MetaLink. Since data warehouses often contain sensitive data, experienced database administrators (DBAs) are aware that they need to protect such data by applying fixes to database security flaws as quickly as possible. Oracle issues Critical Patch Updates to enable organizations to immediately plug security holes that Oracle has identified and provided fixes for. When Oracle issues a Critical Patch Update advisory for its software products, it includes fixes from previous Critical Patch Updates, so all security fixes released to date are included.

Some organizations choose instead to install such security patches when they install Oracle's entire patch sets at pre-scheduled regular intervals (such as once per quarter). Oracle also includes the security fixes in these patch sets giving an organization a choice as to how to implement these important fixes.

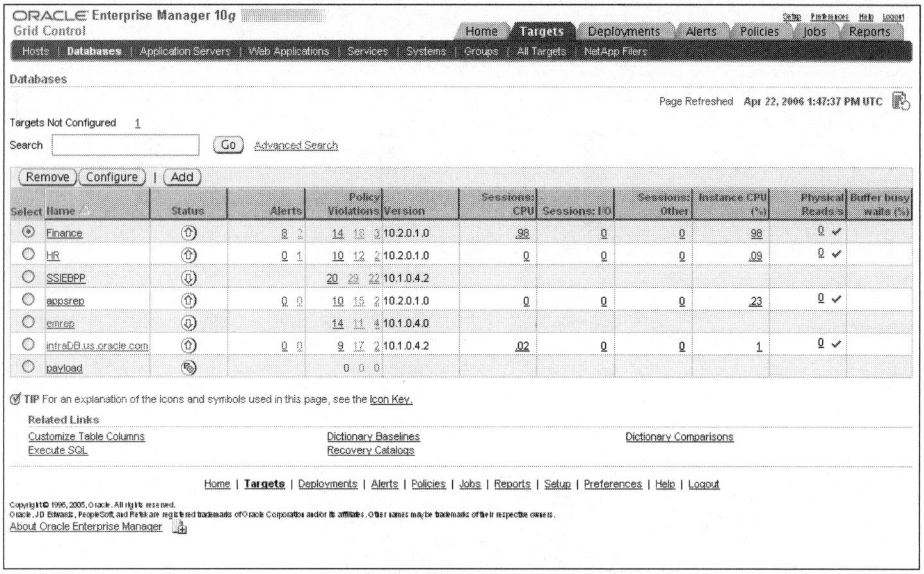

Figure 8-3: Enterprise Manager Grid Control database target status

We next choose the Finance link in the previous Figure 8-3 to take a closer look at the Finance database that is our data warehouse. Figure 8-4 illustrates the home page for this database, including a view of database status, CPU load, active sessions, SQL response time, diagnostics reported by ADDM, space summary, anticipated recovery time, and recent alerts. This page will automatically refresh showing updated statistics based on the View Data setting illustrated in the upper right. Other pages you see tabs for in the following Figure include the performance, administration, and maintenance pages.

METRICS GATHERED BY ADDM

In Oracle Database 10g and newer Oracle database releases, ADDM collects data on over 40 different database metrics, including alert logs, archive areas, database files, database job status, database limits, database services, deferred transactions, failed logins, flash recovery, health checks, invalid objects, recovery, response, Segment Advisor recommendations, sessions suspended, snapshots too old, Streams, tablespaces, throughput, user audits, and waits. Alert thresholds can be set and collections scheduled with upload intervals defined through Enterprise Manager.

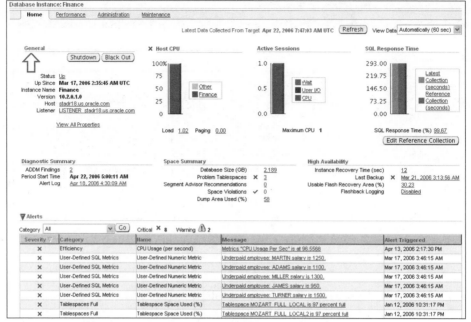

Figure 8-4: Enterprise Manager Grid Control home page for a database

As with other pages, related links are provided. For example, from the database home page, you have links to access, Advisor Central, alert history and logs, all metrics, blackouts, deployments, SQL execution interfaces, jobs, metrics, monitoring, reports, rules, SQL history, and target properties pages. Your ability to execute functions on these pages may require additional privileges beyond those that your Grid Control login allows. If that is the case, you will be prompted for additional login credentials.

Database Performance Monitoring

Optimizing database performance can be a key aspect of managing a data warehouse. We have dedicated the Chapter 9 to this discussion, but for completeness in covering manageability, we'll provide a brief introduction regarding what is possible through Enterprise Manager Grid Control in this section.

Database performance can be viewed in graphic summary form through the database instance performance page illustrated in Figure 8-5. Statistics are automatically gathered as of Oracle Database 10g by ADDM. ADDM can also immediately update the statistics, as illustrated in Figure 8-5. Here, we see monitoring of average load on the host, active CPU sessions, disk I/O, and throughput.

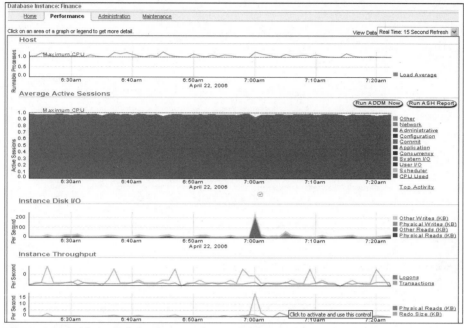

Figure 8-5: Grid Control database performance monitoring

Other links are provided from this page to a top activity page showing top sessions and top SQL data, and pages for hang analysis, search sessions, top consumers, instance locks, snapshots, duplicate SQL, instance activity, SQL tuning sets, blocking sessions, and baseline normalized metrics.

As noted earlier, related links provide access to Advisor Central. The Oracle database offers a number of advisors (since Oracle Database 10g) including ADDM, a memory advisor, mean-time-to-recovery advisor, segment advisor, SQL access advisor, SQL tuning advisor, and undo management. Figure 8-6 shows a typical view in Advisor Central and includes a report of recent advisors run.

The advisors can provide a set of tuning recommendations. Figure 8-7 illustrates what such a set of findings and recommendations might look like and their relative impact.

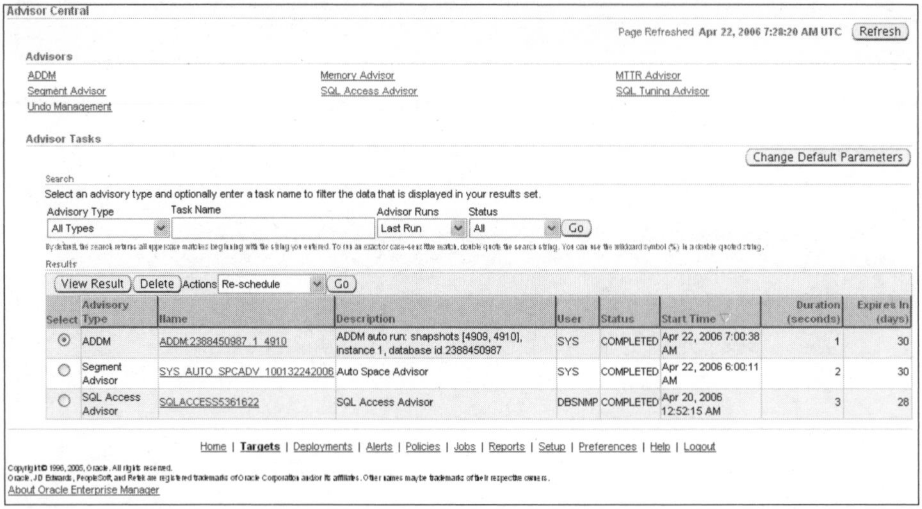

Figure 8-6: Grid Control database Advisor Central

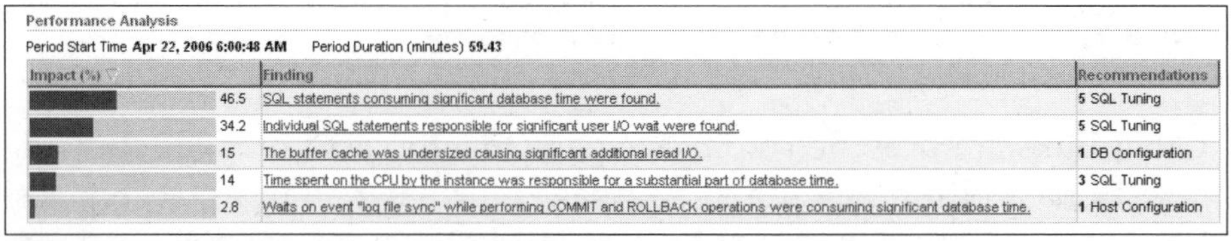

Figure 8-7: Grid Control database performance analysis recommendations

Also from related links, you have access to the Alert History page (as shown in Figure 8-8). Many of these key metrics can have direct implications on performance. Key metrics and their status can be viewed graphically on this page for various recent lengths of history.

Database Administration

The database administration page is used for managing storage, the database configuration parameters, the Oracle scheduler, viewing database statistics, converting databases to clusters or ASM, setting up the resource manager, and managing database objects, programs, and XML capabilities in the database. It is also used for managing users and privileges, managing materialized views, enabling business intelligence and OLAP capabilities, creating user-defined types, and for change management. Figure 8-9 shows the interface to the many administration tasks that are possible from this page.

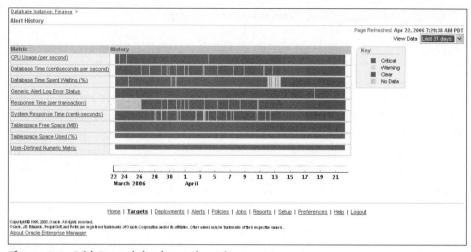

Figure 8-8: Grid Control database Alert History

Database Instance: Finance

| Home | Performance | **Administration** | Maintenance |

The Administration tab displays links that allow you to administer database objects and initiate database operations inside an Oracle database. The Maintenance tab displays links that provide functions that control the flow of data between or outside Oracle databases.

Database Administration

Storage
Control Files
Tablespaces
Temporary Tablespace Groups
Datafiles
Rollback Segments
Redo Log Groups
Archive Logs

Statistics Management
Automatic Workload Repository
Manage Optimizer Statistics

Database Configuration
Memory Parameters
Undo Management
All Initialization Parameters
Database Feature Usage

Change Database
Migrate to ASM
Convert to Cluster Database
Make Tablespace Locally Managed

Oracle Scheduler
Jobs
Chains
Schedules
Programs
Job Classes
Windows
Window Groups
Global Attributes

Resource Manager
Monitors
Consumer Groups
Consumer Group Mappings
Plans

Schema

Database Objects
Tables
Indexes
Views
Synonyms
Sequences
Database Links
Directory Objects
Reorganize Objects

Users & Privileges
Users
Roles
Profiles
Audit Settings

User Defined Types
Array Types
Object Types
Table Types

Programs
Packages
Package Bodies
Procedures
Functions
Triggers
Java Classes
Java Sources

Materialized Views
Materialized Views
Materialized View Logs
Refresh Groups

Change Management
Dictionary Baselines
Dictionary Comparisons

XML Database
Configuration
Resources
Access Control Lists
XML Schemas
XML Type Tables
XML Type Views

BI & OLAP
Dimensions
Cubes
OLAP Dimensions
Measure Folders

Figure 8-9: Grid Control database Administration links

Creating and Managing Tables and Storage

Since a relational database at its simplest level consists of tables containing rows and columns and foreign key relationships to link those tables, a key task is the creation and maintenance of those tables and schema. Oracle provides tremendous flexibility here, including the ability to create schema as third normal form (typical in enterprise data warehouses containing only detailed data), star schema, or a hybrid. (You may recall that we introduced this topic in Chapter 1 and have also discussed it elsewhere in this book.) As of Oracle9i, it is also possible to store data in OLAP Cubes using the Oracle OLAP Option, so we'll describe creating and managing those cubes through Enterprise Manager in a subsequent section of this chapter.

Figure 8-10 illustrates the interface for editing a table in Enterprise Manager. Table column names, data types, size, scale, nulls allowed, and defaults are defined. A variety of actions can be taken including creation of indexes, synonyms, and triggers, generation of DDL, running the segment advisor, shrinking segments, and reorganizing the table. Other links are available as shown in the illustration for defining constraints (For example, foreign key relationships, check constraints), viewing space usage of dependent segments, setting storage parameters (tablespace logging, extent size, space usage, and buffer pools), defining options for row movement, parallel threads and cache, defining partitions, and viewing table statistics, and viewing indexes. The table in this illustration is a sales fact table deployed in a relational star schema.

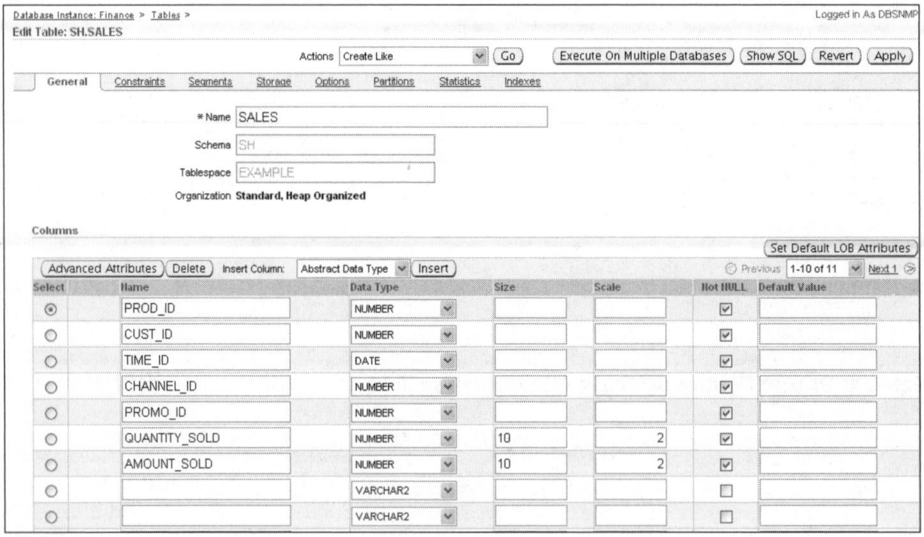

Figure 8-10: Editing a table in Enterprise Manager

A fact table in a star schema is linked to lookup tables that are defined as dimension tables. Dimension tables can also be defined and created through Enterprise Manager as illustrated in Figure 8-11.

The links from fact tables to dimensions are defined by foreign key relationships. Figure 8-12 illustrates foreign key relationships from our sales fact table defined for products, customers, time, channels, and promotions. Figure 8-12 also illustrates all of the possible actions we can take on the sales fact table through the Enterprise Manager interface.

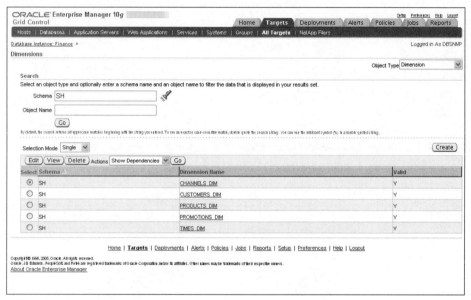

Figure 8-11: Dimensions in Enterprise Manager

When tables are created, they are deployed onto Oracle managed database files. As of Oracle Database 10g, you can leverage Oracle's Automatic Storage Management (ASM) to create disk groups comprised of your available disk storage and simplify deployment of those files. ASM automatically divides the Oracle database files into 1 MB extents and then stripes the files evenly across all disks within the disk group. If you add or remove a disk from a disk group, ASM will redistribute the files for you. You can migrate a database to ASM using a wizard accessible through the Administration interface.

ASM also supports mirroring for high availability on a per-file basis. Each extent can be defined to have one or two mirrors (or none if you prefer to use mirroring providing by your storage device). Figure 8-13 shows information gathered from a disk group deployed using ASM.

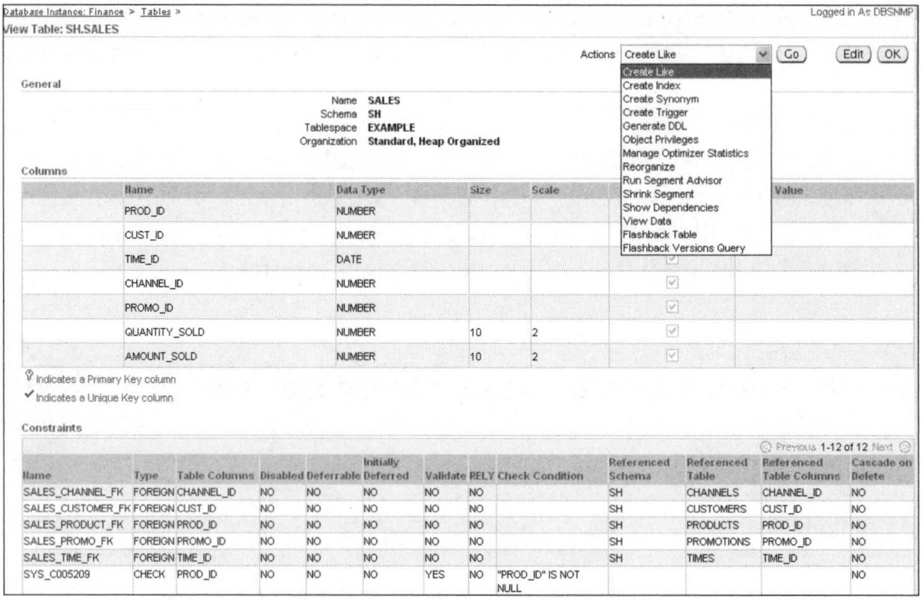

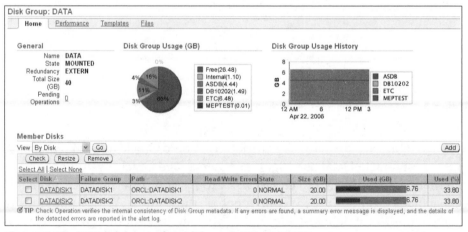

Figure 8-12: Foreign Key relationships designated for sample Sales fact table

Figure 8-13: ASM disk group viewed through Enterprise Manager

Creating and Managing Materialized Views

Materialized views are physical tables in an Oracle database that hold summary-level data. They are built to speed response to queries since business users often analyze data that has been summarized from a more detailed level. For operational reporting, they can provide summary-level information from tables deployed as third normal form. In ad hoc query and analysis, they are often deployed over fact and dimension tables in a star schema. We briefly introduced where you might use materialized views in Chapter 3 and will focus on managing them here. Certainly, a benefit of materialized views is that the Oracle cost-based optimizer will transparently redirect queries to the right view. For query rewrite to occur, the QUERY_REWRITE_ENABLED initialization parameter must be set to TRUE (the default setting during Oracle database installation).

As mentioned previously in this book, creation of materialized views can be recommended automatically by the SQL Access Advisor in Oracle Enterprise Manager in order to speed queries or you might create materialized views in anticipation of how business users will access data. Figure 8-14 illustrates the materialized views page accessible through the administration interface. Here you see the Create button used if you want to create your own materialized views. In this example, you also see materialized views already created for products and times dimension tables.

Updates of data in materialized views after detailed data updates occur are based on the refresh type you specify for the materialized view. Available refresh types include fast (incremental), complete, or force where an incremental refresh will occur if possible, and a full refresh will occur if an incremental refresh is not possible. An incremental refresh to a materialized view can only occur if materialized view logs exist. Refresh intervals can be specified as on demand, on each commit, or scheduled for certain times or dates.

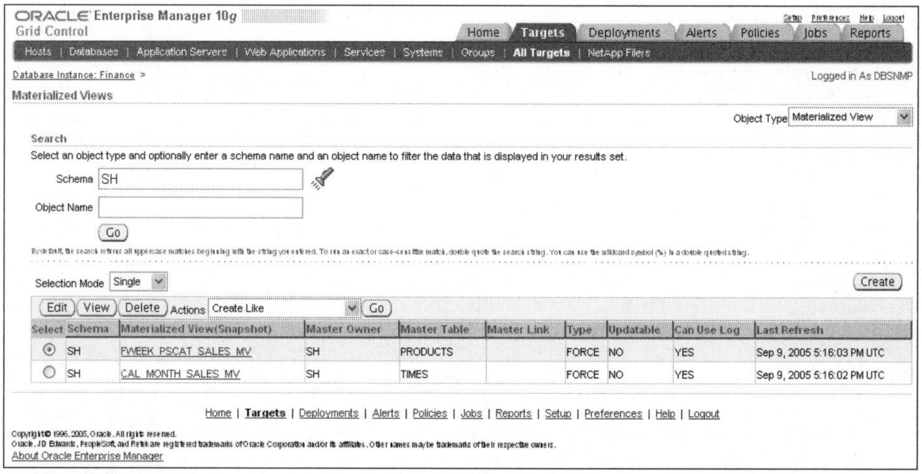

Figure 8-14: Materialized view tables presented through Enterprise Manager

By taking a closer look at one of these materialized views (we clicked on FWEEK_PSCAT_SALES_MV in the above illustration), we see in Figure 8-15 what a query that leverages this materialized view will look like. We can also choose to view an explain of the query to determine the types of refreshes and query rewrites that are possible.

Creating and Managing OLAP Cubes

The star schema and materialized views are recognized by Oracle's cost-based optimizer and, along with Oracle's embedded analytic functions, enable deployment of relational online analytical processing (ROLAP) solutions. However, where a large number of dimensions and many levels exist, it may be desirable to deploy cubes that are prejoined in what are usually called multidimensional online analytical processing (MOLAP) solutions. The Oracle OLAP Option enables you to deploy such cubes in the relational database as objects. Cubes can be created and loaded using a combination of Oracle Enterprise Manager, Oracle Warehouse Builder, and the Analytic Workspace Manager. Since this chapter focuses on managing the data warehouse, we will focus here on using Enterprise Manager to create and manage the cubes.

Figure 8-16 illustrates the Cubes page available through the Administration interface in Enterprise Manager. Two cubes have already been defined in this example, a sales cube and a cost cube. A new cube would be created by selecting the create button.

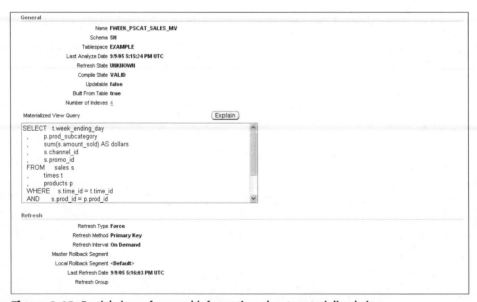

Figure 8-15: Partial view of general information about materialized view

To see more details about the defined cubes, simply select the cube name hyperlink. We've selected the sales cube in our example and in Figure 8-17 we see the dimensions, measures, and aggregations that have been defined for this cube.

From the previous screen, we also have the option of editing the cube and its dimensions, measures, and aggregations. In Figure 8-18, we illustrate the choice of aggregation operators for the measures.

Figure 8-16: The Enterprise Manager interface for Cubes

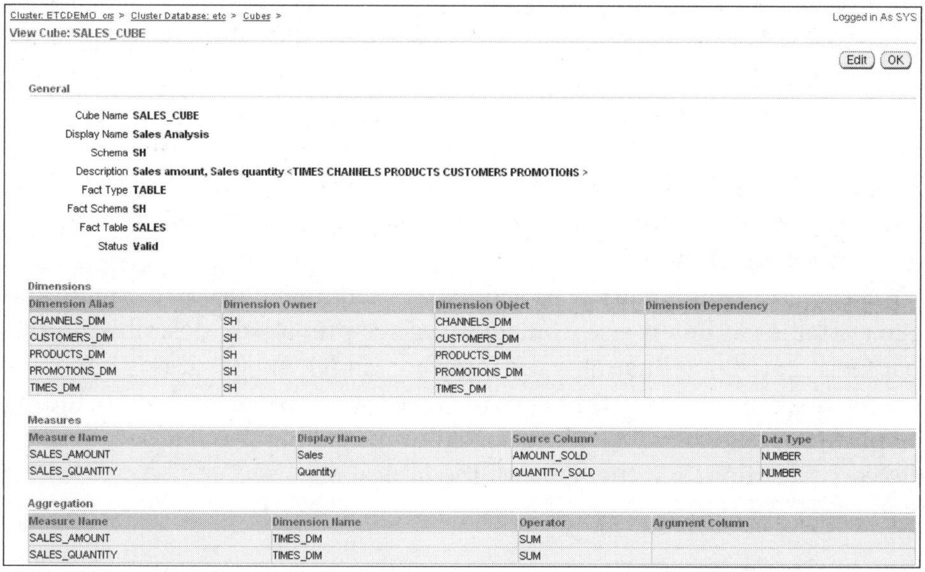

Figure 8-17: Sales cube description

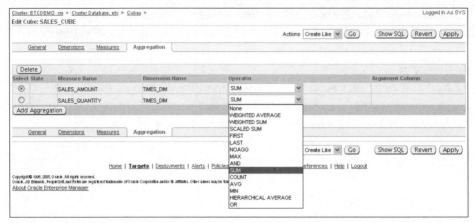

Figure 8-18: Aggregation operators available for Cube measures

After a cube is created in the database, it can be accessed through Oracle's Java OLAP API or, more commonly, through SQL as described in Chapter 6. Cube data population is set up through Oracle Warehouse Builder or the Analytic Workspace Manager.

Managing Partitioning and Database Manageability Impact

The Oracle Partitioning Option was first introduced in Oracle8 primarily to improve database manageability and availability, although there are some performance advantages that can be gained (since the optimizer will not query partitions containing data sets that out of range when the queries are submitted). Since this chapter is about managing the warehouse, we'll focus this discussion on administration of partitioning.

Table 8-1 describes the various partitioning types that Oracle provides in the Partitioning Option.

You can create and manage partitions through the interface to create and manage tables in Enterprise Manager that we previously described in this chapter. Figure 8-19 illustrates the interface under the partitions tab. Here you see a set of range partitions defined for the sales fact table, including the partition names, high values for columns defining what data will go into each partition, and the name of the tablespace used.

Table 8-1: Oracle Partitioning Capabilities in the Partitioning Option

PARTITIONING TYPE	DESCRIPTION
Range Partitioning	Partitions are specified using a defined continuous range of values such as dates (for example, hour, day, week, month, year) or identification numbers or intervals.
List Partitioning	Partitions are specified by a list of specific values such as geographies (region, city, state or province, country).
Hash Partitioning	A hash algorithm determines the partition key for a given row of data.
Composite Partitioning	Various composite partitioning capabilities are available (depending on database release) with range-hash and range-list the most frequently used. In range-hash partitioning, a table of values is first range partitioned and then sub-partitioned using hash partitioning. In range-list partitioning, a table of values is first range partitioned and then sub-partitioned using list partitioning.

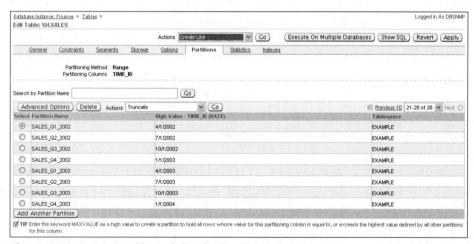

Figure 8-19: Range Partitions defined using Enterprise Manager

An advantage of using the Partitioning Option is that you can keep the rest of the database operational while you perform maintenance tasks on individual partitions. For example, you can create a new partition by choosing the Add Another Partition button in Figure 8-19, load the partition, apply local indexing, and make it available. You can create rolling windows using partitioning where you might take the oldest partition offline and store it to tape when adding a new partition. More likely, as disk prices continue to decrease, you might implement an information lifecycle management (ILM) strategy entirely using disk. Older partitions might be migrated from faster and more expensive disks to slower and cheaper disks since queries of old data may be few and far between.

The use of the Partitioning Option also has positive implications in more traditional backups to tape. Very often, data in older partitions is non-changing. As partitions become read-only, they need not be backed up in subsequent backup cycles. By backing up only the newer and changing partitions, the time required to perform the backup can be significantly reduced for large data warehouses.

In order to reduce the storage needed and minimize budget allocations for additional disk, managers of databases often leverage Oracle's compression capabilities. Introduced in Oracle 9i Release 2, the degree of compression varies depending on the repeating nature of the data values to be stored. Storage reduction of two times is most typical, although a compression ratio of up to seven times has been observed. Since loading data as compressed can take twice as long as loading uncompressed data, many have chosen to compress only older non-changing data residing in dated range partitions while data in newer partitions remains uncompressed.

Managing XML Database in Oracle

The Oracle database is increasingly used for document storage and retrieval to provide another important resource of information used in business intelligence solutions. XML can be used to logically define a model of such documents. For example, an Xpath data model defines document elements, document attributes, parsed character data (PCDATA), and document order. Oracle began supporting storage of native XML datatypes in Oracle's XML DB beginning with the Oracle9i database. Access to such documents is provided by Oracle through SQLX (SQL/XML) and XQuery. Access is also possible through FTP, HTTP, and WebDAV.

Management of Oracle's XML DB, including configuration, resources, access control lists, XML schema, XML type tables, and XML type views (of resource contents and metadata), is through the Administration interface in Enterprise Manager. Figure 8-20 illustrates the interface showing URLs of the XML schema in an Oracle XML DB. Such XML schema can also be created through this interface.

Managing Users and Security

The Oracle database is designed to provide access to data based on user names and privileges given to those users. The best approach to maintain security is to give a user the least amount of privileges needed to do their job. Figure 8-21 illustrates the screen used for creating a user name and password in Oracle Enterprise Manager. Users are assigned to named groups of defined privileges, more commonly known as roles. A user might be given specific system privileges, database object privileges, quotas, consumer group switching privileges, and proxies as illustrated here.

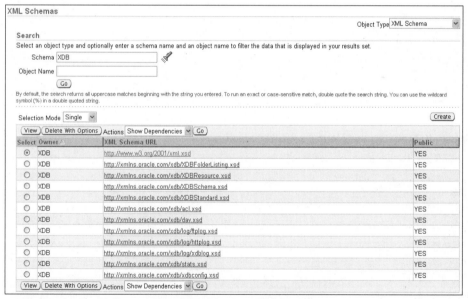

Figure 8-20: XML Schema URLs viewed in Enterprise Manager

At database creation time, SYS and SYSTEM users are created with a special DBA role that includes most system privileges. Additional system privileges are provided in the SYSDBA and SYSOPER roles, and these are typically assigned to database administrators. Since these roles are so powerful, they are generally not widely given out. Figure 8-22 illustrates logging into Enterprise Manager as SYSDBA.

In business intelligence environments, analysts typically connect to the data warehouse through a middle-tier application server. By using proxies, once the application server is authenticated to the database, it can serve as the point at which users authenticate themselves such that they will not need to reauthenticate themselves individually (by providing passwords) at the database. The identity of the user and middle tier is passed to the database enabling auditing.

Figure 8-21: Enterprise Manager database user creation

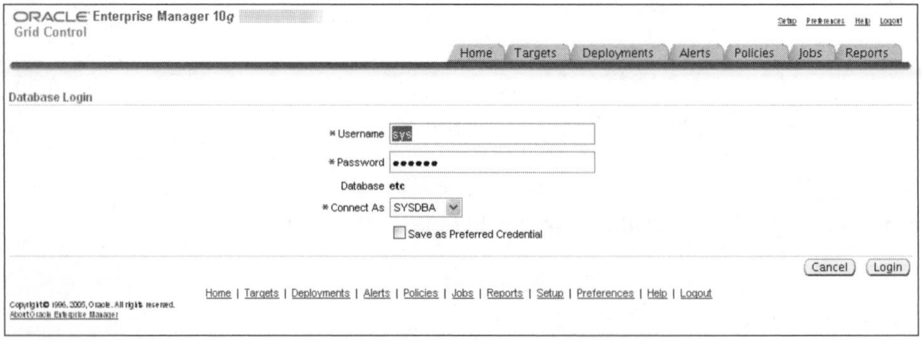

Figure 8-22: Enterprise Manager Grid Control login as SYSDBA

Where analysts access multiple databases, it may be desirable to set up Oracle Enterprise User Security. Using the Oracle Internet Directory, part of Oracle's Identity Management, you can create a single location containing the database users and authentications. Strong authentication is enabled by Oracle's Advanced Security Option and includes support for the use of Kerberos, Public Key Infrastructure (PKI), RADIUS, and the Distributed Computing Environment (DCE).

Oracle provides even stricter security by enabling deployment of a Virtual Private Database (VPD). Policies, defined by DBAs or security administrators, are attached to database objects (tables and views) and are enforced regardless of access method when VPD is deployed. When the Oracle Label Security Option is deployed, access is limited to users who have been given access to rows containing certain values or classification labels.

Of course, users could still try to access data, install software, or perform other tasks in violation of preset policies. Oracle Enterprise Manager Grid Control provides the ability to easily view the number of policy violations, as illustrated in Figure 8-23, in order to more quickly determine if a security risk is present. Fine-grained auditing, also known as policy-based auditing, can be enabled to provide an audit trail of user activities. As of Oracle Database 10g release 2, the audit trails can be stored in XML format as operating system files enabling isolation of the audit trails from database users (including DBAs) with access available to the gathered data even if the database is down.

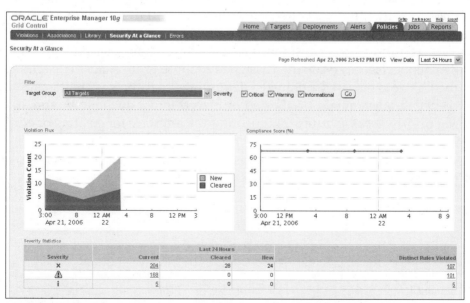

Figure 8-23: Enterprise Manager Grid Control view of policy violations

LIMITING ACCESS TO SPECIFIC COLUMNS, ROWS, AND DATA

Oracle's Label Security Option and Advanced Security Option can further limit access to data. For example, when the Oracle Label Security Option is deployed, to see a certain row of data, the user must have been given the right to view rows containing those specific named labels or classification levels.

It might also be desirable to make certain columns of data unviewable by certain users. To ensure this, the Oracle database Advanced Security Option enables transparent data encryption for data as it is written to disk using 3DES and AES 128-, 192-, and 256-bit encryption. The data is unencrypted transparently when an authorized user attempts to read the data. The Advanced Security Option also provides encryption for data that is transmitted across a network.

As of Oracle Database 10g Release 2, Oracle also began offering a Database Vault Option providing a more granular separation of duties through the creation of realms, thus defining access to data on a need-to-know basis. For example, Database Vault can be set up to block DBAs from seeing sensitive data that is accessed through database applications. Rules can be set to limit specific database commands to certain hostnames and IP addresses. The Database Vault Option is designed to also leverage the Oracle Label Security and Advanced Security Options.

Managing Users and Resource Utilization

For the business user community, managing database resource utilization can be critical. For example, the DBA probably does not want a single user to have the ability to severely impact the query response performance experienced by other users. Oracle features a built-in Database Resource Manager to control this.

The DBA can define consumer groups with certain cost limits or CPU utilization levels. Users are then assigned to those groups. So, for example, if the Oracle cost-based optimizer determines that the cost limit will be exceeded, a query might be aborted or placed into a queue to be run at a lower priority level. Figure 8-24 illustrates the interface for creating or editing consumer groups.

After they have been defined, consumer groups are then assigned to a plan using the interface pictured in Figure 8-25.

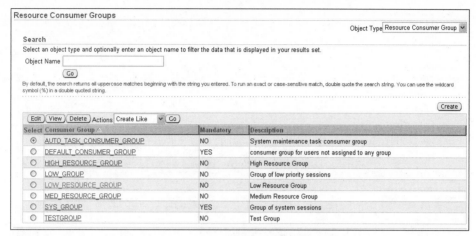

Figure 8-24: Resource Consumer Groups in Enterprise Manager

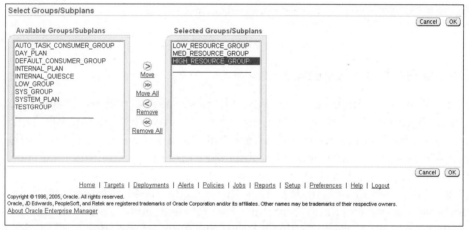

Figure 8-25: Creating a Resource Plan in Enterprise Manager

Figure 8-26 illustrates a completed plan. Users assigned to the HIGH_RESOURCE_GROUP would have unlimited capabilities for degree of parallelism and maximum estimated execution time, whereas users assigned to other groups would have limits as pictured here.

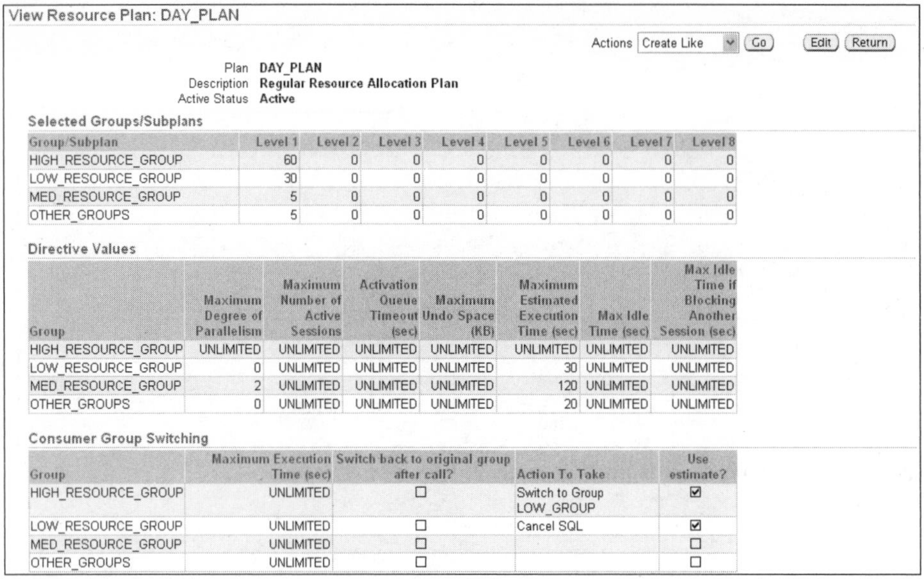

View Resource Plan: DAY_PLAN

Actions Create Like Go Edit Return

Plan DAY_PLAN
Description Regular Resource Allocation Plan
Active Status Active

Selected Groups/Subplans

Group/Subplan	Level 1	Level 2	Level 3	Level 4	Level 5	Level 6	Level 7	Level 8
HIGH_RESOURCE_GROUP	60	0	0	0	0	0	0	0
LOW_RESOURCE_GROUP	30	0	0	0	0	0	0	0
MED_RESOURCE_GROUP	5	0	0	0	0	0	0	0
OTHER_GROUPS	5	0	0	0	0	0	0	0

Directive Values

Group	Maximum Degree of Parallelism	Maximum Number of Active Sessions	Activation Queue Timeout (sec)	Maximum Undo Space (KB)	Maximum Estimated Execution Time (sec)	Max Idle Time (sec)	Max Idle Time if Blocking Another Session (sec)
HIGH_RESOURCE_GROUP	UNLIMITED	UNLIMITED	UNLIMITED	UNLIMITED	UNLIMITED	UNLIMITED	UNLIMITED
LOW_RESOURCE_GROUP	0	UNLIMITED	UNLIMITED	UNLIMITED	30	UNLIMITED	UNLIMITED
MED_RESOURCE_GROUP	2	UNLIMITED	UNLIMITED	UNLIMITED	120	UNLIMITED	UNLIMITED
OTHER_GROUPS	0	UNLIMITED	UNLIMITED	UNLIMITED	20	UNLIMITED	UNLIMITED

Consumer Group Switching

Group	Maximum Execution Time (sec)	Switch back to original group after call?	Action To Take	Use estimate?
HIGH_RESOURCE_GROUP	UNLIMITED	☐	Switch to Group LOW_GROUP	☑
LOW_RESOURCE_GROUP	UNLIMITED	☐	Cancel SQL	☑
MED_RESOURCE_GROUP	UNLIMITED	☐		☐
OTHER_GROUPS	UNLIMITED	☐		☐

Figure 8-26: Completed Resource Plan viewed in Enterprise Manager

Database Maintenance

The database maintenance page provides solutions in three major categories: high availability, data movement, and software deployments. Links are provided to backup and recovery links and Data Guard setup in the high availability category. The data movement capabilities managed through this page includes movement of data rows through import and export, movement of database files through database cloning and transportable tablespaces, and Streams. The last category, software deployments, provides access to collected configuration information.

Backups and High Availability

Backing up the database is a task that Oracle has simplified with succeeding database versions through the Recovery Manager (RMAN). Today, using Enterprise Manager as an interface, you can deploy an Oracle-suggested backup strategy or take a completely custom approach. Figure 8-27 illustrates these choices.

In out-of-the box approaches, you first select a backup destination. Setup of a recovery window for backup management and scheduling of recurring backups follows. Figure 8-28 illustrates the step-wise approach to setting up backups.

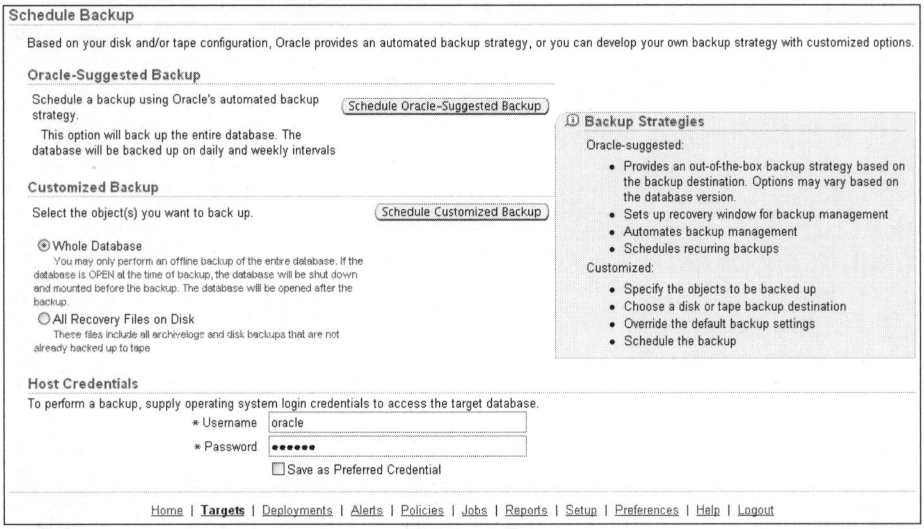

Figure 8-27: Enterprise Manager Schedule Backup choices

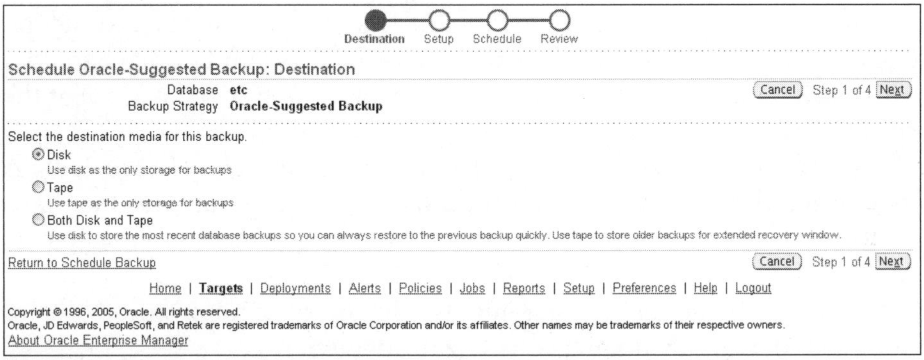

Figure 8-28: Setting destination in an Oracle-suggested backup

In custom backups, the DBA chooses the objects he or she wants backed up and the destination. Default backup settings can be overridden. The DBA also chooses a schedule for recurring custom backups.

A variety of disk and tape settings are possible as pictured in Figure 8-29. Backup and retention policies can be set, including whether to automatically back up the control file and server parameter file (SPFILE) and skip unchanged files that previously had a backup made.

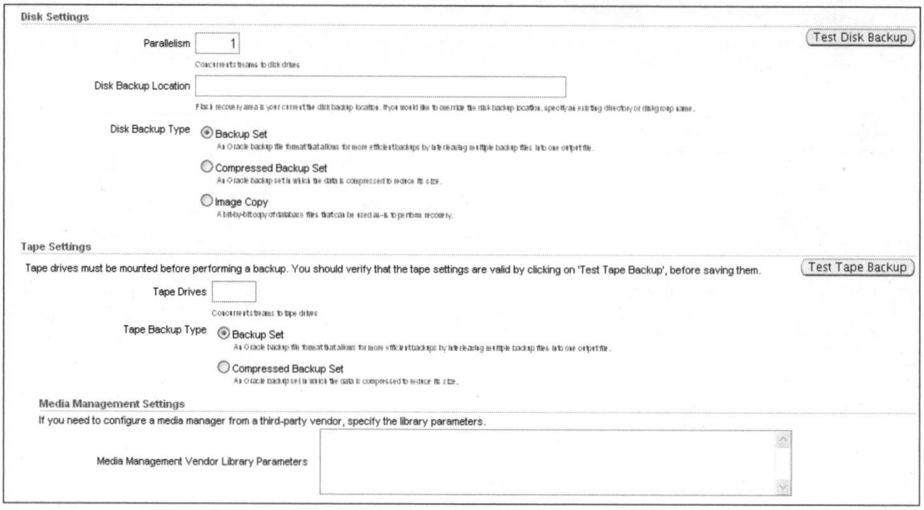

Figure 8-29: Backup settings in Enterprise Manager

Enterprise Manager also enables setup, managing, and monitoring of Oracle Data Guard, used in high availability and disaster recovery configurations. A Data Guard environment consists of a primary or production database with one or more standby databases. A distributed management framework called the Data Guard broker enables centralized control of the primary and standby databases.

Data Guard consistency is maintained through the use of redo logs. A physical standby database will have on-disk database structures that have an identical block structure to that in the primary database. A logical standby database will contain the same data and is updated for consistency through the use of SQL statements. The interface for building both of these types of standby databases is wizard-driven.

Data Movement Maintenance

Enterprise Manager provides interfaces to the database import and export, cloning, transportable tablespaces, and Streams setup and management. For example, exports can be designated for the entire database, specific schema, or tables from schema or tablespaces as illustrated in Figure 8-30. Imports and exports are used for moving both the definitions and the data contained within the selected database, schema, or tables.

Transportable tablespaces provide a means of moving entire tablespaces without going through the export/import process. The most important requirement is that table definitions are consistent at both the source and destination. As of Oracle Database 10g, any limitations caused by operating system characteristics have been removed, so transportable tablespaces can be moved between any two platforms. They are especially useful when exporting and importing data warehouse partitions, publishing structured data to CDs, copying multiple read-only versions of tablespaces, archiving historical data, and performing tablespace point-in-time recovery. Figure 8-31 illustrates the step-wise approach used in generating transportable tablespaces in Enterprise Manager.

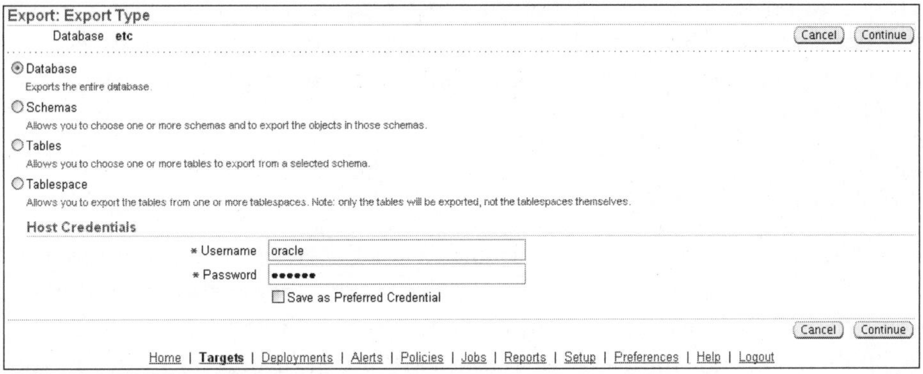

Figure 8-30: Setting export type in Enterprise Manager

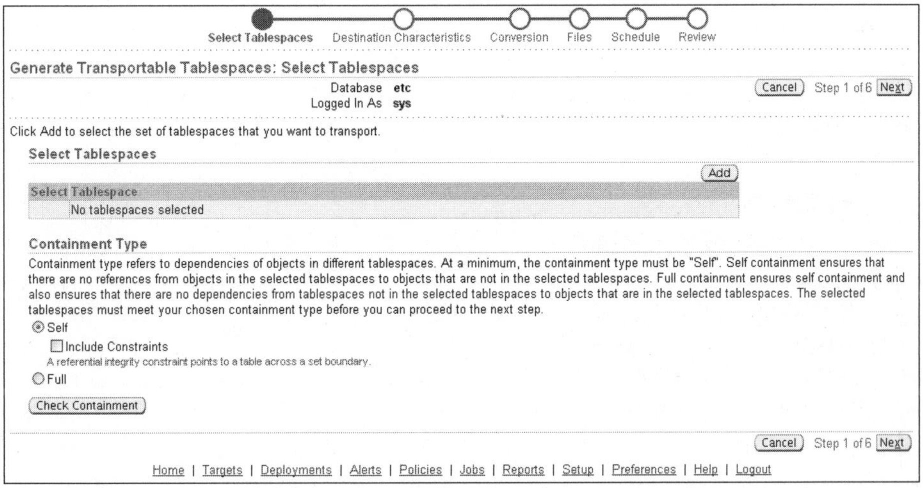

Figure 8-31: Generating transportable tablespaces in Enterprise Manager

Oracle's Streams is typically used to set up messaging between Oracle databases, although Streams can also link to non-Oracle queuing mechanisms by using bridges. Figure 8-32 illustrates the Enterprise Manager interface used to determine the queues available with a create button used to create new queues. Queues can be created as normal or exception. The two types of normal queues are the SYS.ANYDATA datatype to store messages of any type in memory and a queue table and the fixed datatype for storing fixed-type messages in the queue. Exception queues store messages that are not retrieved or processed.

Enterprise Manager features a Streams setup wizard that enables you to set up and replicate an entire database, specific schema, or tables between two databases. A Streams tablespace replication wizard leverages data pump and enables you to set up tablespace replication between two databases.

Software Deployment

The configuration management interface in Enterprise Manager enables viewing of various database configuration parameters. These parameters include instance information, initialization parameters, the system global area (SGA) settings, tablespaces, datafiles, control files, redo logs, rollback segments, high availability settings, and license details.

Figure 8-33 illustrates a typical interface.

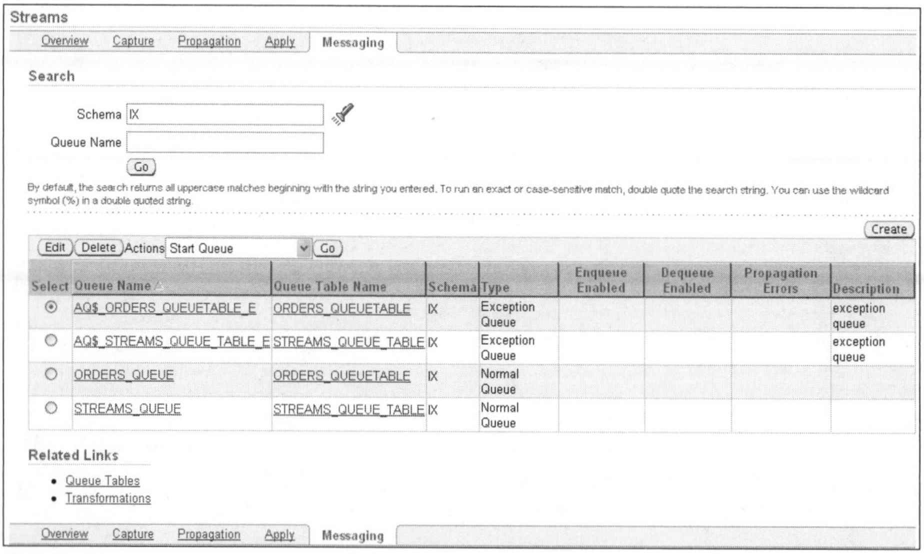

Figure 8-32: Streams viewed through Enterprise Manager

Figure 8-33: Collected Configuration information in Enterprise Manager

Database Topology

The characteristics of Grid computing and Oracle Real Applications Clusters (RAC) were described in Chapter 4. If you are managing a cluster of Oracle database instances using RAC, you will also see a Topology tab when managing your Oracle environment through Oracle Grid Control. Figure 8-34 illustrates a typical view showing a three-node cluster. Through this interface, you can quickly view status of the instances, the number of alerts, and view information on ASM instances, listeners, and interfaces.

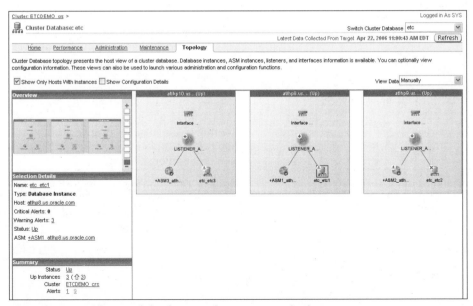

Figure 8-34: Grid Control database performance monitoring

As with other interfaces, you can launch administration and configuration functions provided you have the right privileges.

Management and Management Options

In this chapter, we described how to accomplish key management tasks for Oracle data warehouses using Oracle Enterprise Manager Grid Control. We also illustrated the interfaces used for monitoring performance, administering the database, and maintaining it. We noted how you might leverage some of the database options available for enabling better management and more secure deployment of the database, including the Partitioning Option, Advanced Security Option, and Label Security Option.

Some of the functionality we described in Enterprise Manager is packaged by Oracle in optional management add-on packs. Management packs available for Enterprise Manager or as standalone packs are described in Table 8-2.

Table 8-2: Optional Oracle Management Packs

MANAGEMENT PACK	DESCRIPTION
Database Change Management Pack	Used in reverse engineering database and schema definitions, capture and version baselines, copying database objects (including copies with data), and updating database object definitions.
Database Configuration Management Pack	Provides system inventory collection and reporting, Grid-wide configuration search, system configuration comparisons and history, critical patch advisor, and policy manager.
Database Diagnostics Pack	Includes automatic performance diagnostics leveraging, ADDM, the Automatic Workload Repository, monitoring templates, and advanced event notification/alerting.
Database Tuning Pack	Statistics, SQL profiling, access path, and SQL structure analyses are leveraged in the SQL Tuning Advisor, and includes SQL Access Advisor, and Object Reorganization Wizard.

Table 8-2 (continued)

MANAGEMENT PACK	DESCRIPTION
Application Server Configuration Management Pack	Provides asset and inventory management, incident and problem management, change and release management, policy management and compliance. Includes comparison analysis, change tracking, critical patch advisory, and policy management.
Application Server Diagnostics Pack	Provides user performance monitoring, page performance analysis, interactive transaction tracing and historical request performance diagnostics, and infrastructure component metrics correlation.
Provisioning Pack	Provides automated patching, critical patch facility, software image library, cloning, provisioning, instance to RAC conversion, and Enterprise Security Advisor.
Service Level Management Pack	Includes services dashboards, reports for service availability and performance, Web applications, and root cause analysis.

Optional software is also available from Oracle that enables monitoring of non-Oracle databases, middleware, networks devices, and storage. For example, plug-ins are available enabling monitoring of BEA Weblogic, IBM WebSphere, IBM DB2, Microsoft SQL Server, Microsoft BizTalk Server, Microsoft Commerce Server, Microsoft Internet Information Services, Microsoft Internet Security and Acceleration Server, Microsoft Active Directory, Microsoft .NET Framework, Check Point Firewall, Juniper Netscreen Firewall, NetApp Filers, and EMC Celera Network Attached Storage.

This concludes our introduction to managing the data warehouse. But, since a critical task in data warehouse management is performance monitoring and tuning, we will now take a more detailed look at this topic in Chapter 9.

Data Warehouse Performance Tuning and Monitoring

Let the celebration begin — your team has delivered superior functionality that will provide your organization with needed insight into business operations despite shifting requirements. You likely encountered challenges such as lack of stewardship and suspect data quality. But, your next challenge is that what appeared to be a successful implementation is now in jeopardy as variability in performance and unpredictable service levels begin to overshadow your success. This is not uncommon where a data warehouse solution provides new or enhanced capabilities.

One of the highest risk factors to the long-term success of a data warehouse initiative is performance. Yet the characterization of performance is as much about managing its perception as it is in solving the complexities of hardware, software, and varying business workloads. Business users expect results of queries to return in a predictable and consistent manner when compared with previous interactions and solutions. Although an abundance of features and functions in hardware and software give the developer many design choices that can ensure consistent performance, the key to ensuring the highest levels of business user satisfaction is a comprehensive approach for performance tuning and monitoring.

In this chapter, we will discuss a top-down approach to performance tuning and highlight the key areas for monitoring your data warehouse. In addition, we will use a previously discussed scenario to highlight best practice approaches for tuning and monitoring an Oracle data warehouse using Oracle Enterprise Manager.

Understanding Performance Challenges

Performance challenges are often expressed in complaints from the business-user community when response time fails to meet their expectations. Often, these complaints are centered on variability in response caused by temporary constraints on existing resources or changes in access patterns as business users initiate more complex and resource-intensive queries. Regardless of the cause, the perception that the solution is not performing to expectations can severely damage its viability to the business.

Performance tuning and monitoring are often considered post-production support activities and are not integral to full life-cycle development activities. Although virtually all projects ensure that the functionality needs of the business are captured and properly established, less time is typically spent ensuring that critical business functionality performs to user levels of satisfaction. The cost of this oversight can be significant especially when simple tuning cannot correct the problem.

Figure 9-1 illustrates the increasing complexity associated with deferring performance-related tasks until the initiative is deployed to business users. As the project nears the end of the development cycle, the cost of remediation increases significantly since application code is based on the structural designs. As these applications are moved into production, the cost of remediation can increase as much as four-fold given the potential need to remedy application, database, and infrastructure components. This cost does not include potential down time associated with providing solution remedies.

The risks associated with performance can only be reconciled with a proper approach spanning the solution's life cycle. To better understand how to reconcile performance challenges, we will start by determining the most critical roles and responsibilities for the identification, diagnosis, and remediation.

Who Is Responsible?

It is most often the responsibility of the database administrator (DBA) or technical team to properly identify, analyze, and remediate the impact associated with a performance-related issue. Such efforts are sometimes initiated with little or no information, making the task difficult and time consuming and causing unnecessary delays in performance reconciliation.

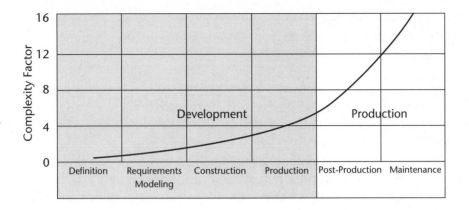

Figure 9-1: Complexity of change

A common mistake, when a perceived performance challenge is reported, is querying the database with the goal of proving that poor performance is not an infrastructure-related issue but is due to improper use of the application. This reactionary approach typically occurs during post-production incidents where support roles and responsibilities have not been formally established. Since few organizations designate a single individual to be solely responsible for performance-related problems, it is important to establish a full life-cycle support infrastructure that can properly identify, analyze, and route performance incidents to the proper team for reconciliation. In an ideal scenario, the responsibility for ensuring performance meets business user expectations is a shared responsibility between a business liaison representing the interests of the application business community and the technical administrative staff.

In our sample support process (illustrated in Figure 9-2), the business community identifies a performance anomaly and contacts the help desk. The help desk captures important information about the incident and generates a support ticket. The business liaison familiar with the solution is contacted to analyze the incident and provides additional information that can be used to determine the root cause of the problem. Some of the key information the business liaison gathers includes:

- What activity was being performed when performance levels degraded beyond current expectations?

- Is the current activity a standard business process, a new query, or an ad hoc query for discovery purposes?

- What are the anticipated data volumes returned from this query?
- At what time of day did the event occur and how often is the query initiated?
- Is the event reproducible?

As further information is gathered, the business liaison engages key members of the technical staff to further diagnose and remediate the incident. To ensure long-term success of the business intelligence solution as it changes to meet the demands of the business, it is necessary to capture all performance incidents and their remediation solutions so they can be used for future diagnostic activities. Although this approach may be viewed as simplistic, where organizations have not integrated their business intelligence solutions into their standard support processes, frustration occurs within the user communities.

Regardless of the process, it is important that the business liaison and support analyst begin the diagnostic process immediately, allowing technical support staff to begin the process of analysis to enable remediation. In the next section, we identify some of the most common causes of poor performance and provide insight into their common characteristics.

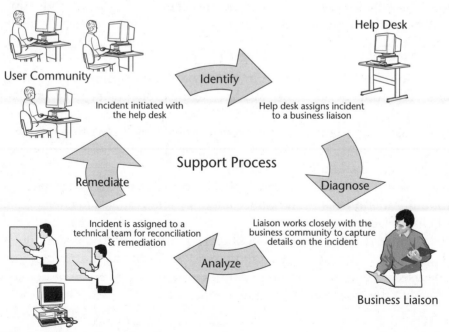

Figure 9-2: Sample support process

Causes of Poor Performance

Poor performance can have a variety of causes such as the wrong combination of hardware, software, and storage for an increasing workload or a poor data model design that doesn't meet the changing requirements of the business. Although the best intentions of architects, administrators, and designers to eliminate performance bottlenecks can be based on predicted usage patterns, it is not uncommon for a new business intelligence initiative to experience performance challenges as business users become familiar with new ways of using the solution.

The interactions of these contributing factors combined with the complexities of an open systems environment often make it difficult to identify and remediate performance challenges. In the following sections, we will highlight the most common causes of poor performance to assist in the diagnostic process.

Educating the Business

New users of business intelligence solutions can have a detrimental impact on the overall performance of the solution and may not leverage it properly. Although excited about the prospect of analyzing critical business data in a timely manner, business users may have a limited understanding of the overall capabilities provided by the solution. To ensure that expectations can be fully realized, a comprehensive training plan can help ensure that these users gain a full understanding and appreciation of the capabilities that the new solution can provide. This training must extend beyond business intelligence tools and applications capabilities to also include representation of business processes and a detailed explanation of the data.

Business Processes

Most business intelligence solutions are aligned to one or more business processes to provide insight into areas of the business such as sales and inventory. Although most business users are familiar with manual processes in their daily tasks, they may not fully understand the scope of information that is available by a reporting and analysis solution. In addition, optimization of business processes and new interfaces can introduce user challenges that impact the overall performance and efficiency of the solution, especially during early deployment.

The project team should use change management techniques to ensure a seamless transition from existing business processes and solutions maps for enhanced processes. Although tools and interface training for business users is important, training on how to gather the proper information and avoid needless generation of less useful queries and reports can also be useful. In addition to saving valuable time, performance of the system can be improved and earlier success can be achieved.

Data

Unfortunately, it is common when deploying solutions to business users to provide little or no explanation about the data provided for analysis. Although most application and reporting tools hide the complexities of physical data representations by providing a layer of abstraction, if only a small percentage of users fully understand the granularity, dimensionality, and join paths, poorly formulated queries become common. Data models can provide a comprehensive view of data, but are more difficult to understand and are best suited for developers and power users.

Many organizations address this challenge by constructing a centralized metadata repository that is used to catalog all corporate data. Although this approach is successful in some larger organizations, these initiatives are difficult to deploy and costly to maintain. The most common scenarios when users lack the necessary understanding of data include ad hoc queries using the wrong data structures, excessive summarization activities, and improperly joined data based on common naming or data characteristics. Although the Oracle optimizer possesses many features to reconcile these challenges, excessive scanning of data can adversely impact the overall performance of the environment.

Hardware

One possible contributor to poor performance can be a poorly designed hardware infrastructure. There are many underlying components that determine hardware performance, including processing capacity, memory, and networking and storage systems. Unlike many other databases, Oracle can be deployed on a wide variety of platforms ranging from large SMP servers to clusters of small lower-priced servers. Although this flexibility and choice has its advantages, it can lead to configuration complexity especially where the administrative staff has limited experience with multiple vendor offerings. A discussion of some of the most common hardware performance challenges follows.

Processing Capacity

A common contributing factor to poor hardware performance is inadequate processing capacity. The number of processors and their speed determines the processing capacity. Business intelligence solutions can be processing intensive and often require significantly more processing capacity when compared to online transaction processing (OLTP) applications. Processing capacity symptoms are relatively easy to diagnose using operating system utilities that measure CPU utilization.

Processing capacity can become an issue where older servers that use slower processors are deployed. In an environment utilizing newer servers, processing capacity challenges are usually due to under-configuration of the server. Although processing capacity challenges affecting business intelligence solution performance can increase over time as the number of users increase and the queries become more sophisticated, expandable configurations can remediate this.

Memory

Constrained memory can significantly impact performance in data warehousing solutions. This most commonly occurs in shared environments where too many business intelligence applications are hosted on a single server and the allocation of memory is restricted. Although the likelihood of memory configurations affecting your business intelligence solution performance typically is environment specific, the effort to remediate most configurations is relatively straightforward provided the server platform memory can be expanded.

Network Infrastructure

A lesser contributing factor impacting the performance of a data warehousing solution is the network infrastructure bandwidth. With the advent of desktop computing placing hundreds to thousands of devices on the desktop, most organizations have enhanced their networking infrastructures to support this environment and have excess capacity to support future growth. However, some global organizations still contend with restricted bandwidth to remote locations where the infrastructure may be limited or cost prohibitive.

Proper networking strategies should include filtering of traffic such that bulk transfers and file movements are isolated from active user communities. In clustered configurations, it is necessary to isolate unwanted traffic from database servers and to dedicate network segments to handle inter-node communications and provide redundancy for highly available solutions.

Storage Infrastructure

One of the most challenging hardware components to design for optimal performance is the storage infrastructure. Storage solutions available today range from dedicated storage to network-attached solutions capable of achieving virtually any price/performance profile. Although such flexibility can provide an effective solution that can span the entire enterprise, configurations designed for transactional systems can yield unacceptable performance for business intelligence solutions.

Many business intelligence environments are I/O intensive, especially where large amount of data is retrieved, and require more channels and bandwidth to storage devices. Such solutions can benefit from many smaller and faster devices. The storage guidelines for business intelligence solutions are often drastically different from transactional counterparts.

Although the likelihood of storage configurations affecting your business intelligence solution performance is noteworthy, the effort required to remediate is high and has a significant cost and time impact. The performance impact of improperly configured storage system can severely limit the value of the solution to the business users.

Software

Software configuration also impacts performance. The composition of business intelligence solutions can be complex especially in environments where specialized best-of-breed software tools are utilized. To fully understand the overall impact of software configurations on a business intelligence solution, we segregate software into two distinct categories: database, and the business intelligence tools and applications.

Database

The flexibility and robustness of the Oracle database is one reason why it is so popular for data warehousing solutions. Oracle introduced dozens of features over several versions specifically designed for data warehousing performance and scalability. Complexities can arise in determining when most appropriately to leverage these features. The most common challenges related to performance include:

- **Database configurations for business intelligence** — A business intelligence environment is configured quite differently for handling transactions, recoverability, and parallel execution when compared to an OLTP configuration. Although such configuration differences are well documented, they are sometimes overlooked in organizations that have never deployed data warehouses. The likelihood of improper database configurations affecting your business intelligence solution performance are most influenced by the experience of the administrative staff, and the effort to remediate can often be performed transparently with a limited amount of effort.

- **Poor optimization execution plans** — There are several causes of poor execution plans that can have a detrimental impact on performance, including poorly written SQL statements by inexperienced users or complex data models. Other causes of poor plans include missing or stale statistics causing the cost-based optimizer to have little insight in generating an optimal plan or embedded hints driving the wrong optimization behavior. These problems were more frequent in Oracle versions prior to Database 10g. Since the likelihood that poorly written SQL will impact performance of your business intelligence solution is fairly common, you should place more emphasis on a structured approach for identification and timely remediation.

▪ **Application of features** — With dozens of features specifically designed for the optimal business intelligence performance, most data warehousing challenges can be efficiently solved by Oracle. As Oracle introduces new features with new database versions, you should evaluate taking advantage of newer features such as composite partitioning variations and embedded high performance ETL as you upgrade. Although features alone will not solve all performance challenges, organizations that deploy new features often have better success in managing performance and scalability challenges with lower remediation efforts.

▪ **Adjusting database parameters** — In older versions of Oracle, one of the first steps in analyzing performance challenges was to review the database configuration parameters found in the `init.ora` configuration file. As more default and dynamic settings for data warehousing were introduced in Oracle 9*i* and newer releases, the overall impact of this exercise has been significantly reduced. Of course, proper parameter configuration does have a positive impact on performance. With the recent advances and embedded database advisors, the level of effort to remediate parameter configurations is minimal today.

▪ **Storage management** — Improper allocation of storage within the Oracle database can have a negative impact on the performance and availability of the data warehouse solution. Quite often, contention is discovered at the data block level, directly correlated to Oracle's ability to find and allocate available storage, and requires intervention by the DBA. Although storage management remains a resource-intensive activity among administrators, a significant number of database features have been introduced that can alleviate management and performance challenges associated with storage allocation.

▪ **Sizing system global area (SGA) memory** — Sizing memory within the SGA for business intelligence solutions was historically assigned to the most senior administrator who was responsible for achieving optimal configuration for scalability and performance. Sizing the SGA too small would have a constraining effect limiting the throughput of the environment. Sizing the SGA too large wasted valuable system resources and introduced unnecessary overhead to the management of the database. With the advent of Oracle 9*i* and further improvement in more recent database releases, much of this effort became automated through memory advisors found in *Oracle Enterprise Manager* and configuration solutions like automatic memory management that will dynamically allocate memory to the Oracle memory caches.

■ **Variability in response** — One of the most frustrating events business users encounter is fluctuating performance for queries. Such unusual situations can be difficult to reproduce and analyze so frequently such variability remains unresolved. The causes of variability can range from capacity constraints within the infrastructure to poorly designed queries that fail to generate an optimal execution plan. Regardless of the underlying cause, variability in performance has a psychological impact on business users' confidence in the solution. The likelihood that some variation in response times will impact your business intelligence solution during its deployment is high but the key to its timely remediation is identifying the key elements of contention. We will discuss in detail successful approaches to performance tuning in later sections.

■ **More data yields slower performance** — Business intelligence solutions often perform well at the time of deployment but as the volume of data increases over time, the performance of the solution can degrade. Usually, this can be traced to a lack of performance and scalability testing prior to deployment, and is often associated to improper partitioning of data or missing indexes. Although any business intelligence solution can suffer from the symptoms caused by increasing data volumes, it is important to have a defined monitoring plan and remediation solution to address this challenge.

Business Intelligence Tools and Application Software

A most important aspect of a business intelligence solution for a business user is the business intelligence tool or application software. This software is the window into the data and provides not only visualization capabilities, but also the ability to explore information without the need to understand or write complex SQL. Although this capability enhances overall productivity and enables users to become proficient much faster, all business intelligence tools and applications are not created equal.

In some organizations, custom applications are developed that address specific business capabilities that cannot be delivered through commercial software. These applications are often targeted toward a select group of users and often lack the flexibility, scalability, and performance necessary to support large user communities. For such applications, performance challenges are secondary to the functionality delivered.

Most organizations choose instead to purchase commercial business intelligence tools and applications that provide a wider range of functionality. The most popular commercial reporting tools provide extensions enabling them to leverage specific features found in the Oracle database. These extensions provide enhanced capabilities and typically increase overall performance by pushing complex calculations and grouping and sorting operations to the database tier. However, such tools sometimes generate complex, sub-optimal SQL that falls short of performance expectations. This is one of the most difficult challenges for administrators where the manual optimization of generated code is not possible without modifications to the underlying database design. Solutions to these performance challenges are never easy to find and can cause business users to accept sluggish performance or endure costly rework of designs.

Application/Database Design

One of the most common causes of poor performance is poor application or database design. Such designs should provide optimal storage and maintainability and access to the underlying data in the most flexible and highly performing manner. To achieve these design goals, the architect and administrator leverage modeling approaches such as star schema and hybrid designs and utilize data warehousing features such as bitmap indexes, partitioning, and materialized views.

Of course, there are circumstances where the current design might not be aligned to meet business needs, causing a significant negative impact on performance. Origins of mismatched database designs are well known and are caused by changes in requirements over time, inadequate design validation, insufficient performance testing, or simply a lack of understanding of the underlying business needs. Poor designs can jeopardize a business intelligence solution by limiting solution adoption and lead to full abandonment and searching for alternative solutions. Although many business intelligence solutions have limited performance caused by a mismatch in database design, experienced architects and designers are commonly called on to correct such designs.

Figure 9-3 highlights the performance challenges discussed previously, the underlying symptoms, the likelihood of occurrence and the anticipated effort to remediate. In the next section, we discuss best practice approaches to effectively remediate the most common data warehouse performance challenges.

Challenge	Symptoms	Probability / Likelihood of Occurrence	Effort to Remediate
Training	• User inability to access necessary data • Slow adoption of new functionality • Slow acceptance of new processes • Reverting to old solutions	High	Low
Hardware: Processing Capacity	• Older, slower processors (32bit vs. 64 bit) • Shared environments • Under configured processing capacity	Increase over time	Configuration dependent
Hardware: Memory	• Shared environments • Under configured environments	Environment dependent	Low
Hardware: Network	• Slow access across multiple applications • Slow access to / from remote locations • Global applications & solutions	Environment dependent	Environment dependent
Hardware: Storage	• Disk "hotspots" • High waits on I/O • Write penalties	Environment dependent & configuration	High
Software: RDBMS	• Improper database configuration • Poor optimizations plans & SQL • Application of database features • Variability in response time	Medium to High	Varies
Software: Application	• Integration challenges • Poorly designed for scalability & performance	Medium	Capabilities often limited
Application Design	• Designs not optimized to meet user needs • Flexibility at the cost of scalability & performance	Varies on Scope	High

Figure 9-3: Summary of performance challenges

Successful Approaches to Performance Tuning

Selecting an approach for monitoring and tuning is critical to ensuring performance of your data warehouse meets anticipated service levels. In addition, when performance challenges are discovered, it is important to have a defined process to identify, analyze, and remediate. The cost of remediation may become prohibitively expensive once the solution is deployed to a wider user community. To reduce the overall risk of poor performance, focus on solving performance challenges during the design and testing cycles to ensure they are not present in production.

The following checklist in Figure 9-4 includes frequently suggested configurations and best practices that can be utilized to reduce your exposure to performance challenges. Although this checklist is based on general guidelines, it can be used as a rule of thumb to validate your configuration. Creating final configurations should be a joint activity performed by your administrator and hardware platform provider.

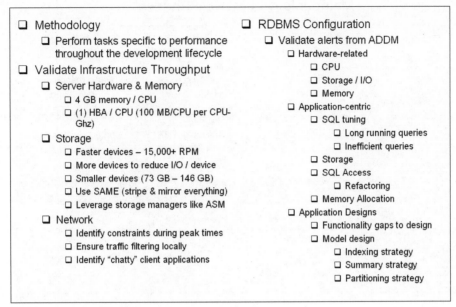

Figure 9-4: Checklist — best practices approach

In the next section, we outline the critical tasks that should be included in your methodology to ensure that performance challenges can be identified and remediated prior to deployment.

Critical Tasks for Performance Tuning Lifecycle

The best approach to avoid performance challenges is to thoroughly understand business requirements and fundamental design principles for data warehousing. Most project teams use some type of development methodology to ensure their project is delivered to a specific engineering approach as constrained by schedule and cost. In Chapter 10, we discuss how a strong methodology enables your organization to scope and effectively deliver business intelligence solutions.

There are many methodology tasks that have correlation to the performance delivered by your business intelligence project. In each phase of the methodology, the associated tasks are designed to ensure the highest levels of performance, capacity, and scale. These are illustrated in Figure 9-5.

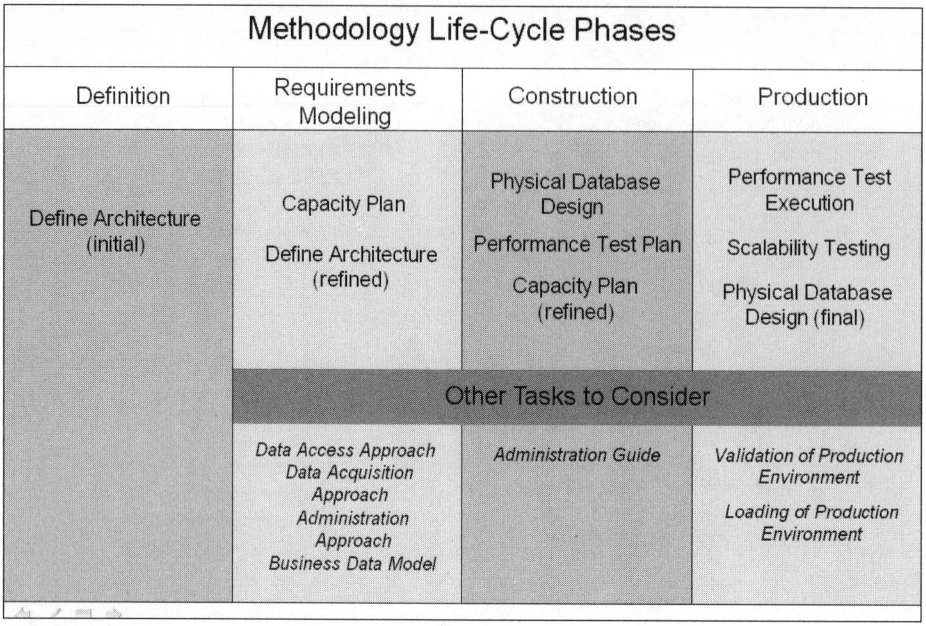

Methodology Life-Cycle Phases			
Definition	Requirements Modeling	Construction	Production
Define Architecture (initial)	Capacity Plan Define Architecture (refined)	Physical Database Design Performance Test Plan Capacity Plan (refined)	Performance Test Execution Scalability Testing Physical Database Design (final)
	Other Tasks to Consider		
	Data Access Approach Data Acquisition Approach Administration Approach Business Data Model	Administration Guide	Validation of Production Environment Loading of Production Environment

Figure 9-5: High-impact performance-related tasks

Definition Phase

The Definition phase commences solution discovery by reviewing business and system objectives while confirming existing documentation and prioritizing the high-level business requirements for the solution. Although there is only one task associated with performance and scalability in this phase, this task is critical in establishing a foundation that will support your data warehouse solution in the future. The following section describes the definition phase task that provides the greatest impact.

Task: Define Architecture

The *Define Architecture* task begins the formulation of the technical design based on initial business requirements. The technical components it addresses include:

- Integration of new initiatives into existing solutions.
- Technical architecture comprised of server, software, and network components.
- Systems management that addresses service levels, high availability, and data archiving strategies.
- Data warehouse management that supports indexing, partitioning, and data summary strategies.

Requirements Modeling Phase

The Requirements Modeling phase begins solution transition from high-level requirements gathered during the definition phase to sufficient detail to ensure that business processes and requirements are met. During this phase, several tasks are established and refined that formulates the foundation for performance and scalability. The following sections describe the Requirements Modeling phase tasks that provide the greatest impact.

Task: Capacity Plan

The *Capacity Plan* task provides an initial pass at defining infrastructure capacities based on current requirements and anticipated future growth. The components the capacity plan addresses include:

- Memory capacity and processor speed and performance.
- Storage infrastructure, including capacity, speed, and performance.
- Network bandwidth and topology.
- Platform configuration, including single node and clustered solutions.

Task: Define Architecture – (Refined)

The *Define Architecture* task is refined during the requirements modeling phase to capture additional details on the technical, data, and application architecture layers. In addition, system management requirements for service levels and availability are formulized to determine the size and scale of hardware that is included as input to the capacity plan.

Task: Others to Consider

There are several other tasks that are addressed during the Requirements Modeling phase. These tasks include *Data Access Approach, Data Acquisition Approach, Administration Approach,* and *Business Data Model.* Although these tasks are not directly related to the performance of your data warehouse, it is helpful to understand the strategies and approach for each to ensure that they will compliment performance guidelines. We introduced earlier in this chapter and in previous chapters the possible influence of data access, data acquisition (bulk transfers), administration, and the data model on performance.

Construction Phase

The Construction phase includes the final design and building of all modules that comprise the data warehouse initiative. During this phase, designs are validated to ensure they meet standards and best practices that will enable them to perform and scale to meet user expectations. The following sections describe the Construction phase tasks that provide the greatest impact on performance.

Task: Physical Database Design

The *Physical Database Design* task provides the translation of the logical database design into physical design constructs for the Oracle database. During the development of this task, key tasks such as modeling, partitioning, and indexing approaches are applied to provide both flexibility and better performance. In addition, the proposed physical design is mapped to the proposed infrastructure to ensure that proposed hardware platforms, software, and storage will meet the specified requirements. When complete, the physical database design will be released to developers to enable construction of data access and acquisition tasks.

Task: Performance Test Plan

The *Performance Test Plan* task provides the planning and test sequencing for performance testing. These tests are comprised of use-cases that represent the most critical business processes and data queries based on functional needs generated by business users. The testing spans both functional and infrastructure components to ensure that all modules work together successfully. Performance criteria are assigned to each use case test to ensure it meets the proposed service levels.

Task: Capacity Plan – (Refined)

The *Capacity Plan* task is refined during the construction phase to support current and near-term infrastructure capacity needs. At the completion of this task, final production configurations are established and released to your platform vendors for final validation.

Task: Others to Consider

Another task to consider during the construction phase is inclusion of performance-related content in an *Administration Guide*. The *Administration Guide* contains the final set of processes and procedures for administering, managing, and monitoring the target environment. This guide is designed for DBAs and reflects the key metrics established for service levels and performance. In addition, the *Administration Guide* confirms the management platform that will be used for monitoring and diagnostic activities.

Production Phase

The Production phase is the culmination of the project when the solution is installed and transitioned to production. During this transition period, the administration and management of the solution are transitioned to the post-production support team. The following sections cover the Production phase tasks that provide the greatest impact.

Task: Performance Test Execution

The *Performance Test* tasks are completed during the production phase and the results are assessed to determine if they meet the functionality and performance requirements. During this initiative, a pre-production validation is performed to ensure that the expected performance metrics are achieved. The components addressed in the performance test include:

- Test iterations by use case
- Analysis of test result by use case and performance metric
- Pre-production validation and assessment
- Index profiles validation
- Summary management and query-rewrite validation
- Scale testing use cases confirmation
- Validation against success criteria

Task: Scalability Testing

The *Scalability Testing* task is designed to execute specific use case tests under increased data volumes and resource loads to characterize the performance. Often these use-cases are the most critical to a data acquisition process or business process where performance and throughput are critical. Some of the key aspects of scale testing include:

- Data volume test against a production and future data volume
- Performance of use case queries at varying degrees of parallelization
- Analysis of execution plans to ensure the most efficient paths
- Exploration of materialized views for increased performance
- Validation against acceptance criteria
- Regression testing where appropriate

Task: Physical Database Design – (Final)

The *Physical Database Design* task is finalized during the production phase and deployed to the production environment for initial data loading. Final modifications and enhancements are made based on feedback from developers and the initial results of performance testing. During this task, only design enhancements that are considered necessary to meet performance and service-level requirements are enhanced.

Task: Others to Consider

The additional tasks during the production phase that impact performance include the *Validation of Production Environment*, results from the *Loading of the Production Environment* and review of *Pre-production Testing Results*. It is important that the administrators and architects understand the initial capabilities of the solution prior to its full deployment into production to ensure it meets both functional and operational needs.

Addressing performance and scalability during the development lifecycle has a significant positive impact on overall performance and reduces production performance complaints. This is especially true when design enhancements are made due to performance challenges. Organizations that invest in the remediation of potential performance challenges prior to production experience fewer help desk incidents and higher user satisfaction and reduce the overall cost of ownership and maintenance.

Hardware Configuration

With continued advances in processor design and speed, performance profiles double in as little as every two to three years providing organizations with cost-effective solutions that alleviate processing constraints. Although some organizations attempt to extend the life of existing servers, many others find that replacing existing servers with faster and less expensive alternatives provide improvements needed to overcome performance challenges. This emerging trend has changed the way many IT organizations view their investments in server hardware, allowing them to purchase capacity on demand with hardware refreshes every couple of years.

Validate Theoretical Throughput

One of the most effective methods to confirm that an existing hardware configuration will scale appropriately is to ensure that the theoretical performance throughput ratios between processor speeds, memory, and I/O subsystems are adequate. All too often, platform performance is constrained by an imbalance restricting throughput and causing inconsistent performance and limited scalability. The configuration in Figure 9-6 provides a sample configuration with the theoretical throughput of each subsystem.

To compute the theoretical throughput capacities, we will review each subsystem in the sample configuration:

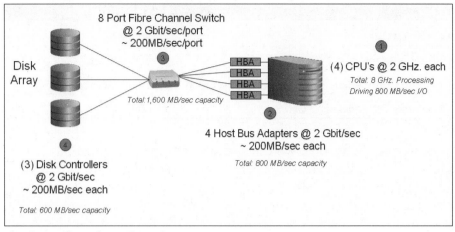

Figure 9-6: Sample configuration

1. The server configuration is comprised of a single node machine with four CPUs running at a speed of two gigahertz each. Based on our rule of thumb metrics, we know that each CPU can drive 200 MB of data per second for each gigahertz of processing power. This enables our configuration to drive 800 MB of data per second.

   ■ The server is comprised of four host bus adapters that have a throughput capacity of two gigabits per second that translates into approximately 200 MB per second per adapter. The total capacity of four host bus adapters (HBAs) is 800 MB of data throughput per second.

   ■ A fibre channel switch provides connectivity between the servers' HBAs and the disk array storage system. In our example, we are utilizing a single eight-port switch that has a throughput capacity of two gigabits per second per port. The total capacity of the eight-port fiber channel switch is 1,600 MB of data throughput per second.

2. The disk array is supported by three disk controllers rated at two gigabits per second throughput that translates into approximately 200 MB per second per controller. The total throughput capacity of the three controllers is 600 MB of data per second.

Now that we have determined the theoretical capabilities of our system, we need to analyze the capacities to determine where configuration constraints can occur:

ITEM	THROUGHPUT
4 CPUs at 2 GHz	800 MB/sec
4 Host Bus Adapters at 2 Gbit/sec	800 MB/sec
1 eight port Fibre Channel Switch at 2 Gbit/sec/port	1,600 MB/sec
3 Disk Array Controllers at 2 Gbit/sec	600 MB/sec

In analyzing the results, we can identify that there is a theoretical constraint caused by the disk array controllers. These controllers have a maximum capacity of 600 MB per second throughput whereas all other components provide a minimum of 800 MB per second throughput. This tells us that if a bottleneck occurs in our system, the likely candidates are the disk array controllers. To alleviate this constraint, additional disk array controllers should be considered.

Additional Infrastructure to Validate

There are other infrastructure components that should be validated to ensure that the throughout of the system is optimal, including network capacity, server memory, and the storage subsystem.

Network capacity can impact performance especially in environments that have undergone recent expansion or are part of aging infrastructures. Measuring network capacity and performance can help determine if there are constraints that impact the overall performance of the infrastructure. Consult your administrator or network engineer for additional assistance in determining if your network is suitable for the planned tools and capacities.

Server Memory

Server memory can become a limiting factor to server performance, especially where multiple solutions reside on the same server. While Oracle Database 10*g* and more recent releases of the database provide dynamic memory allocation and tuning, it is important that there is sufficient resource available to support the environment.

In most configurations, four gigabytes of memory per CPU is sufficient for most data warehousing solutions. When combined with the Oracle OLAP or Data Mining options, the desired configuration might need significantly more memory to operate efficiently. Oracle Enterprise Manager is often leveraged for monitoring and diagnostics when managing memory.

Storage Subsystem

The storage subsystem can have a significant impact on performance if improperly sized and configured. With the cost of storage steadily declining, high performance storage devices have become cost effective, allowing more organizations to benefit from their increased performance. In addition, these devices have increased in density, providing three to five times more storage compared to devices historically.

When selecting storage devices to support a data warehouse initiative, it is important to select the devices with the fastest spindle speed. Devices with slower rotational speeds often become a constraint since the storage subsystem must then wait for information to be fetched from the device. Although it's tempting to use very high-density storage devices, bottlenecks can occur when a higher number of requests are queued per device and spindles are inadequate to handle the workload.

Another important factor in reducing I/O device contention is to ensure that data is spread across as many devices as possible. Most operating systems provide volume manager software that can stripe data across multiple devices. The Oracle database, since Database 10*g*, provides a comprehensive solution to manage storage through *Automatic Storage Management* (ASM). ASM is a high performance virtual storage management solution that significantly reduces and eliminates most manual management activities while optimizing availability and performance. Organizations that have adopted ASM as part of their storage management strategy have seen a significant reduction in storage management and storage-related performance challenges. For more information on Automatic Storage Management, see Chapter 8, and also consult the *Oracle Database Concepts* guide.

The flexibility and choice of hardware and infrastructure components for an Oracle environment can enable your data warehouse solution to perform and scale to higher levels at lower cost. Although capacity constraints can limit throughput and performance, understanding the interactions between these components can reduce incidents that impact performance. In later sections, we provide examples of how to monitor hardware using *Oracle Enterprise Manager* and reference other operating system utilities. In the next section, we discuss configuring software, specifically the Oracle database for data warehousing.

Software Configuration

Configuring the Oracle database for a data warehouse solution is significantly different from online transaction processing systems. A data warehouse solution is often comprised of mixed workloads with long-running transactions that are I/O intensive. There are several added features in recent Oracle versions to consider when configuring Oracle for a data warehouse solution to ensure the highest levels of performance and ease of management. Many of these features were introduced as of Oracle Database 10*g*.

The following sections highlight these key features and provide insight into how they are most successfully utilized.

Instance Configuration

The configuration of the Oracle database instance for data warehousing has undergone significant enhancements since Oracle8*i*. Previously, there were dozens of initialization parameters that were required to efficiently support a data warehouse environment. DBAs were challenged with the complexities of enabling parameters and ensuring that a relationship between multiple parameters was established.

In today's Oracle database versions, there are many fewer parameters that need to be altered from their default values for data warehousing. In upgrades from previous database releases, it is advised that you remove any antiquated settings and reset parameters to their system default values. The following table highlights the most notable parameters that are configured specifically for data warehousing as of Oracle Database 10*g*.

PARAMETER	PURPOSE
PROCESSES	Establishes the maximum number of processes that can be initiated by the instance. This value should be established based on the number of users and degree of parallelism.
COMPATIBLE	Maps to the database release version to enable the latest features. Should reflect the latest RDBMS version to enable the most current features unless there are unique backward compatibility requirements.
SGA_TARGET	Specifies the total size of SGA components including buffer cache, large pool, java pool, and shared pool. The memory advisory framework provides recommendations on properly sizing the SGA_TARGET and supporting components.
STAR_TRANSFORMATION_ ENABLED	Enables the optimizer to estimate the cost of performing star transformation that joins bitmap indexes to fact tables. For star-schema designs, this capability can significantly increase performance while reducing overall I/O.
QUERY_REWRITE_ ENABLED	Query rewrite enables the optimizer to leverage higher-level summary structures or materialized views to optimize query performance transparently to the business user.

PARAMETER	PURPOSE
PARALLEL_MAX_SERVERS	Establishes a resource limit of processes that can be allocated to parallel operations.
DB_BLOCK_SIZE	The database block size determines the amount of data that can be stored in a logical data block. While operating system specific, a larger block size of 8K or greater is beneficial for data warehouse operations.
DB_FILE_MULTI_READ_COUNT	A dynamic parameter that can be used to increase the number of blocks read during a fetch operation, reducing I/O. This is especially useful when full table scans are performed.

When sizing several of these parameters, it will be necessary to understand environmental factors such as the number of concurrent users and the anticipated workload. Although some of these parameters may need adjustments over time as the workload in your environment changes, it is important to note that only a small portion of tuning efforts should be spent on tuning initialization parameters in current versions of Oracle. The *Enterprise Manager* advisory framework can be utilized for fine-tuning many of these parameters.

Automatic Workload Repository

One of the greatest challenges faced by DBAs is gaining an understanding of current and previous workloads that induced a suspected performance challenge. A significant amount of time can be spent in collecting and reviewing historical infrastructure metrics and interviewing users to determine the types of queries that were executed when a change in performance was detected. This triage activity is often time consuming while providing inconclusive evidence as to the root cause of the degradation in performance.

Greatly improving this process as of Oracle Database 10*g* is the *Automatic Workload Repository* or AWR. AWR is an internal database repository used in collecting and maintaining real-time and historical performance statistics and leveraged in database problem detection and self-tuning operations. At periodic intervals that can be set by the DBA, the database workload manager takes a snapshot of vital system statistics and stores this information in the repository. This information is used to determine when automated maintenance tasks such as optimizer statistics refresh is required and schedules these activities during a pre-defined maintenance period.

Automatic Database Diagnostic Monitor

Upon completion of statistics gathering, the *Automatic Database Diagnostic Monitor* (ADDM) executes and reviews statistics to identify the highest resource consumers and determine proactive recommendations to reduce their consumption. Although we introduced ADDM in this book in Chapter 8, it is worth noting here that ADDM includes analysis of key contention components such as CPU utilization, I/O capacity, memory usage by Oracle data structures, connection management, SQL parsing, and high-impact SQL statements.

ADDM prioritizes current resource constraints and provides recommendations accessible through the graphical interface of *Enterprise Manager* enabling the DBA to review and determine if remediation is warranted.

Advisory Framework

As noted in Chapter 8, an advisory framework is also present and accessible through Enterprise Manager (since Oracle Database 10*g*). The advisory framework consists of six major advisors that are responsible for monitoring and optimizing subsystems. With the dynamic nature of a data warehouse environment, these advisors provide significant insight for optimization of performance based on data captured in the AWR.

There are two classes of advisors. The SQL Tuning and SQL Access advisors are aligned to application tuning while the Memory, MTTR, Segment, and Undo Management advisors are primarily focused on the internal operations and optimization of Oracle. This advisory framework is illustrated in Figure 9-7.

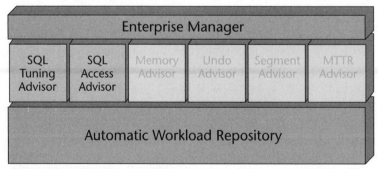

Figure 9-7: Advisory framework

SQL Tuning Advisor

The SQL Tuning Advisor is an internal service responsible for the identification and optimization of top resource-consuming SQL statements. Leveraging the Oracle optimizer, the SQL Tuning Advisor provides highly optimized plans and recommendations based on the current environmental information.

The SQL Tuning Advisor uses this input, as illustrated in Figure 9-8, to provide recommendations on optimizations based on the following processes:

- The advisor relies on the ADDM to identify the SQL statements that utilize the most system resources based on CPU and I/O consumption from information captured in the AWR.

- The advisor submits the plan to Oracle optimizer to determine the overall cost and to determine if the plan can be optimized for better performance accounting for information captured in the AWR.

- The advisor provides recommendations that can be separated into four categories:

  - **Statistics analysis** — Checks query objects to ensure that their supporting statistics are up to date and not stale. Typically, this step is for verification since statistics are gathered by the database and updated by default.

  - **SQL profiling** — Identifies the optimal path of execution using all optimizer settings to achieve the lowest cost plan. It then suggests a profile that can be utilized at runtime. SQL profiling is valuable when the administrator does not have access to application code or where query tools generate suboptimal SQL.

  - **Access path analysis** — Determines if the addition of indexes, materialized views, or other database structures may improve the execution time and lower the cost of the query plan.

  - **SQL structure analysis** — Identifies if changes to the structure of the SQL statement may improve the overall efficiency of the query.

The SQL Tuning Advisor provides the DBA and developers with an effective approach to address query performance beyond tuning SQL. With execution details about current and historical workloads readily available, remediation activities can be focused on the highest priority performance challenges.

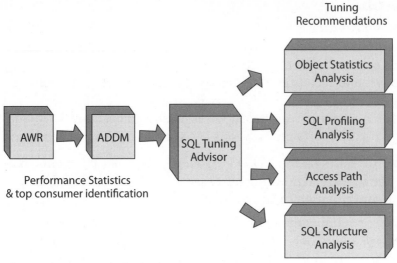

Figure 9-8: SQL Optimization process

It is important to fully understand the types of queries and use cases during the development lifecycle to determine if fundamental function of the environment has changed from the initial design. These use cases can be combined and repeated during the testing phase to gain an appreciation for different workload scenarios enabling the development team to remediate potential performance challenges prior to deployment. The SQL Tuning Advisor allows these combined work sets to be stored and recalled later as new functionality is altered or enhanced.

SQL Access Advisor

Most data warehouse solutions are dependent on architects and designers to ensure that data structures are flexible and meet the needs of the business users while delivering the highest levels of performance. Although the designs may reflect the stated business needs, ensuring levels of performance and functionality is more difficult.

The SQL Access Advisor assesses workload information found in the AWR and SQL plans to provide guidance on where the addition of data structures such as indexes and materialized views would increase performance. This approach, illustrated in Figure 9-9, can be used during the development and post-production cycles to verify that existing designs and structures will benefit from the recommendations without impacting existing designs. Oracle Enterprise Manager provides a simple wizard-based facility to generate the recommendations.

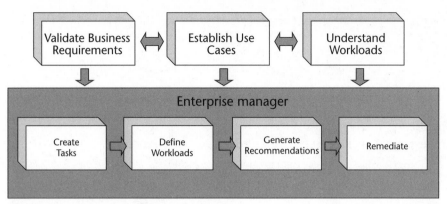

Figure 9-9: SQL Access Advisor process

The key first steps in obtaining a recommendation include architects and administrators validating the business requirements for flexibility and performance, establishing use cases to support the testing cycles, and understanding the anticipated workloads to ensure alignment to capacity plans and service levels. After these steps, the wizards in Enterprise Manager are used to create tasks for analysis, establish workloads, generate recommendations, and determine a plan for remediation.

The introduction of the SQL Access Advisor dramatically changed the approach of development and testing of solutions prior to deployment. Architects and DBAs can reduce and eliminate performance challenges and avoid costly post-production rework. For existing applications that have experienced significant growth or changing requirements, this framework provides an effective approach in performance remediation without the timely and costly efforts of redesign.

Memory Advisor

The proper allocation of memory is critical to the performance of your data warehouse. Prior to Oracle Database 10*g*, the DBA allocated a significant amount of time in sizing memory structures to ensure the highest levels of performance while balancing resources. The memory structures in the Oracle database, pictured in Figure 9-10, are now more sophisticated, providing better caching while increasing the tuning complexity. The Memory Advisor can greatly simplify tuning.

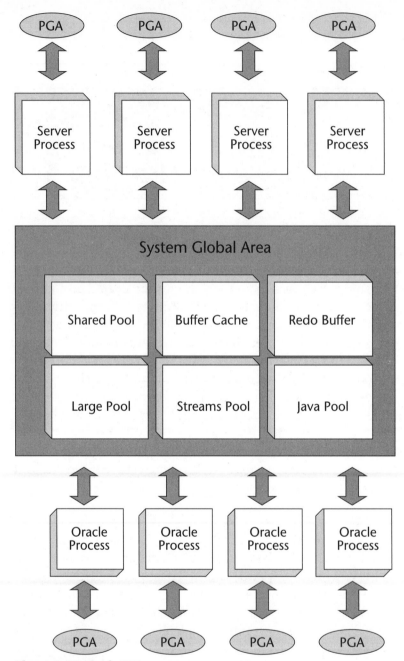

Figure 9-10: Oracle SGA

When the database is first installed, Oracle will estimate the initial size of the SGA based on physical memory available and the type of workload. While this provides a starting point for deployment, additional tuning is necessary. ADDM identifies constraints in memory based on usage patterns and leverages the Memory Advisor to determine the proper ratio and allocation of memory within the SGA. In addition, it provides recommendations as to the overall size of the SGA and Program Global Area (PGA) targets. Within Enterprise Manager, the Memory Advisor can provide graphical recommendations based on a sensitivity analysis of memory allocation to determine if adding or shrinking memory will benefit the application. This approach reduces the need for DBAs to adjust memory based on complex calculations or trial and error efforts.

Segment Advisor

One of the most time-consuming tasks for a DBA is the management of storage. The balance between the over allocation of free storage and preserving storage while managing costs continues in environments that experience rapid data growth and data volatility. Oracle introduced facilities into the database as of Oracle Database 10g designed to address the efficient management and allocation of storage.

The Segment Advisor manages space allocation by analyzing growth trends, identifying storage reclamation opportunities and providing storage usage by object across the entire database. Like many of the other advisors, the Segment Advisor runs automatically to identify opportunities for managing storage more efficiently. The results are displayed in Enterprise Manager allowing the administrator to drill into the recommendations and details.

Other Advisors

The Oracle database has additional advisors that provide significant insight to the DBA for proactive performance and availability management. These advisors are not as important to the overall function of a data warehouse but may be essential in sustaining higher service levels demanded by the business.

The Mean Time to Recovery Advisor or MTTR Advisor assists the DBA in determining the impact of runtime performance to recovery time in the event of a system failure. The advisor considers the size of log files with the associated overhead with memory and I/O management. Since the profile of a standard data warehouse is primarily focused on read activities, recovery service levels are not as essential as compared to OLTP databases. However, as many organizations are classifying their data warehousing environments as mission critical, mean time to recovery sometimes must be comparable to OLTP solutions. Recovery service levels can have a significant impact on the amount of system resources required, so it is important to understand the recovery needs of the business when determining the potential impact to performance and capacity.

Oracle provides a read-consistent image of all transactions through a facility called undo. This ensures that all reads are accurate even though other users may be in the process of altering data. In earlier versions of Oracle, the administrator was required to manage the undo facilities through structures called rollback segments. DBAs often encountered complexities in managing size, storage, and retention period. Oracle has since introduced automatic undo management that automates and manages undo transactions. The Undo Management Advisor provides recommendations for managing transactions based on system activity including long running queries, storage, and retention. Since most transactions for a data warehouse support the loading process, undo management is often isolated to discrete operational windows. For environments that feature near real-time data loading, the management of undo becomes more significant to the operation of the data warehouse.

The advisory framework in today's database versions provides developers and DBAs with tools that can be used in the development and management of data warehouse solutions. This framework can reduce the level of effort in managing a data warehouse, significantly reducing the risks associated with performance-related challenges.

Database Application Design

Proper design of the database application will have perhaps the greatest impact on performance. Applications that deliver the right business information at the wrong time still fail to meet business needs. Poor applications design characteristics range from data structures mismatched to application needs to poor use of technology features.

Chapter 5 discussed some of the key approaches used in designing for usability. Key to ensuring the most flexible and scalable solution is ensuring that the schema design is appropriate. Schema design can have a dramatic impact on the overall performance and scalability of your data warehouse. Designers who select a schema design based on a philosophical approach sometimes introduce flexibility and scalability limitations. The best overall schema design is one that satisfies not only functional requirements but also leverages features built into the database that improve scalability and performance.

The Oracle database is not limited to any specific design for data warehousing, giving the architect and the DBA great flexibility. Since the introduction of the Enterprise Manger framework for tuning and management, performance challenges can be identified and resolved in a fraction of the time and effort. We next describe a typical tuning exercise.

Business Scenario: Tuning Our Sample Solution

In this section we apply several common tuning approaches to our example electronics manufacturing solution from Chapter 5 to ensure that performance meets or exceeds service levels. Recall that our solution in this example enables insight into product profitability, better forecasting, and enhanced data quality within a flexible reporting platform.

The user community we will focus on is the sales organization. The complexity of their queries has grown and become more time consuming causing concerns about current and future performance. We will assume that the configuration of the technical infrastructure is acceptable and will focus on the advisory interfaces in Enterprise Manager that provide insight about the database environment and overall database design.

The sales organization is attempting to identify their highest margin products purchased by zip code over time by customers who are male and married so that they can target these products in a sales initiative to similar prospects. Such queries are complex and resource intensive. The business liaison has asked for assistance in increasing performance to support a faster time to market.

Where To Start

As we described earlier in this chapter, the standard approach for managing performance is based on steps to identify, diagnose, and remediate performance issues. For older versions of the Oracle database prior to Oracle Database 10*g*, the effort to identify and diagnose is typically assigned to senior DBAs and architects who know the environment. Such individuals can become significantly constrained from participation in other activities, including new development, during this time. Help desk and business liaison resources are responsible for identifying and documenting the issues. Application developers are engaged to assist in the diagnostic process to determine the root cause and impact of the performance challenge. This process can become time consuming and may not provide enough information for DBAs and developers to remediate.

Since Oracle Database 10*g*, a more comprehensive management framework enables identification and diagnostic efforts to be combined. Leveraging Enterprise Manager and the advisory framework, the effort to diagnose is significantly reduced, as represented in Figure 9-11, while the recommendations provide options for remediation. Since all diagnostic information is based on runtime statistics captured in the AWR, there is little impact to business users as this evaluation occurs.

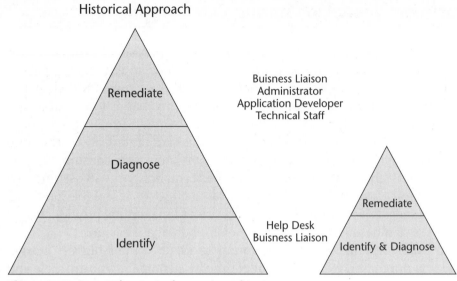

Figure 9-11: Approaches to performance tuning

Enterprise Manager Advisory Framework

The Enterprise Manager advisory framework enables the administrator to systematically identify, diagnose, and remediate performance challenges. Using our business scenario and some of the Enterprise Manager capabilities we previously introduced here and in Chapter 8, we next explore how to use the framework to reduce time in identification and diagnostic activities to enable the remediation of performance challenges.

Analyze the Environment

The first step in our identification and diagnostic activities are to analyze the database environment to identify any constraints in our database configuration. We previously evaluated the technical infrastructure to ensure it is sufficiently configured with ample memory and storage. Our next step is to utilize the Enterprise Manager framework to support our identification and diagnostic analysis efforts.

The Enterprise Manger console, illustrated in Figure 9-12, provides a high-level overview of the database and infrastructure, displaying status information such as CPU utilization, active sessions, database diagnostics, and a summary of storage. Our first observation from the console is that CPU activity appears relatively high and there is a higher percentage of waits. We drill into the performance tab to get a better understanding of host performance, session activity and disk I/O associated with the database instance.

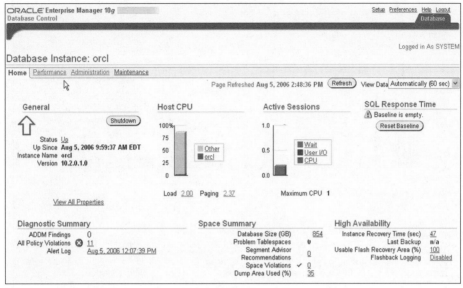

Figure 9-12: Enterprise Manager Framework — Console

From our performance view in Figure 9-13, we can confirm that the queries have a significant impact on both CPU and I/O during several periods during the day. In addition, we can drill to detail during specific time periods to determine the types of activities that were executing and the amount of resource consumed, as illustrated in Figure 9-14.

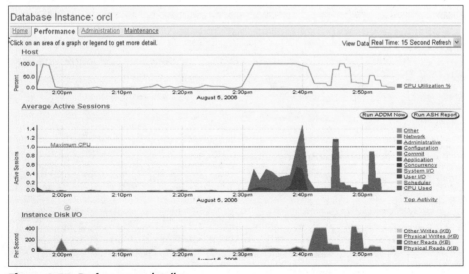

Figure 9-13: Performance details

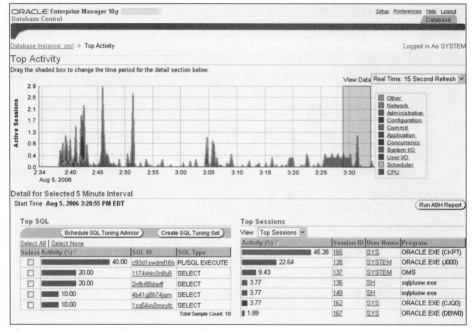

Figure 9-14: Top activity

To continue our analysis, we will navigate to Advisor Central, which provides us access to all database advisors (see Figure 9-15).

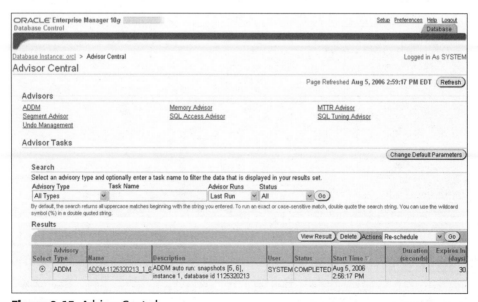

Figure 9-15: Advisor Central

The first task in leveraging the information provided by the advisors is to ensure that ADDM snapshots reflect current information. Figure 9-16 illustrates database activity viewed through ADDM.

From Figure 9-17, you can see that the ADDM has performed a scheduled hourly snapshot of system activity and is up-to-date. In addition, it provides a summary activity graph of resource consumption and an analysis of performance and its impact.

The next step is to investigate each advisor to determine if our system is optimally configured. The first advisor we will investigate is Undo Management, as illustrated in Figure 9-18. Undo Management is responsible for ensuring there is sufficient undo storage to support read consistency and transaction recovery.

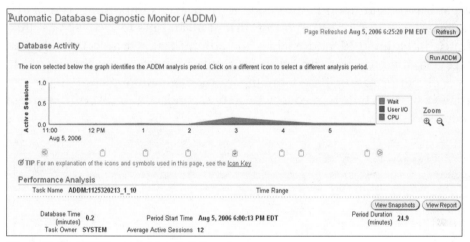

Figure 9-16: ADDM — Database Activity

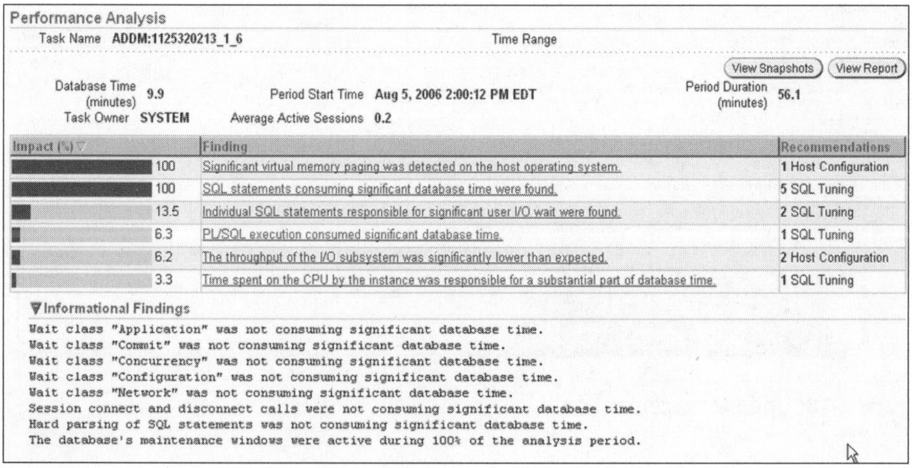

Figure 9-17: ADDM — Performance Analysis

From this figure, we observe that over the past seven days, the Undo Management Advisor has not encountered any problems and there are no recommended modifications. From the system activity graph, we observe that undo storage appears properly sized.

The next advisor we will investigate is the Segment Advisor. The Segment Advisor is responsible for the proper allocation of storage and management of free space. It allows analysis to be performed at the tablespace or schema level. The Segment Advisor wizard guides you through a four-step process to select objects to analyze for storage optimization. Storage optimization recommendations are made if significant storage can be recovered or performance enhanced.

The next advisor we investigate is responsible for recovery performance. For many data warehouses, their functionality is mission-critical to the organization and upon failure, time to recovery is important. The MTTR Advisor provides insight into the current mean time to recovery, as illustrated in Figure 9-19, and enables the administrator to select the desired recovery time to meet service levels while understanding the impact to overall performance. Based on the recommendation pictured, we can achieve a mean time to recovery in sixty seconds at the cost of 20 percent increased I/O.

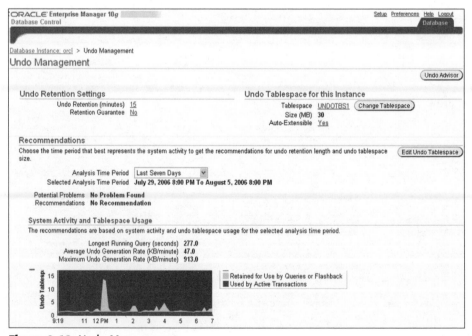

Figure 9-18: Undo Management

The last of the advisors focused on database configuration is the Memory Advisor. The Memory Advisor is responsible for identifying the proper size and allocation of memory for the SGA and PGA. The Memory Advisor provides information on the current state of the SGA and its current allocations to the various pools, as illustrated in Figure 9-20.

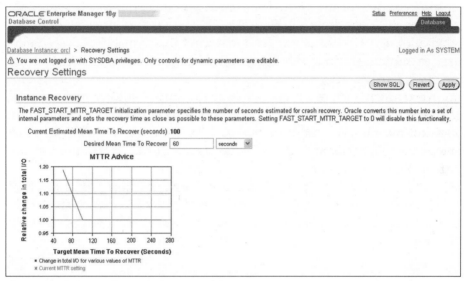

Figure 9-19: Mean Time to Recovery Advisor

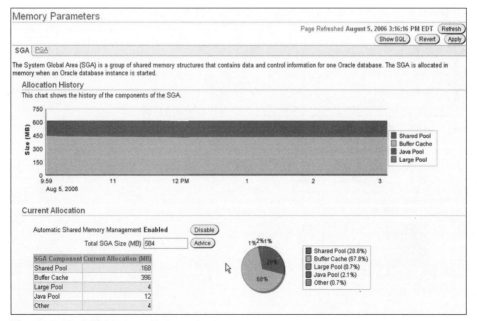

Figure 9-20: SGA Memory Parameters

Reviewing the current allocation, we observe that automatic shared memory management is enabled, allowing dynamic allocation of memory to support workload needs. In addition, the Memory Advisor will provide advice on the proper sizing of the SGA, as illustrated in Figure 9-21, to ensure that the allocation of memory is adequate and efficient.

Our example highlights the percent improvement that can be gained by adjusting the size of the SGA. The same approach is used for tuning the size of the PGA, as shown in Figure 9-22. The PGA is a private memory region allocated to a database server process that is used exclusively for query execution, sorting, bulk load operations and other process-specific, memory-intensive activities. Generally, a larger PGA can significantly improve performance of an operation at the cost of higher memory consumption. Given that each user process is allocated PGA memory, over allocation can be costly and inefficient. Like the SGA, the PGA memory parameters analysis is provided, displaying the current allocation and the maximum allocation with the cache hit percentage.

The PGA Advisor can provide additional insight into sizing the PGA appropriately. From Figure 9-23, we observe that the PGA target size can be achieved with a lower allocation of memory than 193 MB as is currently allocated.

Figure 9-21: SGA Size Advice

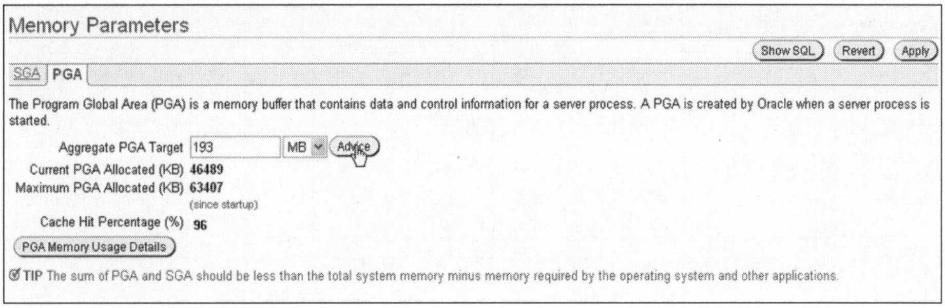

Memory Parameters
Show SQL
Revert
Apply
SGA
PGA
The Program Global Area (PGA) is a memory buffer that contains data and control information for a server process. A PGA is created by Oracle when a server process is started.
Aggregate PGA Target 193 MB Advice
Current PGA Allocated (KB) 46489
Maximum PGA Allocated (KB) 63407
(since startup)
Cache Hit Percentage (%) 96
PGA Memory Usage Details
TIP The sum of PGA and SGA should be less than the total system memory minus memory required by the operating system and other applications.

Figure 9-22: PGA Memory Parameters

PGA Aggregate Target Advice
Cache hit percentage
100%
80%
60%
40%
20%
0%
0 200 400 600 800 1000 1200 1400 1600 1800
Variation of cache hit ratio with PGA target
Current PGA target
Overflow range
Aggregate PGA Target 193 MB
TIP You can click on the curve in the graph to set new value.
Cancel
OK

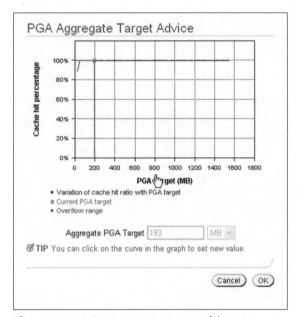

Figure 9-23: PGA Aggregate Target Advice

You can invoke the PGA Memory Usage Details to review the recommended sizes. Based on the queries that have been executed, the advisor recommends a PGA aggregate target optimal size of 48 MB. Figure 9-24 illustrates memory usage details for a PGA target of 48 MB.

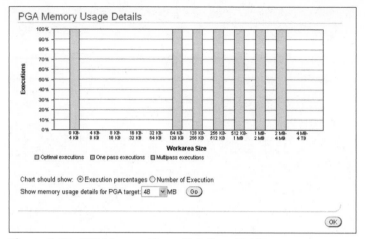

Figure 9-24: PGA Memory Usage Details — 48 MB

This advisor allows the administrator to review various configurations to determine the most appropriate size. Resizing the PGA aggregate target to 24 MB would cause several of the queries to perform multiple executions, as shown in Figure 9-25, due to constrained memory. Larger values will provide better performance for complex queries but at the cost of wasted memory.

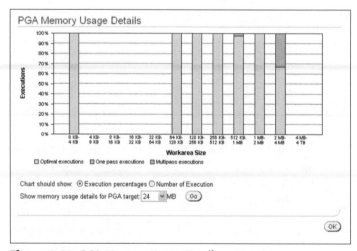

Figure 9-25: PGA Memory Usage Details — 24 MB

This facility provides the administrator many options for configuring memory based on available resources. A comprehensive understanding of the types of queries and the number of connected users is necessary to ensure optimal performance without impacting available capacities.

Analyze the Application

Once the systems environment is analyzed to determine proper function, the administrator can focus efforts on analyzing the application. Most performance challenges are related to application design where data structures or embedded code is inefficient and does not meet the anticipated service level. The first advisor we will investigate is the SQL Access Advisor. This advisor is responsible for identifying modifications or enhancements to data structures like the addition of indexes or materialized views. We will invoke the SQL Access Advisor using the default settings focused on current and recent SQL activity based on information in the AWR, as illustrated in Figure 9-26.

Next, as shown in Figure 9-27, we choose to evaluate the impact of adding both indexes and materialized views to our design and the advisor mode.

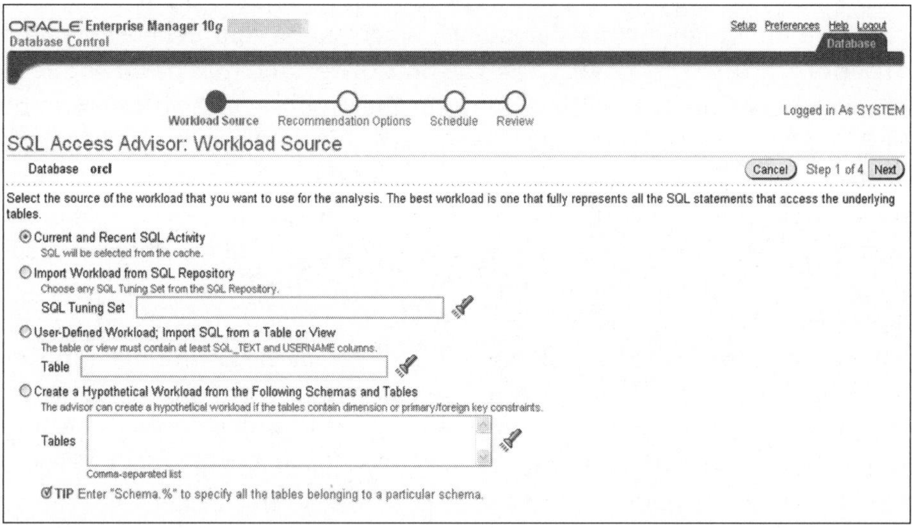

Figure 9-26: SQL Access Advisor

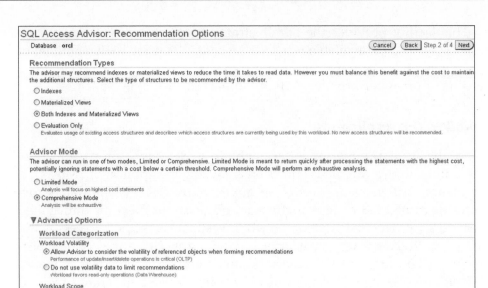

Figure 9-27: SQL Access Advisor — Selection of options

The advisor mode can be set to execute in a limited mode where analysis is focused on only high-impact statements, whereas the comprehensive mode will perform an exhaustive analysis. The time of day and the critical nature of the performance impact or the activity in the environment will determine which mode is most appropriate. Finally, we review the advanced options that enable us to evaluate workload volatility and the scope of the workload. Once complete, we schedule the advisor and review the selected options. When the advisor has completed its analysis, you can evaluate its recommendations for performance improvement, as illustrated in Figure 9-28.

From this figure, you can observe that the advisor discovered only a small percentage of queries that would benefit from the addition of indexes or materialized views. Upon further investigation, this enhancement can yield improvements greater than ten times in performance. When drilling into the recommendations in Figure 9-29, we discover that cost improvement is dramatic with only a limited impact to overall storage.

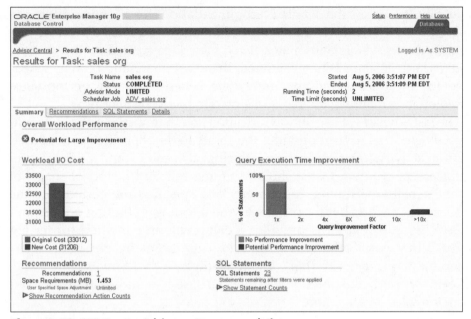

Figure 9-28: SQL Access Advisor — Recommendations

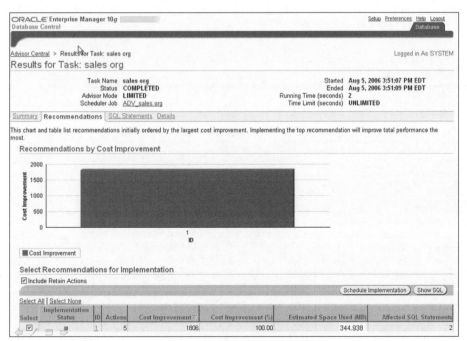

Figure 9-29: SQL Access Advisor — Recommendations by cost improvement

Finally, we review the detailed recommendations for remediation shown in Figure 9-30. The advisor recommends that a materialized view be created on the *sales* table with materialized view logs created on the *products* and *time* dimensions. When validated, this recommendation can be scheduled for execution providing immediate benefit to query performance based on information gathered and stored in the AWR over time.

The last advisor we use for identification and diagnostics is the SQL Tuning Advisor. This advisor provides the ability to tune specific queries based on top activity, queries executed during a specific time periods, predefined sets of queries, snapshots of tuning sets and historical snapshot sets. For real-time tuning, top activity and specific time periods are the most useful method but for pre-deployment testing, gathering queries and classifying into snapshots provides a comprehensive method for testing and scaling workload that will provide significant insight into understanding performance profiles. In our example, we will investigate a specific time period, illustrated in Figure 9-31, based on information gathered from the sales organization.

When we identify the query that performs slower than anticipated, we drill into the details for the query to find that it is CPU-intensive (see Figure 9-32). Then, we can analyze the execution statistics such as read, fetch, and exaction time.

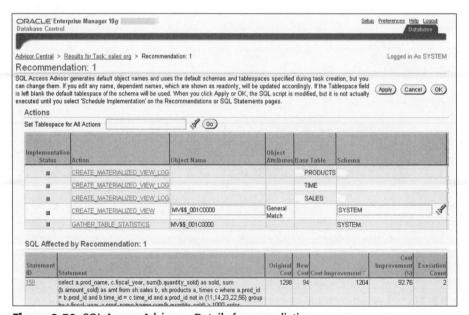

Figure 9-30: SQL Access Advisor — Details for remediation

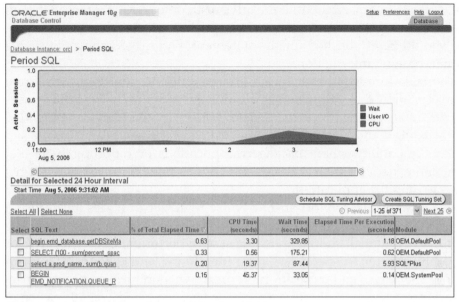

Figure 9-31: SQL Tuning Advisor — Selection of SQL

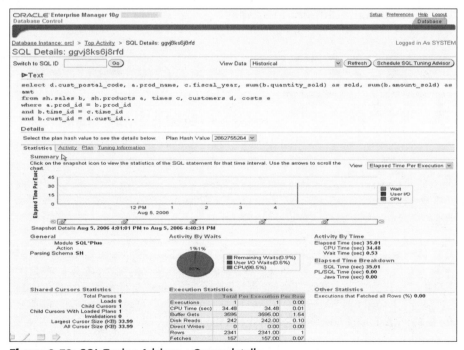

Figure 9-32: SQL Tuning Advisor — Query details

Once satisfied, we schedule the advisor to determine if a more efficient plan can be identified and allow the administrator to decide whether a profile should be established for the statement. Figure 9-33 shows available detailed tuning information.

The SQL Tuning Advisor found a more efficient plan than the current one selected by the optimizer. The administrator can review the differences between the existing execution plan and the proposed plan recommended by the advisor and determine whether to enable the new plan. This is a significant capability where packaged applications or reporting tools that generate generic or poorly designed SQL can now be tuned without the need to alter the application.

The advisory framework in Enterprise Manager provides a significant improvement to the approach of tuning data warehouse applications. The ability to capture all queries and store system performance metrics enables an administrator to spend less time identifying and diagnosing performance challenges and more effort on proactive monitoring and when necessary, remediation. Although our exercise only touched a small portion of the functionality of Enterprise Manager, its performance management and advisory framework with monitoring capabilities make it one of the most robust management solutions available.

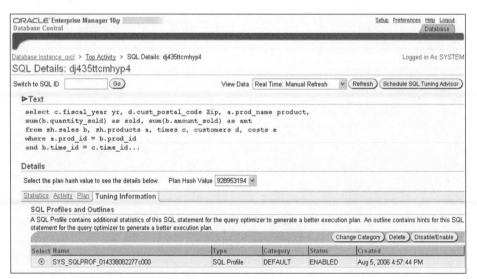

Figure 9-33: SQL Tuning Advisor — Recommendations

Approaches for Success

Poor performance can negatively impact any carefully designed and highly functional data warehouse solution. With a proper approach to satisfying service levels before deploying your solution and a defined approach to solving performance challenges as they arise, administrators can sleep peacefully knowing that their data warehouse environment can provide the insight to all performance-related challenges.

This concludes the section of the book that covers the technologies used in deploying a custom-built business intelligence and data warehousing solution. Of course, more knowledge is required for successful deployment than simply understanding the technologies used in such solutions. Best practices have been developed over a period of years that help to ensure successful projects. That is the subject of the remaining chapters in this book.

Best Practices

In This Part

Scoping the Effort and an Approach for Success

We have all read dreadful stories of business intelligence initiatives that are months behind schedule, millions of dollars over budget or fail to deliver promised functionality. All too often, these projects encounter challenges caused by lack of solid business requirements, complexities within the data, and poor implementation of technology or mismanagement. The success of a business intelligence initiative extends well beyond the selection of technologies or promises of exclusive capabilities or amazing return on investment. A successful implementation requires a precise understanding of the corporate environment, sponsorship by the business, a methodology for execution, and technical and subject-matter expertise supported by strategies that mitigate risk. Although approaches to delivering solutions are as diverse as the people who are responsible, most successful implementations share a set of common principles that ultimately ensure their success.

   This chapter highlights key principles for a successful approach necessary in a business intelligence initiative. We include a discussion on managing well-known risks that such projects often encounter. In addition, we include many of the best practices observed across hundreds of projects and provide some suggestions on how to avoid common mistakes. Throughout, you will be reminded of the need for proper planning and the importance of defining the right scope.

In analyzing successful projects and looking for common characteristics, an approach became evident that consists of principles in five areas. The five principles we describe in this chapter are uncovering business initiatives, securing business sponsorship, endorsing a methodology, staffing the project, and managing risk. Although most projects that reach deployment take into account some or even portions of all of these, significant gaps sometimes remain that can limit risk a project's overall success or even lead to its failure. Our goal is to help you eliminate these gaps through proper planning. Figure 10-1 illustrates these essential principles in creating a successful approach.

Uncovering Key Business Initiatives

In any business intelligence project, a goal is to provide business users with easy access to comprehensive information in a timely fashion. To ensure that the solution satisfies the needs of the business, gaining a precise understanding of the current business climate and future requirements from relevant lines of business is required. Although virtually all project leaders agree that this simple step is beneficial to their initiatives, all too often this elementary task is ignored or not thoroughly completed and the project is jeopardized. Common reasons for not fully uncovering key business initiatives and requirements include not knowing where to start and an inability to identify who is responsible or what is important. In gathering this information, the goal is to gain an understanding of the common themes and direction from a true business perspective (instead of relying on a perspective that might exist in IT that may not match business expectations).

Where to Start

When determining the most important business initiatives and how a business intelligence project can provide a solution, it is necessary to understand many aspects of the current business climate including competitive factors and how that climate might change over time. Business intelligence projects driven from an IT-centric perspective with limited input from the business community often fail to align with the strategic needs and direction the organization is following. To get a better understanding of where to focus attention, the pyramid of influence shown in Figure 10-2 can be useful as you determine sources of information. These sources at each level in the pyramid can help you better understand the needs from the top of the organization (strategic) to the operational levels of the organization (tactical).

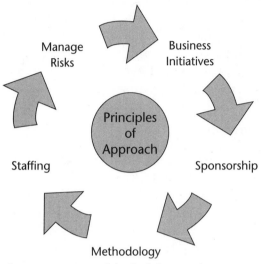

Figure 10-1: Essential principles creating a successful approach

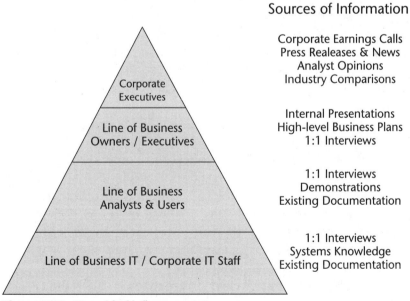

Figure 10-2: Pyramid of influence

Information Sources

Unless the organization is small or the executive board personally endorses the project, top executives may have limited availability to discuss their current views of the project and organization and their vision of the future. Since understanding these views and vision is critical to the success of a business intelligence project, you might look to other sources within your company to gain further insight. Doing some simple homework will help assure that your project is in alignment with current executive views.

Public-Facing Sources of Information

A tremendous amount of information is often publicly available from a company or organization describing current and future goals. Your organization's Internet web site probably includes your mission statement (as viewed by executive management), financial information and corporate earnings calls (if a publicly traded company), and possibly analysts' opinions and competitive analyses.

For publicly traded companies, the most relevant information regarding business intelligence needs for potential projects might be extracted from corporate earnings calls. Such calls usually focus on current performance, continuing business activities such as mergers or acquisitions, and provide future guidance. One of the unique benefits of the earnings call is that for large organizations, there are typically a number of analysts who closely follow the company. In the question and answer portions of these calls, inquiries and responses to past, current, or future challenges can provide additional insight.

Other sources of information for publicly traded companies include current press releases or news events that are linked to financial portals hosted by providers such as Yahoo!, MSN, Dow Jones, and Reuters. You will want to select sites that provide a wide variety of information that is timely and trustworthy. Information here can include company profiles, industry rankings, executive ownership details, and analysts' opinions. You can also gain further insight by reviewing financial profiles of peers within the same industry. This complementary information can help identify what is emerging as top of mind in your management.

If your initiative is at a privately held company or in the public sector (government, education, or non-profit organization) and such information is not as readily available, you might research trade magazines, industry publications or local news outlets pertaining to current events. In many cases, top priorities can be found in public documents with supporting commentary, thus enabling you to better understand the direction of the organization and possible drivers for your project.

Company and Organizational Internal Sources of Information

Internal sources of information provide additional details that are not shared with the public. Most mid-size and large organizations have internal corporate portals that contain links to executive communications as to the overall health of the business, updates on new product and services, and other strategic initiatives and plans for lines of business. If your organization holds periodic town hall forums, attending these can provide valuable information on activities occurring within and across lines of business. Business users within the lines of business might also provide more detailed planning information. Regardless of the source, focus your search for information that can provide additional insight into both the current business needs and challenges that exist within the organization. In most cases, solutions that specifically address these challenges are more likely to receive funding and gain higher acceptance upon completion.

The lines of business executives or owners report to the top-level corporate executives and are often willing to share their vision, knowledge, and experience. They can detail the plan for executing the corporate vision. IT professionals that fail to initiate discussions with this level of management are missing a prime opportunity to gain a first-hand account of the operations of the business. Content created by lines of business leadership for senior management reviews usually highlight the current state of the business and plans for the near term. Interactions between IT and the business at this level are often viewed as a partnership where IT information analysts are taught details of the lines of business operations in return for providing dynamic solutions that solve some of the most difficult information challenges.

Within the lines of business are business analysts and users. These individuals usually provide the most detailed information on the daily operations and the current challenges that exist. Often, these are the individuals who will also provide the most detailed requirements as they understand existing gaps and have well-thought recommendations on how to improve existing processes. Since this group is an important consumer of business intelligence solutions, ensuring their requirements are met is crucial to success.

The final level in the pyramid of influence is within the realm of IT. Although there exists an implicit comfort factor in discussions at this level, information gathered should only be used as a supporting reference. All too often, interviews are conducted at this level only to find the information captured is second-hand and lacks full business credibility needed to be effective. IT discussions are most valuable for providing technical information that may not be apparent to those in the lines of business.

What Is Important

At each level of the pyramid, gather as much information as possible to ensure you are capturing different perspectives about the business. Like a detective story, there are many clues as to what is important and how problems should be solved. It is the responsibility of the IT information analyst to determine the facts that are relevant to the solution and ones that may be misaligned to the corporate vision. Although the questions will vary from level to level within the pyramid, you should expect that a higher degree of detail will be uncovered as you drill lower in the organization. The following is a sample list of topics for questioning that has been shown to have positive results:

- Business process improvement
- Business enablers and differentiators
- Clarity and visibility of information
- Corporate governance
- Strategic pains
- Tactical pains
- Competitive pressures
- Business opportunities
- Return on investment
- Information security
- Financial impact and cost
- Data accuracy
- Data timeliness
- Data granularity

Chapter 11 provides some ideas on how to discuss these with the business by including some sample questions relevant to levels of the pyramid of influence.

Accountability and Securing Business Sponsorship

Accountability in business intelligence initiatives should be shared among all parties involved. This will ensure that each group's interests are managed effectively and the cost and scope of the initiative is appropriate.

Although in the eyes of the business, the project is ready to proceed, all parties must be accountable to their roles and responsibilities to ensure the initiative is successful.

Well-planned projects strategically aligned to the business are sometimes canceled in times of turmoil due to a lack of executive sponsorship, so it is important to formally secure the right level of sponsorship. Neglecting this step is a common mistake when budgets have been allocated and high-level business requirements are defined. When searching for sponsorship, it is best to begin early when the initiative is in the budgeting phase. Start the search for support and sponsorship at the highest levels of the pyramid to ensure the initiative is aligned to meet critical business objectives, properly funded, and has defined success criteria that can be met.

Establish a Steering Committee

When IT-led projects are over budget or delayed, organizations will often allow the line of business to take control over the project to ensure proper management. One of the most critical activities to ensure a successful business intelligence project is the creation and active participation of a steering committee before this occurs. A steering committee should be comprised of key business constituents, financial sponsors, IT management, and the project team. Consultants or senior staff from other lines of business might also be engaged in the steering committee process to provide insight, guidance, and an independent perspective as to the health of the project. Most organizations' steering committee meetings convene on a quarterly basis or at key critical milestones of a project lifecycle to ensure the project remains on schedule and stays within budgetary constraints.

Project Review Board

In addition to a formal steering committee process, most business intelligence projects can also benefit from a project review board that is comprised of IT peers who focus exclusively on IT-centric topics. Such informal committees typically convene at the end of each project phase or at critical milestones to ensure balance between processes, technology, and alignment with corporate standards and goals. In addition, this team provides technical review of approaches used in the areas of architecture, data acquisition, and common use data. Project review boards can provide a positive impact by incorporating synergies from other projects resulting in reduced time of delivery, increased reuse of existing content, and improved functionality.

Endorsing a Methodology

The debate over the most appropriate project methodology, especially within IT, is nothing new. Every few years, we are exposed to the hype that a new breakthrough methodology will eliminate risks and revolutionize the way we approach projects. Nevertheless, an endorsed project methodology is one of the most controllable aspects to ensure success. Although adopting a methodology will not always guarantee success, its framework can be used to manage project scope, duration, and cost. Surprisingly, an alarming percentage of projects fail to adopt or properly follow a methodology. These projects are inevitably at risk of failure and are much less likely to meet the expectations of the business sponsors and users.

Choices of Methodologies

Since not all methodologies are created equal, choose a methodology appropriately aligned with the tasks of implementing your business intelligence project. Historically, classic waterfall methods were adapted in delivery of business intelligence solutions. Although project success could be achievable largely based on the skills of the implementation team, the duration of most implementations, with cycles ranging from twelve months to several years, often failed to meet the needs of fast-moving business environments. Since potential business users were forced to approve their requirements early in the waterfall lifecycle, it was also difficult to modify functionality as the business climate changed.

To address these issues, rapid application development (RAD) methodologies were selectively adopted to enable more timely iterative delivery. While RAD is useful in application-centric initiatives, it does not provide standard structured processes that align well to business intelligence projects. The variety of interpretations of the RAD approach can also make it very difficult to deliver structured and repeatable solutions.

In 1994, the Dynamic Systems Development Method (DSDM) Consortium[1] was formed to focus on combining the disciplines of waterfall methodologies with rapid deployment. The combined discipline, better known as the incremental approach, applies DSDM principles in a unique framework that supports the time constraints demanded by business users for business intelligence projects and the engineering discipline required by IT organizations.

[1]Dynamic Systems Development Method (DSDM) Consortium is a non-profit organization that is focused on the development and evolution of the DSDM framework to enable efficient project delivery to rapidly meet change-business needs. Further information about DSDM can be found at www.dsdm.org.

When viewing a project triangle that depicts the relationships between scope, time, and resource, most commonly scope is fixed while time and resources vary. In contrast, in the incremental approach, resources and duration are constrained while functionality delivered can be changed. As a result, this approach can greatly improve time of delivery while satisfying the most important business requirements. It has been adopted by many systems integrators and is the basis of Oracle's business intelligence and data warehousing approach. Figure 10-3 compares the constraints of traditional waterfall methods to an incremental approach.

A Business-focused Approach

To explore how this approach can work, we'll take a look at Oracle's data warehousing methodology, DWM Fast Track. This is a continuous improvement approach optimized for short lifecycle increments of 90 to 120 days that enables business intelligence and data warehousing solutions to deliver needed business functionality at a faster speed and lower risk. Most business intelligence projects typically start small with limited scope delivering specific information to a single line of business or department and, over time, grow to support a more holistic or enterprise view. Figure 10-4 illustrates how DWM Fast Track's combined approach of waterfall and RAD principles can enable rapid delivery while supporting an engineering discipline.

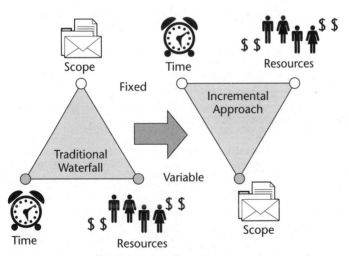

Figure 10-3: Traditional waterfall vs. incremental approach

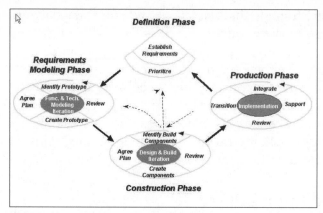

Figure 10-4: DWM fast track lifecycle

Such approaches are designed to provide a framework for project implementation and execution and are not intended to address the creation of a business intelligence strategy. Creating the business intelligence strategy is usually an independent initiative that is formulated and socialized throughout the organization prior to commencing these project-based activities. Developing the strategy requires input from all levels within the pyramid of influence to identify both the business and technology vision. Organizations often dedicate several months in formulating a business intelligence strategy. The resulting dynamic framework can become the basis of corporate standards for all future business intelligence initiatives.

The DWM Fast Track methodology is divided into 4 phases (horizontal) and supported by 13 processes (vertical) that span one or more phases. Figure 10-5 highlights the mapping of processes to phases in DWM Fast Track.

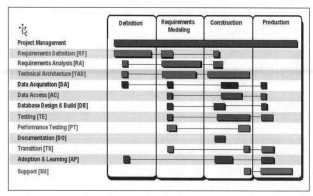

Figure 10-5: DWM fast-track method structure

Only the project management process and supporting tasks span all phases. The remaining processes are comprised of specific tasks of which a few selected tasks are executed multiple times within a specific phase enabling the process of continuous improvement. For example, tasks associated with requirements analysis span across the definition, requirements modeling and construction phases. Although it is expected that requirements would be gathered during the definition and requirements phase, new requirements identified during construction can be captured and prioritized for future increments. This approach ensures that functionality is aligned to the most important business requirements and new requirements that are not satisfied during a current increment are not lost.

The most important principles in using such an incremental approach include:

- Prioritization of business requirements using a must-have, should-have, could-have, and won't-have (MoSCoW) list.

- Use of a time box to limit delivery to the most important functionality.

- Standardization of key deliverables with a supporting repository for documentation.

- Understanding the current business climate to determine the most appropriate duration for each increment.

MoSCoW List for Prioritization

All methodologies provide an approach to capture and prioritize business requirements. Some embed requirements in large documents that make it difficult to extract and reprioritize while others align requirements with business processes. A simple and efficient technique to capture the most important aspects of business requirements is to use the MoSCoW technique. Figure 10-6 highlights the ranking of key project characteristics for MoSCoW.

MoSCoW is a prioritization method where business requirements are captured and rank ordered as *must* have, *should* have, *could* have, and *won't* have. This simple prioritization method allows the assignment of the most important business requirements to initial increments with lower priority requirements to be satisfied in later increments. As new business requirements are uncovered throughout the increment's lifecycle, a reprioritization process considers both old and new requirements and ranks these based on the most critical business needs.

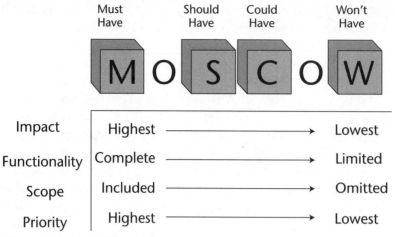

Figure 10-6: MoSCoW technique

Time Box Functionality

A time box approach can be used in delivering functionality that will benefit the most important group of users in the shortest duration. This approach places time limitations on the tasks within a phase to ensure that the project duration stays within pre-defined constraints and core functionality is satisfied. Since 80 percent of functionality can often be delivered in 20 percent of the time, the goal is to eliminate construction of extraneous functionality that provides only limited value. However, those requirements are also captured for future prioritization.

During a time box increment, there are several tasks that can benefit from multiple iterations, including the development and refinement of the MoSCoW list, construction of data models, data quality evaluation and corrective planning and possibly code generation, capacity planning, and architecture planning. Extending the duration of the time box allows for additional iterations of these tasks, but can increase the overall duration of the project. Balancing the duration of the time box is critical since it is often better to deliver limited functionality earlier and avoid elongating a project cycle.

Standard Deliverables with Supporting Repository

Like a blueprint to build a house, standard deliverable templates provide a repeatable roadmap of the functionality and capabilities that a project is to deliver. Most projects have some form of documentation highlighting objectives, requirements, and proposed standards. Such documents should become *living* documents that capture the latest decisions or changes in requirements so that they are not quickly out-of-date.

Unfortunately, bypassing documentation tasks is common when projects are constrained for time. These tasks are often deferred to a later date, but then are never completed. Although the impact to the current project cycle may be minimal, long-term effects can be substantial. When expanding the scope and focus of a business intelligence project, supporting documentation will be needed to define new functionality, even for recently deployed solutions. Such documentation is also critical since the staff involved in the initial project cycle may not be involved in the next cycle.

Although there might seem to be an unlimited number of deliverable templates, it is best to leverage existing industry materials to formulate organizational standards. Most commonly used methodologies include excellent samples that can be customized to meet your organization's needs. There are also numerous sources of templates available from third-party organizations at a nominal fee. Be sure to establish standards for the most critical deliverables first and then expand to the remaining tasks over time.

Most of these documents are beneficial only to selected groups or roles. Such roles include business sponsors who establish objectives and provide requirements, business users who provide requirements and ultimately own the finished product, business analysts who act as a liaison to the business users, and the development team of architects, developers, and database administrators (DBAs) responsible for the design and construction of the project. Table 10-1 shows the most significant deliverable documents from Oracle's DWM Fast Track by phase and denotes the primary beneficiaries. Documents noted with (I) represent documents that span multiple phases and endure multiple iterations and revisions.

Table 10-1: Deliverable Documents and Primary Beneficiary

PHASE	DELIVERABLE	PRIMARY BENEFICIARY
Definition Phase	Business and Systems Objectives	All
	MoSCoW List (I)	All
	Data Source Model (I)	Developers
	Data Standards and Guidelines	All
	Architecture Approach	Architects
Requirements Modeling Phase	Data Quality Approach (I)	All
	Data Acquisition Approach (I)	Developers
	Data Access Approach (I)	Analysts/Users
	Data Architecture (I)	Architects
	Testing Requirements and Approach (I)	Analysts/Developer
	Training Approach	Analysts/Users

(continued)

Table 10-1 *(continued)*

PHASE	DELIVERABLE	PRIMARY BENEFICIARY
Construction Phase	Data Quality Assessment (I)	All
	Capacity Plan (I)	Architects
	Security and Control Approach	Developers
	Backup and Recovery Approach	Developers
	Logical/Physical Database Design (I)	Developers
	Integration Test Plan	Analysts/Developer
Production Phase	User Role Access	All
	Data Validation and Access Test	

To ensure proper communication and access to information, this documentation must be readily available. A portal typically is used to provide access to project information residing in a documentation repository. The structure of the repository may be as simple as a shared file server with supporting directory structures or as complex as a full lifecycle management solution. For larger or more mature organizations that have multiple increments and projects in development, vendors' pre-packaged repositories and software solutions providing comprehensive integrated management can be useful. When evaluating a full lifecycle management repository, the following are features beneficial to business intelligence initiatives:

- **Collaboration** — Provides a flexible solution for communicating information to selected groups based on role and subscription level. This can include advanced capabilities like discussion forums, mailing lists, and distributed capabilities.

- **Version control** — Provides a historical record of changes made to project files with the ability to recover older versions or examine the history of change.

- **Issues tracking** — Provides business users and developers the ability to catalog and track defects and enhancement requests.

- **Search engine** — Enables searching for content within a project and across projects.

- **Document and file management** — Provides file management services such as check in, check out, and versioning of documents.

- **Project dashboard** — Provides current project metrics, status of activities, and overall health of the initiative.

- **Role-based security** — Provides selective access to documents, content, and metrics based on role.

- **Reporting** — Enables a comprehensive view of information pertaining to the current project and across other projects.

Organizations that adopt vendors' software products for content and project management can benefit from increased return on investment, faster time to market, reduction in overall delivery costs, and an improvement in quality. Many find these benefits accrue from better awareness of project status among project sponsors, users, and developers. For organizations that leverage external project resources or participate in distributed development activities, investing in and adopting tools to manage project content can be extremely useful.

Selecting a Project Duration

The duration of a business intelligence project can be the decisive factor in overall success and adoption, regardless of capabilities and functionality delivered. Added requirements and extensions to scope can delay delivery of solutions needed to respond to specific business events. Such business events might drive a need to understand new competitive pressures, how a merger or acquisition changed the competitive landscape or the impact of economic change. The promised business intelligence solutions must be delivered and available in order to take proper business actions.

For example, an executive might anticipate the need for business intelligence linked to the release of a new product or service and changes in corporate strategy. Such planning often occurs at the highest corporate levels, but details on how to measure the overall business performance may not be completely determined. When pushed to the line of business, a significant need for supporting information to execute the strategy and a method to measure the outcome is identified. Such information can be provided from just-in-time solutions developed using the engineering discipline in an incremental approach.

As mentioned earlier, one of the benefits provided by an incremental approach is the ability to predefine the duration and allocation of resources while allowing the scope to vary. Varying the scope to satisfy only the highest priority requirements enables a time-constrained project to become possible. When selecting project duration, there are several influential factors that should be considered:

- **Business climate** — Organizations that encounter changes in business cycles may alter their approach contrary to their strategic direction. Often, the business climate is directly correlated to economic conditions, but other factors might include changes in the competitive landscape, changes in product lifecycles, and reorganization of leadership. These projects will likely be shorter duration and are typically aligned toward meeting tactical or operational business needs.

- **Budget/Funding** — Funding can have the most significant impact in altering the duration of a project. When considering the impact of funding constraints, ensure the balance between funding, scope, and duration to minimize the overall risk.

- **Availability of resources** — The best resources for a given project may not be available or their participation might be constrained. Alternatives can include delaying the project until these resources are available, extending the duration of the project using multiple resources or allocating third-party resources to provide subject-matter expertise or staff augmentation. Since the business climate may prohibit altering start dates, opportunities to leverage external resources may be attractive, especially if the project could benefit from subject-matter expertise. Such experts can assure success by performing critical tasks related to architecture, design and integration, while enabling the existing internal staff to remain on other current projects.

- **Impact of the initiative** — All projects do not have equal impact on an organization. For tactical business intelligence projects, consider minimizing the duration to provide functionality at the earliest possible date. For projects where the end-user community lacks the sophisticated understanding of what would be provided by advanced reporting and analytic solutions, minimize the project duration to accelerate delivery. This enables end-users to begin using new functionality and to better understand how reporting or analytic solutions can provide benefits to their day-to-day activities.

- **Economic conditions** — Changes in economic factors may have a significant impact on scope and duration of projects directly affecting the available resources an organization is willing to allocate. During economic expansion, most organizations align their strategic plans more aggressively for growth to enable them to capitalize on expanding markets. During economic downturns, organizations often take a more conservative approach in allocating capital to only the most strategic initiatives.

- **Risks (technical)** — The risks associated with introducing new technology are often ignored especially if it has been positioned as a means to increase productivity and reduce costs. Consider extending the duration of an increment when new technology is introduced. Examples include introduction of technologies such as ETL tools, metadata repositories or changes in technology platforms. Additionally, data quality and integration activities often require additional time since complexities can be less understood initially.

Although there is no perfect duration for a business intelligence project, it is important to balance the business needs for functionality and timeliness with the IT needs for development quality and engineering standards. All business intelligence projects should be broken into multiple, manageable increments that are aligned to the long-term business objectives. So, you should understand the overall strategy the solution will provide and also influential market factors that may exist.

As little as three years ago, a large majority of projects consisted of increments spanning 9 to 12 months in duration. More recently, durations of increments are typically 3 to 4 months to be more aligned to financial reporting cycles and market factors.

Staffing the Project

There are numerous factors to consider when staffing a business intelligence project. Success will ultimately depend on the ability of the team to efficiently interact, comprehend, and deliver a solution based on requirements that may initially be vague and uncertain. The most dominant factors behind such success are linked to the size, experience, and structure of the delivery organization. While the choices of how to staff are endless, we will describe some common approaches of large and small organizations and the alternatives that are available to ensure success.

Organization Structure

There are several approaches to building an efficient team that is optimal for the construction of business intelligence solutions. Team composition will ultimately depend on the management structure, expertise, location of resources, and the overall size of the organization.

Organizations relatively new to business intelligence projects often start by assigning their brightest developers who possess previous experience or have a unique understanding of the business. These resources will often perform all tasks end to end. Although this approach can be successful, it requires exceptionally talented resources that are familiar with all phases of development and supporting tools. Such an approach becomes difficult to maintain where multiple initiatives become active, resources are reassigned or the resources leave the organization.

A better approach is one where integrated teams of specialists interact to provide a full spectrum of competencies to deliver all aspects of a business intelligence project (see Figure 10-7). For smaller organizations, individuals may be required to fulfill multiple roles or will be augmented by systems integrators and consultants.

Project Management/Portfolio Team

A project management team should include experienced individuals who are responsible for the execution of the project and the management of its portfolio. Ideally, members will possess certifications in project management, have a clear understanding of the business objectives and excellent relationships with project sponsors, and act as the IT representatives for the steering committee. In addition, this team administers a portfolio of assets for reuse during the project or to leverage on future projects.

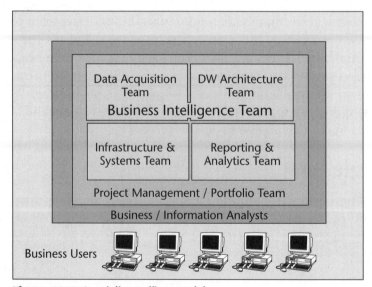

Figure 10-7: Specialist staffing model

To ensure success, a project manager will fulfill many roles and responsibilities, including:

- Ensuring mitigation of financial risk
- Managing project scope and duration
- Reviewing deliverable materials for quality and content
- Managing conflict between competing groups with differing objectives
- Managing resources and staffing
- Creating and maintaining a project management plan

Although the list of responsibilities can seem endless, the project management role is the cornerstone to a successful business intelligence initiative.

Business/Information Analyst

The business/information analyst acts as the translator of business requirements to technical requirements. They are usually not as technical as the developers. The analysts will spend a large portion of time with business users to better understand business processes, data, and functionality requirements in order to ensure that the technical implementation will meet the business needs. The remainder of analyst's time is spent with the delivery staff translating business requirements into technical specifications that are used for the construction of the solution. The most significant roles and responsibilities include:

- Understanding business drivers, objectives, events
- Conducting interviews
- Refining and validating scope and requirements
- Documenting specifications for technical resources
- Creation of business models that enable translation to technology
- Acting as liaison between users and technical resources

In many organizations, analysts from the line of business assist in this role when requirements are complex or rapidly evolving. The information analyst then works closely with the line of business analysts to translate business requirements to technical specifications.

Data Acquisition Team

The data acquisition team is responsible for the extraction of data from source systems, the design and construction of extraction, transformation and load (ETL) code, and assisting in identifying the data elements necessary for the creation of data models. This role provides a bridge between the architects, data modelers, information analysts, and reporting specialists ensuring that source data will provide needed key performance indicators to the business. The most significant roles and responsibilities include:

- Understanding data sources including formats, definitions, frequency of updates, and security requirements
- Providing source-to-target data element mapping
- Designing and constructing ETL modules taking into account error and exception handling
- Supporting the metadata infrastructure
- Assessing data quality

In many organizations, the data acquisition team is comprised of individuals who have ETL tool or coding experience. Organizations that transition from 3GL coding to ETL tools often find that developer productivity increases significantly with fewer defects and higher maintainability. Productivity gains can also be attributed to the easy to use graphical interfaces for data mappings and pre-defined libraries of common transformations present in these tools.

The interrogation and analysis of source systems, including assessment of data quality, helps ensure accurate and comprehensive reporting and analysis. Similar data elements existing in multiple sources should be compared to determine the authoritative source, quality, and completeness during critical review processes. The information analyst or database administrator can provide insight if they were involved in prior projects that included the source systems under consideration.

Reporting and Analytics Team

The reporting and analytics team are responsible for providing business content delivered in a flexible and accessible manner to business users. This content might be delivered in solutions using software vendors' reporting tools that provide both prepackaged and ad hoc query capabilities, or portals and dashboards displaying key performance business indicators. The most significant roles and responsibilities in this team include:

- Identification of the most suitable types of reporting content
- Determining frequency of reporting content (scheduled or real time)
- Providing a platform for ad hoc and analytic discovery activities
- Delivering secure user interfaces aligned to business processes (portals)
- Providing definition and data lineage of reporting content (metadata)

In many organizations, the construction of reporting content now occurs in the line of business. This self-service reporting enables organizations to deliver functionally more rapidly and to be better aligned to business needs while having less reliance on the IT staff. Of course, coordination of development efforts should still occur at a centralized level to ensure that functionality is not duplicated or conflicting results produced.

In a smaller number of organizations, the reporting and analytics team engages in building custom interfaces to support business functionality. Most such custom interfaces are written in Java or other web-based technologies to provide functionality that is not readily available in software vendors' tools. Since this practice maintains a higher cost of development and ownership, it is important to limit these activities to functionality that is unique and differentiates the business.

Infrastructure and Systems Team

The infrastructure and systems team is responsible for the management and configuration of hardware, software, network, and desktop solutions. This team includes systems administrators responsible for the operation of servers, network engineers who maintain the network infrastructure, desktop specialists who support interface devices, production operations staff who maintain and monitor production solutions, and help desk operations staff responsible for the resolution of user service requests. In addition, DBAs are often part of this group supporting and managing the business intelligence infrastructure and, along with support analysts, are deemed very critical in ensuring the infrastructure performs properly.

Support analysts resolve initial functional inquiries from business users. Questions handled can range from complaints of errors in the reporting tools and custom applications to questions about data and data quality, calculations, and derivation of information. The support analyst typically works closely with the information analyst and reporting team to resolve inquiries and log enhancements.

The database administrator performs many roles and may be viewed as the most versatile individual to the overall business intelligence project. In many organizations, the DBA role is divided into production and development roles.

The production DBA is responsible for monitoring and proactive maintenance of business intelligence solutions. Frequently, they manage multiple environments and applications and rely on monitoring tools, such as Oracle Enterprise Manager Grid Control, to ensure that performance and availability remain high.

The development DBA is often the most knowledgeable individual about the features and functions of the database platform. They engage in many roles including assuring best practices for physical design and optimization of processing, engaging in performance tuning activities, and providing database support. They are attuned to the most current database technologies and ensure the solution is flexible and performs to meet business user needs.

Data Warehouse Architecture Team

The data warehouse architecture team is responsible for the design and construction of the data store supporting the business intelligence project. Although this team is primarily responsible for data architecture, it also participates in data acquisition integration, physical design, and assists in defining the application and technical architecture. Some of the significant roles and responsibilities include:

- Data Architecture
  - Establish data movement strategies from acquisition to distribution
  - Perform physical database design and assess data storage requirements
  - Create virtualization to reduce and hide complexities of data locale
  - Design summarization to improve performance
  - Define metadata solutions for accountability, traceability, and lineage of data
  - Assist in definition and deployment of data security
  - Work with DBAs to ensure engineering efforts are consistent with architecture

- Application Architecture
  - Assist in standardization of user interfaces and tools
  - Review design of middle-tier and applications servers
  - Assist in definition and deployment of application security
  - Work with reporting developers to ensure engineering efforts are consistent with architecture
- Technical Architecture
  - Perform capacity planning for hardware and storage
  - Define performance profiles to meet service levels
  - Work with system administrators, database administrators, and infrastructure engineers to ensure architecture is aligned to business-growth models

In most organizations, the data warehouse architecture team provides the tactical and strategic vision to ensure that current and future business objectives are met utilizing the latest technologies in a cost-efficient manner. The data warehouse architect often partners with the DBA to ensure proper delivery of this functionality.

End-User Experience

The success of a business intelligence project can be measured by the usefulness of the solution in the business user community. Well-architected solutions can fail to realize their full potential if the business users have little or no past exposure to reporting solutions, lack the foresight or vision on how using such information might improve their own standing in the business, or have been adversely impacted by the introduction of new technology that is not aligned to business needs. To ensure the highest alignment of proposed functionality to the current aptitude of the end user community, you might assess user capabilities based on a maturity scale for business intelligence (shown in Figure 10-8).

The entry stage on the maturity scale where reporting and business intelligence functionality is first introduced can be called the novice stage. During this stage, most functionality is delivered through pre-defined dashboards and reports meeting operational needs that were previously satisfied by manual procedures. The introduction of key performance indicators enables efficiencies in monitoring the operations of the business. Only the most advanced users require ad hoc capabilities during this stage and typically only after they become familiar with the new tools and began to trust the integrity of the information. For organizations in competitive markets, this transition can occur in as little as six months.

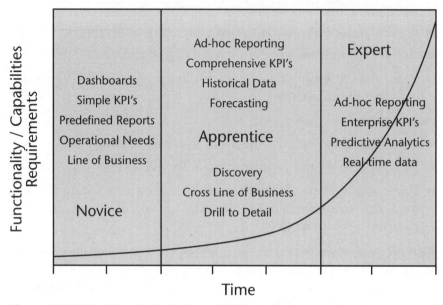

Figure 10-8: Maturity scale for business intelligence

The middle stage of the business intelligence maturity model is the apprentice stage. As users are familiar with the capabilities provided by a reporting platform at this stage, they become interested in working with more data in order to evaluate historical patterns against current and forecasted measures. They rely less on traditional reporting and more on ad hoc query and analysis tools. They will increasingly drill-to-detail enabling discovery of new metrics that include more comprehensive and advanced indicators. Within this stage, organizations rely on information across lines of business and make many strategic decisions. Although many organizations never emerge from this stage, this does not necessarily limit their capabilities. Often, constraints on capital or resources curtail the expansion of reporting and analytic solutions or may not be necessary, especially if the company competes in a mature market where there is stable growth and the barrier to entry is high.

The highest level of the maturity scale is the business expert. These users are most commonly in organizations where there is continuous change and where competition is fierce and margins are narrow. The requests for information often include the need for real-time data, enterprise-wide performance indicators, and predictive analysis to enable real-time decisions. Although few users and organizations evolve to this stage, those that do can react more immediately to sudden changes in business climate and economic conditions.

Engaging the Business: Education and Training

Training is a continuous activity that begins during the requirements gathering phase and continues well after the delivery of the solution. Training is one of the critical responsibilities of the business intelligence team that often is overlooked. Organizations sometimes limit training to skills transfer about how to use query tools or user interfaces, yet the most beneficial training might come from providing a better understanding of definitions of the data. Most users can easily master new query tools or interfaces, but without a strong understanding of the underlying data and its structure, only limited ad hoc discovery analysis can be performed.

When considering methods of training, it is important to consider several factors such as the maturity of the users and the organization as defined by the maturity scale, the availability of resources, and the critical nature of the solution. Traditional formal classroom training is an effective method that is repeatable and can be delivered on demand. It requires a dedicated training staff that is familiar with the solution, the reporting tools, and interfaces.

Many organizations have opted to use alternative methods like train-the-trainer where members of the business intelligence team train selected users of the business community who in turn are responsible for training their teams. This method is a viable alternative since the business is ultimately responsible for ensuring their users are properly trained.

Regardless of the training method, ensure that there is also adequate focus on understanding data including the definition of data elements, quality assessments, data lineage to source, and availability through reporting and ad hoc tools.

Managing Risk

We purchase insurance to protect our most valuable assets from theft, damage, or destruction. Although organizations do not have insurance to protect them against project delays, sponsors want assurance that the project is aligned with business requirements, is financially responsible, and can be delivered within an acceptable timeframe to meet business goals. Therefore, business intelligence projects should be managed and evaluated with the same rigor as other capital projects. A summary of proven techniques to reduce risk follows.

Communication — Managing Expectations

Communication with key stakeholders is critical to the overall success of any project-based initiative. The level of communications between key stakeholders is sometimes limited by lengthy periods between steering committee meetings, especially after initial requirements gathering is complete. Business requirements should be continuously gathered beyond the requirements phase of a project since priorities and functionality needs constantly change. These new requirements should be reflected on a MoSCoW list that becomes the communications method for business users and project team members as they determine needed revisions in scope and priorities. Some key steps to enhance communications during the initiative include:

- Embrace the methodology — incremental data warehousing methodologies are designed to increase touch points with key stakeholders throughout the project lifecycle.

- Ensure weekly status reports are distributed to key stakeholders, project team members and key business users.

- Solicit feedback on modifications and enhancements to the MoSCoW list to ensure priorities are consistent and accurate.

- Communicate project challenges to all key stakeholders providing opportunities for resolution.

- Ensure a single point of contact for the project team to manage consistent communications.

- Provide all stakeholders access to the project documentation repository so they can gain a better understanding of current and past activities.

- Be accountable for mistakes and communicate knowledge of them to key stakeholders to effectively manage expectations.

Although approaches to effective communications may vary in practice, ensure that guidelines are established and acknowledged with key stakeholders so that expectations are properly set.

Contingency Allocation

Even the best projects encounter challenges that may delay delivery or raise initial costs. Causes of delay can include modifications to scope, reallocation of resources, delays accessing key individuals, and changes in the business climate. Regardless of the cause, it is important manage time, functionality, and cost constraints efficiently in order to meet key stakeholder expectations. The most effective method to avoid very bad surprises is to provide a contingency plan for each phase of the initiative. Most often, the project manager will add one or more contingency tasks to each phase of the project to ensure that unknown risks can be mitigated as much as possible. When determining the allocation of contingency within an incremental approach methodology, the guidelines shown in Table 10-2 should be considered.

Table 10-2: Contingency Needs Guidelines and Processes at Risk

PHASE	CONTINGENCY NEED	PROCESSES AT RISK
Definition	Low	Requirements Definition (Scope) Data Acquisition (Approach)
Requirements Modeling	Moderate	Requirements Analysis Technical Architecture
Construction	High	Technical Architecture Data Acquisition Data Access Testing Performance Testing Adoption and Learning
Production	Moderate	Testing Transition Support

Recall that during initial project phases, it may be necessary to defer less important functionality to meet the time constraints. This functionality is placed on the MoSCoW list for re-prioritization and implementation at a later date. As a contingency alternative, it is important to identify additional in-scope functionality that could be deferred to a later date, especially when timely delivery is most critical to the initiatives' overall success.

Financial Risk

The financial investment in a business intelligence initiative is often based on belief in a positive return on investment from added business value or a competitive advantage. Although it may be difficult to eliminate all financial risks, the following recommendations may help reduce their impact:

- Perform financial review during steering committee and project review board events that includes a current run rate against budgeted amount.
- Limit new technology initiatives to enabling capabilities that have the highest business benefits.
- Prioritize, time-box, and MoSCoW.
- Use standardization where possible to reduce cost.
- Invest in training developers and business users.
- Use the methodology as a roadmap to success.
- Add contingency to high-risk tasks.

Although not all projects are delivered to budgetary estimates, long-term benefits can overcome cost overruns. However, projects must deliver an enabling or competitive advantage to realize these benefits. Verifying that key stakeholders understand the financial allocations will ensure that any additional investments will benefit the overall project success.

Technology Risk

Technology will always have the potential to introduce significant risk to any business intelligence initiative. Whether it's the latest upgrade of existing tools or the introduction of new interfaces, new technology can single-handedly delay initiatives even where there appears to be solid reasoning for introducing it. So why do so many projects suffer the wrath of new technology deployment? The answers are simple: We place too much trust in the capabilities and maturity of technology to deliver promised functionality. Some key solutions to reducing technology risks include:

- **Best of breed** — Best-of-breed technology may be appealing for its unique capabilities and functionality. But in many implementations, perceived benefits of best-of-breed technologies are more than offset by complexities associated with integration. Maintenance costs may also be significantly higher and the support process is often more complex where multiple vendors are involved. When considering if best of breed technology is appropriate for your organization, assess the past experiences in adopting new technologies, verify the maturity of the new technology, estimate the level of effort to integrate with existing environments, and determine if the benefits exceed the long-term costs.

- **Stability of technology** — Most technology vendors provide periodic software releases to address fixes or enhancements to their products. Although it is important to adopt the latest enhancements, consider a vendor's reputation in publishing these enhancements to ensure that they will not likely have an adverse effect.

- **Support process** — The support process is critical to ensure that any issues uncovered with the technology can be resolved in the most expedient manner. Since most technology vendors offer multiple levels of support, weigh the costs and benefits to determine the most appropriate solutions.

- **Organizational experience** — Many organizations are reducing the number of vendors they certify in order to reduce the complexities associated with maintenance, support, manageability, and the cost of these. The adoption rate of new technology will vary from organization to organization so it is important to determine the overall risk tolerance and experience of your organization before deploying new technology.

▪ **Cost/Benefit of technology** — For most organizations, it is important to match technology with the overall needs of the organization. Although it is vital to consider future needs and requirements, selecting technology that meets current needs and fits within budgetary constraints is appropriate. Remember that technology decisions are often reevaluated every three to five years due to changes in business requirements or enhanced capabilities found in the marketplace.

▪ **Training** — The introduction of new technology may require formal training for internal developers and infrastructure teams. For tools and interfaces used by business users, a training plan will ensure that they can benefit from the functionality the tools provide. Leverage previously highlighted training approaches to address these requirements.

Although technology is an enabler for every business intelligence project, care must be taken to ensure that the project schedule accounts for the introduction of new technology and reflects necessary contingency to meet delivery expectations. Leveraging external technology expertise can reduce the overall risk, especially in early adopter projects, and ensure that your project will be delivered on time with the highest level of user adoption.

No Place to Shortcut

The approach discussed in this chapter is based on proven techniques and observed best practices yielding successful implementations in hundreds of organizations. The principles in the approach we discussed included uncovering business initiatives, securing business sponsorship, endorsing a methodology, staffing the project, and managing risk.

In the interest of saving time, organizations sometimes will place less emphasis on or completely ignore some of these principles. However, taking shortcuts in these steps will likely put the success of your project in danger. Ultimately, you may find yourself spending more time recovering from a difficult situation than you would have spent in doing more careful up-front planning.

Since incomplete planning is not an option and limited timeframes to meet business needs are likely, we remind you of the other key aspect you control. Limiting scope is a key to successful projects. It is far better to deliver a successful project based on a limited and agreed-upon scope in partnership with your business community. Attempting to deliver a wider scope that is unattainable is not an option.

We mentioned earlier in this chapter that this approach is project centric and that creating a business intelligence strategy is usually an independent initiative. In Chapter 11, we discuss ways you can effectively engage the business and highlight some of the high-yield questions to uncover this strategy. Delivery of business intelligence solutions mapped to this strategy will ensure that your project is highly valued by the organization.

Understanding
Business Needs

In Chapter 10, we identified understanding business needs and initiatives as fundamental to a successful approach in designing and building a business intelligence and data warehousing solution. For technical people, this step is often a challenge. In this chapter, we'll describe how bad business intelligence deployment strategies can impact the lines of business and we provide some sample questions you can ask in the lines of business to call attention to the need for new solutions. We will also discuss some of the typical drivers of these projects in a variety of business types or verticals, including financial companies, healthcare, manufacturing, media and entertainment, retail, transportation and logistics, energy utility companies, educational institutions, and government agencies.

This chapter is meant to give you some ideas as to where to focus your discovery efforts and how to formulate some of the questions you should be asking. It is not meant to take the place of having such discussions within your organization. Each organization has its own unique set of needs and ranking of importance of those needs. The needs are defined by your business constituents and will drive the prioritization you will use in a staged implementation.

Our discussion of project drivers in different business types in this chapter is based on drivers that are commonly present at the time of publication of this book. These drivers sometimes change over time. For example, a few years ago, the focus in the airline industry, a segment of transportation, was gaining a better understanding of what customers wanted and who the most valuable customers were. This led to development of many frequent flyer program data warehouses. As jet fuel prices soared and cheaper air carriers emerged as competition, established airlines changed the focus of their business intelligence efforts to better manage logistics of equipment. Such systems help put the right planes on the right routes at the right time. An impact we sometimes see when traveling is the use of these systems to selectively cancel flights that are not fully booked. Customers are rerouted to other flights with available seats to the same destination. Obviously, this is a much different decision making process than trying to gain market share and grow customer satisfaction.

Before we discuss where you might focus your efforts around problems that are specific to a type of business, let's have a look at how bad deployment choices might drive a need for a new business intelligence solution.

How Bad Deployment Choices Impact the Business

It should be no surprise that bad deployment choices made by IT and technical support organizations within lines of business will negatively impact the ability to deliver meaningful business intelligence. Where business users and IT do not work together, a connection may not be made as to the true nature of the problem. Getting to the root of the problem is required in order to build a case for getting a budget to fix it.

A number of approaches that initially provide short-term fixes to business problems can be the cause of later problems. Examples of bad approaches include deployment of independent data marts, deployment of limited and inflexible reporting solutions, limiting sources of information to internal data, limiting availability of historical data, low-quality data or data that is not timely, and limited growth flexibility.

For each of these, we will describe the nature of the problem from an IT perspective. We also discuss how the lines of business might be impacted and provide you with some sample high-yield questions that can expose that impact.

Independent Data Marts

Data marts can be defined as data warehouses deployed within lines of business or departments to solve problems specific to those departments.

Common where speed of deployment is critical to meet the needs of single departments, these data marts are sometimes built independently of each other and may not be part of a larger enterprise data warehouse strategy. This independence causes a number of issues over time including inconsistency of results when the same business question is asked of systems residing in different departments. The inconsistency can arise from extracting and cleansing data differently within the departments, using different systems as sources, and having different definitions for business terms. Since independent data marts will present stovepipes of information, gaining cross-departmental views is difficult.

To solve these issues, IT organizations build enterprise data warehouses or work with departments to gain agreement on conformed dimensions across departments and create dependent data marts. In Table 11-1, we present some open-ended line-of-business (LOB) questions that can provide a starting point to help lines of business recognize the issues with the independent approach. These are not meant to be the questions for your organization since every business is different. But formulating questions like these and obtaining answers pointing to the difficulties caused by the current environment can prove your point.

You should expect rather complicated answers to each of the questions in the table if the data marts were developed independently. Structure your follow-up questions to help both you and the business user understand the amount of pain the current infrastructure causes and what it would mean from a business standpoint to eliminate this pain. Establishing a financial benefit to solving the business problems can be the justification for the project that you believe should be built.

Table 11-1: Sample LOB Questions to Establish Need for Enterprise Data Warehouse

LINE OF BUSINESS	SAMPLE QUESTION
Finance	How do you determine validity of a financial value?
Sales	How do you assure regional sales values agree with reported totals?
Marketing	How do you determine effectiveness of campaigns within and across sales regions?
Operations	How do you determine costs across the organization?
Human Resources	How do you determine if the number of employees matches business initiatives?

Limited and Inflexible Reporting

If business users can't get the information they need in the format they need it in when using business intelligence solutions with inflexible reporting, they develop workaround procedures. The most common workaround is to download data into spreadsheets to where it can be more flexibly manipulated. This approach, although common, introduces a number of problems.

The business users can become quite savvy in extracting needed data, but such users are really paid to make business decisions. This process leaves less time for actual business analysis. In some situations, users will adjust numbers in the spreadsheets based on their own intuition leading to arguments about whose set of numbers are correct. From a business compliance standpoint, the numbers in the spreadsheets may not be replicable at a future time if the spreadsheet values are altered or deleted, so key business records (that might be used for such critical tasks as briefing financial analysts) can be lost.

Table 11-2 provides a few sample questions you may want to use as a starting point to establishing the need for a data warehousing and business intelligence project that provides more flexible reporting.

The answers to these questions can establish the need for a data warehouse solution containing securely held data coupled with flexible ad hoc query and analysis tools that enable business users to create their own reports.

Table 11-2: Sample LOB Questions to Establish Need for Flexible Reporting

LINE OF BUSINESS	SAMPLE QUESTION
Finance	How do you perform what-if financial analyses and compare to past analyses?
Sales	How do you determine year-over-year performance on an ad hoc basis?
Marketing	How do you determine effectiveness of campaigns as they mature?
Operations	How do you analyze supply chain bottlenecks?
Human Resources	How do you determine top performers using different job classification criteria?

Sources of Information Limited to Internal Data

It may be impossible to understand how the business is truly performing if all of the sources of information are internal. For example, key performance indicators may look good when using only internal data, but the business may be underperforming if like data describing business at a competitor is better and showing improvement at a faster rate. For this reason, many organizations incorporate data from external sources in their business intelligence projects for comparisons and business benchmarking.

Table 11-3 denotes some sample questions that might establish a need for external data.

Answers to the above questions can establish a need to purchase data from third-party data sources and for a project to populate such data in your data warehouse solution and make it available to business users.

Limited Data History

Simple analysis can be performed in transactional systems built upon the Oracle database. In fact, Oracle's E-Business Suite uses materialized views built on transaction tables to provide simple drill-downs in Daily Business Intelligence. However, more sophisticated analyses requiring years of data often leads to a need for a data warehouse in order to deliver necessary performance.

Establishing a need for historical data will be very specific to a line of business problem. Table 11-4 denotes some sample questions that might establish a need for more historical data.

Table 11-3: Sample LOB Questions to Establish Need for External Data

LINE OF BUSINESS	SAMPLE QUESTION
Finance	How do you predict bottom-line implications of an acquisition?
Sales	How do you determine if your sales are growing as fast as sales of your competitors?
Marketing	How do you determine market share trends?
Operations	How do you determine your suppliers' ability to respond to change?
Human Resources	How do you compare employee retention to that of competition?

Table 11-4: Sample LOB Questions to Establish Need for more Historical Data

LINE OF BUSINESS	SAMPLE QUESTION
Finance	How do you determine monthly margin performance over the past five years?
Sales	How do you determine seasonal sales trends over the past seven years?
Marketing	How do you determine the optimal time to replace a marketing slogan?
Operations	How do you determine if inventory reductions are optimal over time?
Human Resources	How do you demonstrate long-term retention as an outcome of training efforts?

Part of this questioning should establish what minimal length of history must be kept and define the optimal length of history needed. Sales and marketing people, in particular, will want to keep very long histories in order to mitigate unusual results caused by events that are anomalies outside the control of the organization. Examples of such events might include weather changes, one-time disasters, and competition entering or leaving a market.

Lack of Current High-Quality Data

Data not available in a timely fashion will be ignored when making business decisions. If the data is suspect, it might also be considered useless, although it could be included in strategic planning if the data issues are considered minor. If inaccuracies are noticeable, business users will shun such information and choose to not use a system at all.

The need for current and high-quality information will sometimes drive the building of a data warehouse that becomes the organization's single version of the truth. The frequency of data updates and loading into the data warehouse should be driven by business needs. A case for near real-time data feeds might be established based on a critical business need for very recent data. However, near real-time data feeds can be impossible to achieve where extensive data cleansing is required and latency results. Where data warehouses exist and the data is of high quality but is not timely, projects might focus on deploying new extraction, transformation, and loading strategies to meet business requirements.

Table 11-5 shows some sample questions that might establish a need for higher quality data or more frequent delivery of such data.

Table 11-5: Sample LOB Questions to Establish Need for Higher Quality Data

LINE OF BUSINESS	SAMPLE QUESTION
Finance	How do you determine exposure to fraud when new transactions and updates occur?
Sales	How do you compare current day's hourly sales versus historical information?
Marketing	How do you determine status and potential success of a campaign in the first 24 hours?
Operations	How quickly can you determine likely supply chain issues when production increases?
Human Resources	How quickly can you determine impact of the departure of a key employee?

Limited Growth Flexibility

In organizations or industries where business change is rampant, flexibility in data warehouse design accommodating growth is important. Changes in deployment strategy might be needed when a company is fond of acquisitions or when business users are planning more sophisticated and detailed analyses. Special considerations should be made as to the flexibility of the data model and the ability to scale the systems when needed.

Table 11-6 shows some sample questions that might expose the need for more flexibility in your approach.

Table 11-6: Sample LOB Questions to Establish Need for Flexibility and Growth

LINE OF BUSINESS	SAMPLE QUESTION
Finance	How do you predict implications on margin as you grow the business?
Sales	How do you identify new up-selling and cross-selling opportunities?
Marketing	How do you measure the impact of an acquisition on customer loyalty?
Operations	How quickly can you analyze the supply chain after an acquisition?
Human Resources	How do you measure the impact of outsourcing?

In Chapter 4, we described some of the scalability choices that can be part of a flexible deployment strategy enabling growth. Scalability can be critical as the questions above usually identify a need for more and different types of detailed data in the data warehouse.

Project Drivers and Business Types

Thus far, we have explored determining business needs driven by business intelligence infrastructure that is less than optimal. However, many projects are driven by a need to provide information that was not previously available but that the business needs to be effective. As mentioned earlier, in commercial corporations, these drivers can change over time.

Drivers are usually tied to goals associated with top-line growth (when business is good) or bottom-line savings (when business is struggling). In government agencies, the goals are different with the most common being the sharing of information with sources of funding (for example, the legislature and their constituents).

We will begin by discussing drivers in commercial companies and end this section with a discussion of drivers of business intelligence projects in government agencies.

Financial Companies

We divide financial companies into two major groups in our discussion based on their historic business strategy emphasis. The first group includes banks and financial advisors that primarily focus on customer relationship management. The second group consists of insurance companies that often focus most of their business strategy on managing risk.

The two groups share some common attributes. Mergers and acquisitions among members in both groups have been occurring for many years. As larger merged versions of these corporations are created, new smaller regional startup competitors emerge promising more personalized service. Both of the financial groups are under the watchful eye of regulators, so meeting compliance requirements is critical. Increasingly, members of each group are exploring opportunities to offer products sold by the other.

Banks and Financial Advisors

Many banks and financial advisors build business intelligence solutions providing customer analysis (including profitability and retention), targeted marketing, and improving the ability to up sell and cross sell services and products. The need to focus on relationship solutions becomes more apparent during the mergers of and growth within these firms. Of course, business intelligence is also used in banking and financial advisor services companies to plan budgets, manage portfolios, determine effectiveness of marketing, determine locations and performance of branch sites, and for other day-to-day business management needs.

Table 11-7 shows a sample of high-yield questions you may want to ask in some of the lines of business present in banks to identify business intelligence needs:

As in the previous section of this book, the intent in the preceding table is to provide some open-ended questions that might be relevant. Your set of questions should be aligned to needs you believe are present in the company you plan to build a solution for. Remember that you'll follow-up the answers you are given with more detailed questions since the goal is to get the business owner to identify business value that a potential business intelligence solution will provide.

Insurance Companies

Insurance companies usually have business intelligence solutions that enable increasing profitability and managing risk. Key performance indicators in such solutions often include sales growth, return on equity, internal growth rate of capital, and product profitability and margins.

Table 11-7: Sample High-Yield Questions Determining Banking Needs

BANKING LINE OF BUSINESS	SAMPLE QUESTION
C-level Executive (CEO, CFO)	How do you measure performance of your various lines of business that provide loans?
Line of Business Executive (Payments and Loans)	How do you monitor selling and servicing of loans?
Enterprise Operations	How do you determine credit risk and deliver the information to the lines of business?
Customer Service	How do you determine who are the best customers and determine appropriate customized services?
Real Estate Management	How do you determine the optimal site to build a new branch?

Recent customer relationship business intelligence projects occurring at insurance companies are driven in response to banks and other financial companies invading their turf. Goals of such projects include improving customer satisfaction, growing numbers of customers, increasing customer profitability, and increasing customer retention. Since the more innovative insurance companies are now also selling policies directly via the Internet, customer web site usage behavior introduces another source of data to evaluate.

Healthcare

Healthcare business management requirements vary based on the degree of government involvement. In this book, we divide the discussion on healthcare into providers and payers. The providers might be the government, health maintenance organizations, independent providers, or a mixture. The payers are insurance companies or the government and their roles depend on the country you are building a solution in. Regardless, a common thread across both of these groups everywhere seems to be the increasing need for quality of care analysis in order to understand the effectiveness of initiatives designed to contain costs.

Healthcare Providers

Healthcare providers often face access to information problems caused by silos of applications (for example, patient management, pharmacy, and so on) and procedures where data is not captured in a database at all (for example, patient charting information or diagnostic images). This information problem is made worse by frequent mergers and acquisitions. The lack of a single source of truth has negative impact on the ability to control costs, make the right diagnoses in a timely manner, and determine the right levels and types of staffing. When efforts are made to bring this information together, secure access to the data on a need-to-know basis is mandated by standards such as the Health Insurance Portability and Accountability Act (HIPAA).

Of course, building a data warehouse and business intelligence solution can bring such information together. Impact can cross lines-of-business providers in areas that include case management (quality assurance and utilization review), care delivery, operations, finance, materials, marketing, and human resources.

Table 11-8 shows some of the key performance indicators important to the lines of business in healthcare providers and should provide you with some ideas on where to focus your high yield questions.

Table 11-8: Sample of Key Performance Indicators important to Healthcare Providers

LINE OF BUSINESS	KEY PERFORMANCE INDICATORS
Executives and Finance	Patient revenue, patient days, average patient days, payer mix, asset turnover, operating margin, days of cash on hand, days in accounts receivable
Operations and Utilization Review	Patient days, average length of stay, percent occupancy, number of outpatient visits, number of admissions, number of Emergency Room visits
Care Delivery	Case mix, mortality rate, complication rate, number of admissions, top 20 DRGs, top DRGs by cost by specialty by physician, post operation infection rate, medication errors, adverse drug reaction, patient falls
Human Resources	Number of occupied beds per nurse, mix of part-time and full-time staffing, hours on medical surgery floor per patient day, hours in ICU per patient day, medical surgery nurse to patient ratio, job vacancy to fill rate
Marketing	Service area, market penetration by service, satisfaction rate, patient complaints, family complaints

Software vendors selling patient management applications are beginning to provide such business intelligence solutions. However, where best-of-breed applications have been deployed in various departments and are unlikely to be replaced in the near term, it probably makes sense to explore a custom data warehouse solution that will address the most serious needs in your organization.

Healthcare Payers

Payers have many of the same issues that providers do. Silos of information make it difficult to bring together needed financial, operational, and clinical (care delivery) information required in claims adjudication and disease management. Other areas that can be impacted include the financial or budgeting office, marketing, and human resources (for example, for managing call center staffing).

Just as for providers, a custom data warehouse project can provide a solution for payers. To establish the business need, we provide some key performance indicators in Table 11-9 that should help you structure useful high-yield questions.

Table 11-9: Sample of Key Performance Indicators important to Healthcare Payers

LINE OF BUSINESS	KEY PERFORMANCE INDICATORS
Executives and Financial Management	Cash on hand, unpaid claims, liquidity, capital benchmark, year over year cost of claims, cost of claims by hospital, cost of claims by doctor
Operations/Call Center	Percent resolution, average talk time, average answer time, number of dropped calls, number of callers on hold (and average length of time)
Claims Adjudication	Claims backlog, claims paid per day, claims in process, average days to pay claims, longest days to pay claims
Membership Marketing	Renewal rate, open enrollment and actual membership, types of membership, number of member lives per year

Manufacturing

Manufacturing companies, as a group, have been relatively slow in adopting advanced data warehousing and business intelligence solutions. The most common focus in manufacturing is in the financial management line of business for budgeting and forecasting. More recently, some manufacturers have put in place business intelligence initiatives to reduce manufacturing cycle times and waste. Today's manufacturers' business models often rely on an ever-growing array of suppliers while the customers of these goods (for example, the retail stores and assemblers) try to reduce their inventory of finished goods and mandate that the manufacturers produce their goods just-in-time.

These trends can increase the unattractive likelihood of being over-capacity or under-capacity. To further complicate the lives of manufacturers, product lifecycles are growing shorter. And since cost is always an issue, many manufacturers are moving key manufacturing processes to the countries where the goods can be manufactured most cheaply.

Key to starting an initiative in this type of business is to understand all of the above business drivers within the company as well as initiatives in competitors. Look for a focus on managing margins in the finance group, increasing supplier visibility and tracking the on-time performance and quality of delivery in business groups managing supply chain, and tracking changes in customer demand and warranty analysis in the manufacturing process planning group.

Media and Entertainment

Most companies selling newspapers and magazines have seen numbers of subscribers decline over many years. Many have reinvented themselves as media companies. They bought radio and television companies and added services via the Internet. For example, many now provide on-line listings of job opportunities and entertainment guides. Since most income is generated through advertisements in each of these forms of media, a focus of business intelligence projects in this group is to track retention of advertisers and total spending of those advertisers across the various media.

The entertainment industry has been slower to embrace the new distribution opportunities arising from the Internet. However, some of these companies are beginning to use business intelligence to track royalties across the various types of media and delivery mechanisms in order to determine the success of new go-to-market strategies.

Retail

The retail business is known for having very thin profitability margins on goods sold. This means it is absolutely essential for a retailer to have the right mix of goods in the right stores at the right time. Because of this, retailers were one of the first business groups to understand the potential value of data warehousing and business intelligence.

Today, much of the focus in retail is to link point-of-sales information to the supply chain to assure the right goods are available for purchase. But a number of other key business requirements also drive retail data warehousing projects. Since stores must be properly staffed to optimally service customers and maximize sales, solutions providing staffing analysis are increasingly deployed. The layout of goods in a store can influence what purchases are made, so customer market baskets are often compared in different stores to determine optimal store layout that will maximize sales revenue. Merchandise loss prevention, analysis of promotion effectiveness, merchandise category management, analysis of customer buying behavior, analysis of gift card sales and redemption, and real estate management are just a few of the other areas typically addressed in retail business intelligence projects.

Table 11-10 shows a sample of some high-yield questions you may want to ask some of the lines of business in a retailer.

Table 11-10: Sample High-Yield Questions Determining Retail Needs

RETAILER LINE OF BUSINESS	SAMPLE QUESTION
C-level Executive (CEO, COO, CFO)	How quickly do you know if new business initiatives are having the desired impact?
Store Management	How do you predict and monitor seasonal store performance?
Merchandise Management	How do you determine when to change the mix of merchandise in a store and how do you determine what that mix should be?
Supply Chain Management	How do you measure supplier performance?
Marketing	How do you determine the success of a marketing campaign?
Human Resources	How do you determine if a store is properly staffed?
Real Estate Management	How do you determine whether leasing or buying property is optimal?

The need for more detailed data containing customers' individual transactions (to determine market basket buying behavior) and supply chain analyses resulted in retail businesses deploying some of the first multi-terabyte–sized data warehouses. The emerging use of RFID tags on goods and the use of the tags in tracking where the goods are located will result in significantly larger retail supply chain data warehouses in the future.

The greatest data volume, however, is present in non-traditional dot-com retailers. These retailers often track buying behavior through the customer mouse clicks they capture. They sometimes use this information to make recommendations and present web pages displaying products that have been proven to sell to similar customers. Such techniques rely on very large data warehouses behind the scenes that compare the path these customers are taking as they navigate the web site to the past behavior of customers.

Telecommunications

Telecommunications companies have some of the largest data warehouses known. Their data volume is driven by the need to store call detail records, especially when analyzing network elements and events. Although many early telecommunications data warehousing projects focused on quality of service and time for repairs, more recent projects are focused on gaining and retaining the customer.

Telecommunications companies are adding more services to traditional local, long distance, and cellular offerings. New offerings often include cable television and high-speed Internet. Of particular interest in these companies is the use of business intelligence to analyze the effectiveness of cross selling and to up selling these new services through targeted packaging and marketing. Other areas of increased interest include determining the lifetime value of customers and determining the likelihood of customer churn in response to promotions.

Other Business Types: Transportation and Utilities

A list of commercial business types can be extensive. We have covered some of the major categories, but two others are worth mentioning here. Both transportation/logistics companies and energy utility companies commonly build business intelligence solutions.

Transportation and logistics companies focus on cost containment and schedule optimization when faced with increased fuel and other transportation costs. Such companies make decisions on a real-time basis on when to reroute passengers and packages based on availability of equipment, percentage of capacity filled, and the importance of the customer who might be inconvenienced by rerouting. Business intelligence solutions are also commonly deployed for determining the right schedules for equipment nearing planned maintenance, most efficient equipment usage, and crew and driver scheduling.

Energy utility companies often use business intelligence in determining the right time to buy or sell energy on the energy grid. Some of these companies have plans to determine when to bring more power online by analyzing energy usage data populated in their data warehouses by automated meters located in homes and businesses.

Educational Institutions

Business intelligence initiatives in educational institutions are quite different in elementary and secondary school districts and systems (K through 12) and in higher education institutions (colleges and universities). We'll describe some typical initiatives in each and the business drivers.

Elementary and Secondary Schools

Administration styles in elementary and secondary schools might be most comparable to government agencies. In public schools, increases in spending are approved by voters. Funding comes from tax revenue and the government.

More recently, the government (especially in the United States) mandated measurement of education quality through testing procedures, sometimes linking funding levels to the education quality delivered. Elementary and secondary school districts increasingly find themselves competing for the best students with other public school districts and other private schools.

For these reasons, much of the focus on business intelligence initiatives among school districts and school systems is currently aimed at reporting test results. The districts use portals and reporting tools to display test results that are mandated by No Child Left Behind and other programs. These solutions make the data easily available to government officials and parents who want to understand how well a school district is meeting objectives. Districts that are not building such solutions increasingly find themselves at a disadvantage in attracting the best students and are forced to use slower manual methods to report results back to the government. News media sometimes indicate that districts without easy access to such information are intentionally trying to make access difficult.

School districts also typically use business intelligence for budgeting and financial forecasting. Relevant information needed in such planning includes information on new housing starts, changes in the tax base, and changes in population demographics.

Higher Education

Institutions of higher education, the colleges and universities, have more complex business intelligence needs than primary and secondary schools. As a result, a different variety of business intelligence initiatives are common.

Presidents, chancellors, and boards of regents are most commonly interested in the effectiveness of academic and research programs and their rankings among such institutions. Analysis of enrollment trends and expenses is also often desired in this level of management in the university.

Academic leadership, such as the provosts, need to understand student achievement and retention trends. They also want to understand faculty effectiveness, faculty retention, and ability to generate grants.

Financial management is critical, so budget analysis initiatives are common. Since fundraising is a key portion of income generation, business intelligence initiatives sometimes include analysis of alumni and their satisfaction with the university. Some universities offer special programs for alumni and target specific companies or types of businesses and then measure the effectiveness of such programs.

Table 11-11 denotes some sample high-yield questions that can be asked when determining the need for a business intelligence solution in an institution of higher education.

Table 11-11: Sample High-Yield Questions Determining Higher Education Needs

LEVEL OF INSTITUTION	SAMPLE QUESTION
Presidents, chancellors, board of regents	How do you determine if spending is matching emerging trends in enrollment?
VP of Academic Affairs, VP of Research	How do you measure value of a faculty member to the university?
Budget Director, Budget Analyst, Fundraising Director	How do you determine when you should launch a new fundraising campaign?

Government Agencies

Government agencies use business intelligence for budgeting, but in a different way than businesses do. Since the money is allocated for an entire fiscal year and profit is not a goal, financial business intelligence is directed at understanding the percentage of budget spent and providing information after it is spent back to the funding authority. In addition to sharing financial information with the legislature, a common goal is the sharing of information about agency services and initiatives with both the legislature and the taxpayers. We'll now take a quick look at how business intelligence is used in a variety of agencies.

Defense, Military, and Intelligence Agencies

Business intelligence is widely used in defense and intelligence agencies. Of course, there are special requirements for secure data access and control since the audience seeing such data is much more limited than in civilian agencies. However, just as in business, successful projects are critical in order to make both strategic and tactical decisions. Solutions often have a similar mix of deployment technologies including portals and reports showing key performance indicators, and ad hoc query, analysis, forecasting, and data mining tools. For example, data mining is sometimes used in such agencies for risk identification.

Table 11-12 contains sample high yield questions that could help define the type of business intelligence project needed. In defense and intelligence agencies, the need for such projects is often established by requirements mandated by the legislature or to fulfill a mandated mission, but the agency leaders also sell the legislature on the project need when obtaining their budget.

Table 11-12: Sample High-Yield Questions Determining Defense Needs

ROLE	SAMPLE QUESTION
Secretary, General Officer	How do you measure readiness across different functional areas?
Mission Operations	How do you track scarce resources, including manpower and material?
Finance / Budgeting / Comptroller	Describe your confidence in internal controls, financial reports, and budget submissions.
Human Resources	How do you know if you have the right personnel at the appropriate grade sufficiently trained?
Logistics	How do you determine the material requirements and readiness?
Procurement	How do you determine weapons system lifecycle costs?

Civilian Agencies, State, and Local Government

Civilian agencies and local government use business intelligence to share information and allocate limited resources. Table 11-13 contains typical sample questions that point toward business intelligence solutions that would enable an agency to better report on the performance of the agency and to accomplish agency goals.

Asking questions specific to an agency is a better approach to uncover more compelling business needs. To illustrate this point, Table 11-14 contains sample high-yield questions that could help determine needs for business intelligence projects in a Health and Human Services agency.

Table 11-13: Sample High-Yield Questions Determining Civilian Agency Needs

ROLE	SAMPLE QUESTION
Agency Head	How do you measure performance across the agencies within your Department?
Finance/Budgeting/ Comptroller	How do you monitor performance, budget formulation, and execution for projects?
Investigative Audit/ Inspector General	How do you deliver audit risk statistics to senior agency management?
Human Resources	How do you assess if you have the right personnel with the right skills to accomplish agency goals?
Chief of Procurement	How do you achieve economies of scale with your most important suppliers?

Table 11-14: Sample High-Yield Questions Determining Health and Human Services Needs

ROLE	SAMPLE QUESTION
Administration	How do you determine if services are eligible for reimbursement?
Finance	How do you determine high-cost contributors that should be proactively managed?
Case Management	How do you ensure problem trends are identified for further follow-up?
Call Center Response	How do you determine staffing and skill levels required at various times of the day?
Human Resources	How do you determine employee retention rates and compare those with number of caseloads handled, salary, and training?

Of course, governments consist of many types of agencies. Rather than attempting to provide sample high yield questions for all of them, we'll instead summarize common initiatives in a few types of agencies:

- **Corrections and prison systems** — Determine effectiveness of rehabilitation programs and optimize staffing levels.

- **Emergency management** — Logistical management of supplies and support personnel in times of disaster.

- **Labor** — Determine current and future trends in skilled labor availability and demand for specific needed job skills.

- **Law enforcement and justice** — Predict crime hotspots, assign officers to the right locations, determine staffing and skills requirements, and augment crime information with data from other agencies.

- **Taxation and revenue** — Determine likely tax audit candidates.

- **Trade and commerce** — Determine trends in foreign trade and impact of trading agreements and protective legislation.

- **Tourism** — Track visitor statistics such as visitor purpose, mode of arrival, and visitor preferences to develop better targeted marketing campaigns.

- **Transportation** — Predict traffic and passenger loads, and determine optimal toll and fare structures.

Developing Scope and Gaining Business Support

Now that we have presented a variety of high-yield questions and you understand some potential needs for business intelligence in commercial businesses and government agencies, you should feel more comfortable formulating your own questions. As you ask these questions, try to determine the importance of the benefits that the business owners believe a business intelligence solution will deliver, both in initially solving their business problem and as a solution on an ongoing basis. Whenever possible, get the business owner to estimate the financial value provided by such a solution.

Remember that the project plan you develop should be deployed in manageable and rapid increments. Establishing a defined scope of deliverables in the order of priorities based on business importance and chosen by the business owners will be critical. But gathering this information by itself may not be enough to gain support for starting the project.

Business owners will often have trouble visualizing the solution you will propose. One technique you might use to improve clarity in this process is to ask the business owners what key performance indicators are most important to them for display on a dashboard. You might then draw a diagram of how such a dashboard could appear and get their buy-in as to whether you are on the right track.

A bit more involved technique that can be used at this point is to build a very small proof of concept. Since you should now have a defined business problem and identified some needed key performance indicators, with skilled business intelligence developers or a willing partner vendor, you could build a demonstration of a potential solution. The demonstration should be of very limited scope, ideally completed within a week, and would show what the finished dashboard could look like. Probably only one or two of the key performance indicators should be populated with live data since the goal is to produce something tangible quickly. You shouldn't think of this effort as part of the actual project building effort. Focus on educating and gaining confidence of potential sponsors who have spending authority for money that could be budgeted. Building such a demonstration can also be used to help refine the scope.

Figure 11-1 shows a dashboard that could be used in demonstrating the value of a banking business intelligence project to the CFO of a bank. This demonstration dashboard includes typical key performance indicators that would be of likely interest.

Figure 11-1: Typical demonstration dashboard for a banking executive

In some organizations, building a business case to start a project or continue to the next increment of a project requires that a positive potential return on investment (ROI) be identified. Such ROI computations must be based on benefits projected by the business owners to be believed. This is a very inexact undertaking. But, using the answers you obtain in response to high yield questions similar to those in this chapter, you should be able to identify benefits that will become part of the ROI computation. We describe the steps in determining ROI next in Chapter 12.

Justifying Projects and Claiming Success

Beauty is in the eye of the beholder — this is often true for business intelligence projects when determining their value to the organization and whether investments in hardware, software, and other resources positively impact the business. All too often, organizations are excited at the prospect of providing business insight to the desktop only to find costs have exceeded budgets and functionality has fallen short of expectations. Most project teams believe they can deliver a superior solution provided that they obtain the necessary funding and are given sufficient time. But the task is becoming more difficult in today's corporate climate where numerous initiatives often compete for a limited pool of resources. Although there is no guarantee that a project will be delivered on time and within budget and provide the desired functionality, a number of key factors can help ensure that there is agreement as to the project value. The measure of such value can be complex and includes tangible items that can be measured and intangible items that often can only be estimated.

The goal of this chapter is to assist you in understanding the key financial metrics required to build a comprehensive justification for a business intelligence initiative. This chapter highlights approaches that have proven successful in justifying projects leading to proper sponsorship and funding. We discuss common methods that can be used in the formulation of a value assessment supported by tangible measures, such as total cost of ownership, and intangible measures that can determine the overall return on investment. In addition, we describe proven techniques for measuring value that meet the criteria of both the business constituents and the project team.

Concept to Project

Project concepts often start with goals such as changing how an organization will go to market or solving a critical business problem that will enable operations to run more efficiently. As many organizations churn through business cycles, they understand that better business information can improve business performance or provide a competitive advantage. Regardless of whether a business cycle occurs during an economic expansion or economic downturn, it is prudent to provide sufficient business and cost justification to ensure the concept becomes a funded project and ultimately survives.

Business Constraints

Business constraints can limit a great concept from ever becoming reality. Today, few solutions that promise to deliver differentiating functionality to achieve a competitive advantage receive immediate funding without being scrutinized. Although many organizations do not possess a formal justification process, most require some due diligence before funding is allocated. Even where projects are initially well aligned to business needs and possess the proper sponsorship, funding can be rescinded later as a result of reorganization or a key stakeholder leaving the organization.

Where to Start Justification

In determining where to start constructing the justification for an initiative, first understand how the organization measures value. The challenges are clear: provide a compelling business case that includes business objectives and a credible financial plan with necessary business sponsorship. Capturing the business objectives can be straightforward if they align to specific business deficiencies that can be solved by providing better visibility into operations. Most often, the objectives are aligned to operational parameters used in measuring the business, new initiatives such as entry into a new market, or in response to competitive pressures. Align these objectives to the vision of the business to ensure the highest levels of support.

Unlike uncovering objectives, obtaining business sponsorship is a complex and political task that requires consensus and compromise. As previously highlighted in this book, the pyramid of influence provides an approach to obtaining sponsorship in the most efficient and expedient manner and enables focus on the most critical step: financial justification. Regardless of perceived value of a business intelligence initiative, sufficient funding is needed to turn a concept into reality. Recent studies and experience indicate that preparing a financial justification for a proposed initiative leads to funding, on average, in nearly half the time. This is significant since most requested initiatives are time sensitive and require quick delivery. Unfortunately, IT organizations have historically performed cost analyses to justify projects but have rarely linked these initiatives to business results. In the next section, we will discuss how organizations measure value and discuss many of the key metrics that are evaluated prior to funding a project.

Measuring Value

Measuring the value of a business intelligence initiative can be divided into two broad perspectives: intrinsic or perceived value, and financial return. Intrinsic value is the simpler since the project will be funded based on anticipated overall impact and positive influence in the organization regardless of cost. Fewer current business intelligence projects are funded solely because of intrinsic value and more often require financial justification to ensure the proposed investment reflects the best use of the organization's capital. Although financial measurements vary from organization to organization, most focus their analysis on models that consider factors such as the initial outlay of capital, annual reoccurring costs like maintenance and support, asset life expectancy, the sources of capital, opportunity cost, and overall value to the business. When combined, the perceived intrinsic value and strong financial justification provide the necessary incentive to justify the project.

Figure 12-1 illustrates the factors used in measuring overall value. In the next section, we will discuss some of the most common metrics that are used for measuring business intelligence initiatives that form the building blocks for analyzing the total cost of ownership and return on investment.

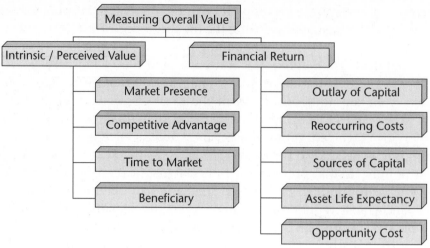

Figure 12-1: Factors for measuring overall value

Common Metrics to Measure

To construct financial justification using total cost of ownership and return on investment, let's start with the most common metrics that are used in measuring IT investments. The detailed information gathered during this process is similar to that found in income and cash flow statements, enabling analysis of cost structures and the impending benefits realized from cost savings or positive cash flows. The metrics needed for financial justification can be divided into cost elements and elements associated with value generation. When accompanied by common budgeting techniques, a comprehensive view of the proposed initiative develops and the business can analyze its overall value in direct comparison to initiatives from other areas of the business.

Elements of Cost

The elements of cost are the easiest metrics to capture, because they reflect familiar purchased components that are part of almost any business intelligence or IT initiative. These elements are not limited to initial costs, as it is necessary to consider hidden elements that impact cost over the entire life of the solution. The sections below highlight the most common elements of cost: hardware, software, storage, and human resources. In addition, we explain many of the details that should be included as part of an analysis when determining true cost over an entire solution lifecycle and specifics pertaining to an Oracle environment.

Hardware

The hardware is the capital expenditure that provides the physical platform supporting the data retrieval, calculations, and level of performance for a business intelligence initiative. It is important to understand the various architectural options when selecting hardware since processing resources are required to support the database tier, OLAP or analytics tier (where deployed separately), and the application server tier for user reporting and analysis tools. We described hardware platform choices earlier in Chapter 4, but to summarize here, the top factors to consider when estimating the cost of hardware include:

- **Capacity requirements** — Determine the capacity requirements necessary to support the business intelligence initiative. At the database tier, this includes understanding the number of users who will have access to the environment and what percentage is anticipated to query the database concurrently. If metrics are not available, we recommend using a factor of 10 percent of the total user population to represent concurrent activities. In addition, it is important to understand the overall type of work the users perform. This is classified into three types based on the type of queries executed. Type I queries are operational in nature, scan only a few rows, and execute in only a minimal amount of time. Type II queries range from complex operational to historical inquiries where a large data set is scanned to provide results of varying size. Execution times of these queries will vary in time ranging from three to five times that of Type I queries. Type III queries are the most complex, scanning large sets of data while performing multiple calculations that consume large amounts of computing resources. The execution times of these queries are several times that of Type II queries or longer. The mix of Type I, II, and III queries is significant in determining the amount of computational resource that is needed. Although query mix will vary by solution, we recommend a starting mix of 60/30/10 for initial discussions.

- **Technical architecture** — There are several ways technical architecture can be deployed for Oracle business intelligence solutions. The choices range from large SMP configurations to horizontal, grid-based solutions. When considering the most appropriate architecture, it is important to consider existing corporate standards, cost constraints, scalability needs, and the future architecture direction established by the IT organization.

- **Scalability** — There are three common approaches to scaling Oracle business intelligence solutions: vertical, horizontal, and hybrid solutions. Vertically scaled solutions are based on single SMP configurations that have substantial growth available within the platform to provide additional resources. Although such a configuration requires the purchase of a larger platform that will support future growth, expansion is relatively simple until the configuration reaches capacity. Horizontally scaled solutions are based on multiple smaller SMP platforms (nodes) where capacity is increased by adding nodes. These configurations possess several benefits, including high availability, ability to pay as you grow, and unlimited scalability with few limitations. A hybrid solution combines the best of vertical and horizontal scale by providing short-term scalability through vertical expansion and unlimited scalability through horizontal growth.

- **Life expectancy** — The life expectancy of hardware is often measured by its depreciation schedule. When fully depreciated, aging equipment becomes a candidate for repurposing or replacement. Since significant enhancements in hardware performance and scalability occur about every two years, many organizations are accelerating depreciation schedules or repurposing hardware. Given these rapid advances, it is important to understand IT investment strategies and align them to minimize the long-term impact of upgrades.

- **Maintenance and support** — Part of the ongoing cost associated with hardware is support and maintenance. These contractual agreements provide needed maintenance and services to ensure that the hardware is operating at its prescribed capabilities. As the hardware ages and nears obsolescence, the cost of maintenance and support often increases significantly encouraging organizations to upgrade to faster and newer models that have a lower maintenance cost. An emerging trend is to purchase excess capacity when organizations lower their costs through the use of commodity hardware. Since low-cost, commodity hardware typically has a shorter life span due to rapid advancements in processing speed and performance, it is often less expensive to replace defective equipment than to maintain existing, aging servers.

- **Training** — Hardware related training costs are often limited to the initial acquisition period when administrators become familiar with the new platform. For more mature organizations, this cost is often minimal or not required.

- **Experience** — Experience with and knowledge of the proposed hardware platform is important in ensuring the highest levels of performance and availability. Although new platforms may promise higher performance and a lower cost of acquisition, the long-term cost of operations and the risks associated with switching classes of hardware or operating systems need to be factored into the overall calculations. We recommend analyzing past experiences within the IT organization to determine if experiences in the adoption of new technologies have an adverse impact on operations.

Software

Another capital expenditure for a business intelligence initiative is software. Software powers data retrieval, reporting, security, analytics, and specialty functions. The selection of software can provide an organization a competitive advantage through better visibility into operations or the optimization of business processes. Although many organizations continue to debate the alternatives of best-of-breed software solutions, an emerging trend is consideration of software suites. Although suites sometimes lack the equivalent functionality of their best-of-breed counterparts, the overall cost of ownership is often considerably lower when considering maintenance, training, integration costs, and the complexities of support and upgrades. The top software classifications that comprise a business intelligence initiative include:

- **Operating system software** — Operating system software is responsible for the management of processing resources, file management, and other computing services that provide integration between the hardware and application software. When selecting an operating system for business intelligence initiatives, it is important to understand the level of platform support provided by your software vendors. Selecting mainstream platforms often provides a higher level of stability since more have been deployed and the latest functionality is readily available. Although commercial operating system software provides the benefits of maturity and wide-spread adoption, many organizations are choosing to move to open source alternatives (for example, Linux) at a significantly lower cost. When considering open source alternatives, ensure that your application software providers are committed to future development and support.

- **Database software** — Database software is the most critical software component for a business intelligence initiative as it provides data management, storage, and security. The Oracle database includes features designed specifically for data warehousing as we have discussed throughout much of this book. To support the demands of growth and scalability, Oracle Real Application Clusters enables capacity to be increased seamlessly without modifications to the data or technical architecture. Supported on the most popular hardware platforms and operating systems, the Oracle database provides organizations great flexibility when designing and configuring a technical architecture. Oracle's scalability and features also enable the consolidation of many disparate repositories of information, providing the business a single source of information.

- **Reporting suites/tools** — Reporting tools provide broad functionality, including reporting, analysis, scorecards, dashboards, and event management. Although most organizations are moving to thin-client, web-based interfaces, eliminating the need for desktop installations and maintenance, desktop configurations sometimes continue to be mandated for power users who desire local processing power and capacity to satisfy resource-intensive queries. Today, most reporting tool suites can be deployed to application servers and provide everything from high-fidelity formatting to computational analysis in highly available and load balanced configurations. When selecting reporting suites and tools, it is important that they are aligned to your architectural configurations and leverage the existing infrastructure when possible. As more analytic capabilities are moving from the reporting suites to the database tier, it is increasingly important to validate that your suite of tools will provide native database access and benefit from the embedded database analytics.

- **Management and monitoring tools** — Many operating systems and database vendors include management and monitoring tools as part of their software suites. Most operating systems are bundled with baseline tools for monitoring the utilization of CPU, I/O, and memory. Advanced tools often provide graphical interfaces with repositories that provide the ability to compare metrics over time. The Oracle database includes Enterprise Manager, enabling the management of business applications, end-user services and supporting infrastructure. Enterprise Manager 10g Release 2 and newer releases automate many time-consuming, error-prone administrative tasks. Features such as automatic memory tuning, automated storage management, backup, and health monitoring reduce the time administrators spend managing configurations and deployments.

- **Specialized software** — Many organizations leverage additional software to perform analytics and advanced forecasting. Much of the analytic functionality is now available in the database engine, enabling computations to occur where the data is stored. Oracle added statistical functionality in the database accessible through standard SQL. Advanced functions such as ranking, linear regression, distribution, linear algebra, and predictive analytics enable reporting suites and tools to benefit from the processing power found at the database tier. In addition, Oracle embedded its OLAP and data mining technology into the database providing a scalable, secure platform for advanced forecasting, modeling, and analytical processing. When determining usage of these capabilities or selecting other specialized software, it is important to consider the architecture, capabilities to scale, security provisions, and the level of effort to integrate into the existing infrastructure. The associated cost of ownership should also be weighed against the overall value.

- **Maintenance and support** — Maintenance and support are recurring software-related costs. Most software companies bundle both maintenance and support into annual contracts enabling access to support analysts to solve issues encountered and access to periodic maintenance releases. Software maintenance releases often include new functionality as well as fixes to existing problems. Larger organizations consolidate software to fewer vendors, where possible, to reduce costs associated with multiple maintenance and support contracts. Although this practice must balance specialized functionality provided by best-of-breed software with cost of maintenance, many organizations realize the cost benefits and faster time to resolution provided by single vendor support.

- **Training** — Software training is important to the overall success of any business intelligence initiative to ensure that return on investment is fully realized. Although training is critical to maintain productivity of developers and administrators, business users are often the largest group needing formal training. Though many methods can be effective in training users, the desire for training repeated on demand and relevant to the current needs of the user community is common, regardless of the method used.

Remember to include each software package in your financial justification to reflect the true overall benefits and associated costs. This allows key decision makers to understand the impact of each software component on the overall business intelligence solution.

Storage

As business intelligence initiatives become more strategic to the daily operations of business, additional years of history and details about transactions and events are stored. Growing amounts of data challenge IT organizations to stay within their budgets for storage. As much as 60 percent of added cost can be due to management and acquisition of storage. A huge miscalculation can occur if the IT organization has not considered the expansion of storage in their financial justification. Nonetheless, there are some advanced solutions available today that can help reduce the overall cost of storage while the need grows. The top factors to consider when estimating the cost of storage include:

- **Performance** — An increasing number of storage options provide organizations with choices that have a direct impact on performance and cost. Your organization can select from traditional storage, network attached storage (NAS), or a storage area network (SAN). Many IT organizations are choosing multiple storage solutions. When determining the best price-to-performance criteria for data warehouse storage, the following guidelines can be applied:

  - More spindles often reduce contention for data
  - Faster spindles enable faster data access
  - More channels to storage provides additional access paths
  - Large capacity disk devices are not always better

  Given the cost of storage can vary dramatically based on its architecture and configuration, ensure that the performance of your storage system meets or exceeds service levels established by the business.

- **Capacity** — Capacity planning for a business intelligence initiative requires estimating initial capacity needs, determining the rate of growth of data, and confirming requirements for retaining historical data. Such capacity estimates should be adjusted if business needs radically change. Keep in mind that recurring costs can be reduced by leveraging hardware and software solutions such as data compression. A best practice when estimating storage is to increase overall storage by 10 to 15 percent to account for unexpected growth and for administrative purposes.

- **Configuration** — The configuration of storage has a significant impact to the overall performance and long-term cost to a business intelligence solution. Modern storage systems provide configurations called RAID that optimize capacity, availability, and reliability to achieve the best price-to-performance ratio. We described popular RAID configurations for data warehousing in Chapter 4. When working with your storage provider, ensure that the suggested RAID configuration is capable of meeting performance and scalability needs. Most business intelligence solutions are resource intensive and have high throughput requirements.

■ **Expansion** — As the data volumes grow and more history is retained for reporting and analysis, additional storage is needed. Adding storage can require additional supporting infrastructure. When estimating the long-term costs associated with the growth of data, it is important to understand the expansion capabilities of the storage infrastructure to ensure that it can support the anticipated growth targets and to understand the point when additional infrastructure will be required.

■ **Information lifecycle management** — Information lifecycle management consists of a set of strategies used in the management of storage solutions. ILM can provide a significant reduction in cost, especially where large amounts of storage are used. Most ILM solutions utilize a combination of storage technologies that enable the most frequently accessed data to reside on the fastest devices while older, less frequently accessed data is moved to slower, lower-cost devices over time. Data that is most commonly accessed resides within the current week, month, or quarter. As data ages, its frequency of access is significantly reduced and the value of high-speed access is diminished. When planning and configuring your storage solution, you may want to determine if an ILM strategy can significantly reduce the overall cost. Oracle first included ILM capabilities in Oracle Database 10g Release 2 and continued to improve these capabilities in subsequent database releases and through introduction of an ILM Assistant.

■ **Maintenance and support** — Just as in our hardware discussion, storage solutions require maintenance and support. Even with advances in technology, the annualized failure rate of enterprise storage devices is commonly thought to approach 1 percent per year. When estimating the annualized cost of storage maintenance and support, the total cost ownership is often higher and may include costs associated with data center infrastructure, installation, configuration, and internal resources.

■ **Training** — Training costs related to the management of storage is similar to the training requirements for hardware. Once administrators become familiar with the supporting management software and administration, the future costs are normally minimal.

When estimating the cost of storage for financial justification, it is often beneficial to estimate the total cost per gigabyte for usable storage. This metric can be used for estimating the cost of storage associated with current and future growth of data.

Human Resources

Human resources remain one of the largest line item costs found in IT budgets. Business intelligence and data warehousing IT specialists are often highly prized for their skills in constructing solutions that provide better operational efficiencies or better visibility into business activities. To better understand the cost of resources associated with business intelligence solutions, the following factors should be considered:

- **Roles and responsibilities** — When estimating the cost of human resources for a business intelligence initiative, it is important to understand the roles and responsibilities of assigned persons and the current state of the project lifecycle. In Chapter 10, we discussed the approaches to staffing a business intelligence engagement and described a specialized team comprised of a project manager, information analysts, data acquisition specialists, reporting specialists, architects, and infrastructure support. During new development activities, it is necessary to estimate the level of effort to support full life-cycle development that includes all roles. When the initiative is delivered, support is typically limited to analysts, trainers, and administrators. Analysts remain engaged with the user community to validate that the solution delivered meets the current business needs and identify new requirements for future phases. Trainers are responsible for ensuring that business users are properly trained to use the new solution. When estimating training costs, first estimate of the number of users and then amount of hours of training per user. Since administrators are often assigned to monitor and maintain additional systems, their cost might be apportioned appropriately based on their administration workload for each system.

- **Experience** — There is no substitute for experience in developing and delivering business intelligence solutions. Countless projects have encountered cost overruns that are mainly attributable to lack of experience. When estimating the cost of a new initiative, account for the experience level of the team and ensure sufficient time and funding is allocated to offset any risk.

- **Professional services** — Leveraging professional services has strong appeal to organizations searching for subject matter expertise or best practices for developing and delivering business intelligence solutions.

The use of professional services can reduce the overall risk associated with the initiative while providing mentoring and guidance to educate employees on best practices. Many organizations use professional services to perform staff augmentation activities. When such resources are engaged in construction activities, organizations can focus their own limited resources on the most important activities, such as design and architecture. Although professional services consultants can be higher cost than internal employees, they can be engaged on demand for short durations without the overhead associated with hiring. When selecting a professional services organization, understand their core competencies, validate references, and understand their contract process. If requirements are unclear and risks are considered high or if multiple service firms are engaged, it can be beneficial to request fixed-price service contracts. Although the cost of such a contract is typically more expensive, the contract will eliminate unplanned costs if risks are realized.

When estimating the cost of resources for financial justification, it is often beneficial to provide detailed cost estimates by role to show the level of effort assigned in the project. Be sure to include factors that reflect the level of staff experience needed such that a higher level of experience is allocated additional time or resources. When estimating the cost of employees, ensure that cost factors are fully burdened to include costs of benefits and leverage pre-defined rates negotiated between the business and IT. Finally, engage the business to take an active role in the project to ensure proper alignment with their goals.

The identified costs are just a sample of what is included in a financial analysis. Remember that providing sufficient detail gives the business a clearer understanding of the costs of the proposed initiative when determining overall value compared to initiatives from other areas of the business.

Elements of Value

When performing a cost/benefit analysis to justify a business intelligence initiative, it is necessary to demonstrate the value the solution provides in the form of cost savings, operational visibility, and economic impact to the organization's bottom line. Although it is more difficult to place value on intangible benefits, it might be important to emphasize their significance to ensure the initiative receives consideration for funding. The section below highlights the most common elements of value considered when performing financial analysis for business intelligence initiatives. We provide details to consider when determining the value of the solution and scenarios of how to measure the results.

Resource Reallocation

One of the simplest measures of value is savings achieved by reducing or eliminating full time equivalents needed to perform a data collection or preparation activity. The measurement of value appears to be simple — the annualized cost of the resource is captured and the elimination of this work is defined to be a benefit of the project. Though this work may be eliminated, in reality, the person is rarely eliminated and thus no real savings are actually realized. They simply are assigned another task.

To account for this, review resource cost and time allocation before and after the project and place a value on the savings in terms of full-time equivalents (FTEs). The following scenario highlights the value gained in resource reallocation:

> *Scenario 1: Executives require a weekly sales report for all divisions to determine if the company is meeting its forecast. It takes one day to collect data from their ten divisions, two days to reconcile this information, and one more day to reformat the details into an executive summary that compares current sales to last year's sales and build a forecast. The report is made available on the fifth day, as pictured in Figure 12-2. The current process requires three FTEs to collect the data, reconcile it, and create the executive summary. The proposed business intelligence solution will automate the collection of sales information from all the districts and build the historical comparison and forecast. The new solution will provide information to the executives daily and requires only one FTE to validate results and perform a more detailed analysis on request. The other FTEs will be reallocated to new business initiatives.*

In scenario one, two FTEs will now be allocated to new business initiatives eliminating the need for the organization to hire two additional resources.

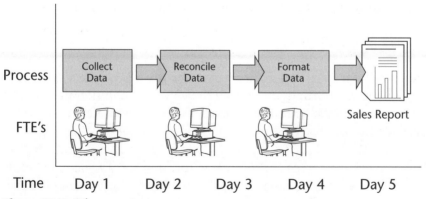

Figure 12-2: Sales report process

Productivity Enhancements

Productivity enhancements are more difficult to measure financially. The most common approach is to determine the amount of time eliminated from a common business process. This requires a decomposition of the business process into discrete activities where each activity is assessed to determine the complexity and level of effort. This process is commonly referred to as activity-based management and is often used in supply chain, manufacturing, and service industries where the marketplace is competitive, processes are inefficient, and overhead costs are excessive.

In scenario one, there is a reduction of two FTEs that were previously allocated to collect, reconcile, and reformat the sales report prior to deployment of the automated reporting solution. The productivity enhancements enable the remaining FTE to focus on activities such as report validation and analysis. Figure 12-3 illustrates this optimized sales report process. When measuring productivity enhancements, one must determine the optimization achieved through automation and assign a value. This value may be vague and difficult to measure, so use conservative estimates based on the value assigned to the newly assigned tasks.

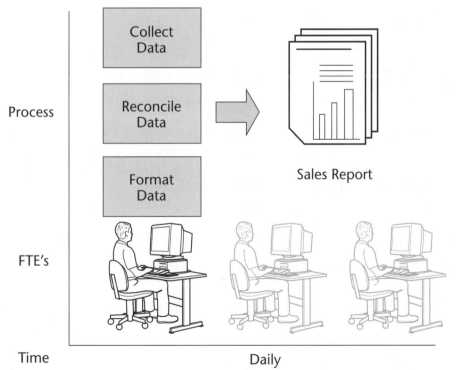

Figure 12-3: Optimized sales report process

Cost Avoidance

Another simple measure of value is cost avoidance where funds set aside for a specific expenditure can be reclaimed and reallocated to another investment. In most financial justification exercises, the funds are reapplied to the new project to build additional functionality. The following scenario highlights the value gained in cost avoidance:

Scenario 2: The marketing department purchased a reporting tool suite several years ago and pays $25,000 in annual support and maintenance. This year, the tool suite is scheduled for a major upgrade that will require an additional license fee of $50,000 and $25,000 in professional services to perform the upgrade. This company also owns an enterprise license for a competing reporting suite, so the marketing department is considering an alternate plan to instead abandon their current tool, migrate to the company-owned enterprise reporting suite, and spend $60,000 in professional services to convert their existing reports. Figure 12-4 illustrates the costs of these choices.

Upgrade		**Migration**	
Expense	Cost	Expense	Cost
Annual Support	$25,000	Annual Support	$0
Additional License Fee	$50,000	Additional License Fee	$0
Professional Services	$25,000	Professional Services	$60,000
Budgeted Amount	$100,000	Budgeted Amount	$60,000
Cost Avoidance: $40,000			

Figure 12-4: Cost avoidance decision

In scenario two, the marketing department is budgeting for a $100,000 annual expenditure to upgrade and support the existing environment. By migrating to the enterprise tool suite, the marketing department will avoid the cost of the annual support contract and the additional license fee, but will incur an additional $35,000 in professional services. The cost avoided in marketing is $40,000.

Of course, replacement functionality should be comparable or superior so that business needs are met. The overall value will be reduced if proposed functionality introduces new gaps or fails to address current requirements. An additional risk when considering cost avoidance is time to market. Scenario two assumes that the migration can occur in a similar timeframe as the upgrade. When constructing the financial justification, ensure that the proper time and resources are included in the plan and all detailed costs are properly captured.

Revenue Preservation and Enhancement

It can be more difficult to identify scenarios where a business intelligence initiative has a positive impact on revenue. Although these scenarios are subtle, most such opportunities can be discovered in process optimizations or the capitalization of lost opportunities. When searching for such scenarios, identify situations where current constraints impact revenue and more accurate, timely, and comprehensive information would be used to improve business. The following hypothetical scenario highlights how increasing and preserving revenues are realized by timely information and better visibility into operations:

Scenario 3: A large supermarket chain is having difficulty in managing their perishable inventory, especially milk products. The local supplier delivers one thousand milk units per week to the supermarket distribution center. A distribution report available shows that milk is sold at $3 at a cost of $2.65 (product + distribution) yielding a $0.35 per unit margin or 12 percent. Although the purchasing department is satisfied, operations have discovered a potential problem when they talked to the store managers. The store managers at certain stores reported that a total of 220 units currently on the shelves are going to expire. What finance had forecasted as $350 in profits this week has now become a loss $310 because of expired product. Even worse, several stores temporarily ran out of milk further impacting revenue. And this was not the first time this had happened. Figure 12-5 illustrates this scenario.

Forecast View		Store View		Revised View	
Units / Week Received	1,000	Units / Week Sold	780	Units / Week Sold	980
Cost / Unit	$2.50	Expired Units / Week	220	Expired Units / Week	20
Distribution Cost / Unit	$0.15	Sales Margin	$273.00	Sales Margin	$343.00
Selling Price / Unit	$3.00	Loss (Expired Product)	($583.00)	Sales Loss (Expired)	($53.00)
				Additional Distribution *Pickup & Redistribution (.30 / unit)*	($66.00)
P&L / Unit	$0.35	P&L / Unit	($0.31)	P&L / Unit	**$0.23**
Forecasted Margin	$350	Actual Margin	($310)	Actual Margin	$224
Margin %	12%	Margin %	-10%	Margin %	8%

Figure 12-5: Revenue preservation and enhancement

In scenario three, the distribution report showing milk as a profitable product line was not an indication of the true nature of the business. Management was unable to determine where stock shortages existed in the stores in this report or see a current inventory view of aging products. To solve this challenge, this organization constructed an inventory reporting solution that enabled operations to better understand current inventory levels at the store level and recognize their exposure to expiring products. Instead of allowing products to expire on the shelf while other stores are short of available inventory, this organization moved expiring inventories from overstocked stores to stores low on inventory. Although profit margins may not have matched the forecasted view, the product line returned to profitability through better timeliness and visibility into inventory enabling operational strategies to be implemented.

Competitive Advantage

The business strategy goals of most organizations are to continually increase profitability at the expense of competitors by controlling costs and differentiating goods and services. Cost advantages can be obtained by better availability of inventories, faster time to market, or greater efficiencies in the manufacturing process. Differentiation of goods and services can be attributed to better brand recognition, market domination, or superior offerings. A key factor in gaining competitive advantage can come through access to better information providing a clear understanding of business. The following scenario highlights how increased revenues can be realized by timely information and better visibility into operations:

Scenario 4: A mid-sized regional bank recently struggled to grow its profitable customer base. Many of the large national banking competitors continue to lure away their most profitable customers by offering free services and slightly better rates. The regional bank has strong ties to the community with a reputation for excellent branch service and the widest coverage in the region. Executives have recently noticed that not all lines of businesses are as profitable as before the entry of the large national banks into the region. The credit card line of business continues to struggle — showing higher than normal turnover and complaints of poor customer service. While the asset management line of business continues to grow, there is concern that several large clients have been lost due to an inability to provide a comprehensive package of services.

Scenario four reflects a common situation in the financial services industry where significant consolidation has occurred. In the mid-sized regional bank, each line of business has its own reporting solution focused exclusively on products and services sold to a subset of the bank's customers. These reporting silos have negatively impacted the overall performance of the bank. Upon further investigation, the credit card line of business finds that only a small percentage of their customers have additional products and services such as checking, savings, or retirement accounts. The asset management line of business does not possess the full portfolio of retirement, insurance, and credit services their clients require. Each line of business believes they own the relationship with the customer and do not actively share information with other lines of business.

To reduce the risk of being acquired by a larger financial institution, the regional bank chooses to refocus on its core values that provided it a competitive advantage for so many years: customer service. Like many other financial institutions, the bank establishes a strategy to move from a product-centric approach to a customer-centric approach where customer relationships are owned by all lines of business. To facilitate this change in the business, the creation of a centralized enterprise repository of customer information is mandated to enable all lines of business to view all of the current products and services each customer owns. This information will provide the bank the foundation for determining a customer's value to the bank based on their entire portfolio, not just a single product or service.

The results of this initiative will give the regional bank a competitive advantage in building customer profitability, better retention, and the ability to cross-sell additional products and services during all customer interactions. This advantage will be enabled by an enterprise reporting solution providing a single view of the customer and linking their portfolio of products and services.

Market Presence

Market presence is perhaps the most difficult element of value to measure. It is often easier to gain presence by starting with better business management on a smaller scale. For example, the ability to inform trading partners of current order status or inventory levels is essential to profitability by enabling reduction of carrying costs of raw materials and excess inventory. This solution can also help the same organization expand its operations and presence in new geographies, build awareness of products and services, invest in retaining existing customers, and convey a clear value proposition. The following scenario highlights how an increased market presence is converted into increased revenues:

Scenario 5: A small parts manufacturer maintains a competitive advantage by custom manufacturing the finest parts in the shortest duration at a competitive cost. Although the business maintains strong profit margins, growth is limited to its local geography. In an effort to expand, the manufacturer establishes an Internet presence and regional satellite offices. In addition, the manufacturer begins advertising in national trade publications and participates in several regional trade shows. The manufacturer decides to support the expansion initiative by deploying a business intelligence system that enables customers to cross match expensive, hard to find parts at a fraction of the time and cost. This system enables the customer to provide engineering specifications, place orders, and track the process.

In scenario five, a traditional organization that has a physical presence in a geographical market leverages the Internet to span geographic boundaries. The new market presence is established by leveraging the fundamentals that enabled the manufacturer to dominate a local market. By exposing candidate customers to unique services at a competitive price, the manufacturer used their ability to cross match parts from hundreds of manufacturers with engineering specifications, providing customers a single source for all their parts needs.

In the next sections we discuss the most common budgeting techniques organizations leverage to justify projects and provide insight into the financial measurements: total cost of ownership and return on investment.

Common Budgeting Techniques

In estimating the total cost of ownership and the overall return on investment, we rely on the same capital budgeting techniques described above for justifying new manufacturing equipment, real estate, or potential acquisition targets. Factors such as time value assessment, overall risk, total return, valuation, and the cost of capital for decision purposes can be considered. These fundamentals of capital budgeting can be split into two techniques: unsophisticated and sophisticated.

Unsophisticated techniques are relatively simple to calculate but do not explicitly consider the time value of money. Examples of unsophisticated techniques include the average rate of return and payback period. Sophisticated techniques are more complex and include the critical time component representing discounting of cash flows. Examples of sophisticated techniques include profitability index, internal rate of return, and net present value. Theses metrics, illustrated in Figure 12-6, represent a sampling of common building blocks used in capital budgeting process and are discussed in more detail to provide a general understanding for selecting the best approach for calculating total cost of ownership and return on investment.

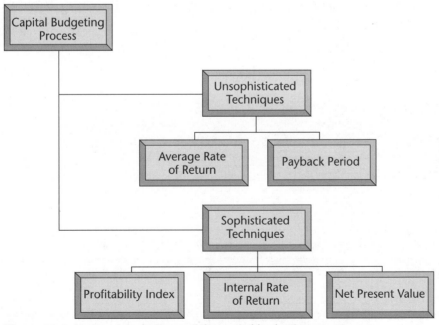

Figure 12-6: Common techniques of the capital budgeting process

Figure 12-7 shows data for three sample projects that we use in illustrating common budgeting techniques in the following sections. If you are going to use techniques similar to these, you should obtain guidelines from your organization's finance department since there could be standard techniques already defined in your organization.

Average Rate of Return

The average rate of return is a simplistic and unsophisticated calculation that can be based on existing, historical accounting data. This simple calculation is based on dividing the average net return achieved by the project by the capital cost of the investment. The simplicity of calculating this measure does have its drawbacks. The average rate of return fails to account for maximization of profitability and it is unable to recognize the time value of the investment. Figure 12-8 illustrates calculating the average rate of return.

In this example, the customer profitability project has the highest average rate of return, although it provides the lowest cash flow among all projects. The organization has determined that the decision point for candidate projects must exceed 6 percent average rate of return. Based on this condition, the marketing and customer profitability projects qualify for funding while the executive dashboard would be excluded from consideration. Based on choosing the best average rate of return, the customer profitability project would be the one to select.

Sample Projects Investment & Cash Flows

	Marketing Reporting Project	Customer Profitability Project	Executive Dashboard Project
Initial Investment	$1,100,000	$1,000,000	$1,200,000
Year	Cash Flow	Cash Flow	Cash Flow
1	$100,000	$320,000	$600,000
2	$300,000	$320,000	$400,000
3	$400,000	$320,000	$300,000
4	$600,000	$320,000	$100,000
Total Cash Flow	$1,400,000	$1,280,000	$1,400,000

Figure 12-7: Sample projects for investment

Figure 12-8: Project average rate of return

Payback Period

The payback period is also a simplistic and unsophisticated calculation that determines the exact amount of time required for an organization to recover its initial investment based on the generation of cash flows. The payback period is a more accurate measure than the average rate of return since it considers the timing of cash flows. Payback period is more commonly used as a measure of risk and is often used as supplemental criteria to more sophisticated techniques. Figure 12-9 illustrates calculating the payback period.

In the example, the executive dashboard project has the fastest payback period compared to the other projects. Unlike the average rate of return where the executive dashboard was the last project to be considered, based on the rapid cash flows generated by this project, it exhibits the lowest financial risk. The organization has determined that the decision point for payback for the candidate projects must be less than three years. Based on this condition, the executive dashboard project is the only project qualifying for funding and would be selected.

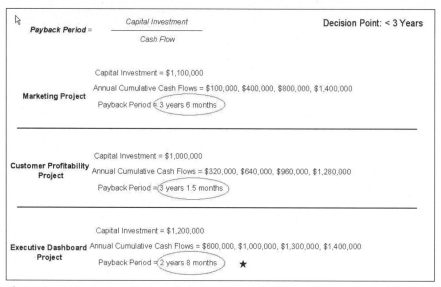

Figure 12-9: Project payback period

Net Present Value

The net present value (NPV) is a sophisticated budgeting technique that is used to analyze the profitability of an investment in terms of today's dollars, accounting for inflation and future returns. It can be calculated by subtracting the project's initial capital investment from the present value of cash flows discounted at the organization's cost of capital. The cost of capital or opportunity cost is the rate of return an organization must earn on its project investments to maintain its market value to attract funds. NPV is perhaps the most versatile measure since the results are expressed in terms of today's dollars and account for alternative investment of funds. Figure 12-10 illustrates calculating the net present value.

The decision point for net present value is to select the project with the highest return on investment. Therefore, any project with a positive net present value will provide the organization with value above and beyond other investments at their cost of capital. In this example, the decision point is for projects that have a positive NPV. The customer profitability project is the only project to meet this characteristic over four years. The highest impacting factors in calculating net present value are the cost of capital and the time recognition of positive cash flows. The cost of capital is perhaps the most significant factor. As the cost of capital declines, the present value increases (see Figure 12-11). This is true since lower interest rates allow more projects to qualify for funding since their return has a lower threshold to achieve. When the cost of capital rises, few projects qualify for funding since the threshold for return is considerably higher.

| Net Present Value = $\sum\limits_{i=1}^{n} \dfrac{\text{Cash Flows}}{(1 + \text{cost of capital})^i}$ | | Where n = number of cash flows
Where i = number of periods (years) | | | Cost of Capital : 10%
Decision Point: + NPV | |

Marketing Project

NPV: ($50,823)

Year	0	1	2	3	4
Cash Flow	($1,100,000)	$100,000	$300,000	$400,000	$600,000
PV Interest Factor	1.000	0.909	0.826	0.751	0.683
Present Value	($1,100,000)	$90,909	$247,934	$300,526	$409,808
Cumulative PV	($1,100,000)	($1,009,091)	($761,157)	($460,631)	($50,823)

Customer Profitability Project

★ NPV: $14,357

Year	0	1	2	3	4
Cash Flow	($1,000,000)	$320,000	$320,000	$320,000	$320,000
PV Interest Factor	1.000	0.909	0.826	0.751	0.683
Present Value	($1,000,000)	$290,909	$264,463	$240,421	$218,564
Cumulative PV	($1,000,000)	($709,091)	($444,628)	($204,207)	$14,357

Executive Dashboard Project

NPV: ($30,271)

Year	0	1	2	3	4
Cash Flow	($1,200,000)	$600,000	$400,000	$300,000	$100,000
PV Interest Factor	1.000	0.909	0.826	0.751	0.683
Present Value	($1,200,000)	$545,455	$330,579	$225,394	$68,301
Cumulative PV	($1,200,000)	($654,545)	($323,967)	($98,573)	($30,271)

Figure 12-10: Project net present value

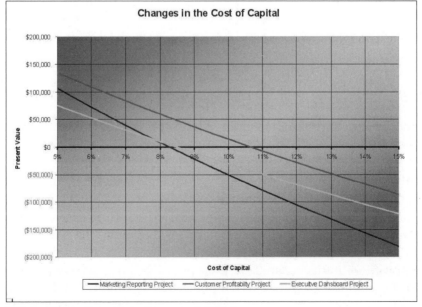

Figure 12-11: Changes in the cost of capital

The second factor is the amount of time in which positive cash flows are achieved. The greater the positive cash flow earlier in the cycle, the higher the present value will be. Given two projects with equivalent cash flows, you will discover that generating cash flows earlier in the cycle will provide a better return. Work with your finance department to determine your organization's cost of capital, how to measure cash flow, and in determining the proper duration of the analysis.

Internal Rate of Return

The internal rate of return (IRR) is a sophisticated budgeting technique where the cost of capital equates the present value of all cash flows to zero. Similar to the net present value calculation, the concept for IRR is simple — an organization should invest in an internal project if it can earn a higher return than investing its capital elsewhere. Internal rate of return assumes that the cost of capital remains constant over time. Figure 12-12 illustrates calculating the internal rate of return.

In this example, we are searching for the project that has an internal rate of return greater than the cost of capital. Although the marketing and executive dashboard projects possess internal rate of return slightly greater than 8 percent, the customer profitability project exceeds both projects and the cost of capital that was set at 10 percent. The internal rate of return calculation helps us understand at what point our projects become financially viable. Given the provided metrics, if the cost of capital could be acquired at 8 percent or less, all projects would be viable and the decision criteria would rely on other business decision points such as critical needs or time to market.

Profitability Index

The profitability index is another method closely aligned to net present value and internal rate of return. It provides a relative index value for comparison of projects. The Profitability index is a calculation of the sum of the present value of cash flows divided by the initial investment. Figure 12-13 illustrates calculating a profitability index.

In the example, the decision criteria are based on selecting a project that has the greatest profitability index that is greater than one. When the profitability index exceeds one, the net present value is greater than zero providing the profitability index and net present value approaches the same acceptance/rejection criteria. When comparing these projects in the example, the customer profitability project is the only project with a profitability index greater than one, confirming a positive net present value.

Internal Rate of Return

Cost of Capital: 10%

Decision Point: IRR > Cost of Capital

Year	0	1	2	3	4	IRR
Marketing Reporting Project	($1,100,000)	$100,000	$300,000	$400,000	$600,000	8.27%
Customer Profitability Project	($1,000,000)	$320,000	$320,000	$320,000	$320,000	10.66%
Executive Dashboard Project	($1,200,000)	$600,000	$400,000	$300,000	$100,000	8.49%

Marketing Project

IRR: 8.27%

Customer Profitability Project

IRR: 10.66% ★

Executive Dashboard Project

IRR: 8.49%

Figure 12-12: Project internal rate of return

$$\text{Profitability Index} = \frac{PV\ of\ Cash\ Flows}{Initial\ Investment}$$

Cost of Capital: 10%

Decision Point: PI > 1.0

Year	0	1	2	3	4	Σ Cash Flows
Marketing Reporting Project	($1,100,000)	$90,909	$247,934	$300,526	$409,808	$1,049,177
Customer Profitability Project	($1,000,000)	$290,909	$264,463	$240,421	$218,564	$1,014,357
Executive Dashboard Project	($1,200,000)	$545,455	$330,579	$225,394	$68,301	$1,169,729

Marketing Project

$$\frac{\$1,049,177}{\$1,100,000} = 0.95$$

Customer Profitability Project

$$\frac{\$1,014,357}{\$1,000,000} = 1.01 \star$$

Executive Dashboard Project

$$\frac{\$1,169,729}{\$1,200,000} = 0.97$$

Figure 12-13: Project profitability index

What's the Best Solution?

We have analyzed five different budgeting approaches — each with varying approaches. Which approach provides the best solution? Figure 12-14 summarizes the analyses we performed for our examples.

Comparison of Approaches

Budgeting Techniques	Marketing Project	Customer Profitability Project	Executive Dashboard Project
Average Rate of Return	6.8%	7.0%	4.2%
Payback Period	3 years 6 months	3 years 1½ months	2 years 8 months
Net Present Value	($50,823)	$14,357	($30,271)
Internal Rate of Return	8.27%	10.66%	8.49%
Profitability Index	0.95	1.01	0.97

Figure 12-14: Comparison of approaches

When analyzing the data, all but one measure identified the customer profitability project as the most financially sound. When determining what measure is the most appropriate, most organizations will insist on using sophisticated measures to provide financial justification. The three sophisticated measures — net present value, internal rate of return and profitability index should all be utilized. Net present value (NPV) focuses on measuring cash flow over time base in today's dollars based on the cost of capital. Once captured, the internal rate of return (IRR) and profitability are reference points that can be used for comparison purposes. Although NPV is the theoretical superior choice, many financial mangers will insist on the use of IRR as it reflects the rate of return in place of actual dollars. Work with your finance department to determine your organization's preferred method.

Total Cost of Ownership

Total cost of ownership (TCO) is one of the most common measures used in the justification of technology initiatives. TCO analyzes the true cost of the opportunity over its entire useful life. The calculations are straightforward in that all the pertinent costs are added together and the opportunity with the lowest overall cost is the best financial value. Today, most organizations require their IT staff to minimally provide a total cost of ownership report for capital purchases and large projects.

Modeling Total Cost of Ownership

Before beginning to model total cost of ownership for your next project, consult your finance department to determine if they have a standard template to be used for the exercise. If one does not exist, don't despair. The process is simple and there are many approaches that can be used in modeling TCO. To provide the highest flexibility in creating financial models, spreadsheets are the tool of choice for sophisticated financial analyses and graphing. The starting point in constructing a TCO model is to divide the analysis into four major categories: capital expenditures, expensed purchases, resources, and the duration of the analysis. These classifications of costs are not intended to align to an accounting view but are logically divided for planning purposes.

Capital Expenditures

Capital purchases are large expenditures that are expected to provide benefit to the organization for longer than one year and exceed a standard cost threshold. Capital expenditures associated with a business intelligence initiative include hardware, enterprise software, storage, and large-scale services associated with the construction or migration of the initiative.

Expensed Purchases

Expensed purchases are items that are typically smaller than capital expenditures. These are incremental costs associated with the project with a useful lifetime of one year or less. Expenses often associated with business intelligence initiatives include support services, maintenance, and small training initiatives.

Resources

Resources are an important cost associated with any business intelligence initiative. Although these costs are capital expenditures from an accounting point of view, we list them separately here to reflect that these are human resources providing project and support staffing. Project resources are assigned to the construction of the initiative and are often listed by role to provide detail associated with staffing. Support resources are often shared resources that participate in both the construction and long-term support of the initiative.

Analysis Duration

The duration of the analysis is important in determining the overall total cost of ownership. Establish a time frame that reflects real expectations of the solution and its alignment to the strategic direction of the organization. Considerations should include hardware life cycles and replacement strategies, anticipated life expectancy of a solution, and the business problem that the solution addresses.

TCO Example

In the following scenario, illustrated in Figure 12-15, we analyze the organization's requirements and highlight the detailed components that comprise a total cost of ownership model.

> *The sales organization plans to undertake the construction of the customer profitability solution to enable better visibility into their existing customer base and to better manage discounting policies. The purchase plan includes a new server for the production database, additional storage to integrate into an existing SAN, database and monitoring software. The construction of the project is anticipated to last for six months and have a useful life of four years. It is anticipated that the number of users and data will grow by 10 percent per year. Standard support will be required for new hardware and software purchases. Professional services will be engaged to reduce the overall risk of the project and the remaining staff will be internal teams.*

1. **Capital expenditures** — This section of the analysis includes items that are anticipated to provide benefits for greater than one year and, in our analysis, includes hardware, software, and training costs needed to establish the environment. Although from an accounting point of view, other line items will be capitalized, we have logically grouped these for the analysis to ensure completeness. Some highlights from this section include new hardware, additional storage to be added to existing SAN, operating system, database, and monitoring software, and training to support the new technology.

2. **Expensed costs** — This section reflects maintenance and other short-term costs associated with developing the solution. In this section, costs are associated to support and maintenance of new hardware and software. Although maintenance and support costs for existing development and test environments are not included in this analysis due to their prior existence, many organizations apportion these costs across all projects based on their size and usage patterns.

Capital Expenditures	Initial	Year 1	Year 2	Year 3	Year 4	Total
Production Hardware	$150,000	$0	$15,000	$0	$15,000	$180,000
Development / Test Hardware	$0	$0	$10,000	$0	$10,000	$20,000
Production Storage	$50,000	$0	$10,000	$10,000	$10,000	$80,000
Development Storage	$0	$0	$5,000	$0	$5,000	$10,000
OS Software	$21,000	$0	$0	$0	$0	$21,000
RDBMS Software	$60,000	$0	$20,000	$0	$0	$80,000
Monitoring Software	$10,000	$0	$0	$0	$0	$10,000
Training (technology)	$20,000	$0	$0	$0	$0	$20,000
Total Capital Expenditures	$311,000	$0	$60,000	$10,000	$40,000	$421,000

Expensed Costs	Initial	Year 1	Year 2	Year 3	Year 4	Total
Production HW / SW Support	$30,000	$30,000	$30,000	$0	$3,000	$93,000
Dev / Test HW / SW Support	$0	$0	$0	$66,726	$70,063	$136,789
Storage Maintenance / Other	$10,000	$0	$0	$153,110	$160,764	$323,874
Database SW Maintenance	$14,000	$14,000	$18,000	$18,000	$18,000	$82,000
Total Expensed Costs	$54,000	$44,000	$48,000	$237,836	$251,827	$635,663

Resources	Initial	Year 1	Year 2	Year 3	Year 4	Total
Projects						
DW Architect	$55,000	$0	$0	$0	$0	$55,000
ETL Specialist	$100,000	$0	$0	$0	$0	$100,000
Development DBA	$45,000	$0	$0	$0	$0	$45,000
DW Reporting Analyst / Developer	$100,000	$0	$0	$0	$0	$100,000
Support						
Production DBA	$80,000	$80,000	$80,000	$80,000	$80,000	$400,000
System Administrator	$45,000	$45,000	$45,000	$45,000	$45,000	$225,000
DW Application Support Analyst	$60,000	$60,000	$60,000	$60,000	$60,000	$300,000
Professional Services						
Professional Services	$150,000	$0	$0	$0	$0	$150,000
Total Resources	$635,000	$185,000	$185,000	$185,000	$185,000	$1,375,000
Total Cost of Ownership	$1,000,000	$229,000	$293,000	$432,836	$476,827	$2,431,663

Figure 12-15: Total cost of ownership scenario

3. **Resources** — This section includes the project team, a support team that is allocated for the full life expectancy of the solution, and professional services that will be engaged during the strategy phase of the project. Since the construction of the project is anticipated to be complete in six months or less, project resources are estimated accordingly.

4. **Life expectancy** — The life expectancy or usefulness of the project is anticipated to be four years. It is important to capture the anticipated life expectancy of an initiative since there are costs for expansion and enhancements that will occur several years after development is complete. More importantly, there are business benefits associated with the solution that will add value to its overall return on investment.

5. **Additional investments** — Additional investments are anticipated throughout the life cycle of the initiative and provided during enhancements introducing new functionality. In our analysis, additional hardware, storage, and software licenses were required in the second year and the fourth year that reflect the projected growth targets of the solution. In addition, support costs will be adjusted accordingly to support the growth in infrastructure.

6. **Support resources** — The support resources for the solution exist over the entire life cycle of the solution. The technical resources support database administration tasks and systems administration that is shared among several environments. Although the analyst position is not a full-time role, this role is critical in identifying new requirements, ensuring that existing functionality meets the current needs and assisting the business in realizing the overall value of the solution.

7. **Totals** — The totals reflect the sum of the initial cost and additional costs incurred during the life cycle of the solution and do not consider the time value of money in the calculation. This can be easily calculated by applying the net present value to each cash flow stream.

8. **TCO** — The total cost of ownership line reflects the sum of all expenditures for a given year and a grand total for all expenditures. Similar to the line item totals, this calculation does not consider the time value of money.

Return on Investment

Over the past decade, the return on investment (ROI) calculation has been the standard for measuring performance. ROI measures the overall value of an investment by calculating the financial performance of an investment. Although ROI can be measured as a pure percentage similar to return from money in a bank account, many organizations require additional detail and rely on fundamental budgeting techniques to provide the true picture. ROI computation is similar to that of TCO with the addition of business benefits as discussed earlier. By including the business benefits, the cash flows generated by the solution are included in the overall value assessment. This type of analysis may be required especially during economic downturns where projects need to be self-funded.

Modeling Return on Investment

Just as in other examples, it is important to consult your finance department to determine if they have a standard approach for ROI analysis. Most often, the ROI modeling is accomplished by extending the analysis performed for total cost of ownership. By including business benefits in the analysis, ROI exposes additional information providing a comprehensive view to the decision process.

Business Benefits

Business benefits measure the value the initiative provides directly or indirectly in terms of positive cash flow. Benefits like reduction or reallocation of resources, cost avoidance, revenue preservation, competitive advantage, productivity enhancements, or the establishing of a market presence are just a few factors of how business intelligence initiatives can impact cash flows. Although many of these factors are difficult to measure, your finance department has approaches and experience in measuring overall value.

ROI Example

We build on the TCO scenario by adding business benefits and calculate many of the measures that provide decision makers essential information to analyze the overall value of the initiative (see Figure 12-16).

The sales organization has completed their total cost of ownership analysis and wishes to extend this analysis to include the business benefits that the customer profitability solution will provide. The value proposition includes:

- Savings that will be achieved in reallocating existing resources to other business initiatives
- Avoiding the cost of constructing additional profitability reposts on the existing mainframe
- Bypassing future hardware upgrades to an aging AS-400 environment
- Savings achieved in deploying a consistent discounting policy across the sales organization
- Enabling the sales organization to understand competitor's offerings in the marketplace
- Consistent policies across sales strategies enabling better focus on who are the most profitable customers

1. **Business benefits** — There are several business benefit factors that over time can have a positive impact on cash flows. Value is realized for many of these factors within the first year. The overall approach to estimating savings and cash flows was provided by finance.

2. **Expenditures** — The expenditures in this section are based on information captured from the total cost of ownership analysis and include expenditures for capital purchases, expensed purchases, and resource requirements.

3. **Life expectancy** — Consistent with the total cost of ownership analysis, it is important to determine the overall life expectancy to provide the most comprehensive view of the value of the initiative.

4. **Totals** — The totals reflect the sum of the benefits and costs over the life cycle of the solution and do not consider the discounted cash flows in the calculation. Discounted cash flows are summarized in the analysis section of the justification.

5. **Cash flow** — The cash flows reflect the sum of all costs and benefits for each year of the initiative's life expectancy. This information is used in determining the overall financial value.

6. **Analysis** — The analysis provides the summary of details enabling decision makers the most comprehensive view of the initiative. In this scenario, it highlights the sophisticated measures used in further analysis and decisions.

Return on Investment

Cost of Capital: 10%

Business Benefits	Initial	Year 1	2	3	4	Total
Resource Reallocation	$0	$80,000	$80,000	$40,000	$40,000	$240,000
Cost Avoidance	$0	$150,000	$0	$150,000	$0	$300,000
Revenue Preservation	$0	$150,000	$150,000	$150,000	$150,000	$600,000
Competitive Advantage	$0	$250,000	$200,000	$150,000	$100,000	$700,000
Market Presence	$0	$50,000	$100,000	$100,000	$100,000	$350,000
Productivity Enhancements	$0	$200,000	$150,000	$100,000	$100,000	$550,000
Total Business Benefits	$0	$880,000	$680,000	$690,000	$490,000	$2,740,000
Total Capital Expenditures	($311,000)	$0	($60,000)	($10,000)	($40,000)	($421,000)
Total Expensed Costs	($54,000)	($44,000)	($48,000)	($237,836)	($251,827)	($635,663)
Total Resources	($635,000)	($185,000)	($185,000)	($185,000)	($185,000)	($1,375,000)
Total Costs	($1,000,000)	($229,000)	($293,000)	($432,836)	($476,827)	($2,431,663)
Discounted Costs	$1,000,000	$208,182	$242,149	$325,196	$325,679	$2,101,206
Discounted Benefits	$0	$800,000	$561,983	$518,407	$334,677	$2,215,067
Discounted Cash Flow	($1,000,000)	$591,818	$319,835	$193,211	$8,997	$113,861
Cumulative Discounted Cash Flow	($1,000,000)	($408,182)	($88,347)	$104,864	$113,861	

Analysis		Year 1	2	3	4	Total
Return on Investment		66%	94%	106%	105%	
Sophisicated Techniques						
Net Present Value	$113,861					
Internal Rate of Return	6.8%					
Profitability Index	1.11					
Unsophisticated Techniqes						
Average Rate of Return	7.7%					
Payback Period	1 Year 11 Months					

Figure 12-16: Return on investment scenario

Claiming Success

A business intelligence initiative can provide remarkable impact on the efficiency and profitability of an organization and how it operates. In many enterprises, investment and reliance on timely, comprehensive information is critical to the overall success. Building a foundation for successful project delivery based on strong financial justification and a strong business case enables future project initiatives to achieve support and approval more rapidly.

Although many IT professionals feel uncomfortable in providing a financial justification, the process is relatively straightforward if a standard approach is used. Financial justification provides details of costs and perceived benefits leading to a strong business case that identifies the value of the initiative. Financial teams, in most organizations, are eager to assist in calculating the numbers but need visibility into the costs and the supporting justification prior to completing a full analysis. Although the financial justification is important in determining the overall value, it is only one consideration in determining where to invest. Although a potential low TCO or high ROI are important, assessment of risk must also be considered since unmitigated risk could jeopardize the entire investment.

IT can play a critical role in the success of any organization and can provide capabilities that differentiate a business from competitors. Financial responsibility does not end once the project is approved. But, by continuing to deliver on the commitments promised in the business case, IT can share in the success achieved by the organization.

Index